The Global Rule of Three

"Coming out of the current COVID crisis, many expect further industry consolidation across sectors. *The Global Rule of Three* lifts the curtain on what this future could look like. The book is packed with great insights into the dynamic forces shaping most industries: above all, that those who know how to truly serve will be the long term winners."
—Paul Polman, *Co-founder and Chair, IMAGINE and former CEO, Unilever*

"Congratulations for writing a seminal book on how industries evolve, grow, plateau and revitalize over time! Simultaneous coexistence of both the volume driven full line competitors (oligopoly) and the margin driven niche players (monopolistic competitors) is unique to competitive positioning Globally."
—Philip Kotler, *S.C. Johnson & Son Distinguished Professor of International Marketing (emeritus), Kellogg School of Management, Northwestern University, USA*

"*The Global Rule of Three* is an eye opener! It provides a blue print on how to compete globally especially against growing competition from Multinationals from the Emerging Markets such as China and India. Buy it, you will like it!"
—Ram Charan, *Best-Selling Author and Advisor to Global Enterprises*

"*The Global Rule of Three* offers a plethora of historical as well as contemporary examples to chronicle the evolution of hypercompetition leading up to the current pan-industrial revolution. A must read for every manager interested in the spiraling competition from multinationals of emerging markets such as China and India."
—Richard D'Aveni, *Bakala Professor of Strategy, Tuck School of Business, Dartmouth College, USA*

"The merger of T-Mobile U.S.A. and Sprint is a great example of the Rule of Three. The next battleground in global wireless networks will be won by those companies that implement strategies to take advantage of the Global Rule of Three. This is just the tip of the iceberg and will be followed by shakeout of streaming services. *The Global Rule of Three* will provide leaders an invaluable guide on how to navigate the turbulent waters ahead."
—Ralph de la Vega, *Former Vice-Chairman, AT&T, and Founder of the De La Vega Group, USA*

"*The Global Rule of Three* is the international extension of Jag Sheth's original insights into the strategic path of industries from telecom and media, to finance, manufacturing, services, and consumer products. He offers more than compelling theory, but also proven realities. This book reveals the ongoing competitive strategic priorities large global enterprises use to become number one or two competitors globally through their leveraging large domestic market advantages for companies from nations such as China and India. There is no book like this with such clear vision through the fog of competitive battle and no top leader who can risk not gaining this insight."

—Jeffrey A. Sonnenfeld, *Senior Associate Dean for Leadership Studies and Lester Crown Professor of Leadership Practice, Yale School of Management, Yale University, USA*

"A compelling and deep exploration of the causes of the consolidation of global markets, and the consequences of being governed by the 'Rule of Three.' The authors pose provocative questions that strategists must anticipate and address to avoid driving their company into 'The Ditch.'"

—George S. Day, *Geoffrey T. Boisi Professor Emeritus at the Wharton School of the University of Pennsylvania, USA*

"Since the rule of three and four was first proposed by Henderson in 1976 to explain industry structure, globalization and technology have reshaped competition. *The Global Rule of Three* is a must read for any manager interested in whether and how industry ecology has shifted."

—Martin Reeves, *Chairman of the BCG Henderson Institute and Managing Director and Senior Partner, Boston Consulting Group, USA*

"A fact of economic life has been the growth of oligopolies within countries around the world, as well as in sectors dominated by multinational companies. Greater concentration has been observed in industries over the past 40 years. While some may quibble with the provocative focus of this book on the number 'three' (as opposed to say 'two' or 'four') the authors provide many insights on the reorganization of industries which will be useful to strategists and consultants, as well as sparking testable hypotheses among scholars who research industrial concentration and M&A. The authors have been especially bold in predicting, by name, the three companies in several sectors which they say will dominate in the year 2030."

—Farok J. Contractor, *President-Elect, Academy of International Business and Distinguished Professor, Rutgers Business School, USA*

Jagdish Sheth • Can Uslay • Raj Sisodia

The Global Rule of Three

Competing with Conscious Strategy

Jagdish Sheth
Emory University, Goizueta Business School
Atlanta, GA, USA

Can Uslay
Rutgers University, Rutgers Business School
Newark and New Brunswick, NJ, USA

Raj Sisodia
Babson College, Olin Graduate School of
Business
Wellesley, MA, USA

ISBN 978-3-030-73083-3   ISBN 978-3-030-57473-4   (eBook)
https://doi.org/10.1007/978-3-030-57473-4

Cover illustration: © posteriori, shutterstock 381607369

This Palgrave Macmillan imprint is published by the registered company Springer Nature Switzerland AG.
The registered company address is: Gewerbestrasse 11, 6330 Cham, Switzerland

Preface

The genesis of this book goes back to the late 1970s, when the Carter administration announced wholesale deregulation of several industries including airlines, utilities, and trucking. This was a desperate effort to kickstart the economy which was massively impacted by the energy crisis and stagflation. The Big Bang deregulation, as it was referred to, led to massive industry consolidation and more than 70 airlines with regional monopolies went out of business. The three survivors were United, American, and Delta Airlines.

At the same time, several niche carriers had emerged successfully. This included PSA in California, Southwest Airlines in Texas, and People Express in New York/New Jersey area. While the big full-service carriers were struggling, the niche players were thriving. This pattern of survival, struggle, and consolidation of full-line generalists and, at the same time, thriving growth of focused niche players was repeated across industries including the automotive, appliances, and consumer electronics (television). It was also observed in several services industries such as accounting (Big 8 to Big 4), advertising agencies, and consulting services.

Finally, the real "aha" moment came from observing the shopping centers where we saw full-line department stores as three anchors and lots of specialty retailers in between them. It was obvious that the anchor stores' strategy was high volume with low margin, while the specialty retailers' was high margin low volume. In economic theory, the anchor stores represented the oligopoly form of competition and the specialty stores represented the monopolistic competition (monopoly rents commanded through differentiation). What struck us was that both forms of competition co-existed and were symbiotic in the short run but competitive in the long run. It is a cycle of competition between the specialists and the generalists.

In the early 1990s, the government policies changed toward liberalization of trade as a growth engine and especially trade between the advanced economies and the emerging markets such as Brazil, Russia, China, and India. The formation of the World Trade Organization (WTO), replacing the General Agreement on Tariffs and Trade (GATT), was an active policy intervention to promote global competition. Today, virtually all industries have global competition even if a company remains domestic.

It seems that the Global Rule of Three has emerged across most industries. Regardless of the scope of the contested market (ranging from the local to regional to national to global), all industries get organized into three large generalist competitors and lots of smaller niche players. While we have economic theories of competition, we don't have a theory of how product or service industries are born, get organized, grow exponentially, and revitalize after reaching maturity.

The Global Rule of Three not only provides the description of how industries evolve but also articulates competitive strategies for the big three, as well as niche players, and those who are in the ditch. We have researched hundreds of product or service industries to validate the Global Rule of Three.

Atlanta, GA   Jagdish Sheth
New Brunswick, NJ   Can Uslay
Wellesley, MA   Raj Sisodia

Acknowledgments

We would like to thank our co-authors, editors, and anonymous reviewers, and countless executives who have helped shape our thinking over the years. Our undergraduate, MBA, EMBA, PhD students, and colleagues at the University of Illinois Urbana-Champaign, University of Southern California, Emory University, Chapman University, Rutgers University, George Mason University, Bentley University, and Babson College have also helped our work with their perspectives and insightful questions.

We would like to thank Nicole Lobo for her design work on some of the figures, Ashley Acevedo for helping with the endnotes of an earlier version, Anjana Chandra and especially Shivani Srivastava for their assistance with the appendix, abstracts, index keywords, and key takeaways of several chapters. Xiaoru Gao and earlier Akshay Malik also assisted with identifying market share data. Also, many thanks to Angel Harris, Laura Hilado, and Beth Robinson for preparing the original PowerPoint presentations used for the book. We would also like to thank the editorial team members at Palgrave Macmillan, in particular Marcus Ballenger, Madison Allums, Sophia Siegler, and Divya Anish. Their collective efforts have significantly improved the manuscript. It goes without saying that any remaining errors are our own.

Finally, we would also like to acknowledge Bruce Henderson (Founder and late Chairman of the Boston Consulting Group [BCG]) who first made some observations about the Rule of Three in a BCG Perspectives note in 1976. In addition, Can Uslay would also like to thank the BCG Strategy Institute for its support of empirical research on the Rule of Three and market structure, and his co-authors—Kate Karniouchina, Ayca Altintig, and Bob Winsor.

Contents

1   What Is the Rule of Three?   1

2   Strategies for Generalists, Specialists, and Ditch Dwellers   39

3   How Industries Evolve, Mature, and Revitalize   73

4   Ten Ways to Innovate and Revitalize Industries   101

5   Evolving to the Global Rule of Three   135

6   The New Triad Power: Impact on Global Markets, Resources, and Politics   175

7   Global Expansion Strategies for Multinationals from Emerging Markets   195

8   Epilogue: What Does the Global Future Hold?   227

Appendix: Past, Current, and Future Top Three Players in Global Markets   249

Index   271

About the Authors

Jagdish N. Sheth, Ph.D. is Charles H. Kellstadt Professor of Marketing at the Goizueta School of Business at Emory University, USA.

Can Uslay, Ph.D. is Associate Professor of Marketing and Vice Dean for Academic Programs and Innovations at Rutgers Business School, USA, and Chair of the Entrepreneurial Marketing Special Interest Group of the American Marketing Association.

Rajendra S. Sisodia, Ph.D. is F.W. Olin Distinguished Professor of Global Business and Whole Foods Market Research Scholar in Conscious Capitalism at Babson College, USA.

Abbreviations

AI	Artificial Intelligence
ASEAN	Association of Southeast Asian Nations
B2B	Business to Business
B2C	Business to Consumer
EMNC	Emerging Market Multinational Corporations
FMCG	Fast-Moving Consumer Goods
IMF	International Monetary Fund
M&A	Mergers and Acquisitions
MES	Minimum Efficient Scale
NAFTA	North American Free Trade Agreement
OEM	Original Equipment Manufacturer
R&D	Research and Development
ROA	Return on Assets
SKU	Stock Keeping Unit (retailing)

List of Figures

Fig. 1.1 The Rule of Three. (Source: Adapted from "Competitive Positioning: The Rule of Three" presentation by Jagdish N. Sheth, 2017) 5

Fig. 1.2 The shopping mall analogy. (Source: Adapted from "Competitive Positioning: The Rule of Three" presentation by Jagdish N. Sheth, 2017) 6

Fig. 1.3 How markets evolve. (Source: Adapted from "The Global Rule of Three" presentation by Jagdish N. Sheth, 2017) 9

Fig. 1.4 Stages of industry evolution over time. (Source: Adapted from "Competitive Positioning: The Rule of Three" presentation by Jagdish N. Sheth, 2017) 11

Fig. 1.5 How margin players get pulled in. (Source: Adapted from "Competitive Positioning: The Rule of Three" presentation by Jagdish N. Sheth, 2017) 15

Fig. 1.6 How volume players get pushed in. (Source: Adapted from "Competitive Positioning: The Rule of Three" presentation by Jagdish N. Sheth, 2017) 17

Fig. 3.1 A typology of strategic options. (Source: Adapted from "The Global Rule of Three" presentation by Jagdish N. Sheth, 2017) 75

Fig. 3.2 Market pathways to scale and efficiency. (Source: Adapted from "The Global Rule of Three" presentation by Jagdish N. Sheth, 2017) 78

Fig. 3.3 Drivers of market revitalization. (Source: Adapted from "The Global Rule of Three" presentation by Jagdish N. Sheth, 2017) 84

Fig. 4.1 Industry life cycle. (Source: Authors' creation based on Ted Levitt's seminal article. Levitt, Theodore (1965), "Exploit the Product Life Cycle," *Harvard Business Review*, November, (43), 81–94) 102

Fig. 4.2   A taxonomy of industry structures. (Source: Adapted from "Competitive Positioning: The Rule of Three" presentation by Jagdish N. Sheth, 2017)   103

Fig. 5.1   The Global Rule of Three circa 2000. (Source: Adapted from "The Global Rule of Three" presentation by Jagdish N. Sheth, 2017)   150

Fig. 5.2   Global passenger car tires. (Source: Adapted from "The Global Rule of Three" presentation by Jagdish N. Sheth, 2017)   152

Fig. 5.3   Global auto manufacturers. (Source: Adapted from "The Global Rule of Three" presentation by Jagdish N. Sheth, 2017)   154

Fig. 5.4   Global aircraft manufacturers. (Source: Adapted from "The Global Rule of Three" presentation by Jagdish N. Sheth, 2017)   158

Fig. 5.5   Global airline industry and alliances. (Source: Adapted from "The Global Rule of Three" presentation by Jagdish N. Sheth, 2017)   160

Fig. 7.1   Twelve strategies and six differential advantages of EMNCs. (Source: Jagdish N. Sheth presentation on "Global Expansion Strategies of Multinationals from Emerging Markets," 2018)   200

Fig. 7.2   The reverse brand life cycle, (Source: Jagdish N. Sheth presentation on "Global Expansion Strategies of Multinationals from Emerging Markets," 2018)   203

Fig. 8.1   The relationship between collaboration and competitive intensity. (Source: Authors' creation)   234

List of Tables

Table 1.1   Market share of U.S. brewers   18
Table 2.1   Characteristics of generalists and specialists   41
Table 3.1   Evolution of markets across stages   80
Table 5.1   2019 GDP indexed to purchasing power parity (PPP)   143
Table 7.1   Differential advantages of EMNCs   214
Table 8.1   Revenue and share of the top ten firms in the aerospace and
            defense industry (2018)   236
Table A.1   Accounting/consulting firms   250
Table A.2   Advertising agencies   250
Table A.3   Aerospace companies   250
Table A.4   Agricultural equipment makers   251
Table A.5   Aircraft engine makers   251
Table A.6   Aircraft alliances   251
Table A.7   Aluminum producers   252
Table A.8   Apparel companies   252
Table A.9   Appliance makers   252
Table A.10 Athletic apparel companies   253
Table A.11 Banks (custodial)   253
Table A.12 Banks (full service)   253
Table A.13 Banks (investment)   254
Table A.14 Beer producers (sub-category of alcoholic beverages)   254
Table A.15 Beverage companies (alcoholic)   254
Table A.16 Beverage companies (non-alcoholic)   255
Table A.17 Biotechnology companies   255
Table A.18 Brokerage firms/wealth management   255
Table A.19 Candy makers   256
Table A.20 Chemical companies   256

Table A.21	Communications equipment companies	256
Table A.22	Computer disk drive manufacturers	257
Table A.23	Coal companies	257
Table A.24	Consumer electronics manufacturers	257
Table A.25	Contact lens makers	258
Table A.26	Cosmetics companies	258
Table A.27	Credit card companies	258
Table A.28	Cruise lines	258
Table A.29	Defense contractors	259
Table A.30	Engineering and construction companies	259
Table A.31	Entertainment producers	259
Table A.32	Forest products companies	260
Table A.33	Global retailers	260
Table A.34	Grain companies	260
Table A.35	Ground coffee companies, non-durable	260
Table A.36	Health care insurers	261
Table A.37	Hotel chains	261
Table A.38	Insurance companies, full line	261
Table A.39	Insurance companies, property, and casualty	262
Table A.40	Investment securities	262
Table A.41	Meat producers	262
Table A.42	Medical supply companies	262
Table A.43	Mining companies	263
Table A.44	Mobile phone manufacturers	263
Table A.45	Movie theater chains	263
Table A.46	Music publishers	264
Table A.47	Office copier manufacturers	264
Table A.48	Office furniture manufacturers	264
Table A.49	Online travel agencies	264
Table A.50	Overnight couriers	264
Table A.51	Paper and pulp companies	265
Table A.52	PBX equipment manufacturers	265
Table A.53	Personal computer companies	265
Table A.54	Pharmaceutical companies	265
Table A.55	Power plant companies	266
Table A.56	Quick service restaurants	266
Table A.57	Railroads	266
Table A.58	Security systems makers	267
Table A.59	Semiconductor chip manufacturers	267
Table A.60	Shipbuilders	267
Table A.61	Steel companies	267
Table A.62	Tire manufacturers	268

Table A.63   Tobacco companies   268
Table A.64   Toy makers   268
Table A.65   Web portal companies   268
Table A.66   Wireless carriers   269

List of Boxes

Box 1.1   The Case of a Successful Specialist: Zara   7
Box 1.2   Why Three?   14
Box 1.3   Never the Twain Shall Meet   20
Box 1.4   The Innovation Leader: #3   22
Box 2.1   Online Dating   50
Box 2.2   The Limited   55
Box 2.3   The Quandary of the Ditch Dwellers   55
Box 3.1   When Scale Is Not Enough: Economies of Scale, Scope, and the
          Minimum Efficient Scale   81
Box 3.2   Sony's Soul-Searching   91
Box 4.1   The Diffusion of Innovations and Crossing the Chasm   103
Box 4.2   Quartz Watches   112
Box 4.3   Line Pruning and Divestments   122
Box 5.1   Owner-Managed Businesses: The Case of Professional Services   148
Box 5.2   The Case of BF Goodrich   155
Box 5.3   Beyond Global: The Universal Rule of Three   163
Box 8.1   Why More Mergers Are Inevitable in Aerospace and Defense   235
Box 8.2   Coinstar: Unleashing the Power of Tri-Sector Collaborations   239

1

What Is the Rule of Three?

Consider the history of the U.S. telecom market. Twenty-two Baby-Bells (operating telephone companies) were divested after the breakup of AT&T by the U.S. government in 1982. Baby-Bells initially organized into seven players by region. Subsequently, roughly 240 firms engaged in reselling long-distance calls, and AT&T's market share collapsed from 90% to under 40%. After a period of shakeout and mergers, there were three survivors—AT&T, MCI, and Sprint. Interestingly, MCI was not only the largest competitor but also the largest customer of AT&T. Today, in wireless communications, three major players are also emerging with #1 AT&T (which was ironically acquired in 2005 by one of the former Baby-Bells, SBC a.k.a. Southwestern Bell), #2 T-Mobile-Sprint, and #3 Verizon. Similarly, the Pay TV market also went through the same journey and three players dominate the market—Comcast with 24% market share, followed by DirecTV with 21%, and Dish Network with 15% share.[1]

Akron, Ohio came to fame as the Rubber City after Benjamin Franklin Goodrich moved his small rubber business from Jamestown, N.Y., to Akron in 1870. Iconic brands such as Goodyear (1898), Firestone (1900), Cooper Tire (1914), and General Tire and Rubber (1915) were all founded in Akron where at one time almost two-thirds of U.S. tire production was concentrated.[2] *Three large players (Goodyear, Firestone, and BF Goodrich) emerged historically, whereas others such as Cooper tire remained viable specialists. Decades later, there are still three large players and Goodyear is still the U.S. market leader, yet it is also the sole remaining U.S.-owned tire manufacturer. Michelin (of France which bought BF Goodrich), and Bridgestone (of Japan which bought Firestone) round up the top three, while specialist Cooper has been bought by Apollo from India.*

Sometimes convergence to the "big three" can happen organically and relatively quickly. The battle to deliver food to homes is only a few years old. However, 55% of Americans aged 18–24 already use online restaurant delivery services.[3] *GrubHub*

© The Author(s) 2020
J. Sheth et al., *The Global Rule of Three*, https://doi.org/10.1007/978-3-030-57473-4_1

started out as an online restaurant order platform in 2011 but pivoted after five years and began to deliver restaurant food in 2016. Seeing proof-of-concept, Uber became a delivery player with Uber Eats in 2017 and DoorDash joined in 2018. The players in the restaurant delivery market are experimenting and thriving: DoorDash rents space in San Francisco to enable third party chefs who only serve their cuisine via the delivery apps, and Uber states 17% of all of its rides hailed globally is for deliveries.[4] As of May 2020, DoorDash had the lead with 45% share of the market, and GrubHub (soon to be acquired by Just Eat Takeaway for $7.3 billion) with its 23% share barely edged over Uber Eats' 22%.[5] Uber Eats is poised to become #2 soon, however. In July 2020, it announced it is acquiring Postmates (and its 8% market share) for $2.65 billion.[6]

Duopoly broken, revolution in action: Founded in 1901, Gillette (acquired by P&G for $57 billion in 2005)[7] ruled the razor market for over a century and had more than 70% market share in the U.S. earlier in the last decade. Today, it is down to about 50% with Schick commanding another 15% and both are bleeding shares fast.[8] Dollar Shave Club and Harry's came in with their direct-to-consumer subscription models in 2012 and 2013 respectively and disrupted the market. The market may be mature; however, Dollar Shave Club (acquired by Unilever for $1 billion in 2016)[9] captured more than half of online sales within five years of inception and currently plans to launch a deodorant line.[10] Meanwhile, Edgewell Personal Care (parent company of Schick and Wilkinson razor brands) has acquired Harry's for $1.37 billion.[11] We may finally see the emergence of the rule of three in this space.

Race to the cloud: AWS (Amazon Web Services), Azure (Microsoft), and Google Cloud are quickly emerging as the three leaders in cloud services. By 2020, AWS is predicted to have 52% market share, followed by 21% for Azure, and 18% for Google in the U.S.[12] Other players such as IBM, Oracle, and Salesforce will likely persist as specialists.

Over the past several years, the world economy, principally in the developed free-market economies of North America and Europe, has witnessed a unique combination of economic phenomena: mergers as well as demergers (i.e., spin-offs of non-core businesses) at record levels with no signs of slowing down. "Since 2012, M&A activity has increased dramatically in both number of deals and size of transaction, with the yearly value of global M&A deals tracking above $4.5 trillion for the past four years."[13] Just weeks before the U.S. presidential elections, October 2016 set a monthly record for U.S. merger activity aided by the biggest acquisition of the year (AT&T's acquisition of Time Warner for $85.4 billion), and one that created the world's largest tobacco company (British Tobacco's acquisition of Reynolds American for $47 billion).[14]

Overall, the deals announced in October 2016 alone amounted to almost a quarter of trillion dollars ($248.9 billion).[15] The number of billion-dollar transactions was up by 25% and the number of megadeals exceeding $25 billion in value increased by more than 100% in 2018![16] According to a 2019 mergers and acquisitions (M&A) trends report by Deloitte, 76% of M&A executives, and 87% of M&A leaders at U.S. private equity firms expect to close more deals over the next year (up from 69% and 76% the year before respectively).[17] Furthermore, they expect the sizes of these transactions to be more significant. Meanwhile, more than 80% of the executives also stated they intended to divest units or portfolio companies in 2019, up from 70% the year before.

Consequently, the landscape of just about every major industry has been changing in a significant way, a process that has been further accelerated by the COVID-19 pandemic. Industries as varied as wireless communications (T-Mobile-Sprint), aluminum (M&A deals in metals surged 90% in 2018),[18] banking (SunTrust and BBT merger worth $66 billion),[19] pharmaceuticals (Bristol-Myers Squibb bid for Celgene),[20] and airlines (acquisition of Virgin America by Alaska Air) are in the midst of rationalization and consolidation, moving inexorably toward what we call the *Rule of Three*.[21] And for the oil industry, "[i]n five days in late October [2018] alone, corporate consolidation saw a bona fide frenzy with Denbury buying Penn Virginia for $1.7 billion, Chesapeake bidding $4 billion for WildHorse, and EnCana acquiring Newfield for $4.2 billion."[22] Indeed, the great recession of 2007, the threat of Brexit, the trade wars of the Trump administration, and COVID-19 have slowed but not halted this fundamental evolution, nor has it altered its basic direction.

The Wall Street Journal argued that the pace of mergers demonstrates "how strong the urge is for [firms] to combine at a time of persistently sluggish economic growth."[23] However, this argument fails to explain why corporate spin-off activities are keeping brisk pace with record levels of acquisitions and why the two activities go in hand.[24] Why, for example, did Dell's announcement that it may spin-off VMware propel its stock price up by 14%?[25] We argue that there is a more powerful explanation that explains the M&A and spin-off surge: the Rule of Three.

What Is the Rule of Three?

Just as living organisms have a reasonably standard pattern of growth and development, so do competitive markets, and our research involving hundreds of industries has revealed that markets evolve in a highly predictable fashion, governed by the "Rule of Three."

Through competitive market forces, markets that are largely free of regulatory constraints and major entry barriers (such as very restrictive patent rights or government-controlled capacity licenses) eventually get organized into two kinds of competitors: full-line generalists and product/market specialists. Full-line generalists compete across a range of products and markets and are volume-driven players for whom financial performance improves with gains in market share. Specialists tend to be margin-driven players, who actually suffer deterioration in financial performance by increasing their share of the broad market beyond a certain level. Contrary to traditional economic theory, then, evolved markets tend to be simultaneously oligopolistic as well as monopolistic.

Figure 1.1 plots financial performance and market share, illustrating the central paradigm of the Rule of Three: in competitive, mature markets, there is only room for *three* full-line generalists, along with several (in some markets, numerous) product or market specialists. Together, the three "inner circle" competitors typically control, in varying proportions, between 70% and 90% of the market. To be viable as volume-driven players, companies must have a critical-mass market share of at least 10%. As the illustration shows, the financial performance of full-line generalists *gradually* improves with greater market share, while the performance of specialists drops off *rapidly* as their market share increases.

There is a discontinuity "in the middle"; mid-sized companies almost always exhibit the worst financial performance of all. We label this middle position the "ditch," the competitive pothole in the market (generally between 5% and 10% market share), where competitive position (and, thus, financial performance) is the weakest. The rule of competitive market physics is straightforward—those closest to the ditch are the ones most likely to fall into it. Therefore, the most desirable competitive positions are those furthest away from the middle. Firms on either side of the ditch—especially those close to it—need to develop strategies to distance themselves. If a firm in a mature industry finds itself in the ditch, it must carefully consider its options and formulate an explicit strategy to move to either the right or the left.

The Shopping Mall Analogy

The Rule of Three applies (and renews itself) at every stage of a market's geographic evolution—from local to regional, regional to national, and national to global. A useful analogy to mature competitive markets is a shopping mall. Mature markets are "anchored" by a few full-line generalists, which are akin to the full-service anchor department stores (such as Macy's and JC Penney) in a mall. In addition, a number of other players are positioned as either product specialists or market specialists. In a mall, a store such as Foot Locker is clearly a product specialist, whereas Zara is more of a market specialist. While Foot locker sells primarily athletic shoes, Zara has a well-defined target

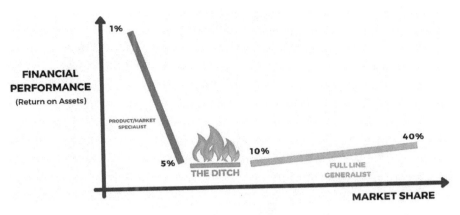

Fig. 1.1 The Rule of Three. (Source: Adapted from "Competitive Positioning: The Rule of Three" presentation by Jagdish N. Sheth, 2017)

market—young, price- and trend-conscious urban women (and men)—and caters to a wide range of their fashion needs.[26]

Shopping malls come in different sizes and architectures but are invariably characterized by (typically three) anchor stores which are full-line volume-driven generalists.[27] These generalists can sell anything as long as it generates profits through turns or volume. However, in between these generalists, there are numerous specialty retailers which are predominantly margin-driven. In the same shopping mall, monopolistic competition is represented by the smaller vendors (specialty retailers), whereas the oligopolistic competition takes place between the anchor stores competing on volume. Examples of such generalists are Target, JC Penney, Macy's, Nordstrom, Lord & Taylor, Sears, and (and in the old days) Montgomery Ward. The anchor stores attract traffic and co-exist with specialty retailers in malls across the world today. Examples of specialty retailers include Foot Locker, GameStop, Kay Jewelers (product specialists); and Benetton, Coach, and Five Below (market specialists). Finally, there are usually a few restaurants and a food court in the center.

For example, whereas Sears (a full-line generalist) used to carry shoes for men, women, and children; and dress shoes, casual, and athletic shoes (3 × 3 segments), Foot Locker (product specialist) primarily focused on athletic shoes for men. They have subsequently expanded into athletic shoes for women and kids with Lady Foot Locker and Kids Foot Locker respectively. Foot Locker does not offer a one-stop-shop to a family as a generalist does. Meanwhile, it tends to command a 20% premium over the generalist for the same stock keeping units (SKUs).[28]

In exclusive and super niche markets, the high price itself may actually represent prestige and value as in expensive perfumes, handbags, and gowns further reinforcing the margins of these retailers. Hence, the shopping mall

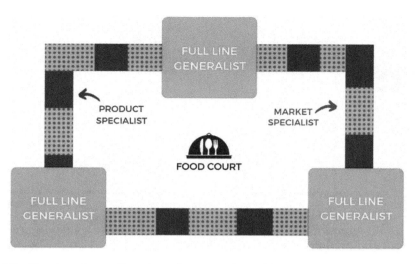

Fig. 1.2 The shopping mall analogy. (Source: Adapted from "Competitive Positioning: The Rule of Three" presentation by Jagdish N. Sheth, 2017)

analogy is very fitting to explain the margin versus volume dichotomy and the corresponding dynamics for other industries. The organization of a typical shopping mall is depicted in Fig. 1.2.

There is usually considerable overlap between the offerings of specialists and generalists. Yet the specialists enjoy significant price premiums over generalists. So why would customers opt to pay 20% more for the same shoes about 100 yards apart in the same mall? The answer is that a specialist such as Foot Locker is able to add value in ways a generalist cannot. The value difference may not be in the particular shoe/product which is identical to what Sears might sell, but rather in the service and selection of offerings. Whereas a Sears' employee may typically lack specific knowledge of the product and is more of an order taker, Foot Locker employees are required to be active in at least two sports and they tend to be young athletes with vast personal experience and knowledge of the brands and shoes. Naturally, they are better equipped to educate consumers and engage in consultative selling. Foot Locker also offers a broader selection of shoe sizes and deeper variety of offerings for specific sports. Moreover, their superior margins are not only a consequence of their price premiums but also of their lower procurement cost. Foot Locker is a bigger customer for Nike, Adidas, and Under Armour athletic shoes than Sears, since it specializes in the athletic shoe category whereas Sears' procurement is divided across multiple shoe segments sourced from different suppliers. This helps explain why Sears is struggling to survive today (it is now part of an entity called TransformCo, which also owns Kmart).

Of course, you may be wondering whether the shopping mall analogy is still relevant when a third of the 1200 or so enclosed malls in the U.S. are either dead or dying.[29] As a matter of fact, this very phenomenon can also be explained by the Rule of Three.

Box 1.1   The Case of a Successful Specialist: Zara[32]

Founded in Spain in 1974, and ranked the 25th most valuable brand in the world by Interbrand in 2018 (with brand equity value in excess of $17.7 billion),[33] Zara has redefined specialty retail for decades. Keenly focused on changing customer taste and preferences, Zara offers more products (styles and choices) than most competitors do, and yet it can be considered the consummate market specialist. Thanks to its short and frequent production runs, while most competitors are happy to get to market in a few months, Zara can modify existing merchandise in as little as two weeks, and ship brand-new designs in another two to four. Furthermore, short production runs provide inherent flexibility so that the company does not have to place big bets on next season's fashion trends. Limited batch production also ensures lean inventory, and creates a sense of urgency with the customers since any given item could sell out immediately.

Zara has created a loyal following among its target demographic of 24–35-year-old women, who visit Zara stores 17 times a year as opposed to three times for competing stores. It sells 85% of its merchandise at full price (vs. 60% industry average) and carries only 10% unsold inventory (vs. industry averages ranging from 17% to 20%). Such customer loyalty ultimately enables Zara to enjoy 12 inventory turns per year whereas most competitors merely average 3–4 turns.

Rather than discounting or spending heavily on advertising like most of its competitors, Zara invests to maintain a lean and agile supply chain which enables 48-hour deliveries to most markets. This, in turn, enables it to respond to consumer preferences in each market very quickly, setting Zara apart from its generalist as well as direct competitors.

While retailers around the world (including the very generalists such as Sears, JC Penney, and Macy's we have referenced as well as specialists such as Victoria's Secret) are struggling, consumers around the world have not decreased their spending. If anything, global consumption has exploded. Consumers have simply been moving their purchases online, hence the phenomenal growth of one-stop e-tailers such as Amazon and Alibaba. E-tailers have been effectively stealing share from the malls and their tenants which put many retail giants such as Sears on the chopping block as they get deeper and deeper into the ditch. Amazon alone has effectively become a phantom generalist for an increasing majority of U.S. households.[30] And with the Whole Foods acquisition, the phantom now has a body for itself leaving other retailers in a frail state. Thus, shopping malls will have to reinvent themselves as showroom, recreation, or service malls. Attempts are underway, and whether or not a family experience can revive our favorite malls remains to be seen.[31] Meanwhile, the Rule of Three in retailing has now become omni-channel where full-line generalists strive to establish leadership in both online and physical stores. Walmart, Amazon, and Target co-exist with numerous specialty retailers such as Zara, Motherhood Maternity, Tom's Shoes, Lululemon, Tiffany, and others.

How Competitive Markets Evolve

By observing how numerous markets have evolved, we have identified the primary drivers of change and a pattern of evolution. In the auto industry's late nineteenth-century infancy, for example, some 500 manufacturers were building cars in the U.S. alone, none on a truly national scale. It took the 1909 launch of the Model T and Henry Ford's innovations in mass production to establish a standard and initiate the process of industry consolidation. By 1917, the number of manufacturers dwindled to just 23; by the 1940s, the market had consolidated further into three full-line players (GM, Ford, and Chrysler) and several niche players such as American Motors (which failed in its attempts at becoming a generalist and was acquired by Renault and then by Chrysler), Checker, and Studebaker. Eventually, the Rule of Three prevailed, with GM, Ford, and Chrysler dominating the U.S. market.

Two driving forces shape markets: efficiency and growth (see Fig. 1.3). Growth comes primarily from creating customer demand while efficiency is a function of optimized operations. In cyclical pursuit of these objectives, markets get organized and reorganized over time.

Although early entrants can specialize in different ways, almost all tend to be product specialists. Young markets tend to have few technical standards, low barriers to entry and exit, and a decidedly local geographic focus. Newly created markets are typified by rapid growth and the presence of numerous competitors jockeying for position. This quickly leads to excess capacity as the market attracts more entrants than it can support.

Even though viable start-up markets grow rapidly in pursuit of scale economies, they tend to be highly inefficient; firms within the industry lack economies of scale, operational experience, and tools to automate production and distribution tasks. They tend to be vertically integrated, producing many of their own inputs, since a well-defined supply function has yet to emerge in the fledgling industry. Consequently, during the growth phase, the drivers of

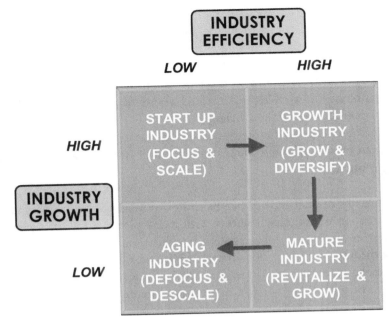

Fig. 1.3 How markets evolve. (Source: Adapted from "The Global Rule of Three" presentation by Jagdish N. Sheth, 2017)

market evolution are geared to creating efficiency by enhancing scale economies and lowering costs. There are four key processes by which this happens:

Creation of Standards: Market processes often result in the creation of a de facto standard. The standard could be for products (as with Windows in personal computing or Google for search engines) or processes (as with the assembly-line manufacturing process pioneered for the Model T or six-sigma/lean manufacturing).

Shared Infrastructure: The market might also create efficiency through the development of a shared infrastructure. Infrastructure costs are generally too high to be loaded on to the transactions generated by any one company. Consequently, the government may take the lead in creating or organizing the infrastructure or one company could develop an infrastructure for its internal needs and then make it widely available. For example, banks benefit greatly from shared infrastructures for check clearing, credit card transactions, and automated teller networks. Airlines require shared infrastructures for reservations, air traffic control, and ground services.

Governmental Intervention: If it sees that an important market is failing to achieve efficiency on its own, the government may intervene. In the U.S., this occurred in the telephone and railroad markets when too many companies started laying cable and setting up tracks. Each one wanted monopoly power and so made themselves incompatible with the others. The government intervened and created standards and sanctioned "natural monopolies" to generate efficiency.

Consolidation: Finally, market processes create efficiency in a highly fragmented market through the consolidation of small, inefficient players into larger ones.

Eventually, market growth begins to slow down and the drive for efficiency transforms an unorganized market with many players into an organized one with far fewer players. After a start-up industry achieves a high level of efficiency through the realization of scale economies, the focus shifts toward the achievement of scope economies. This typically occurs through market expansion (from local to global) and/or product line expansion (from specialty to full line).

When a market is in its infancy, all the players are on the left side of Fig. 1.1. Then, one player makes the turn and becomes a broad-based supplier, through acquisitions (as General Motors (GM) did in the automobile industry), the creation of a *de facto* standard, and so on. It is at this point that the market's natural evolution toward the Rule of Three manifests itself, allowing room for two additional players to evolve into full-line generalists.

Over time, as growth slows and the industry becomes mature, the forces of technological change, shifting regulations, market shifts and changing investor expectations may give rise to a "revolution" or revitalization of the industry. Through such periodic upheavals, the potential exists for the competitive landscape to be redrawn in a substantially different way. Savvy incumbents are able to sustain or improve on their leadership positions, while aggressive newcomers replace others.

Some industries eventually enter a phase wherein growth slows dramatically and industry efficiency declines. Survivors in such industry focus on improving financial performance through "descaling" processes such as capacity reduction, the outsourcing of non-core functions, the breakup of vertical integration and/or exiting the industry and focusing resources elsewhere. Figure 1.4 summarizes this process.

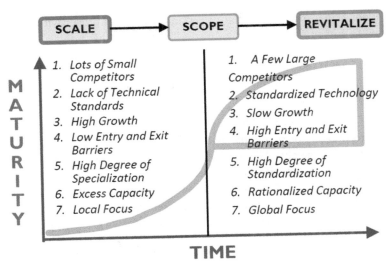

Fig. 1.4 Stages of industry evolution over time. (Source: Adapted from "Competitive Positioning: The Rule of Three" presentation by Jagdish N. Sheth, 2017)

Common Elements in Market Evolution

By analyzing the evolution of hundreds of competitive markets, we have arrived at the following generalizations:

A typical competitive market starts out in an unorganized way, with only small players serving it. As markets expand, they get organized through a process of consolidation and standardization. This process eventually results in the emergence of a small handful of "full-line generalists" surrounded by a number of "product specialists" and "market specialists." Contrary to the prevailing wisdom that they only occur when an industry matures or shrinks, such shakeouts often take place during market expansion (e.g., wireless telecom industry).

With uncanny regularity, the number of full-line generalists that survive this transition is three.[34] In the typical market, the market shares of the three eventually hover around 40%, 20%, and 10%, respectively.[35] Together, they generally serve between 70% and 90% of the market, with the balance going to product/market specialists.[36] We have found that the extent of market share concentration among the big three depends on the extent to which fixed costs dominate the cost structure.

The Rule of Three applies (and renews itself) at every stage of a market's geographic evolution—from local to regional, regional to national, and national to global.

The financial performance of the three large players improves with increased market share—up to a point (typically 40%). Beyond that point, diminishing returns and *dis*economies of scale set in, along with the potential for regulatory problems related to heightened anti-monopoly scrutiny.[37] Therefore, divestiture and international expansion should become priorities for market leaders with more than 40% share.

If the top player commands 70% or more of the market (usually because of proprietary technology or strong patent rights), there is often no room for even a second full-line generalist. When IBM dominated the mainframe business many years ago, all of its competitors had to become niche players to survive. When the market leader has a share between 50% and 70%, there is often only room for two full-line generalists. Similarly, if the market leader enjoys considerably less than 40%, there may (temporarily) be room for a fourth generalist player.

A market share of 10% is the minimum level necessary for a player to be viable as a full-line generalist. Companies that dip below this level are not viable as full-line players, and must make the transition to specialist status to survive; alternatively, they must consider a merger with another company to regain a market share above 10%. In the U.S. airline industry, US Airways, Northwest, and America West all succumbed to the ditch; and each eventually had to merge with one of the Big Three (American, United, and Delta) in order to survive. Even earlier ditch players, such as Eastern, Braniff, Pan Am, and TWA, have already perished.

In a market suffering through a downturn in growth, the fight for market share between #1 and 2 often sends the #3 company into the ditch. For example, this happened in soft drinks (RC Cola wound up in the ditch), beer industry (Schlitz), aircraft manufacturing (Lockheed first, then McDonnell Douglas), and automobiles (previous battles between GM and Ford drove Chrysler perilously close to extinction several times).

Nevertheless, in the long run, a new #3 full-line player usually emerges. For example, in the U.S. soft drink market, Coca-Cola and Pepsi may have top-of-mind share, but do not count out Keurig Dr. Pepper, which is a product of vigorous M&A activity. Even prior to the 2018 acquisition by Keurig, Dr. Pepper Snapple was viable and comfortably #3 with an 18% share against 43% for Coca-Cola, and 26% for PepsiCo respectively.[38]

The number one company is usually the *least* innovative, though it may have the largest R&D budget. Such companies tend to adopt a "fast follower" strategic posture when it comes to innovation.

The number three company is usually the *most* innovative. However, its innovations are usually "stolen" by the number one company unless it can protect them. Such protection becomes more difficult to attain over time.

The extent to which the third-ranked player enjoys a comfortable or precarious existence depends on how far away that player is from the "ditch."

The performance of specialist companies deteriorates as they grow market share within the overall market (through undifferentiated offerings), but improves as they grow their share of a specialty niche (with ever-more differentiated offerings).

Reckless growth can rapidly lead specialists into the ditch. The airline People Express is a classic example; after a few years of heady growth, the Newark (NJ)-based carrier flamed out as it sought to add flights across the continent and to Europe.[39] More recently, Virgin Atlantic also got into trouble as its market share got closer to 5%.[40]

Specialists can make the transition to successful full-line generalists only if there are two or fewer incumbent generalists in the market.

Alternatively, specialists serving a niche that has gone mainstream can sell out to full-line generalists, as Mennon, Maybelline, and Gatorade have done.

Successful product or market specialists typically face only one direct competitor in their chosen specialty. Uber and Lyft can be considered as examples of this, as well as many branded versus generic drugs.

If they face excessive competition in their niche, specialists can move up to become supernichers. For example, some cruise lines have made this transition, as have many boutique practices. Similarly, after its foray into affordable luxury sports car (with Porsche Boxster) depreciated its margins, Porsche also decided to go up-market.

Successful superniche players (that specialize by product *and* market) are, in essence, monopolists in their niches, commanding 80–90% market share.

Companies in the "ditch" exhibit the worst financial performance and have a very difficult time surviving.

Ditch dwellers can emerge as big players by merging with one another, but only if there is no viable third-ranked player to block them. General Motors achieved this in the early years of the automobile industry.

A better strategy for ditch companies may be to seek a merger with a successful full-line generalist. The ditch can be a very attractive source of bargains for full-line generalists looking to rapidly boost market share.

Ditch dwellers can emerge as specialists only if they are able to identify a defensible niche in which they have a sustainable competitive advantage through unique resource endowments. Woolworth department stores redefined itself as a specialty retail chain, and PC-maker IBM has sustained itself as a service provider.

The evidence in support of these generalizations is strong and consistent. There is a powerful logic driving market evolution in this direction. The Rule of Three draws on fundamental truths about consumer psychology (e.g., the "evoked set" of brands typically considered by most consumers consists of three alternatives), competitive dynamics, and the balance of power (see Box 1.2).

Box 1.2   Why Three?

Though our formulation of the "Rule of Three" is based primarily on empirical observation, there are a number of important reasons why a market structure based on three major players tends to be both viable and sustainable.

First, it is important to emphasize that this theory applies to markets rather than industries (as we normally define them). Thus, while aviation is an industry, commercial aviation is a distinct market within that industry. Markets are impacted by industrial dynamics (e.g., scale and scope economies) as well as consumer psychology. Market boundaries are thus defined by customer perceptions, wants, and needs in addition to economic and technological concerns.

The primary logic in postulating the existence of three major players is that a market with three players is both more stable and more competitive than one with two players. With just two players, the outcome is either mutual destruction or collusion that is ultimately damaging to customers. Either scenario eventually leads to a *de facto* monopoly. This is why the Rule of Three structure should be preferable from a policy viewpoint as well.

To create a balance or equilibrium, three entities are needed. With three main players, there is less predatory competition as well as a lower likelihood of collusion. In most markets, a coalition of two out of the three is strong enough to block any predatory intentions that the third might have. Just that threat prevents an attack since the would-be "victim" can always seek the assistance of the third to counterbalance.

The Rule of Three structure results in an optimal level of choice and selection for customers, the ability of companies to generate healthy returns for investors and to be able to pay their employees good wages. In the absence of this structure, all the stakeholders suffer. Thus, the Rule of Three is very compatible with a stakeholder-oriented approach to business, rather than one that is purely shareholder-centric.

Why not more than three? Since only three players are needed to create a balance of power, the fourth player becomes expendable in the market's push toward efficiency. More important, however, we believe that the Rule of Three is strongly linked with the theory of consumer "evoked sets," the short list of purchase options considered by a consumer. Research suggests that most consumers consider only three choices in making their purchases.[41] Their share of preference may be akin to the market shares of the generalists in the Rule of Three (e.g., 40%, 20%, and 10%). Likewise, customers in industrial and commercial markets typically do not consider more than three suppliers. For industrial buyers, #1 and #2 vendors may be chosen based on price/value and the #3 can be a strategic vendor who is experimenting with new processes/technology.[42] Ultimately, more than three choices appear to be unnecessary (in fact, choice overload can even turn off consumers and decrease their purchase and consumption),[43] and fewer than three is sub-optimal. Hence, the Rule of Three emerges consistently. Consideration of three options even extends to the market for higher education where MBA candidates typically have three schools in their all-important short list. Getting into the "inner circle" for volume-oriented competitors is thus a matter of being one of the top three brands.

The Ditch

The Rule of Three posits a model of market competition in which two diametrically opposed strategies can be viable and successful. However, a veritable Bermuda Triangle of competitive strategy lies in the middle. Firms can generate attractive returns regardless of where they fall on the graph in Fig. 1.1—except the ditch—provided they follow strategies appropriate to their position on the chart. Failing to do so has but one consequence: a slide into the ditch, and a long and possibly fatal attempt to climb back out. It is far better to stay out of the ditch in the first place.

How Margin Players Get Pulled In

Margin-driven players are often lured into the ditch, tempted by the possibility of higher volumes (see Fig. 1.5). For example, in the global business of manufacturing pens, BIC, a high-volume French player driven by market share, dominates the mass market. The number two player in the mass market is Newell Rubbermaid, followed by Pilot.[44] On the other side of the graph are the margin-driven specialists: companies such as Mont Blanc, Pelikan, Cross, and many others, all of which operate with low volumes and high margins for their elegant offerings.

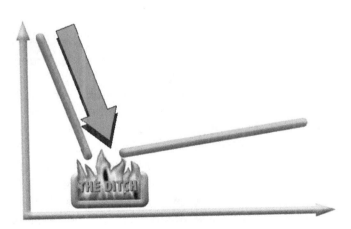

Fig. 1.5 How margin players get pulled in. (Source: Adapted from "Competitive Positioning: The Rule of Three" presentation by Jagdish N. Sheth, 2017)

Consider what would happen if a fictional left-side pen manufacturer (Excalibur) were to become tempted to do business with a classic fictional right-side retailer (MegaMart). Here is how such a "marriage" of incompatibles might evolve:

Year 1 (The Selling of the Soul): Excalibur, under pressure from its shareholders to grow, seeks to broaden its market reach, and approaches MegaMart to carry its offerings. After much haggling, MegaMart agrees to carry the product, provided Excalibur lowers the price and invests in creating an electronic link with its ordering system. Excalibur, buoyed by the sudden growth in volume at a relatively modest reduction in its margins, reports record sales, market share, profits, and stock price.

Year 2 (The Pound of Flesh): MegaMart asks Excalibur to further lower its price, hinting that it has alternative suppliers ready and waiting to offer comparable products on better terms. Excalibur, now hooked on the higher volumes, and having committed to an expansion of its manufacturing facilities, has little choice but to agree. Sales increase further, market share climbs, but profits head down. Investors, sensing distress, start selling.

Year 3 (Deja Vu All over Again): Here we go again. Excalibur is once again asked by MegaMart to lower its price. The company pleads with the retailer that it has already taken as many costs as it can out of the system. Its high-quality metallic cylinder requires precision machining and expensive materials. Then comes the fateful question: *"Could you make it in plastic?"*

The only way for Excalibur to salvage this situation is to decide which side of the graph it wants to play on. If it wants to go back to the left side, it must systematically exit certain markets and drop some products. It must reestablish its quality image. If, on the other hand, the firm wants to become a volume-driven player, it must recognize that its effort to climb the curve on the right-side will be immediately opposed by the #3 incumbent on that side: Pilot. A costly fight for market share will likely ensue, and profits will dry up completely for perhaps several years. One fact is eminently clear: Excalibur cannot stay in the middle. The ditch is not a hospitable home for any competitor.

There are numerous examples of misguided attempts to grow out of specialty status. AMC, the automobile maker, went into the ditch after being a great niche player by trying to expand into a full line of automobiles, since the Rule of Three was already in place in the industry. Lacking the resources to compete with the Big Three, AMC came up with a single car (the Hornet) masquerading as everything from an "econobox" to a luxury sedan. Not surprisingly, the strategy failed, and AMC was subsequently purchased by Chrysler.

How Volume Players Get Pushed In

On the right side of the graph, the most vulnerable is the #3 company, because it is closest to the ditch. In a growing market, the third full-line player continues to survive. However, when market growth slows, the two leaders aggressively fight for share. In the process, the #3 player (and any other aspiring full-line generalist) often gets pushed into the ditch (see Fig. 1.6). This is most common during tough economic times (such as the high inflation 1970s, the low-growth early 1990s, or the great recession following 2007) when overall market growth shrinks or is negative. This impels the #1 and #2 players to raise the competitive stakes and take market share away from the easiest target: the #3 player. For example:

Aircraft Manufacturing: In the recession of the late 1970s, the intense fight for market share between Boeing and McDonnell Douglas pushed Lockheed into the ditch. Lockheed, which had been #3 behind Boeing and McDonnell Douglas before the emergence of Airbus, was forced to exit the commercial aviation market and focus on the military market. Trailing badly behind Boeing and Airbus in the globalized commercial aviation market in the mid-1990s, McDonnell Douglas sought a deal with Taiwan Aerospace to make the fast-growing Asian market its second "home" and particularly to position itself for the fast-growing China market (with its $20 billion in backlog orders). When the U.S. government disallowed this deal, McDonnell Douglas' options were limited; it could have emerged as a spe-

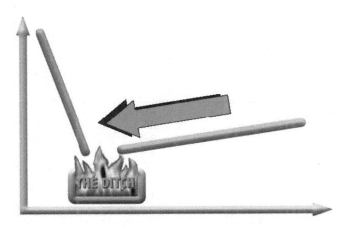

Fig. 1.6 How volume players get pushed in. (Source: Adapted from "Competitive Positioning: The Rule of Three" presentation by Jagdish N. Sheth, 2017)

cialist producer of short-haul jets based on its MD-80 platform or exited the commercial aviation market. In 1997, the company chose to accept a merger with Boeing, leaving the commercial aviation business without a third full-line generalist. We believe this condition is temporary, and that a new full-line generalist will eventually emerge.

Beer: Founded in 1852, Anheuser-Busch eventually became the first nation-wide brewer in the U.S. after over a century-long journey in the 1950s. Then Miller, another early entrant (founded in 1855), became the second national brewer. In the late 1970s, Anheuser-Busch and Miller battled each other for market share following the introduction of Miller Lite in 1975; in the process #3 player (Schlitz) was driven out. Coors (founded in 1873) emerged as an innovative brewer (introducing the first aluminum cans in 1959) and finally began national distribution to become the third-largest brewer in 1991. However, in 2005, Coors merged with Molson making Molson Coors fifth globally, which then subsequently merged with SABMiller to become MillerCoors.[45] European and Japanese brewers have also gone through a similar consolidation process (the journey from domestic to global markets is discussed in Chap. 5). Table 1.1 demonstrates the evolution of market shares among brewers in the U.S. market as the market globalizes. Constellation Brands positioned as a high-end beverage company eventually became the #3 player thanks to its Mexican heritage beers, Corona and Modelo.

Autos: Chrysler's descent into the ditch in the mid-1970s had little to do with Japanese competition and everything to do with the fight between GM and Ford. After the 1974–1975 energy crisis, GM redesigned the Chevrolet Caprice, a car that had great fuel efficiency and was rated by *Consumer*

Table 1.1 Market share of U.S. brewers

Brewer/importer	2009 market share (%)	2017 market share (%)	2019 market share (%)
Anheuser-Busch InBev	48.8	41.6	39.9
MillerCoors, LLC	29.5	24.3	22.6
Constellation	5	8.9	10.6
Heineken USA	4	3.8	3.3
Pabst Brewing	2.7	2.3	n/a
Boston Beer	0.9	n/a	2.5
Other domestic and imports	9	19	21

Source: Compiled by the authors from America's Beer Distributors (2018), "Industry Fast Facts," NBWA.org, accessed September 24, 2019, and America's Beer Distributors (2020), "Industry Fast Facts," NBWA.org, accessed July 25, 2020. https://www.nbwa.org/resources/industry-fast-facts

Reports as a "Best Buy" for several years running. As a result, GM's market share in full-size cars jumped significantly. Ford was able to keep pace, but Chrysler couldn't. It went into the ditch and then reemerged following its bailout as a marginal full-line player with an emphasis on minivans. Chrysler could have remained in the ditch, giving Toyota or Honda an opportunity to become the No. 3 player in the U.S. market. However, Chrysler pulled ahead through its acquisition of AMC from Renault, while Honda failed to rapidly expand its product line to include minivans and sports utility vehicles.

In the short run, the third player may exit during market slowdowns or period of intense rivalry. At the end of such a period, there is usually another third player who emerges—usually not the one that left. Importantly, niche players are not significantly affected by the competitive tumult among the generalists. The competitive challenge from full-line generalists primarily affects other generalists and would-be generalists. Successful specialists are generally secure in their own niches. For example, the beer battles left micro-breweries unscathed, the cola wars had little impact on sports drink maker Gatorade, and corporate jet makers prospered even as the generalists fought for dominance in the commercial aviation market.

Strategies for Generalists Versus Specialists

Full-line generalists are first and foremost volume-driven players, while specialists tend to be margin-driven. In addition, successful generalists and specialists follow different strategies and have very different operating characteristics.

Because they are large, volume-driven players, generalists depend on economies of scale and the potential for selective cross-subsidization for much of their competitive advantage. They have large fixed assets in place, and their success depends heavily on their ability to maximize the use of those assets. Such players create (and constantly must improve) an "asset-turns" advantage—the ability to reuse the same large variable and especially fixed assets (which could be retail floor space, a large factory, a national telecommunications network, or financial assets such as working capital and inventory) continuously and efficiently.

Generalists achieve their value positioning through internal synergies, such as integrated operations, and external synergies, such as a single corporate identity. The cost savings enabled by these two factors, along with efficiency advantages derived from scale economies, enable generalists to offer superior value to many customer groups.

Specialists, by contrast, tend to emphasize service and selectivity rather than size and speed. Most specialists are also margin-driven players, due to the fact that they tend not to invest heavily in fixed costs.[46] Since variable costs are high, and sales volumes are low, profitability is driven by increasing the margin, either by raising the price (accompanied by further differentiation of the product), or lowering costs through greater efficiency.

Box 1.3   Never the Twain Shall Meet

Full-line generalists and product/market specialists have inherently different approaches to business that rarely mix well. Specialist manufacturers who start selling through generalist retailers are headed for trouble (recall the example of Excalibur and MegaMart earlier). Likewise, it is almost impossible for generalists and specialists to work together in an alliance. The inherent contradictions between a margin-driven and a volume-driven player are too great to be readily overcome.

Generalists who try to run specialty businesses in addition to their core business find that they have no talent for it. For example, Sears' downfall has been linked to its "socks and stocks" strategy in the 1980s. Sears bought Dean Witter Reynolds stock brokerage and Coldwell Banker & Co, a real estate broker. It even managed to fail in a pre-web portal joint venture (Prodigy) which was ahead of its time in many ways and offered email, games, news, weather, and shopping. Most of these holdings would be divested in the 1990s.[47] Similarly, then the leading domestic U.S. airline, United Airlines used to own Westin and Hilton hotel chains, and the world's biggest car rental company, Hertz. These had to be divested later when Wall Street did not agree with the company's assessment that these were "natural market extensions." Similarly, Kmart's attempt to foster a range of specialty businesses, such as Walden Books and Sports Authority, also failed. [48]

The only way generalists can succeed with such a strategy is by maintaining a strict separation between the two sides. Any attempts at extracting synergy between the operations by creating overlapping assortments, sharing brand names, and so on, will fail—they dilute the uniqueness and specialty nature of the specialist.

Of course, the absence of synergies begs the question of why a stable of successful businesses should be saddled with added corporate overhead and sluggish bureaucracy—questions answered mostly in the negative during the 1980s, when numerous diversified companies were acquired in hostile takeovers and then split up. In an interesting case of reversal of strategy, F.W. Woolworth Department Stores realized through trial and error that it could not be a generalist and specialist simultaneously and eventually chose to become a specialty retail chain and is the predecessor of today's success story, Foot Locker.[49]

Cost Structure

The cost structure of a full-line player is dominated by fixed costs: extensive manufacturing facilities, sophisticated flexible manufacturing systems, huge amounts of retail floor space, hundreds of airplanes or hotels, and so on. For the incremental transaction, variable costs tend to be low. The opposite is true for most successful specialists: they invest in a minimum of fixed assets and are thus able to scale their costs down rapidly if needed.

Scope of Offerings

Successful generalists offer a wide range of products and services and are able to meet the needs of customers for ancillary products as well, through either horizontal integration or alliances with other firms. Specialists, on the other hand, either offer a wide range of products to a well-defined market segment (market specialists) or a narrow range of products to all comers (product specialists, such as the various "category killers" in retailing, e.g., Staples). For example, Toys"R"Us successfully took over the toys category from the department stores such as Macy's but then ironically lost the category to Amazon, whereas BestBuy in consumer electronics has managed to co-exist based on its showroom and price-matching strategy.

Similarly, Blockbuster lost its video-rental category leadership to Netflix which delivered DVDs straight to your home. However, the market has morphed into streaming and the demand for on-demand video services has exploded where Netflix remains the leader with roughly 50% share followed by Amazon Prime (30%) and Hulu (15%) with more competition (e.g., Disney) imminent.[50]

Positioning and Branding

Generalists must pursue a broad market positioning and promote a single corporate identity. Broad-based Japanese companies have shown us for decades that brand names are far more powerful when defined broadly and applied widely (such as Yamaha, Panasonic, and Mitsubishi). Full-line generalists must use umbrella branding, offering varied products to diverse segments under a common market identity. The corporate positioning must be broad enough to allow for wide applicability across products and segments.

Increasingly, we see the use of dual brands—one for the broad market and one for the premium segment (e.g., Toyota and Lexus). This applies if the premium market is large enough to offer economies of scale advantages, as is the case in the automobile market. It is also the case in a rising number of industries, as income distributions in countries like the U.S. flatten out instead of being bell-shaped; there is now a much larger high-income segment as well as a larger low-income segment than there used to be, while the middle-income segment has diminished in size.

Specialists must be positioned differently than generalists. Product specialists need an identity that is virtually synonymous with a product category (or sub-category), whereas market specialists have to define themselves almost entirely in terms of their (ideal) customers. Since each brand stands for something distinct, specialists with more than one focus must keep the identity of each separate.

Box 1.4   The Innovation Leader: #3

For years, RC Cola was the most innovative of the big three soft drink companies. It was the first to use aluminum cans (a move that took Coke years to respond to) and the first to introduce a diet cola (Diet-Rite), playing on Coke's historical reluctance to change its formula.

In the automobile industry, perennial #3 Chrysler was known for decades as an innovative engineering company and then as a leader in innovative product design. It invented the minivan and sold over four million of them in a decade. It reintroduced the convertible to the mass market and then pioneered the successful "cab-forward" design.

In the long-distance telephone market, the #3 player was Sprint. The company had a history of pioneering innovations, most of them related to its technology. It was the first company to invest heavily in fiber optics, creating the first fully digital phone network. Sprint was also the first telecommunications company to combine long-distance, local, and cellular services, a move mimicked by its rivals. It was the first to introduce Asynchronous Transfer Mode (ATM) technology into its network and the first to offer voice-activated calling. Sprint's relative lack of market success was due to the extraordinary marketing prowess of its chief rival MCI.

Since they cannot afford to play by the rules of #1 and #2, #3 companies must compete on new flanks. For example, RC Cola looked for something Coke could not easily duplicate. They decided to attack Coke in an area where it had little flexibility: its bottling operations. Coke utilized thick, recyclable glass bottles. RC Cola introduced the aluminum can. It required huge investment for Coke to make the change to aluminum; they couldn't do it immediately.

A second move by RC Cola was predicated on its belief that Coke would never change its recipe. RC Cola invented Diet-Rite, the first low-calorie soft drink in 1958. Pepsi countered very quickly and Coke responded much later with Tab, which was not a big success. The introduction of Diet Coke would have to wait until 1982.

Distribution Channels

To attain maximum market coverage, generalists must be easily accessible to all customers. They thus utilize complex hybrid distribution systems, while specialty businesses tend to use much more focused distribution channels. Importantly, specialty businesses typically distribute their products through specialty retailers, rather than through volume-driven mass merchandisers.

Organization and Operations

Successful volume players today also focus on integrating as many aspects of their offerings as possible, striving for seamlessness and shared operations and services. WeChat from China and Facebook can be considered examples of this. One-stop shop integration reduces duplication of effort and leads to higher asset turns. Such companies also make extensive use of "flexible" fixed assets, that is, those that can be readily reconfigured to meet different kinds of demand. Generally speaking, software is more flexible than hardware. For example, cloud computing is a flexible resource with high applicability in many different sectors. Specialty businesses tend to be divisionalized rather than integrated organizations since synergies across businesses are minimal. Each business within the umbrella has its own dedicated operations.

When the Rule of Three Does Not Apply

The Rule of Three applies wherever competitive market forces are allowed to determine market structure with only minor regulatory and technological impediments. It would, therefore, not apply in markets where the following factors are significant:

Regulation. In certain markets such as utilities, having one company was viewed to be more cost-efficient for the society than having more competitors. If regulatory policies hinder market consolidation (as they have in Japan or the banking sector in the U.S.) or allow for the existence of "natural" monopolies (as was the case with the local telecommunications market in the U.S.), the Rule of Three is not operational. With deregulation, it comes into play, as was the case with the U.S. airline and trucking industries. In the case of telecommunications, the Rule of Three was observed among long-distance players, the baby bells, and for wireless service! The theory of natural monopolies is being scrutinized, and the support for it has been waning.

Exclusive Rights. If patents and trademarks are major factors in a market, it must be viewed as a collection of sub-monopolies and is thus not subject to market forces. In the chemical and pharmaceutical markets, therefore, we are less likely to see the Rule of Three govern market evolution. However, in recent years, the pharmaceutical industry has seen a large number of mergers and appears to be gradually moving toward the Rule of Three; this is due to the fact that large pharmaceutical firms are now participating in the growing generic sector as well as patented drugs, and patent-based sub-monopolies are being eroded as firms target the same therapeutic class with multiple drug formulations.

Licensed Economy. The Rule of Three cannot operate in economies in which companies are not free to adjust their production levels up or down based on market conditions. This used to be the case for the communist bloc, India, China, and Brazil. However, as these markets are deregulated, the Rule of Three is also expected to apply. For example, with the passing of the infamous "license Raj" of old, market forces have come increasingly to the fore in India, leading many companies to achieve greater economies of scale through production growth as well as mergers. Subsequently, when the media sector was deregulated, three major networks (TAR, ZTV, and Sony) emerged. The WTO has been a prime driver in raising the competitive intensity of industries internally as well as from the outside.

Major Barriers to Trade and Foreign Ownership of Assets. In this case, we are likely to see the Rule of Three operate at the national level, but not at the global level. The Rule of Three may still be seen in the formation of global groups or alliances, as we expect to occur in the global telecommunications market.

Markets with a High Degree of Vertical Integration. To the extent that certain customer groups are captive to in-house suppliers or vice-versa, the emergence of three full-line players in the supplier market is unlikely. Vertical integration does not allow competitive market forces to operate. It ties up suppliers and customers internally so they are not free to buy or sell in the open market.

Markets with Combined Ownership and Management. If ownership and management are combined, as in the case of professional services, the market process is not allowed to work. Ownership creates an emotional attachment and inhibits rational economic decision-making which would lead to mergers and demergers. In recent times, we have seen the accounting services market move from the Big 8 to the Big 6, Big 5, and now the Big 4 (Deloitte, Ernst & Young, KPMG, and PricewaterhouseCoopers).

Empirical Evidence Regarding the Rule of Three

The Rule of Three was first observed by the Boston Consulting Group Founder Bruce Henderson in a BCG Perspectives note in 1976.[51] More than three decades later, another BCG Perspectives note observed that the rule "remains relevant more than three decades after its conception—in a business environment that is, in many respects, profoundly different—and its implications continue to provide guidance for decision makers…"[52]

Using industry data from more than 10,000 firms from 1975 through 2009, the note confirmed that: "…the rule of three and four has remained a predictor of the evolution of industry structures in 'stable, competitive' industries over the decades…[t]he prevalence of industries with no more than three generalists (the 'three' part of Henderson's rule) was striking."[53] The note also found that the three-generalist configuration was the most common and the most profitable market configuration over the 35-year time-frame examined. The Rule of Three structure was characterized as a stable basin of attraction toward which markets gravitate.

For example, 15 years ago Avis, Enterprise, Hertz, and Vanguard each had over 10% market share. However, Enterprise acquired Vanguard in 2007 to take the lead and bring about the Rule of Three structure. In 2012, Hertz acquired specialist Dollar Thrifty to solidify its number two position. In fact, since 2009 Avis is no longer #2 in the industry, it had to try even harder to not succumb to the ditch! However, with Hertz in bankruptcy due to COVID-19, it may yet again be able to reclaim its perennial #2 position.[54]

Profit Impact of Market Strategies (PIMS) is a widely used database that has been the source of dozens of seminal empirical academic studies of the relationship between market share and financial performance since the 1970s.[55] The vast majority of the PIMS data came from Fortune 500 companies. One of the key findings of the PIMS project was that market share and profitability are positively related. This finding stood out so much so that some scholars referred to PIMS as the "Profit Impact of Market Share."[56] Please note that this positive association happens to be true for the right-hand side of the Rule of Three chart, for the full-line generalists where the PIMS data came from in the first place. On the contrary, we posit that the opposite association holds true for oversized specialists on the left side of the chart. Hence, our understanding remains very much incomplete if only examined from the oligopolistic view of large firms.

The Rule of Three indeed holds up when subjected to rigorous empirical analysis. Using a sample of roughly 1500 firms from 164 U.S. industries, two time periods, and numerous performance measures (such as return-on-assets (ROA), return-on-sales (ROS), and cumulative abnormal stock market returns (CAR)), a study (led by Uslay) published in a top peer-reviewed academic journal (*Journal of Marketing*) subjected the claims of The Rule of Three to empirical testing, and reported that the mode number of generalists was indeed three for the industries in the extensive sample.[57]

More interestingly, the Rule of Three (R3) industries clearly outperformed others. For example, firms in R3 conforming industries had an average operating ROA of 15.10% in 2002, whereas industries with fewer or more than three generalists averaged only 4.89% and 6.98% respectively. These findings were persistent even after controlling for other possible explanations such as firm size and

(continued)

(continued)

age, market-to-book ratio, market concentration, and market share. Moreover, the study also provided support for the hockey stick (or swoosh effect) argument depicted by the Rule of Three. For example, the generalists' operating ROA for the firms in one of the time periods was 10.58% and the specialists fared even better with 13.58%, but those stuck in the middle averaged merely 6.29%. The performance bonus for being in an R3 structure reached 209%, whereas the penalty for being stuck in the middle was as great as −54%! The results were also persistent after using a number of other measures and definitions.

It is important to point out this structure benefits all stakeholders, not just shareholders. Employees are better paid and more engaged; customers can choose from a range of offerings without getting overwhelmed with choice; suppliers can have stable and profitable relationships, and communities benefit from having robust, resilient businesses that provide steady employment and generate healthy tax revenues.

A more recent longitudinal study of market share and financial performance utilized an even more comprehensive sample of roughly 220,000 firm-years representative of the U.S. economy over four decades and reported that "the results indicate that being 'stuck in the middle' is a prevalent and empirically generalizable phenomenon that persists decade after decade even as average industry profitability decreases."[58] That study too concluded that businesses with an intermediate market share between specialists and generalists consistently find themselves at significant financial performance disadvantages across industry groups such as manufacturing, transportation, communications, and utilities, wholesale, retail, and services. Finally, game-theoretical experimental findings also echo the Rule of Three hypothesis and other empirical findings that a three-player market structure provides optimal industry performance.[59]

The empirical findings thus far have been strongly supportive of the theory, and business leaders would highly benefit from paying close attention to their implications.[60] Overall, based on our cross-sectional as well as longitudinal analyses of hundreds of markets, we find that no matter how large the market, the Rule of Three principles ultimately prevail.

These exceptions are mostly disappearing as most industries become market-driven through deregulation, privatization, and influence of the WTO. When these barriers begin to fall, markets start moving toward the Rule of Three as we have seen in India, China, Brazil, Russia, and elsewhere.

Conclusion

The Rule of Three is much more than an interesting theoretical construct; it is a powerful and robust empirical reality that must be factored into corporate strategizing. Understanding the likely end-points of market evolution is critical to the ability of executives to develop strategies that will result in success.

The lure of greater market share to niche players is a powerful one, and has caused many successful specialist companies to sacrifice their distinguishing characteristics and dilute their competencies in a headlong pursuit of growth, only to end up in the "ditch." As we have pointed out, such strategies are only viable if a clear (i.e., unblocked) opportunity to occupy a generalist position exists. If not, firms are generally far better off deploying the same resources into a geographic expansion within existing niches, or creating new niches.

Just as many specialist companies wrongly aspire to be generalists, many struggling generalists would deliver greater value to their stakeholders by merging with other generalists or reverting to specialist status. Profitable share matters much more than market share *per se*; as a senior Chrysler executive put it, "We would rather sell two cars at a profit than three at a loss." Eminently reasonable and seemingly incontestable though that concept may be, too many companies fail to grasp it.

Ultimately, the Rule of Three is about the search for the highest level of operating efficiency in a competitive market and having a positive impact on all stakeholders. Industries with four or more major players, as well as those with two or fewer, tend to be less efficient than those with three major players. The role of the government is to ensure that free-market conditions do indeed prevail, to allow industry rationalization and consolidation to occur naturally, and to step in when an industry seeks to consolidate too far, that is, to a level where fewer than three players control the lion's share.

The greatest impact and potential dislocations arising from the Rule of Three occur when an industry makes a major geographic transition—from regional to national or, even more dramatically, from national to global. The impact of this transition on a number of industries, including tires, appliances, automobiles, telecommunications, and hotels has been the emergence of a new core of inner circle companies, with, at times, surprising winners and losers.

The Rule of Three framework offers a more conscious approach to strategy formulation. The strategic guidelines we offer for players that occupy various positions in the market are all aligned with better value creation for all stakeholders, including customers, employees, suppliers, investors, communities, and society as a whole.

Finally, an implicit understanding of the Rule of Three lies behind General Electric's well-known "Number 1 or Number 2" approach to restructuring in the 1980s. When Jack Welch laid down these guidelines—that GE would have to be number 1 or number 2 in any business that it remained in—he was recognizing the constant pressures and pulls on businesses that are #3 in their market. The strategic implications of the Rule of Three are many and varied, however, and thus go considerably beyond this simple dictum.

As more markets become globalized or get transformed through technology in the coming years, managers everywhere will have to reassess their corporate positioning and strategic goals. For some, this will spell a once-in-a-lifetime opportunity to seize the initiative and firmly establish their companies on a larger stage. For many others, it will require hard thinking about strategic choices, and the courage to make painful but necessary decisions about markets not served and products not offered.

The rest of this book is organized as follows. In Chap. 2, we dissect the differences between the generalists and specialists and prescribe the best offensive and defensive strategies for each player including those stuck in the ditch. Subsequently, we revisit the industry life cycle and discuss the stages of introduction, growth, maturity, and the evitable decline or revitalization (Chap. 3), and ten ways through which industries are innovated (Chap. 4). Then, we introduce the Global Rule of Three and discuss how the Rule of Three extends to increasingly global markets (Chap. 5). Then, we introduce the new triad power and its impact on global markets, resources, and politics (Chap. 6), and discuss the global expansion strategies for multinationals from emerging markets (Chap. 7). We conclude with an Epilogue Chapter regarding the future (Chap. 8), and the current and predicted standing of global players in a variety of global markets is presented in the Appendix.

Key Takeaways

- Over the past several years, the world economy has witnessed a unique combination of economic phenomena: mergers as well as demergers at record levels with no signs of slowing down. Industries are moving toward what we call the *Rule of Three*.
- Through competitive market forces, markets get organized into full-line generalists and product/market specialists. In competitive, mature markets, there is only room for *three* full-line generalists, along with several product or market specialists.
- To be viable as volume-driven players, full-line generalists must have a critical-mass market share of at least 10%.
- The financial performance of full-line generalists *gradually* improves with greater market share, while the performance of specialists drops off *rapidly* as their market share increases.
- The ditch is a competitive pothole in the middle of generalists and specialists where companies exhibit the worst financial performance. Those closest to the ditch are the ones most likely to fall into it. The most desirable competitive positions are those furthest away from the middle.
- The Rule of Three applies to every stage of a market's geographic evolution: local, regional, national, and global.
- Like a typical shopping mall, mature markets are usually anchored by three full-line generalists among many specialty retailers. There is overlap between

(continued)

the offerings of specialists and generalists, but specialists tend to have more selection in their chosen category and command higher premiums.

- Consumers have been shifting their purchases online, hence the phenomenal growth of one-stop e-tailers such as Amazon and Alibaba. This shift makes it difficult for retailing giants to stay in business.
- The Rule of Three in retailing has now become omni-channel where full-line generalists strive to establish leadership in both online and physical stores.
- The drivers of market evolution are geared to creating efficiency by enhancing scale economies and lowering costs. This happens through four key processes: Creation of Standards, Shared Infrastructure, Governmental Intervention, and Consolidation. This leads to an organized market with fewer players.
- If the top player commands 70% or more of the market, there is often no room for even a second full-line generalist.
- In a market suffering through a downturn in growth, the fight for market share between #1 and 2 often sends the #3 company into the ditch.
- The performance of specialist companies deteriorates as they grow market share within the overall market but improves as they grow their share of a specialty niche.
- Successful specialists can become "supernichers." They are essentially monopolists in that industry.
- The existence of three players rather than two is more stable and competitive, leading to equilibrium. The structure of three creates an optimal level of choice for customers, according to the theory of evoked sets in consumer behavior.
- Full-line generalists are volume-driven players, while specialists tend to be margin-driven. Generalists achieve their value positioning through internal synergies, such as integrated operations, and external synergies, such as a single corporate identity. Specialists emphasize service and selectivity rather than size and speed. It is not feasible for generalists and specialists to work together in an alliance.
- The cost structure of a full-line player is dominated by fixed costs while the opposite is true for specialists.
- The number three player is typically the leader in innovation.
- Generalists utilize complex hybrid distribution systems while specialty businesses tend to use much more focused distribution channels.
- Successful volume players today focus on integrating their offerings for seamless and shared operations and services. Specialty businesses tend to be divisionalized.
- The Rule of Three would not apply where the following factors are significant: regulation, exclusive rights, licensed economy, major barriers to trade, foreign ownership of assets, markets with high degrees of vertical integration, and markets with combined ownership and management.
- The empirical findings have been strongly supportive of the Rule of Three. This structure benefits shareholders as well as other stakeholders. Employees are better paid and more engaged, customers choose from a variety of offerings without being overwhelmed by choice, suppliers can have stable and profitable relationships, and communities benefit from having robust, resilient businesses that provide employment and generate tax revenues.

Notes

1. Statista (2019), "Cable TV in the US," accessed September 23, 2019. https://www-statista-com.proxy.libraries.rutgers.edu/study/41973/cable-tv-in-the-us/
2. Akron Beacon Journal (2019), "Tire Company Headquarters Come and Go; Goodyear is Steadfast," accessed July 12, 2020. https://www.ohio.com/akron/business/tire-company-headquarters-come-and-go-goodyear-is-steadfast
3. Statista (2019), "Internet Users in the United States Who Have Used Food Delivery Services to Deliver a Restaurant Meal as of February 2018, by Age," accessed September 23, 2019. https://www-statista-com.proxy.libraries.rutgers.edu/statistics/921887/internet-users-usage-of-food-delivery-services-to-deliver-meals-by-age-us/
4. Schuhmacher, Tracy and Sarah Taddeo (2018), "Food Delivery Apps are Impacting Your Favorite Restaurants, Taking Bite out of Profits," DemocratandChronicle.com, August 16, 2018, accessed July 12, 2020. https://www.democratandchronicle.com/story/lifestyle/rocflavors/2018/08/16/doordash-grubhub-uber-eats-rochester-restaurant-online-food-delivery-services-swillburger-dogtown/833124002/
   Simonite, Tim (2019), "How Data Helps Deliver Your Dinner on Time," Wired.com, February 27, 2019, accessed July 12, 2020. https://www.wired.com/story/how-data-helps-deliver-your-dinner-on-time-warm/
5. Yeo, Liyin (2020), "Which Company is Winning the Food Delivery War?" Second Measure, June 15, 2020, accessed July 12, 2020. https://secondmeasure.com/datapoints/food-delivery-services-grubhub-uber-eats-doordash-postmates/
6. Isaac, Mike, Erin Griffith, Adam Satariano (2020), "Uber Buys Postmates for $2.65 Billion," *The New York Times*, July 5, 2020, accessed July 12, 2020. https://www.nytimes.com/2020/07/05/technology/uber-postmates-deal.html#
7. CBSNews (2005), "Procter & Gamble Acquires Gillette," CBSNews.com, accessed July 12, 2020. https://www.cbsnews.com/news/procter-gamble-acquires-gillette/
8. Green, Dennis (2017), "Gillette is Facing a New Threat from One of Its Oldest Rivals," BusinessInsider.com, May 24, 2019, accessed July 12, 2020. https://www.businessinsider.com/gillette-facing-a-new-threat-from-its-oldest-rival-schick-2017-5
9. Primack, Dan (2016), "Unilever Buys Dollar Shave Club for $1 Billion," Fortune.com, July 19, 2019, accessed July 12, 2020. http://fortune.com/2016/07/19/unilever-buys-dollar-shave-club-for-1-billion/
10. Statista (2016), "Sales Share of the Leading Online Blades and Razor Brands in the United States in 2016," accessed September 23, 2019. https://www-

statista-com.proxy.libraries.rutgers.edu/statistics/670586/us-sales-share-leading-online-blades-razor-brands/

    Alcantara, Ann-Marie (2019), "Dollar Shave Club's Evolution Continues with a Whole New Line of Deodorant Products," AdWeek.com, March 5, 2019, accessed September 23, 2019. https://www.adweek.com/digital/dollar-shave-clubs-evolution-continues-with-a-whole-new-line-of-deodor-ant-products/

11. Merced, Michael J. de la (2019), "Shaving Start-Up Harry's Will Be Sold to Owner of Schick for $1.37 Billion," nytimes.com, May 9, 2019, accessed September 23, 2019. https://www.nytimes.com/2019/05/09/business/deal-book/harrys-edgewell-acquisition.html

12. Statista (2019), "Market Share Prediction of Cloud Services Providers in the United States by 2020," accessed September 23, 2019. https://www-statista-com.proxy.libraries.rutgers.edu/statistics/805942/worldwide-market-share-cloud-service-providers/

13. Fondrevay, Jennifer J. (2018), "After a Merger, Don't Let "Us vs. Them" Thinking Ruin the Company," hbr.org, May 21, 2018, accessed September 23, 2019. https://hbr.org/2018/05/after-a-merger-dont-let-us-vs-them-thinking-ruin-the-company

    Statista (2019), "Value of Mergers and Acquisitions (M&A) Worldwide from 1985 to 2018 (in billion U.S. dollars)," accessed September 23, 2019. https://www.statista.com/statistics/267369/volume-of-mergers-and-acquisitions-worldwide/

14. Cimilluca, Dana and Dana Mattioli and David Benoit (2016), "Merger Deals Set Monthly Record, Even as Election Looms," wsj.com, October 28, 2016, accessed September 23, 2019. http://www.wsj.com/articles/merger-deals-set-monthly-record-even-as-election-looms-1477614934

    Brandchannel (2018), "AT&T's $85 Billion Merger with Time Warner Approved in U.S.," brandchannel.com, June 12, 2018, accessed September 23, 2019. https://www.brandchannel.com/2018/06/12/att_time_warner_merger_approved_in_us/

    The Guardian (2017), "British American Tobacco completes acquisition of Reynolds to create world's biggest tobacco firm," Scmp.com, July 20, 2017, accessed September 23, 2019. https://www.scmp.com/business/companies/article/2103355/british-american-tobacco-completes-acquisition-reynolds-create

15. Of course, not all announced deals will close. A number of recently proposed M&A deals have been challenged by the government such as the $160 billion acquisition of Allergan by Pfizer. President Trump blocked what would have been the largest tech acquisition of all time—Broadcom's hostile takeover of Qualcomm for $117 billion in March 2018. Similarly, the Chinese government challenged what would have been the second biggest technology acqui-sition of all time—Qualcomm's acquisition of NXP Semiconductors for $39

billion and the deal fell apart in July 2018 (#1 Tech M&A honor still belongs to Dell's acquisition of EMC/VMware for $67 billion in September 2016).

Bylund, Anders (2018), "Trump Stops a Chip Deal: How the Broadcom-Qualcomm Deal Collapsed," *USA Today*, March 13, 2018, accessed September 23, 2019. https://www.usatoday.com/story/tech/columnist/2018/03/13/what-you-need-to-know-about-trump-stopping-broadcoms-takeover-of-qualcomm/32886339/

Cimilluca, Dana and Dana Mattioli and David Benoit (2016), "Merger Deals Set Monthly Record, Even as Election Looms," wsj.com, October 28, 2016, accessed September 23, 2019. http://www.wsj.com/articles/merger-deals-set-monthly-record-even-as-election-looms-1477614934

16. Barclays (2019), "Beyond the Megadeal: M&A Outlook for 2019," Barclays.com, January 11, 2019, accessed September 23, 2019. https://www.investmentbank.barclays.com/our-insights/2019-global-mergers-and-acquisitions-outlook.html

17. Deloitte (2019), "The State of the Deal: M&A Trends 2019," accessed September 23, 2019. https://www2.deloitte.com/us/en/pages/mergers-and-acquisitions/articles/ma-trends-report.html\

18. Egbaria, Fouad (2019), "This Morning in Metals: World Gold Council Launches Responsible Mining Principles," Agmetalminer.com, September 12, 2019, accessed September 23, 2019. https://agmetalminer.com/category/ma-activity/

19. Beals, Rachel Koning (2019), "SunTrust Banks and BB&T Combining in Merger Worth About $66 Billion," MarketWatch.com, February 7, 2019, accessed September 23, 2019. https://www.marketwatch.com/story/suntrust-banks-and-bbt-combining-in-merger-worth-about-66-billion-2019-02-07

20. Bristol-Myers Squibb (2019), "Bristol-Myers Squibb Provides Update on Pending Transaction with Celgene," News.BMS.com, February 20, 2019, accessed September 23, 2019. https://news.bms.com/press-release/corporate-financial-news/bristol-myers-squibb-provides-update-pending-transaction-celge

Bristol-Myers Squibb (2019), "Bristol-Myers Squibb to Acquire Celgene to Create a Premier Innovative Biopharma Company," News.BMS.com, accessed September 24, 2019. https://news.bms.com/press-release/corporate-financial-news/bristol-myers-squibb-acquire-celgene-create-premier-innovative

Wikipedia (2019), "List of Largest Pharmaceutical Mergers and Acquisitions," en.Wikipedia.org, accessed September 24, 2019. https://en.wikipedia.org/wiki/List_of_largest_pharmaceutical_mergers_and_acquisitions

21. Sheth, Jagdish N. and Rajendra S. Sisodia (2002), *The Rule of Three: Surviving and Thriving in Competitive Markets*. New York: The Free Press.

22. Eberhart, Dan (2019), "Oil Sector Primed for Major Merger and Acquisition Activity," Forbes.com, January 14, 2019, accessed September 24, 2019. https://www.forbes.com/sites/daneberhart/2019/01/14/oil-sector-primed-for-major-merger-and-acquisition-activity/#edd3f3e7759a

23. Cimilluca, Dana and Dana Mattioli and David Benoit (2016), "Merger Deals Set Monthly Record, Even as Election Looms," WSJ.com, October 28, 2016, accessed September 24, 2019. http://www.wsj.com/articles/merger-deals-set-monthly-record-even-as-election-looms-1477614934

24. Davis, Alexa (2014), "Record Year in Reach For Spinoffs Thanks To Activist Appetite, Sluggish Growth," Forbes.com, June 12, 2014, accessed September 24, 2019. http://www.forbes.com/sites/alexadavis/2014/06/12/record-year-in-reach-for-spinoffs-thanks-to-activist-appetite-sluggish-growth/#756af3441700

25. Bary, Andrew, (2020), "Dell Wants to Spin Off VMware—and Wall Street Loves It," Barron's, July 16, accessed July 17, 2020. https://www.barrons.com/articles/boeing-delivered-20-planes-in-the-second-quarter-heres-how-bad-it-is-51594753379

26. Zara Retailer, "Fashion Target Market," accessed September 24, 2019. https://sites.google.com/site/zararetailer/fashion-target-market

27. When there are more than three anchor stores, the anchors (especially #4) do not do well and when there are fewer than three anchor stores, mall traffic tends to be less than ideal which hurts viability.

28. A specialist with less than 20% margin premium over the generalist may find it hard to survive. In fact, the healthy premium for superniche companies may be as high as 40%.

29. Rutgers Business School (2018), "Dan Schulman, PayPal CEO Keynote Address," YouTube.com, April 26, 2018, accessed September 24, 2019. https://www.youtube.com/watch?v=iqv18iuz3V0&feature=youtu.be

30. La Roche, Julia (2019), "59% of US Households Are Amazon Prime Members, According to Analyst," Yahoo Finance, July 15, 2019, accessed July 26, 2020. https://finance.yahoo.com/news/amazon-prime-members-59-per-cent-of-us-households-rbc-150743767.html

31. Brandchannel (2018), "Cirque du Soleil Is Coming to Shopping Malls in 2019," brandchannel.com, June 15, 2018, accessed September 24, 2019. https://www.brandchannel.com/2018/06/15/cirque_du_soleil_shopping_mall/

32. This box is drawn from: SCM Globe (2020), "Zara Clothing Company Supply Chain," January 4, 2020, accessed July 12, 2020. https://www.scmglobe.com/zara-clothing-company-supply-chain/

33. Interbrand (2018), "Best Global Brands 2018 Rankings," Interbrand.com, accessed September 24, 2019. https://www.interbrand.com/best-brands/best-global-brands/2018/ranking/

34. For example, Uslay, Altintig, and Winsor (2010) and Reeves et al. (2012) both report convergence to a three-generalist structure over time.

Uslay, Can, Z. Ayca Altintig, and Robert D. Winsor (2010), "An Empirical Examination of the 'Rule of Three': Strategy Implications for Top Management, Marketers, and Investors," *Journal of Marketing*, 74 (March), 20–39.

Reeves, Martin, Mike Daimler, George Stalk, and Filippo L. Scognamiglio (2012), "BCG Classics Revisited: The Rule of Three and Four," BCG Perspectives, #468, 12/12.

35. Henderson, Bruce D. (1979), *Henderson on Corporate Strategy*. Cambridge, MA: Abt Books.

Reeves, Martin, Mike Daimler, George Stalk, and Filippo L. Scognamiglio (2012), "BCG Classics Revisited: The Rule of Three and Four," BCG Perspectives, #468, 12/12.

36. As Fig. 1.1 also implies, super-specialists with less than 1% market share underperform larger specialists. This arguably occurs because the brand, customer, and channel equity of the super-specialists are all significantly lower. They also have neither the capability nor the resources to fully capitalize on their innovations and drive the market. "Typically, those that come up with a potential breakthrough innovation are either acquired quickly and get subsumed by a larger company or they quickly grow to become successful and legitimate specialists with more than 1% share and do not stay in this minimal market share range for long" (Uslay, Altintig and Winsor 2010, p. 25).

Meanwhile, an Harvard Business Review (HBR) study examined 1345 large mergers completed over 13 years and concluded that after going through three stages, the top three companies in each industry ultimately claim as much as 70–90% of the market.

Uslay Can, Z. Ayca Altintig, and Robert D. Winsor (2010), "An Empirical Examination of the 'Rule of Three': Strategy Implications for Top Management, Marketers, and Investors," *Journal of Marketing*, 74 (March), 20–39.

Deans, Graeme K., Fritz Kroeger, and Stefan Zeisel (2002), "The Consolidation Curve," *Harvard Business Review*, December, accessed July 12, 2020. https://hbr.org/2002/12/the-consolidation-curve

37. For example, both U.S. and EU antitrust commissions afford additional scrutiny and typically block mergers that enable a player to possess more than 40% market share.

Cohen, Michael P.A., Matthew Gibson, Eric Greenberg (2011), "United States: Cumulus/Citadel: Is 40% Market Concentration the Threshold for JSA's and Station Group Deals?" Mondaq, September 21, 2011, accessed July 12, 2020. http://www.mondaq.com/unitedstates/x/146030/Antitrust+Competition/CumulusCitadel+Is+40+Market+Concentration+The+Threshold+For+Jsas+And+Station+Group+Deals

It is very likely that high market shares…indicate a dominant position…more likely to be found in the market share range of 40% to 50%…although also undertakings with market shares below 40% could be considered to be in a dominant position…

Maher M. Dabbah, (2004), "EC and UK Competition Law: Commentary, Cases and Materials" 330, Korah, supra note 4, 121–123.

38. Carnevale, Chuck (2013), "In the Beverage Industry, Don't Overlook Dr. Pepper Snapple Group," Forbes.com, October 25, 2013, accessed September 24, 2019. http://www.forbes.com/sites/chuckcarnevale/2013/10/25/dr-pepper-snapple-dont-overlook-this-beverage-contender/#334ae8544811

Conway, Jan (2019), "Soft Drink Market Share by Company in the U.S. from 2004 to 2018*," Statista.com, July 19, 2019, accessed September 24, 2019. https://www-statista-com.proxy.libraries.rutgers.edu/statistics/225464/market-share-of-leading-soft-drink-companies-in-the-us-since-2004/

39. Sheth, Jagdish N., Fred C. Allvine, Can Uslay, and Ashutosh Dixit (2007), *Deregulation and Competition: Lessons from the Airline Industry*, Thousand Oaks, CA: Sage Publications.

40. Beresnevicius, Rytis (2019), "Flybe Becomes Virgin Connect; A Move Crucial for Virgin Atlantic," Aerotime, October 16, 2019, accessed June 29, 2020. https://www.aerotime.aero/rytis.beresnevicius/24075-flybe-virgin-connect?page=1

41. Howard, John and Jagdish N. Sheth (1969), *The Theory of Buyer Behavior*. New York: John Wiley & Sons.

42. Malhotra, Naresh K. and Can Uslay (2018), "Make, Buy, Borrow or Crowdsource? The Evolution and Future of Outsourcing," *Journal of Business Strategy*, 39 (5), 14–21.

Of course, a conglomerate such as P&G may ship to 100,000 retailers and source from 20,000 vendors so we are referring to primary suppliers at the component/SKU/service level.

Brady, Shirley (2018), "Sustainability at Scale: Q&A with P&G Chief Brand Officer Marc Pritchard," Brandchannel.com, June 13, 2018, accessed September 24, 2019. https://www.brandchannel.com/2018/06/13/sustainability-scale-qa-pg-chief-brand-officer-marc-pritchard/

43. Fenstermaker, Scott, "Too Much Choice: The Jam Experiment," Scottfenstermaker.com, accessed September 24, 2019. https://peopletriggers.wordpress.com/2013/08/31/too-much-choice-the-jam-experiment/

44. BIC Group (2017), "Registration Document," BICworld.com, accessed September 24, 2019. https://www.bicworld.com/sites/default/files/2018-03/BIC-registration-document-2017.pdf

45. MillersCoors (2019), "History of Coors Brewing Company," MillerCoors. com, accessed September 24, 2019. https://www.millercoors.com/breweries/ coors-brewing-company/history

46. Even for service industries where fixed costs tend to dominate such as the airline industry, a specialist player might choose to lease the physical asset or arrange for the costs of the asset to be linked to usage levels.

47. Delventhal, Shoshanna (2019), "Who Killed Sears? Fifty Years on the Road to Ruin," Investopedia.com, July 1, 2019, accessed September 24, 2019. https://www.investopedia.com/news/downfall-of-sears/

48. Cole, Robert J. (1985), "United Airlines Set to Buy Hertz from RCA in $587 Million Deal," *New York Times*, June 18, 1985, accessed September 24, 2019. https://www.nytimes.com/1985/06/18/business/united-airlines-set-to-buy-hertz-from-rca-in-587-million-deal.html

49. Funding Universe (2019), "Foot Locker, Inc. History," FundingUniverse. com, accessed September 24, 2019. http://www.fundinguniverse.com/company-histories/foot-locker-inc-history/

50. Watson, Amy (2019), "Share of Consumers Who Have a Subscription to an On-Demand Video Service in the United States in 2017," Statista.com, August 8, 2019, accessed September 24, 2019. https://www.statista.com/statistics/318778/subscription-based-video-streaming-services-usage-usa/

51. Henderson, Bruce (1976), The Rule of Three and Four, BCG Perspectives, No.187.

52. Reeves, Martin, Mike Daimler, George Stalk, and Filippo L. Scognamiglio (2012), "BCG Classics Revisited: The Rule of Three and Four," BCG Perspectives, #468.
    This research was performed in collaboration with Can Uslay, Ekaterina V. Karniouchina, and Z. Ayca Altintig.

53. Reeves, Martin, Mike Daimler, George Stalk, and Filippo L. Scognamiglio (2012), "BCG Classics Revisited: The Rule of Three and Four," BCG Perspectives, #468.

54. Kelly, Jack (2020), "Hertz Files for Bankruptcy after 16,000 Employees Were Let Go and CEO Made over $9 Million," Forbes, May 23, accessed June 28, 2020. https://www.forbes.com/sites/jackkelly/2020/05/23/hertz-files-for-bankruptcy-after-16000-employees-were-let-go-and-ceo-made-over-9-millio n/#17fe478f2bca
    Reeves, Martin, Mike Daimler, George Stalk, and Filippo L. Scognamiglio (2012), "BCG Classics Revisited: The Rule of Three and Four," BCG Perspectives, #468.

55. Farris, Paul and Michael J. Moore (2004), *The Profit Impact of Marketing Strategy Project: Retrospect and Prospects.* Cambridge, UK: Cambridge University Press.

56. Buzzell, R.D. (2004), "The PIMS Program of Strategy Research: A Retrospective Appraisal," *Journal of Business Research*, 57, 478–483.

57. Uslay Can, Z. Ayca Altintig, and Robert D. Winsor (2010), "An Empirical Examination of the "Rule of Three": Strategy Implications for Top Management, Marketers, and Investors," *Journal of Marketing*, 74 (March), 20–39.

This article was selected as the first runner-up for two of the most prestigious awards in marketing: the Harold H. Maynard Award for most significant contribution to marketing theory and thought, and the MSI/H. Paul Root Award for most significant contribution to the advancement of the practice of marketing. Empirical research findings based on the Rule of Three have also been presented in numerous academic conferences all over the world such as the INFORMS Marketing Science Conference (Singapore; Cologne, Germany; Istanbul, Turkey), Corporate Finance Conference (Los Angeles, USA), Marketing Dynamics Conference (Istanbul, Turkey), Global Research Conference on Marketing & Entrepreneurship (Rio de Janeiro, Brazil; London, UK), American Marketing Association Educators' Conference (Las Vegas, USA), Strategic Management Society Conference (Glasgow, UK), Academy of Marketing Conference (London, UK). One of these presentations was recipient of the 2019 AMA EMSIG Abdul Ali Promising Research Award. Finally, the research findings have been ackowledged in a book about Empirical Generalizations About Marketing Impact published by the Marketing Science Institute.

58. Uslay, Can, Ekaterina Karniouchina, Ayca Altintig, and Martin Reeves (2017), "Do Businesses Get Stuck in the Middle? The Peril of Intermediate Market Share," September 28, 2017, accessed July 11, 2020. https://papers.ssrn.com/sol3/papers.cfm?abstract_id=3043330.

59. Huck, Steffen, Hans-Theo Normann, and Jorg Oechssler (2004), "Two Are Few and Four Are Many: Number Effects in Experimental Oligopolies," *Journal of Economic Behavior & Organization*, 53 (4), 435–46.

60. For example, Uslay, Altintig, and Winsor (2010) study results were even robust when using different cut-offs to identify generalists, specialists and ditch players. Similarly, Uslay et al. (2017) use relative market share in addition to absolute market share and find full support for the ditch phenomenon and Uslay et al. (2020) replicate and extend these results using market share elasticities.

Uslay, Can, Ekaterina Karniouchina, Ayca Altintig, and Martin Reeves (2017), "Do Businesses Get Stuck in the Middle? The Peril of Intermediate Market Share," September 28, 2017, accessed July 11, 2020. https://papers.ssrn.com/sol3/papers.cfm?abstract_id=3043330.

2

Strategies for Generalists, Specialists, and Ditch Dwellers

Strategy matters. It is the difference between perishing, merely surviving, and thriving. The goal of strategy-making used to be rooted in maximizing profits. It is evolving toward optimizing value creation for all stakeholders. The Rule of Three offers strategic prescriptions that are rooted in this broader understanding of the role and purpose of strategy.

In this chapter, we further explore the governing industry dynamics of the Rule of Three. Figure 1.1 (see Chap. 1) is indeed very illuminating when used to analyze industry structure. It is essentially a plot of market share versus a measure of market value such as return on assets, P/E ratio, Tobin's q (i.e., market value/book value), return on equity, or cumulative abnormal stock market returns. Those on the left-hand side of the figure are specialty (niche) players. Super niche players such as high-end bridal boutique Vera Wang may have even higher margins than other niche players such as Red Bull. However, the downslope is rather sharp for a superniche player that wants to grow, making it more likely to head into the ditch. Specialists can be pressured into growing too fast by venture capitalists or by misguided executive compensation plans pegged to sales growth, and in the process, they typically end up losing their appeal of exclusivity and see their margins shrink. Silicon Valley firms in social media and sharing economy spaces are going through similar struggles due to their preoccupation with user growth and scaling up ("eat or be eaten"). Hence, due to the sharp slope, they could end up in the ditch if they grow too fast (and become food for bigger fish).[1]

Meanwhile, there is only room for three volume-driven players on the right-hand side, not four or more. The major players strive for growth

© The Author(s) 2020
J. Sheth et al., *The Global Rule of Three*, https://doi.org/10.1007/978-3-030-57473-4_2

primarily through mergers and acquisitions (M&A) until the structure reaches three players.

The number three firm tends to be the most innovative of the big three. Number one or two may have bigger R&D budgets, state-of-the-art labs, and more patented inventions. However, they do not perform the best where it counts the most: they are not on top when it comes to the commercial success of their innovations. Due to internal resistance and inertia, most of their investments tend to be steered toward old technology. Number 3 companies, on the other hand, as a matter of survival must continuously innovate to stay away from the ditch and are the best positioned to be innovative, to challenge, and to change the paradigm.

For example, in the 1990s, it was not AT&T or MCI but Sprint that offered affordable long-distance calls (10 cents per minute was the flat charge rather than a convoluted system of peak-off peak pricing). Contrary to industry tradition, they also used a celebrity spokesperson (Candice Bergen) in their ads to promote their innovations. More recently, this role was assumed in the mobile phone service industry by #3 player T-Mobile which has led the way in introducing new pricing schemes to the U.S. (several of which were borrowed from its parent company Deutsche Telecom mirroring the dynamic industry practices in the EU). Similarly, it was not General Motors (GM) or Ford but Chrysler that led major innovations in the automobile market, such as inventing and successfully commercializing the minivan, repositioning Jeep as an SUV, and reviving the convertible segment.

Interestingly, #3 player Google Cloud has to be the most innovative to gain share at the expense of the cloud computing leader Amazon Web Services (and #2 Microsoft Azure), whereas #3 player Amazon is expected to return the favor to market leader Google (and #2 Facebook) in digital advertising; it has already has surpassed Google for product search.[2]

Meanwhile, the fate of the #3 player is not always in its own hands. When #1 and #2 fight for market share in a stagnant market, #3 often becomes the casualty. For example, when GM and Ford fought for market share in the 1970s energy crisis, Chrysler was wounded, though it survived. When Boeing and McDonnell Douglas fought for share, Lockheed became a casualty. In the next round, when Boeing and Airbus fought for share, McDonnell Douglas was the casualty. Similarly, RC Cola found itself in the ditch when Coca-Cola and Pepsi engaged in the so-called Cola Wars in the early 1980s,[3] and Pabst and Schlitz ended up in the ditch and several local brewers became casualties when Anheuser-Busch and Miller engaged in prolonged beer wars during the 1970s and 1980s.[4]

To accomplish dominance, generalists rely on their scale and speed, product line, and network and alliances, whereas specialists emphasize selectivity and service. Overall, the cultures, processes, business models, and procurement practices, and sometimes even the infrastructures that are used by generalists and specialists are different. Furthermore, since the right-hand side of the Rule of Three (see Fig. 1.1) depicts only a mild slope, the implication is that incremental market share does not generate a high financial return for generalists. Ironically, significant share gains and sales growth (which are all too important for the C-Suite and executive compensation) do not stem from advertising campaigns, aggressive sales promotions, or price wars, which are all too common. These marketing approaches will typically not impress unless they perform surprisingly better than expected (which cannot be consistently relied upon). However, share gains from acquisitions are much more assured and significant than the incremental share gains from marketing campaigns and can be relied upon systematically which explains why M&A is so common among the large players in the corporate world as a generic strategy, as discussed previously. Mergers also result in a decreased intensity of competition, to a level more compatible with achieving sustainable financial performance as well as providing for the well-being of other stakeholders.

In Table 2.1, we recap the main differences between the generalists and specialists. Next, we offer detailed guidance for each strategic firm type and subsequently for varying market ranks.

Table 2.1 Characteristics of generalists and specialists

Characteristics	Specialists	Generalists
Sources of advantage	Economies of exclusivity and differentiation	Economies of scale, scope, and speed
	Service and selection driven	Asset-turns advantage
Competitive advantage	Image/service	Value/promotion/convenience
Cost structure	High variable costs	High fixed costs
Scope of offerings	Limited/focused line of products/services	Full line of products/services
Positioning and branding	House of brands	Branded house
	Specialty business, target market positioning	Broad market, one-stop-shop positioning with single brand (corporate) or dual (upscale and mainstream) brand identity
	Separate stops shop	
Distribution channels	Focused channels	Omni-channel
Organization and operations	Decentralized, multi-business enterprise, dedicated operations/resources, vertical integration	Integrated Enterprise, shared resources/operations, networks and alliances Horizontal integration

Source: Adapted from "Competitive Positioning: The Rule of Three" presentation by Jagdish N. Sheth, 2017

Strategies for Generalists

Generalists have volume advantages but they typically struggle capitalizing on any advantages of speed, which is increasingly a necessity. One exception to this phenomenon was McDonald's which invested in smart cash registers early on. Another exception was Walmart which invested in cash registers and inventory systems to improve both accountability and speed.[5] In fact, considering how Walmart overtook Kmart and Sears to become the largest employer in the world is telling. From the outset, Walmart focused on markets that its competitors ignored. For example, Sears focused on metropolitan areas with 500,000 to 1 million or more in population. Historically, Kmart capitalized on this; it did not compete directly with Sears and emphasized lower density locations instead (focusing on 250,000–500,000 density), and co-existed initially before it could challenge Sears. Sam Walton's unique idea was that in small towns with 15,000 or less population, he did not and would not have competitors. Not surprisingly, Walton's motto for business success was "hit'em where they ain't!"[6] By choosing locations proximate to these underserved customers, he was able to supply them from central warehouses and get concessions from large suppliers by consolidating demand.

Importantly, as detailed in his autobiography *Made in America*, Sam Walton was also guided by a higher purpose: his decision to locate in smaller towns was strategically brilliant, but was also motivated by his realization that residents of such towns had lower incomes but paid higher prices for most goods. They also lacked access to the wide variety of products that city residents took for granted. From these realizations was born Walmart's stated purpose: "Save people money so they can live better." This purpose served the company extraordinarily well—until Walton passed away. After that, the company focused resolutely on low prices that increasingly relied on paying employees as little as possible and squeezing suppliers as much as possible. Under Walton, employees and suppliers were treated with respect. The company was able to lower prices because it created extraordinary operating efficiencies, pioneering a host of innovative supply chain practices that would eventually transform the retailing sector.[7]

Ironically, Sears also started out by targeting the rural population by selling a broad range of products to farmers by catalog in the late 1800s and early 1900s. But it was Sam Walton who recognized that the largest market waiting to be unlocked was small towns. Walmart aggregated rural America for economies of scale, served them efficiently, and the rest is history.[8] If it can navigate cultural differences, Walmart still has boundless potential to grow in emerging markets with the same approach.

Amazon with its Prime shipping has made significant progress in terms of velocity, and it is currently introducing free one-day delivery. An oft-ignored factor, economies of speed tends to be equally important for success for a generalist as economies of scale.

The ability to turn over assets (measured by dividing revenue by assets) is critical for generalists. They must become one-stop shops comprised of both products and services. Branding gurus generally advise a singular clear message for brand positioning purposes. However, for a true generalist, this approach can be restricting. For example, what does Amazon stand for? Can it really be simplified to one concept or dimension? Can one concept truly capture the essence of a mega-brand?

Consider the case of Unilever, which in 2018 announced that its 26-strong sustainable living brand portfolio grew 46% more than the rest of its business and delivered 70% of its turnover growth. Twenty-two of these sustainable brands were also among the company's top 40 brands.[9] While then-CEO Paul Polman was rightly passionate about the need to move sustainability to the center of the company's strategy (given all the challenges the world faces, especially climate change), does that mean Unilever should anchor its future primarily to sustainability? Inspired by Unilever's example and competing to keep up, Procter and Gamble (P&G) in 2018 pledged total commitment to recycling and announced that it would entirely cease sending consumer manufacturing waste to landfills by 2020 and switch to 100% renewable energy in its manufacturing plants by 2030.[10] Such moves by its competitors help Unilever advance toward its stated purpose to "make sustainable living commonplace." However, even Unilever leaders would agree that sustainability cannot be the sole driver of its success in the market; customers also care about other dimensions. Hence, the brand positioning for generalists must be broad rather than focused on a singular dimension. Value is always the top consideration in mass markets. Generalists must therefore compete based on their broad value proposition.

What can generalists of all industries learn from pizza chains? You can dine in, pick it up, or have it delivered. Similarly, generalists should not restrict themselves to any particular channel. Contrary to conventional thinking, we posit that the more channels a generalist utilizes, the better off it is. Whereas specialists are advised to avoid channel conflict and not try to manage it, generalists, especially in the age of e-commerce, must have omnipresence and master how to manage channel conflict. Many businesses that have historically relied on channel members for their success can no longer ignore selling direct to customers. They must join the omni-channel movement and enable their consumers to convert on any channel.[11]

Successful generalists emphasize a common brand, common corporate overhead structure, and dominate several segments at once. Rather than being content with a simple holding structure, they strive to become integrated enterprises. Hence, the architecture of their revenues and costs must be integrated as opposed to independent divisions running as separate business units. Their operations must be shared such that different product lines can be manufactured in the same plant. Their sales channels must be shared so that distribution is optimized across product categories and a well-trained sales force can sell multiple products to the same customer. Overall, they must be organized from a total process and architecture point of view. For example, a generalist retailer such as Amazon can truly sell anything and everything. Indeed, it carried 119,928,851 different products as of April 2019 and it is on pace to become the top-selling fashion retailer in the U.S.![12]

Similarly, it is very common for business-to-business (B2B) generalists to have a corporate umbrella brand (single corporate identity) in order to achieve economies of scale, scope, and speed. A few decades ago, it was not even imaginable that mass merchants rather than jewelry stores would carry precious stones. Today, the largest diamond seller in America is Walmart. Similarly, generic-brand luggage sells more than Samsonite if Walmart offers it. Whether in Canada, Mexico, or China—it makes no difference. Omnipresence does not mean emphasizing online or direct selling while deteriorating traditional channels. Manufacturers have to remember to respect their retail partners and treat them as their customers and partners.

In packaged or fast-moving consumer goods (FMCG) categories, the Rule of Three is applicable at the brand level. For example, in the U.S. hair care market, L'Oréal (Redken, Kiehl's, Garnier) is the market leader with 21% market share, followed by Unilever (Suave, Axe, Tresemme) with 17%, and P&G (Head & Shoulders, Pantene, Herbal Essence) which was the market leader a decade ago has 14% market share.[13] Companies such as Nestle, Unilever, and P&G have numerous diversified product lines with a different set of competitors in each. Even though they are treated as one entity, they resemble conglomerates that need to be analyzed at the product/brand level instead of the aggregate level that would apply to other generalists.

For example, there is very little synergy between the coffee division and the detergent division at P&G. On the other hand, it is possible for these conglomerates to achieve brand identity in major categories as P&G has done with Tide and Pantene. The value proposition of these global master brands supersedes cultural differences. However, in the world of consumer packaged goods (CPG), there are many more brands than needed, and these brands, like the numerous castles across the Rhine river, are nice to observe but very expensive to maintain. Unless a generalist already has a significant market share, the margins will simply not be sufficient to maintain too many brands. And even for a generalist with significant share and lead, excessive brand proliferation can become a drag on margins. Therefore, many CPG companies such as Nestle, Unilever, and P&G are focused on pruning their brand portfolio to a handful of master brands. P&G's reduction of its detergent and shampoo brands to focus on the 80 brands that generate 95% of its profits and sale of the iconic Folgers coffee brand to Smucker for $3 billion are examples of this.[14]

Toyota, which has consistently been one of the top automakers globally, has long operated with a single volume brand. The Toyota corporate logo is affixed to all its sub-brands (the Scion experiment ended in Toyota killing off the brand, renaming remaining models as Toyota 86, Toyota Yaris iA, and Toyota Corolla iM).[15] They also own the Lexus luxury brand; however, the volume brand Toyota has a coherent broad corporate identity based on reliability.

Meanwhile, GM (which lost global auto leadership to Toyota in 2008) simply has too many brands each requiring considerable attention and support to maintain a unique market position.[16] Their current brands include Buick, Cadillac, Chevrolet, GMC, Holden, and Wuling. Former brands included McLaughlin, Oakland, Oldsmobile, Opel, Pontiac, Hummer, Saab, Saturn, and Vauxhall. With so many brands to support, they lack economies of scale in manufacturing, marketing, and distribution. Akin to Toyota/Lexus architecture, they would be better off with Chevrolet as their volume brand and Cadillac as their luxury brand.

Strategies for Specialists

Specialists do not compete on value or price but on brand image, exclusivity, and sometimes customer support services. They need to think of after-sales, in addition to pre-sale and sale activities for differentiation. Specialty manufacturers and retailers need to be much more end-user driven than generalists. Generalists may get away with serving just buyers/payers but that will not suffice for specialists to command higher margins (through procurement as well as higher price points). Thus, the notions of positioning and competition are very different for specialists. They must also be very focused when it comes to channel selection.

For example, a major quandary that specialty manufacturers face is that they may align with a volume retailer in order to grow sales. Historically, this was a major mistake by the successful specialist Levi's which came under public pressure to grow after going public in the 1970s and aligned itself with JC Penney and Sears. Prior to this alignment, Levi's was just sold through its own stores as well as specialty retailers. Subsequently, Levi's began competing heavily against its own stores. It then outsourced manufacturing to lower labor costs, cut corners, but became associated with cheap goods and damaged its own brand equity in the process.

As alluded to in Chap. 1, for the budding specialist seeking aggressive growth through mass market channels, things go great at first. The first year of operations creates tremendous sales volume for the manufacturer which more than justifies the price cut to the volume retailer. However, in the second year, the volume retailer will simply ask for more price concessions, the third year even more and so forth. The manufacturer by now has invested in larger facilities in anticipation of future sales growth and becomes dependent on the volume retailer's business. To maintain the account, extreme cost-cutting and compromised quality follow the price concessions. A slippery slope indeed which can only end up in the ditch! Hence, the choice of channel partners (or franchisees or dedicated sales force, if applicable) is critical for specialists.

Unlike generalists, specialists should *not* integrate their operations (except for back-office operations) in search of cost savings. Furthermore, they need to maintain separate margin-driven brand names/storefronts as opposed to a master brand. Specialists' core competency stems from design as opposed to manufacturing. They can utilize designers to project exclusivity advantage. They cannot be one-stop shops and must carefully select their markets. Thus, the motto for the specialists is focus, focus, and more focus; and target, target, and target some more where each brand occupies a unique position in the market.

It is important to observe that it is very difficult to be a generalist and specialist simultaneously. We caution our readers to not defy this warning. Many have tried and most have ended up in the ditch. In an industry that is already organized into the Rule of Three structure, it is very difficult for a fourth firm to emerge as a viable generalist. For example, American Motors (AMC) tried to scale up with its Jeep acquisition and failed. Renault which bought AMC also failed to break through and sold it to Chrysler. There are many routes to success for specialty businesses other than becoming a generalist, and it is a very risky proposition for a specialist to even try. Tesla is a prime example of this and its future as an independent company remains uncertain as it is consistently among the most shorted U.S. stocks.[17] To take a shot at the most valuable automaker in the world (Tesla is valued at $183 billion in June 2020 as opposed to Toyota at $176 billion) may appear counter-intuitive. However, please also note that Tesla sold only 192 K vehicles in the U.S. in 2019 versus Toyota's 2.38 million. It would be truly a remarkable achievement for Tesla to stay the distance as an independent concern.[18]

A primary reason why Kmart and Sears are on life support is because they tried to get into specialty retailing by acquiring specialty retailers. For example, Kmart eventually had to divest OfficeMax, PayLess Drug Stores, Pace Membership Clubs, Coles Myer, Borders, Walden Books, The Sports Authority, and Builders Square. Similarly, Sears expanded into financial services and home brokerage business.[19]

These generalists thought that they could succeed by pumping investments from volume into the margin side of the business and appease investors by providing volume and margin simultaneously. This just doesn't work! The strategy process is not really complex. A business must decide whether they are a volume- or margin-driven player, then organize and execute everything accordingly.

As mentioned before, exceptions may exist in the case of luxury divisions (e.g., Lexus for Toyota, Infiniti for Nissan, Acura for Honda, and Audi for Volkswagen) but then the divisions are run separately. A parent company may have two divisions—one for volume and the other for margin-driven businesses. For example, volume-driven products and margin-driven services can be maintained as separate businesses by the same umbrella organization. When Siemens envisioned a separate organization for maintenance contracts, it was able to create a high-margin global services business. Similarly, Apple's service business is its fastest growing source of revenue, and at 17.7% share of revenue for the fiscal year 2019, generated almost double the revenue Apple earned from its Macs.[20] On the other hand, the traditional way of organizing—tying services to related products does not work as well, as has been the case with GE Energy, and Phillips.

Next, we discuss the strategies for the top three generalists, ditch, and niche players.

Defensive and Offensive Strategies for Competitors

The traditional generic strategies in the literature refer to low-cost, differentiation, and focus, or interchangeably operational excellence, innovation, or customer intimacy. However, our view of strategic options differs based on the market rank and standing of the players. Next, we discuss two types of strategies for each player. One is defensive, that is, how do you defend your turf? The general principles of market defense and retaliation for the incumbents have been established, and include speed, intensity, breadth (e.g., number of marketing mix variables used), and market domain responses.[21] And the other strategy which is more challenging is offensive that is, how do you grow your business?[22]

Strategies for #1 Generalists

The first viable defensive strategy for a market leader with 30–40% market share is to be a fast follower rather than a pioneer. Indeed, it is rare for a leader like Microsoft to come up with and commercialize a breakthrough innovation. Other leaders in the tech space such as Google, Amazon, and Facebook are also fast followers. A fast follower strategy can be employed through own R&D as well as through acquisitions. In fact, the safest and quickest way for a generalist to get to 40% market share is typically through M&A.

Arguably, Facebook would have lost its social media leadership by now if it had not acquired the then 18-month-old Instagram for $1 billion in 2012.[23] Overall, #1 companies should pay especially close attention to what the #3 player is doing. Recall from Chap. 1 that the most successful innovations tend to come from the third player, a notion we will discuss in more detail later in this chapter. Coca-Cola did not invent the diet soda; however, it is currently the leader of the category with Diet Coke thanks to its fast follower strategy. It intently watches new offerings and the consumer response very closely and is quick to acquire or develop its own version if there is validated potential. For example, its acquisition of a 77% stake of Flipkart in 2018 for $16 billion instantly gave Walmart online apparel and fashion leadership in the Indian market over Amazon.[24]

On the other hand, if the market leader is a pioneer that created the market with a large R&D investment, being a fast follower may prove to be a difficult logic to follow. For example, Bell Labs (and Kodak and Xerox) have always been inclined to pioneer as opposed to follow—they suffered from the NIH (not invented here) syndrome, which contributed to their eventual downfall. IBM, on the other hand, used to be a great fast follower in the last century, and Microsoft maintains the fast-follower tradition in the current one.

As powerfully argued for by Renee Mauborgne and Chan Kim in their best-selling book *Blue Ocean Strategy*,[25] a more aggressive option for the market leader is to focus on growing the total market as opposed to being preoccupied with its direct competitors. Fighting for market share is not only costly but can also invite antitrust scrutiny. The market leader is better served by growing the market than by trying to gain share in a stagnant market. For example, Coca-Cola focuses on global/emerging markets where they can convert non-users to customers of bottled water and beverages. It is redefining its heritage as the global beverage leader (as opposed to soft drinks) in the process. Among the aging populations of the world, consumption of carbonated beverages is inevitably lower. Fighting for market share through price wars and sales promotions may consolidate the market further (e.g., failure of 7 Up enabled the growth of Sprite). However, that is not where the real value lies. The highest per capita consumption and the highest growth in the consumption of Coca-Cola beverages are in emerging markets.

Similarly, 3M and GE are prioritizing China and India over the U.S. Counter-intuitively then, the most effective aggressive strategy for the #1 generalist is to stop fighting for share and focus on growing the pie. Strategy is about realizing market potential rather than expanding market share. Growing the pie also elevates the role and prominence of marketing in the organization. For example, Carnival has redefined itself as a vacation provider as opposed to a cruise-line operator.

In many cases, acquiring users from among non-users (Uber vs. taxi-users, Uber vs. public transportation) can be easier and more profitable than acquiring them from competitors (Uber vs. Lyft). In other cases, getting new eyeballs makes more business sense than trying to engage current users even further. For example, whereas roughly 80% of the U.S. population had at least one social media profile in 2019, the percentage is much lower globally, under 35%.[26] Similarly, the per capita consumption of Cola products in China and India is a mere fraction of the figures for Argentina or Australia.[27]

Huawei Technologies of China is expanding the market globally and is very active in Africa where it entered over two decades ago.[28] From its humble beginnings as a low-cost mobile network builder, it now has operations in over 40 African nations and has become one of the top three providers worldwide. The same global market development approach also applies to consumer packaged goods category leaders such as P&G and Unilever.

The performance of the market leader is typically optimized around 40–45% market share. Anything beyond these levels tends to dampen margins and potentially attract antitrust scrutiny. In protecting or seeking market share, the leader may start subsidizing product lines or markets, especially foreign markets considered as strategic. Contrary to prevailing wisdom, market leaders with close to 45% share may actually want to deselect segments and shed share points and begin to boost their margins instead.

> **Box 2.1 Online Dating**
>
> Once considered to be taboo, online dating is now a fast-growing market.[29] About one in five consumers have sought courtship online. Match Group focused on online dating early on and has been a fast follower and buyer of promising start-ups before they became legitimate challengers. Alongside its mainstream platform Match.com, it actually owns over 45 dating businesses including popular sites such as OkCupid, Plenty of Fish, Hinge, Meetic (Europe), Eureka (Japan). Match had revenues of $2.1 billion in the year ended March 31, 2020 (and a market cap of $28 billion), and 34% market share.[30] A distant number two player is eHarmony with about 11% share. Everyone else is a specialist with no full-line contender in sight. That is until Facebook rightfully decided to be a player in this lucrative market.[31]
>
> We fully expect it to challenge and dislodge Match.com from their seemingly secure leadership position utilizing their analytics prowess and the scale of the Facebook nation (which had 2.6 billion monthly active users as of March 2020). But this is only case of the U.S. of course. In the global picture, Match.com will also be likely surpassed by a Chinese platform such as Jiayuan, which already has 135 million members.[32] To compare their respective monetization potential, as of the first quarter of 2019, the entire Match Group had 8.6 million paying members.[33] Jiayuan could become a global leader simply by leveraging its domestic scale advantage (also see Chap. 7).

Strategies for #2 Generalists

Number 2 generalists have a choice. They can decide to co-exist with the leader (defensive strategy option) or they can challenge the leader head-on (aggressive option). Co-existing is a better option especially if the share distance to the leader is large (e.g., a #2 player with 10–15% share vs. a leader with 40–45%). This was the case in the 1960s for IBM versus the seven dwarfs, when IBM held 65% of the market versus Burroughs, Sperry Rand, Control Data, Honeywell, General Electric, RCA, and NCR.[34]

And this is currently the case for Google versus Bing, Mozilla, and others in search engines where Google holds over 90% market share globally.[35] Number 2 players can emphasize the markets where #1 does not have the capacity or interest, rather than challenging it in its focal markets. For example, generic drug manufacturers co-exist peacefully with brand-name drugs in most categories. Among Chinese telecom service providers, China Mobile has the clear lead with about 60% share followed by China Unicom 20.4% share and China Telecom 19.6% share, so the #2 and #3 compete more with each other rather than co-challenge the leadership of China Mobile.[36]

Going from defense to attack is a sequential process. MCI, Avis, and EDS all co-existed before they were ready to challenge the market leaders AT&T,

Hertz, and IBM respectively. While Pepsi was happy to co-exist with Coca-Cola for several decades by focusing on northern states initially, a review of its later campaigns since the 1980s (a.k.a. the Cola Wars) suggests a shift in strategy. Finally, PC manufacturer Lenovo became #2 globally in 2011 and then successfully challenged HP to become the global leader in 2014. However, HP made a comeback in 2017 and competition for market leadership was neck-and-neck for 2018.[37] Whereas Lowe's (the original home improvement leader founded in 1921 which succumbed its leadership in 1990) attempts to regain leadership from Home Depot have been unsuccessful, Haier was successfully able to challenge the leader in each continent and became the #1 white goods manufacturer globally.

Interestingly, even though price competition alone rarely represents a good long-term strategy, the price elasticities applicable to the #2 player tend to be higher than those applicable to the leader. That is, price cuts and sales promotions of the #2 player are more impactful than those of the #1 player, everything else being equal, especially if the #2 and #1 are not close in market share.[38]

It is important to consider what the #2 is doing because the price earnings ratio (and thus shareholder value) not only is a function of market share and return on assets (ROA) of the leader but also depends on #2 player's conduct. The market capitalizations of both firms are interdependent, and future expectations about the intensity of competition can significantly impact these figures. The theory of mutual forbearance also suggests that a high degree of interdependence should mitigate rivalry and lead to co-existence.[39]

Strategies for #3 Generalists

The #3 generalist should try to insulate itself from directly competing with #1 and #2 to the extent possible as a defensive strategy. It should strive to dominate a segment of the market with 55–70% share even though its overall market share may be more modest such as 11–12%. If #3 can dominate a segment with three or four times the share of its overall share, it can have a significant fall back market in case #1 and #2 engage in price wars.

For example, Uniroyal was primarily an OEM tire manufacturer with more than half of its business from GM, which insulated it from the competition. Similarly, FedEx focused on the airmail (documents) niche in its early days and insulated itself from USPS competition. Later on, it built mini-warehouses for its largest clients such as Boeing near Memphis and insulated itself from competition with the new entrant DHL. Similarly, Coors initially emphasized a non-pasteurized beer without preservatives and gained almost a cult-like following, which insulated it from brands with broader distribution.[40]

The high risk-high reward aggressive strategy for the #3 player is to innovate with the hope of changing the market order before the innovation can be emulated. The #3 player should strive to find out what it is that #1 and #2 are not doing right and pursue markets where they cannot follow due to their higher incumbency investments. For example, Chrysler was the first company to position Jeep as an SUV, and also invented the minivan. Sprint was the most innovative in long-distance communications. Its network configuration, billing, collection, and processes were superior, and it also introduced the use of a celebrity spokesperson and simplified flat-rate pricing. In contrast, the #3 player in India, Reliance Jio has been very innovative and overtook #1 and #2 Vodafone and Bharti Airtel, respectively, to become #1 by offering highly affordable data plans. It is in fact projected to extend its lead by capturing 45% of the market by 2022 (also see "Reverse Innovation" section in Chap. 7).[41]

In the fast-growing cruise industry which projected 40 million passengers and $9 billion + earnings from $60 billion gross revenues in the next decade (pre-Covid-19 pandemic), three cruise lines (Carnival, Royal Caribbean, and Norwegian) control 85% of the global cruise market.[42] However, it was #3 Norwegian that pioneered "freestyle" cruising which represented an innovation vacationers welcomed when introduced in 2000. Traditional cruise ship dining required passengers to choose between early or late seating for formal, sit-down dinners. The tablemate companions as well as the restaurant dined would be the same every night. Norwegian's "freestyle" enabled guests choose when and where they would dine and also switched the dress code from formal to casual. Freestyle proved to be a significant success and "today even the most traditional of luxury cruise lines are ditching assigned for open seating and opting for elegant casual dinner attire over strict, multi-tiered dress codes. Modern-day ships offer a plethora of dining venues, from quick and casual to date-night fancy and ethnic specialties from around the world."[43] Similarly, Norwegian introduced waterfront dining in 2013. Indeed, the concept of having "bars and restaurants with outdoor seating along a quarter-mile oceanfront promenade" makes a lot of sense in hindsight.[44]

Overall, we would like to emphasize that the convention that a generalist must follow either a low-cost (operational excellence) or differentiated position in the marketplace is misguided. Indeed, the generic low-cost proposition often represents a race to the bottom with a single winner, if any (e.g., IKEA), while focusing on differentiation requires continuously upping the

R&D ante and depresses margins. Thus, the most appropriate approach depends on the market standing as well as the defensive versus offensive stance of the business as opposed to a simplistic choice between low-cost versus differentiation strategies.

Strategies for Niche Players

Specialists come in three types: product specialists (e.g., Red Bull and WD-40), market specialists (e.g., In-N-Out), and supernichers (e.g., USAA, Gentex, Porsche, and Lamborghini) that specialize in both. Superniche players can actually dominate their well-defined *segments* and effectively enjoy monopolist status. For example, both Tesla and Netflix were near monopolists in their superniche segments before they grew the segment substantially and attracted mainstream competitors (which for Netflix now includes Amazon, Disney, HBO, NBC, and others). Other nichers can enjoy the rule of two in larger segments (Krispy Kreme and Dunkin' Donuts, but watch out for Duck Donuts; or Martin and Taylor for acoustic guitars) or even Rule of Three if the niche is substantial (e.g., Five Guys, Smashburger, In-N-Out; Chick-fil-A, KFC, and Popeyes).

If left unchecked, aggressive growth can drive superniche players into the ditch, especially following an IPO. Successful product specialist La-Z-Boy expanded and became just another furniture company with a 4.8% market share of U.S. household furniture manufacturing.[45] Similarly Bed Bath and Beyond has recently been more "Beyond" than Bed and Bath; its future may require more trimming and getting back to the basics. Chipotle also expanded aggressively but only found its path to profitability after shutting down dozens of locations and emphasizing food delivery partnerships.[46]

There is plenty of room for successful niche players to dominate their well-defined segments and thrive in global markets.[47] The challenge is to stay independent even as investors and private equity do not mind paying a hefty multiple if they think they can perform even better. As stock buybacks can only carry them so far, conglomerates have also been looking for ways to supplement their portfolios and ways to invest their retained earnings. Hence, the first and most common option for a niche player is to sell to a generalist. Maybelline, Honest Tea, Gatorade, LinkedIn, ResearchGate, Snapple, and Banana Republic are all examples of this. In the brewing sector, over 70 specialist craft brewers such as Anchor Brewing, Wicked Weed, Karbach Brewing, and Revolver Brewing have been acquired by the generalists such as Sapporo, Constellation Brands, and AB InBev.[48] The founding team can grow a business to 3–4% share and then sell at a premium. There is also an opportunity for them to become serial entrepreneurs, which is commonplace in high-tech.

Maybelline used to strictly focus on mascara; it tried to diversify but did not do very well in make-up products, and was subsequently sold to L'Oréal.[49] Gatorade, invented at the University of Florida to serve student-athletes, was later sold to Quaker Oats, which consisted of basically a collection of niche brands such as Snapple and Captain Crunch cereals. Unable to compete against the Rule of Three, that is, Kellogg's, General Mills, and General Foods in the cereal market, Quaker Oats was ultimately bought by Pepsi for $13.4 billion in 2000.[50] Similarly, Volkswagen group has bought controlling stakes in high-end specialists Bentley, Lamborghini, Bugatti, Ducati, and Porsche respectively.

About half of the growth of J&J (the global leader in health care) has come from acquisitions, mostly of specialists. Acquiring specialists is such a commonplace practice that even a handbook for *Building a Market-Ready M&A Brand* is available from Interbrand to encourage the practice.[51] Unilever's acquisitions of eco-friendly cleaning brand Seventh Generation for $700 million and Dollar Shave Club for $1 billion are additional recent examples.[52]

The other strategic option for specialists is to descale/harvest the original business and move up to a superniche position and improve margins further. Rolls-Royce (the aerospace and power systems company, not the automaker, which is part of BMW) can be considered as a prime candidate for this.[53] Similarly, in order to fend off Japanese competitors such as Citizen and Seiko, the Swiss watchmakers had to reinvent themselves and move superniche upscale for much higher price points (also see Box 4.2 in Chap. 4 "Quartz Watches").

In the cruise industry, Carnival, Royal Caribbean, and Norwegian represent the three generalists, and Disney is a niche player. SeaDream Yacht Club remains one of the few independent ultra-luxury cruise lines after Royal Caribbean bought a controlling stake in the ultra-luxury Silversea Cruises in early 2018.[54] Meanwhile, American Cruise Lines and Viking Cruises focus on river cruises. Supernichers tend to have excellent margins; however, as they grow further, their margins collapse, especially with a franchising system. For example, Krispy Kreme struggled financially as it tried to expand too quickly, and diluted its brand equity and experiential appeal by selling its doughnuts through grocery and convenience stores.

Specialists in need of capital infusion can also attract strategic investments from generalists for non-controlling rights and pave the way or keep their options open for future exit acquisitions. Toyota's recent $1 billion investment in Grab, the largest car-hailing service of Southeast Asia is an example.[55] Coca-Cola bought a 40% stake in the Honest Tea in 2008 which it purchased outright in 2011. The original investors made a 2500% return.[56]

Box 2.2   The Limited

The Limited (founded in 1963) came out of a class project at Ohio State University. The target market was a narrowly and precisely defined yet very fast-growing segment—young (18–30-year-old), affluent, college-educated, professional, and slim women—and catered to a wide range of their fashion needs. These women were fashion-conscious, modern, and wanted to be breadwinners. The Limited hired its employees from the same demographic profile and incentivized them to wear from The Limited through discounts. Hence, the store image, customer image, and employee image all blended into one harmonious mix. However, when the original market it catered to became mainstream, the company fell into the temptation of opening too many stores and also added Limited Express, Victoria's Secret, and Lane Bryant (for plus-sized women) to its holdings. Losing brand equity, loaded with debt, and unable to appeal to changing customer needs, the company declared bankruptcy in 2017.

Box 2.3   The Quandary of the Ditch Dwellers

As Michael Porter observed: "There are two basic types of competitive advantage: cost leadership and differentiation ... A firm that engages in each generic strategy but fails to achieve any of them is 'stuck in the middle' ... In most industries, quite a few competitors are stuck in the middle."[58] In this section, we further elaborate on what we mean by the ditch and why it matters so much for its tenants. The 2016 Sheth Medal recipient and Harvard Business School Distinguished Professor Michael Porter is known for synthesizing the vast body of knowledge in industrial economics and for developing several parsimonious and seminal management frameworks including the five forces of competition, the value chain, and competitive cluster development. Among these, Porter also described three generic strategies: cost leadership, differentiation, and focus. One of the fundamental axioms of strategic management, Michael Porter's generic strategy framework suggests that firms that try to implement more than one strategy perform significantly worse than those committed to a single generic strategy.[59] As a result, the dictum to avoid being "stuck in the middle" remains among the reigning takeaways from the business schools.[60]

Michael Porter prescribed that it was typically not feasible to differentiate and minimize cost simultaneously, and business units that did not commit to a generic strategy or tried to implement more than one would get "stuck in the middle."[61] Focus was related to the scope at which the remaining two strategies would be implemented. However, since low-cost strategy by and large needed large scale (and market share to utilize that scale), the focus decision was practically deemed secondary. Porter himself noted that the two basic types of competitive advantage are cost leadership and differentiation. Subsequently, many researchers omitted the focus dimension of generic strategies in their research design. Overall, Porter's generic strategies framework remains among the most disseminated in the field of business strategy.

(continued)

Box 2.3   (continued)

The Rule of Three succinctly suggests that firms with 5–10% share of their markets typically get stuck in the middle, or in other words, end up in the ditch. These firms tend to have lower financial performance and market capitalization than both larger generalists and smaller specialists. In some cases, they err in pursuing both strategies simultaneously. They try to be special but then try to serve the general market. Meanwhile, they have no scale or uniqueness/differentiation advantage. Firms end up in the ditch either due to intensive competition (too many undersized generalists may exist due to regulation preventing consolidation or during the early stages of an industry life cycle, or a price war between #1 and #2 can push #3 in the ditch) or due to the lure of growth.

Market share is undeniably a fundamental variable in business strategy practice and research. Thus, it is critical to understand its relationship with performance. Despite the prevailing dictum for more market share, *there is concrete empirical evidence that being stuck in the ditch is so common that it can be characterized as a law-like empirical generalization*. Using ROA as the dependent variable, four-digit standard industry classification codes for market definition, and data that is representative of the entire U.S. economy (using roughly 220,000 firm-years from over four decades), a research team (led by Uslay and supported by the Boston Consulting Group Strategy Institute) reported that being stuck in the middle is a prevalent and empirically generalizable phenomenon that persists decade after decade.[62] They found that the ditch can be as wide as 3–11% with its nadir at around 7–7.5%. The team also examined industry groups such as manufacturing, transportation/telecommunications/utilities, wholesale, retail, and services and industries such as computer manufacturing and found that the results were remarkably consistent. Their sample size was also more than 150 times larger than that of the typical academic research study on market share and performance. Another research paper utilized five-digit North American Industry Classification System codes and also found strong support regarding this issue.[63] Thus, it is very unlikely that these results are due to sampling or market definition issues. Indeed, the performance penalty for getting stuck in the ditch can exceed 50% (e.g., sample ROA for generalists was 11%, and for specialists it was 14%, but those in the ditch averaged merely 6%)![64]

These research efforts have collectively provided the evidence that other leading scholars had suspected a long time ago: "Whatever strategy they adopt to fight off the challenge of the larger form makes them more vulnerable in competition with small organizations, and vice versa. That is, at least in a stable environment the two ends of the size distribution ought to outcompete in the middle."[65] The middle of the industry distribution is "a bad place to be for firms in any strategic dimension such as size, location, and price."[66]

In the case of retailers, the emergence of Amazon as a dominant e-tailer with such a large scale has wreaked havoc on physical retailers, many of which have been pushed into the ditch. The Rule of Three predicts that when there is excessive competition due to too many generalists or when #1 and #2 firms engage in price wars, #3 usually ends up in the ditch. Right now, there is an ongoing war between Amazon and brick-and-mortar retailers which is pushing some large players into the ditch as Amazon challenges and displaces the leaders one by one. In fact, both Amazon and Walmart's online sales of toys and baby products

(continued)

Box 2.3 (continued)

had already surpassed that of Toys"R"Us in 2016,[67] so when it declared bankruptcy in September 2017, it surprised no one.[68]

Other retailers that have gone bankrupt in the last few years pre-Covid-19 include Aerosoles, Alfred Angelo, American Apparel, Aeropostale, A'Gaci, Art Van Furniture, Barneys New York, BCBG Max Azria, Beauty Brands, Bluestem Brands, Charlotte Russe, Charming Charlie, Cornerstone Apparel (Papaya), Destination Maternity, Diesel, Eastern Outfitters, Forever 21, Fred's, Gander Mountain, Gordmans, Gymboree, Henri Bendel, HHGregg, Innovative Mattress Solutions, Modell's Sporting Goods, Pacific Sunwear, Payless ShoeSource, Performance Bicycle, Perfumania, Pier 1, Radio Shack, Rue 21, SFP Franchise Corp., Shopko, Sports Authority, The Limited, Things Remembered, True Religion, Vanity, Vitamin World, Wet Seal, and Z Gallerie.[69]

Moreover, Covid-19 pandemic added household names such as Aldo, Brooks Brothers, Centric Brands, GNC, Gold's Gym, G-Star Raw, J.C. Penney, J. Crew, Lucky Brand, Neiman Marcus, Roots USA, Stage Stores, Sur La Table, Tuesday Morning, and Victoria's Secret UK to the growing bankruptcy list.[70]

These specialists had become accustomed to sustaining their growth by continuously adding new stores in the old days. When the tide turned, they found themselves as outsized specialists in the ditch only able to revive themselves after closing hundreds of stores and painful downsizing, if at all. Counter-intuitively, for those that are able to come out of Chap. 11, future vitality will depend on their going small and improving their margins rather than getting larger.

Nevertheless, the idea that all firms must grow is still taken for granted. But as Peter Drucker observed, growth is only meaningful if it improves the productivity of resources, and volume alone is not relevant. According to Drucker, if growth does not improve the productivity of resources, it should be considered fat to be sweated off. Growth that results in diminished productivity is akin to cancer that calls for radical surgery. "By itself there is no virtue in business growth."[71] Therefore, it is important for managers to not fixate on growth for the sake of growth and astutely analyze their market(s) and decide on the best standing and necessary growth for their firms. This requires an understanding of what is optimal for the organization based on its strategic type and objectives rather than a quest for maximum size.

For example, while the storied piano-maker Steinway continues to dominate the high end of the market with more than 80% share, it can be considered to be in the ditch when it comes to upper middle and lower middle grand piano segments. Banking on growth, the company acquired the largest piano key manufacturer of Europe in 1998 and the largest piano plate manufacturer of the U.S. in 1999. Management estimated its overall market share to be 9% in 2004, which is not a tenable position. Within a decade, the company was in the hands of a hedge fund for $512 million and continues to struggle.[72]

That is not to say that small firms that are already doing well should avoid growth. "A company needs a viable market standing. Otherwise it soon becomes marginal … in effect, the wrong size. And if the market expands, whether domestically or worldwide, a company has to grow the market to maintain its viability. At times a company therefore needs a very high minimum growth rate …"[73] Therefore, avoiding the ditch can be a tricky proposition, and once a

(continued)

The case of The Limited illustrates a maxim—that the optimal way for a specialist to grow healthily is by spawning new specialists without growing any of them excessively so as to saturate the market and grow into the ditch.

To reiterate, the Rule of Three points to commonly observed misalignments between size and strategic performance objectives. "Being the wrong size is a chronic, debilitating, wasting—and a very common—disease. There are industries in which a big business and a small business can prosper. But the in-between businesses, the fair-sized business, is the 'wrong size.' The middle size is becoming the wrong size."[57] This argument put forth powerfully by Peter Drucker is entirely consistent with the subsequent work on the Rule of Three and the notion of the ditch. Thus, anchored to efficiency and growth, the Rule of Three organizing principle is of paramount importance. It is also vital to note that growth comes not only from market share/increased concentration but through successful scope diversification of products and markets. This includes geographic expansion as well as product diversification (e.g., Boeing, Airbus, Walmart, and Starbucks). Scope diversification essentially makes a player a viable generalist; the lack of it makes it a ditch dweller.

Strategies for Ditch Dwellers

As heroic as it sounds, it is very hard (but not impossible as exemplified by the resurgence of T-Mobile in the U.S.) to exit the ditch through organic growth.

Therefore, the first strategy for ditch players is to downsize and become a specialist especially if they fell in the ditch as a volume-driven player. For example, A&P, the first large supermarket in the U.S., sold its own private label products (like Sears used to). Supermarkets receive significant sums from manufacturers in terms of slotting fees, and in some cases, the fee received for a product can amount to more than the money they make from selling it. Without the benefit of slotting fees, many independent supermarkets could not endure the competition from rivals like Kroger and Safeway. A&P closed locations and tried cost-cutting but lost its customer appeal in the process. It became a smaller specialty niche retailer and ultimately did not survive.[77]

BF Goodrich (also see Box 5.2 on BF Goodrich in Chap. 5) was also stuck in the middle when it decided that its core competency was specialty chemicals as opposed to tire manufacturing and sold to Uniroyal and subsequently Michelin. Service Merchandise was a catalog company which tried showroom retail locations, grew too fast and collapsed, and did not survive after downsizing. However, Godfather's Pizza is a different story. The pizza chain aggressively expanded in late the 1970s (in fact, it was the fastest-growing fast-food chain in the U.S. 1977–1979) and early 1980s to become to third-largest pizza chain the U.S. in 1985.[78] However, Pillsbury bought Godfather's and watched it lose ground against other chains before selling to a leveraged buyout group led by Godfather's own executives in 1990. The group closed about 200 locations and eliminated thousands of jobs but was able to bring the chain back to profitability as a nimbler specialist.[79]

Following its bankruptcy, the storied fashion brand Brooks Brothers' future story also remains uncertain. As one pundit observed: "middle of the market is untenable for classic men's clothing. Perhaps the only way out is to go back upmarket … or go further downmarket to the point where it's even less inspiring. Mid-tier retailing with a large number of stores seems to be a dead business model in fashion."[80] Of course, we already exemplified in Chap. 1, the danger of going downmarket, and the stuck in the ditch phenomenon applies to more than fashion brands.

Sometimes, new players may go into the ditch from the start. Iridium Satellite (which emerged out of Motorola) had plans to dominate the market for wireless communications with its low orbit satellites surrounding the earth. However, it could not overcome a host of regulatory, marketing, and technical challenges, and more importantly, the phones were too bulky and the service was unaffordable for most consumers and Iridium ended up in the ditch. However, it too reemerged from bankruptcy as a much nimbler player focusing primarily on B2B markets.

More recently, Kodak has reemerged from bankruptcy as a significantly smaller specialist and produced its first annual profit, three years after bankruptcy in 2017.[81] It is currently focused on B2B products and services, such as making film for the movie industry. Similarly, formidable smartphone leader Blackberry was disrupted by Apple's iPhone and subsequently Samsung's offerings and was taken private to fend off bankruptcy in 2013 and had to exit smartphone manufacturing altogether to become a viable software company in 2016.[82]

Alternatively, ditch dwellers may need to find a consolidator to join them together, like JP Morgan did for steel and electric power in the heydays and AB InBev seems to be doing in alcoholic beverages. In fact, AB InBev made 21 acquisitions over the past decade including the $103 billion SABMiller acquisition in 2015, and the $52 billion Anheuser-Busch acquisition in 2008. Alternatively, private equity firms can also serve as consolidators.[83] Insurance companies were among the first holdings that Warren Buffet added to the portfolio of Berkshire Hathaway.

Historically, GM was also a consolidator. As Ford's Model T caused the collapse of dozens of auto-manufacturers, GM co-founded by Billy Durant consolidated the industry. It continued to do so when the Great Depression caused the failure of more automakers. GM bought many household brands such as Chevrolet, Buick, Pontiac, Oldsmobile, Cadillac, and even surpassed Ford in the process. The reason many conglomerates are called "general" (General Motors, General Electric, General Mills, General Foods, General Dynamics, etc.) is that they were all consolidators (of failing firms) of their industries following the Great Depression. They were able to extract value by transforming themselves into volume-driven players. Similarly, Coors became #3 not by organic growth but by buying breweries in various locations that were collapsing due to price wars. Today, consolidators are just as likely to emerge from emerging markets as they are from advanced markets. (See Chap. 7 for strategies for firms from emerging markets.) For example, Anhui Conch of China is the #2 cement manufacturer in the world, and Cemex of Mexico, despite its government-induced divestitures, is still #4 globally.

Overall, William-Sonoma, Chick-fil-A, and Red Bull can be considered to be representative of specialists; Brookstone; Abercrombie and Fitch, Sprint, and Avon are representative of ditch players, whereas McDonald's, Amazon, Google are generalists. In the next chapter, we revisit the industry life cycle to explain how industries evolve, mature, and get revived.

Key Takeaways

- The Rule of Three enables managerial implications and guidance that is rooted in a broader understanding of the role and purpose of strategy.
- When #1 and #2 fight for market share in a stagnant market, #3 often becomes the casualty.
- Share gains from M&A are much more significant than the incremental share gains resulting from marketing campaigns, which explains why M&A is so common among the large players as a generic strategy.
- Generalists have volume advantages but struggle to capitalize on any advantages of speed, which is increasingly a necessity.
- The ability to turn over assets is critical for generalists. They must become one-stop shops comprised of both products and services. Brand positioning for generalists must be broad focused, as value is always the top consideration in mass markets.
- In the age of e-commerce, generalists must have omnipresence and master how to manage channel conflict. Omnipresence does not mean emphasizing online or direct selling while deteriorating traditional channels.
- Specialists compete on brand image, exclusivity, and customer support services. They need to think about end-users to command higher margins and must be focused on channel selections.
- Specialists can be pressured into growing too fast, and in the process, they typically end up losing their appeal of exclusivity and see their margins shrink.
- A major quandary that specialists face is that they may align with a volume retailer in order to grow sales. This can lead to a position in the ditch.
- Specialists should *not* integrate their operations in search of cost savings. They should rather focus and target to occupy a unique position in the market.
- It is nearly impossible to be a generalist and a specialist at the same time. The exception is the case where the parent company may have two divisions—one for volume and the other for margin-driven businesses.
- *Strategies for 1# Generalist:* The first viable defensive strategy is to be a fast follower rather than a pioneer. Number 1 companies should pay especially close attention to what the #3 player is doing. A more aggressive strategy is for the market leader to focus on growing the total market as opposed to being preoccupied with its direct competitors. Expanding the market can also lead to the elevated prominence of marketing in a firm.
- Market leaders with close to 45% share may actually want to deselect segments and shed share points and begin to boost their margins instead.
- *Strategies for #2 Generalist:* Number 2 generalists can decide to co-exist with the leader (defensive strategy option) or challenge the leader head-on (aggressive option). Co-existing is better when the market leader's share is much greater than #2's.
- *Strategies for #3 Generalist:* The #3 generalist should try to insulate itself from directly competing with #1 and #2 to the extent possible as a defensive strategy. If #3 can dominate a market segment with three or four times the share of its overall share, it can have a significant fall back market in case #1 and #2 engage in price wars.
- The high risk-high reward aggressive strategy for the #3 player is to innovate with the hope of changing the market order before the innovation can be emulated.

(continued)

- *Strategies for Niche Players:* Specialists can fall into three categories: product specialists, market specialists, and supernichers. The most common option for a niche player is to sell to a generalist. There is also an opportunity for them to become serial entrepreneurs, which is commonplace in high-tech. Much of the growth of generalists comes from acquiring growing specialists.
- *Strategies for Ditch Dwellers:* One strategy for such firms is to downsize and become a specialist especially if they fell in the ditch as a volume-driven player. Another is to merge among other ditch players or scale up through acquisitions. Ditch dwellers may need to find a consolidator to join them together.
- The other strategic option for specialists is to descale/harvest the original business and move up to a superniche position and improve margins further.
- The optimal way for a specialist to grow healthily is by spawning new specialists without growing any of them excessively so as to saturate the market and grow into the ditch.
- Growth comes not only from market share/increased concentration but through successful scope diversification of products and markets. This includes geographic expansion as well as product diversification.
- The Rule of Three succinctly observes that firms with 5–10% share of their markets end up in the ditch. Firms end up in the ditch due to intensive competition or the lure of growth.
- There is concrete empirical evidence that being stuck in the ditch is so common that it can be characterized as a law-like empirical generalization.

Notes

1. Of course, this does not present much of a problem for the venture capitalists (VCs) as their portfolios generate healthy returns regardless, whether their firms eat or are eaten. Thus, they constantly broker such arrangements, and they may even be the vested party to both the target and the acquirer. Also see:
   Masulis, Ronald W. and Rajarishi Nahata (2011), "Venture Capital Conflicts of Interest: Evidence from Acquisitions of Venture Backed Firms," *Journal of Financial and Quantitative Analysis*, 46 (2), 395–430.
2. Salinas, Sara (2019), "Amazon's Ad Business Will Steal Market Share from Google This Year, Says eMarketer," CNBC.com, February 20, 2019, accessed September 24, 2019.
   https://www.cnbc.com/2019/02/20/amazon-advertising-business-stealing-market-share-from-google.html.
   Alaimo, Dan (2018), "Amazon Now Dominates Google in Product Search," RetailDive.com, September 7, 2018, accessed September 24, 2019.
   https://www.retaildive.com/news/amazon-now-dominates-google-in-product-search/531822/.

3. Paracha, Nadeem F. (2017), "Cola Wars: A Social and Political History," Dawn.com, April 28, 2017, accessed September 24, 2019. https://www.dawn.com/news/1329368.

4. Ascher, Bernard (2012), "Global Beer: The Road to Monopoly," The American Antitrust Institute, accessed July 12, 2020. http://www.bluedustpgh.com/uploads/1/0/3/0/10309574/global_beer_road_to_monopoly.pdf.

5. Hess, Alexander E.M and Robert Serenbetz (2014), "15 Biggest Employers in the World," *USA Today*, August 24, 2014, accessed September 24, 2019. https://www.usatoday.com/story/money/business/2014/08/24/24-7-wall-st-biggest-employers/14443001/.

6. Beckwith, Harry (1997), *Selling the Invisible: A Field Guide to Modern Marketing*, New York: NY, Warner Books.

7. Walton, Sam and John Huey (1993), *Sam Walton: Made in America*, New York: NY, Bantam Books.

8. Rumelt, Richard (2011), *Good Strategy, Bad Strategy*, New York: NY, Random House.

9. Buss, Dale (2018), "Unilever's Sustainable Living Brands: Why Doing Good Is Good For Business," BrandChannel.com, May 10, 2018, accessed September 24, 2019. https://www.brandchannel.com/2018/05/10/unilever_sustainable_living_brands_good_business/.

10. Brady, Shirley (2018), "Sustainability at Scale: Q&A With P&G Chief Brand Officer Marc Pritchard," BrandChannel.com, June 13, 2018, accessed September 24, 2019. https://www.brandchannel.com/2018/06/13/sustainability-scale-qa-pg-chief-brand-officer-marc-pritchard/.

11. Verhoef, Peter C., P.K. Kannan, and J. Jeffrey Inman (2015), "From Multi-Channel Retailing to Omni-Channel Retailing: Introduction to the Special Issue on Multi-Channel Retailing," Sciencedirect.com, March 31, 2015, accessed September 24, 2019. https://www.sciencedirect.com/science/article/abs/pii/S0022435915000214.

12. ScrapeHero (2019), "How Many Products Does Amazon Sell?" https://www.scrapehero.com/number-of-products-on-amazon-april-2019/.

13. Chaudhuru, Saabira (2019), "Shampoo Giants Go Head to Head," The Wall Street Journal, October 17, accessed November 2, 2019. https://www.wsj.com/articles/unilever-cuts-prices-as-shampoo-rivalry-grows-11571302051?mod=hp_lead_pos8.

14. Bhattarai, Abha (2008), "Smucker to Pay $3 Billion for Folgers Coffee," NYTimes.com, June 5, 2008, accessed September 24, 2019. https://www.nytimes.com/2008/06/05/business/05folgers.html.

Abrams, Rachel (2014), "Procter & Gamble to Streamline Offerings, Dropping Up to 100 Brands," NYTimes.com, August 1, 2014, accessed September 24, 2019.
https://www.nytimes.com/2014/08/02/business/procter-gamble-to-drop-up-to-100-brands.html.

15. Mays, Kelsey (2016), "Scion Is Toast: What It Means to Owners and Shoppers," Cars.com, February 3, 2016, accessed September 24, 2019.
https://www.cars.com/articles/scion-is-toast-what-it-means-to-owners-and-shoppers-1420683373148/.

16. Marr, Kendra (2009), "Toyota Passes GM as World's Largest Automaker," WashingtonPost.com, January 22, 2009, accessed September 24, 2019.
http://www.washingtonpost.com/wp-dyn/content/article/2009/01/21/AR2009012101216.html.

17. Garber, Jonathan (2018), "Tesla Short-Sellers Mauled with $2.5B Loss," Fox Business, February 3, 2020, accessed June 22, 2020. https://www.foxbusiness.com/markets/tesla-stock-short-sellers-lose-2-5b.

18. Routley, Nick (2020), "Tesla is Now the World's Most Valuable Automaker," Visual Capitalist, June 16, 2020, accessed July 12, 2020.
https://www.visualcapitalist.com/tesla-is-now-the-worlds-most-valuable-automaker/.

19. Delventhal, Shoshanna (2019), "Who Killed Sears? Fifty Years on the Road to Ruin," Investopedia, July 1, 2019, accessed September 24, 2019.
https://www.investopedia.com/news/downfall-of-sears/.

20. Delventhal, Shoshanna (2020), "Apple's 5 Most Profitable Lines of Business," Investopedia.com, March 10, 2020, accessed June 29, 2020.
https://www.investopedia.com/apple-s-5-most-profitable-lines-of-business-4684130#:~:text=For%20fiscal%20year%202019%2C%20the,generated%209.8%25%20of%20total%20revenue.

21. Kuester, Sabine, Christian Homburg, Thomas S. Robinson (1999), "Retaliatory Behavior to New Product Entry," *Journal of Marketing*, 63 (October), 90–106.
Uslay, Can (2005), "The Role of Pricing Strategy in Market Defense," doctoral dissertation, Georgia Institute of Technology.

22. Kotler, Philip and Kevin Lane Keller (2016), *Marketing Management*, 15th ed., Upper Saddle River, NJ: Pearson.

23. Moffitt, Ashley, and Can Uslay (2016), "Periscope's Dawn: Up or Down?" *Rutgers Business Review*, 1 (1), 123–139.

24. Sharma, Nishant (2018), "This Is Why Amazon Hasn't Beaten Flipkart In India Yet," Bloombergquint.com, March 23, 2018, accessed September 24, 2019.
https://www.bloombergquint.com/business/2018/03/23/this-is-why-amazon-hasnt-beaten-flipkart-in-india-yet#gs.KaQHHLs.

25. Kim, W. Chan and Renée Mauborgne (2005), *Blue Ocean Strategy: How to Create Uncontested Market Space and Make the Competition Irrelevant,* Boston, MA: Harvard Business School Press.
26. Clement, J. (2019), "Percentage of U.S. Population Who Currently Use Any Social Media from 2008 to 2019," Statista.com, March 6, 2019, accessed September 24, 2019.
     https://www.statista.com/statistics/273476/percentage-of-us-population-with-a-social-network-profile/.
     Clement, J. (2019), "Number of Social Network Users Worldwide from 2010 to 2021 (in billions)." Statista.com, May 28, 2018, accessed September 24, 2019.
     https://www.statista.com/statistics/278414/number-of-worldwide-social-network-users/.
27. Coca-Cola Company (2013), "Per Capita Consumption of Company Beverage Products," Coca-ColaCompany.com, accessed September 24, 2019.
     https://www.coca-colacompany.com/cs/tccc-yir2012/pdf/2012-per-cap-ita-consumption.pdf.
28. Rukato, Wadeisor (2016), "What Huawei Has Done Right in Africa," FromAfricatoChina.com, August 10, 2016, accessed September 24, 2019.
     https://fromafricatochina.com/2016/08/10/what-huawei-has-done-right-in-africa/.
29. Statista (2019), "Online Dating," Statista.com, accessed September 24, 2019.
     https://www.statista.com/outlook/372/100/online-dating/worldwide.
30. Cardona, Frank (2019), "The Rise of Online Dating, and the Company That Dominates the Market," VisualCapitalist.com, March 23, 2019, accessed September 24, 2019.
     https://www.visualcapitalist.com/online-dating-big-business/.
     Gillies, Trent (2017), "In 'Swipe Left' Era of Mobile Dating, eHarmony Tries to Avoid Getting 'Frozen in Time'," CNBC.com, February 11, 2017, accessed June 28, 2020.
     https://www.cnbc.com/2017/02/11/in-swipe-left-era-of-mobile-dating-eharmony-tries-to-avoid-getting-frozen-in-time.html.
     Statista (2020), "Revenue of the Match Group from 1st Quarter 2014 to 1st Quarter 2020" Statista.com, accessed July 12, 2020.
     https://www.statista.com/statistics/449390/quarterly-revenue-match-group/.
31. Kraus, Rachel (2019), "Facebook Dating is coming to the U.S. in 2019," Mashable.com, April 30, 2019, accessed September 24, 2019.
     https://mashable.com/article/facebook-dating-comes-to-usa-facebook-f8-2019/.
32. Visa Hunter (2019), "The 5 Best Online Dating Sites in China," VisaHunter.com, accessed September 24, 2019.

https://www.visahunter.com/articles/the-best-online-dating-sites-in-china/.

33. Clement, J. (2019), "Number of Paid Subscribers Registered to the Match Group from 1st Quarter 2014 to 2nd Quarter 2019 (in 1000 s)," Statista. com, August 9, 2019, accessed September 24, 2019.
     https://www.statista.com/statistics/449465/paid-dating-subscribers-match-group/.

34. Dvorak, John C., "IBM and the Seven Dwarfs—Dwarf One: Burroughs," Dvorak.org, accessed September 24, 2019.
     http://www.dvorak.org/blog/ibm-and-the-seven-dwarfs-dwarf-one-burroughs/.

35. Statcounter GlobalStats (2019), "Search Engine Market Share Worldwide," gs.Statcounter.com, accessed September 24, 2019.
     http://gs.statcounter.com/search-engine-market-share.

36. Waring, Joseph (2019), "China Telecom Narrows Subs Gap to Unicom," Mobileworldlive.com, January 22, 2019, accessed September 24, 2019.
     https://www.mobileworldlive.com/asia/asia-news/china-telecom-narrows-subs-gap-to-unicom/.

37. Holst, Arne (2019), "Global Market Share Held by the Leading PC Vendors from 2006 to 2018," Statista.com, January 15, 2019, accessed September 24, 2019.
     https://www-statista-com.proxy.libraries.rutgers.edu/statistics/273675/global-market-share-held-by-pc-manufacturers-since-2006/.

38. Increasing the sales promotion budget or cutting the price by the same percentage amount is much more costly for the market leader, while there is also less room to lift the sales of the leader based on this price cut or sales promotion.

39. Kang, Wooseong, Barry L. Bayus, and Sridhar Balasubramanian (2010), "The Strategic Effects of Multimarket Contact: Mutual Forbearance and Competitive Response in the Personal Computer Industry," *Journal of Marketing Research*, 47(June), 415–427.

40. Bell, Emily (2016), "The True Coors Bootlegging Story Behind Smokey And The Bandit," Vinepair.com, March 29, 2016, accessed September 24, 2019.
     https://vinepair.com/wine-blog/smokey-and-the-bandit-and-coors/.

41. Wire Agency (2019) "Reliance Jio Market Share May Jump to 45%: India Ratings," LiveMint.com, August 29, 2019, accessed September 24, 2019.
     https://www.livemint.com/companies/news/reliance-jio-market-share-may-jump-to-45-india-ratings-1567084595812.html.

42. Cruise Industry News (2018), "Cruise Industry Targets 40 M Passengers and Net Earnings of $9 Billion-Plus," CruiseIndustryNews.com, May 30, 2018, accessed September 24, 2019.
     https://www.cruiseindustrynews.com/cruise-news/19068-cruise-industry-targets-40m-passengers-and-net-earnings-of-9-billion-plus.html.

43. Silverstein, Erica (2019), "11 Jaw-Dropping Cruise Ship Innovations," Cruisecritic.com, accessed September 24, 2019.
    https://www.cruisecritic.com/articles.cfm?ID=1697.

44. Silverstein, Erica (2019), "11 Jaw-Dropping Cruise Ship Innovations," Cruisecritic.com, accessed September 24, 2019.
    https://www.cruisecritic.com/articles.cfm?ID=1697.

45. Seeking Alpha (2019), "La-Z-Boy: Far from Lazy," SeekingAlpha.com, March 13, 2019, accessed September 24, 2019.
    https://seekingalpha.com/article/4248413-la-z-boy-far-lazy.

46. Meyer, Zlati (2018), "Chipotle to close up to 65 stores this year," USAToday.com, June 27, 2018, accessed September 24, 2019.
    https://www.usatoday.com/story/money/2018/06/27/chipotle-close-55-65-stores-year/740245002/.

47. Simon, Hermann (2017), "Why Germany Still Has So Many Middle-Class Manufacturing Jobs," *Harvard Business Review*, May 2,
    Simon, Hermann (1992), "Lessons from Germany's Midsize Giants," *Harvard Business Review*, March/April, 115–123.
    Simon, Hermann (1996), *Hidden Champions: Lessons from 500 of the World's Best Unknown Companies*, Boston: Harvard Business School Press.

48. Vinepair (2019), "The Definitive Timeline Of Craft Beer Acquisitions," Vinepair.com, accessed September 24, 2019.
    https://vinepair.com/craft-beer-sales/.

49. Wayne, Leslie (1995), "L'Oreal to Buy Maybelline in Cash Deal," NYTimes.com, December 11, 1995, accessed September 24, 2019.
    https://www.nytimes.com/1995/12/11/business/l-oreal-to-buy-maybelline-in-cash-deal.html.

50. Sorkin, Andrew Ross and Greg Winter (2000), "PepsiCo Said to Acquire Quaker Oats for $13.4 Billion in Stock," NYTimes.com, December 4, 2000, accessed September 24, 2019.
    https://www.nytimes.com/2000/12/04/business/pepsico-said-to-acquire-quaker-oats-for-13.4-billion-in-stock.html.

51. Brandchannel (2018), "M&A Insider: How Johnson & Johnson Makes Big-Little Mergers Work," Brandchannel.com, June 15, 2018, accessed September 24, 2019.
    https://www.brandchannel.com/2018/06/15/johnson_and_johnson_jnj_merger_acquisition_interbrand-panel/.

52. Battelle, John (2016), "What Everyone Missed in the Unilever/Seventh Generation Deal," Shift.newco.co, September 20, 2016, accessed September 24, 2019.
    https://shift.newco.co/what-everyone-missed-in-the-unilever-seventh-generation-deal-41258b5a2248.
    Primack, Dan (2016), "Unilever Buys Dollar Shave Club for $1 Billion," Fortune.com, July 19, 2016, accessed September 24, 2019.

http://fortune.com/2016/07/19/unilever-buys-dollar-shave-club-for-1-billion.

53. BBC News (2018), "Rolls-Royce Announces 4600 Job Cuts," BBC.com, June 14, 2018, accessed September 24, 2019.

     https://www.bbc.com/news/business-44479410.

54. Cruise Arabia & Africa (2018), "Mixed Reactions as Royal Caribbean Buys Controlling Stake in Silversea," CruiseArabiaOnline.com, June 14, 2018, accessed September 25, 2019.

     https://cruisearabiaonline.com/2018/06/14/mixed-reactions-as-royal-caribbean-buys-controlling-stake-in-silversea/.

55. Buss, Dale (2018), "Unilever's Sustainable Living Brands: Why Doing Good Is Good For Business," BrandChannel.com, May 10, 2018, accessed September 26, 2019.

     https://www.brandchannel.com/2018/05/10/unilever_sustainable_living_brands_good_business/.

56. Buss, Dale (2018), "Honest Branding: 5 Questions with Honest Tea Co-Founder Seth Goldman," BrandChannnel.com, July 27, 2018, accessed September 26, 2019.

     https://www.brandchannel.com/2018/07/27/5_questions_seth_goldman_honest_tea_at_20/.

57. Drucker, P.F. (1973), *Management: Tasks, Responsibilities, Practices.* New York: Harper & Row. pp. 664–665.

58. M. E. Porter (1985), *Competitive Advantage,* New York: The Free Press, pp. 3, 16.

59. M. E. Porter (1985), *Competitive Advantage,* New York: The Free Press.

     M. E. Porter (1980), *Competitive Strategy*, New York: The Free Press.

     M. E. Porter (2008), *On Competition: Updated and Expanded Edition*, Boston: MA, Harvard Business Review Publishing.

60. Porter (1980) coined the term "stuck in the middle" to refer to businesses that commit to none of the generic strategies (low cost, differentiation, focus) or those that attempt to pursue more than one simultaneously. He also argued that this choice could result in a U-shaped relationship between market share and business performance (1980, p. 43; 1985). We adopt this second interpretation of being stuck in the middle based on market share and performance.

     M. E. Porter (1980), *Competitive Strategy*, New York: The Free Press.

     M. E. Porter (1985), *Competitive Advantage,* New York: The Free Press.

61. For example, a specialist could preemptively invest and achieve a dominant focus and low-cost position within a niche market or a generalist could create loyalty through differentiation while maintaining cost-leadership. However, it is very challenging to sustain performance through such dual strategies which is the essence of Porter's stuck in the middle proposition.

62. Uslay, Can, Ekaterina V. Karniouchina, Z. Ayca Altintig, and Martin Reeves (2017), "(How) Do Businesses Get Stuck in the Middle?" working paper, accessed July 11, 2020.

   https://papers.ssrn.com/sol3/papers.cfm?abstract_id=3043330.

   Also see Schwalbach, J. (1991), "Profitability and Market Share: A Reflection on the Functional Relationship," *Strategic Management Journal,* 12(May), 299–307.

63. Uslay, Can, Z. Ayca Altintig, and Robert D. Winsor (2010), "An Empirical Examination of the 'Rule of Three': Strategy Implications for Top Management, Marketers, and Investors," *Journal of Marketing,* 74 (March), 20–39.

64. Uslay, Can (2015), "The Rule of Three: Market Share and Performance," in *Empirical Generalizations about Marketing Impact,* D. M. Hanssens ed., Cambridge, MA: Marketing Science Institute, 17–18.

65. Hannan, M.T., Freeman, J. (1977), "The Population Ecology of Organizations," *American Journal of Sociology,* 82 (5), 929–964, p. 946.

66. Kalnins, A. (2016), "Beyond Manhattan: Localized Competition and Organizational Failure in Urban Hotel Markets Throughout the United States, 2000–2014," *Strategic Management Journal,* 37 (11), 2235–2253, p. 2236.

67. Green, Dennis (2017), "Walmart and Amazon are Already Picking at the Carcass of Toys R Us," BusinessInsider.com, September 20, 2017, accessed September 26, 2019.

   http://www.businessinsider.com/walmart-amazon-beat-toys-r-us-online-sales-2017-9.

68. Debter, Lauren (2017), "Toys 'R' Us Files for Bankruptcy, But Will Keep Stores Open," Forbes.com, September 19, 2017, accessed September 26, 2019.

   https://www.forbes.com/sites/laurengensler/2017/09/19/toys-r-us-bankruptcy/#1a5f8c29574a.

69. McCoy, Kevin (2017), "Payless Emerges from Bankruptcy Court Protection After Closing More Than 673 Stores," *USA Today,* August 10, 2017, accessed September 26, 2019.

   https://www.usatoday.com/story/money/2017/08/10/payless-emerges-bankruptcy-court-protection-after-closing-more-than-673-stores/555790001/.

   Thomas, Lauren (2017), "Here are the Retailers That Have Filed for Bankruptcy Protection in 2017," CNBC.com, September 23, 2017, accessed September 26, 2019.

   https://www.cnbc.com/2017/09/23/here-are-the-retailers-that-filed-for-bankruptcy-protection-in-2017.html.

Cain, Aine and Bethany Biron (2019), "These 17 Retailers Have Filed for Bankruptcy or Liquidation in 2019," BusinessInsider.com, September 26, 2019, accessed September 26, 2019.
https://www.businessinsider.com/bankrupt-companies-retail-list-2019-3.
Peterson, Hayley (2019), "More than 9300 Stores are Closing in 2019 as the Retail Apocalypse Drags On—Here's the Full List," Business Insider, December 23, 2019, accessed July 12, 2020.
https://www.businessinsider.com/stores-closing-in-2019-list-2019-3.

70. Retail Dive Team (2020), "The Running List of 2020 Retail Bankruptcies," Retail Dive, June 30, 2020, accessed July 12, 2020.
https://www.retaildive.com/news/the-running-list-of-2020-retail-bankruptcies/571159/.

71. Drucker, P.F. (1982), *The Changing World of the Executive*, New York: Times Books. p. 87.
Drucker is often credited with influencing GE CEO Jack Welch, in thinking to develop "become #1 or #2 or exit" strategy which is a simplistic but consistent way of executing a strategy based on the Rule of Three.

72. Batt, Robert and M. Eric Johnson (2007), "Strengthening the Distribution Channel at Steinway & Sons," Vincent L. Lacorte Case Series, Tuck School of Business at Dartmouth, Case: #6–0027.
https://digitalstrategies.tuck.dartmouth.edu/wp-content/uploads/2016/10/6-0027.pdf.
Mangan, Dan, (2016), "Steinway & Sons CEO Out Three Years After Billionaire John Paulson Purchase," CNBC Markets, August 22, 2016, accessed July 12, 2020.
https://www.cnbc.com/2016/08/22/steinway-sons-ceo-out-three-years-after-billionaire-john-paulson-purchase.html.

73. Drucker, P.F. (1973), *Management: Tasks, Responsibilities, Practices*. New York: Harper & Row. pp. 774–775.

74. Whalen, Peter, Can Uslay, Vincent J. Pascal, Glenn Omura, Andrew McAuley, Chickery J. Kasouf, Rosalind Jones, Claes M. Hultman, Gerald E. Hills, David J. Hansen, Audrey Gilmore, Joe Giglierano, Fabian Eggers, Jonathan Deacon (2016), "Anatomy of Competitive Advantage: Towards a Contingency Theory of Entrepreneurial Marketing," *Journal of Strategic Marketing*, 24 (1), 5–19.
Alqahtani, Nasser and Can Uslay (2020), "Entrepreneurial Marketing and Firm Performance: Synthesis and Conceptual Development," *Journal of Business Research*, 113 (May), 62–71.

75. Rewers, Mark (2018), "Sprint and T-Mobile Senate Hearing Exposes Merger Has Little Resistance—Sprint Short Positions Pressured," SeekingAlpha.com, July 27, 2018, accessed September 26, 2019.
https://seekingalpha.com/article/4191391-sprint-t-mobile-senate-hearing-exposes-merger-little-resistance-sprint-short-positions.

76. Brandchannel (2017), "Westfield and Unibail-Rodamco Merge Premium Shopping Centers," Brandchannel.com, December 12, 2017, accessed September 26, 2019.
http://www.brandchannel.com/2017/12/12/westfield-unibail-rodamco-merger/.
77. Progressive Grocer (2018), "A&P Sells Remaining Banners, Brands," ProgressiveGrocer.com, May 2, 2018, accessed September 26, 2019.
https://progressivegrocer.com/ap-sells-remaining-banners-brands.
78. Berg, Eric N. (1988), "Godfather's Pizza Sold by Pillsbury," *New York Times*, September 26, 2019, access September 26, 2019.
https://www.nytimes.com/1988/09/20/business/godfather-s-pizza-sold-by-pillsbury.html.
79. Wikipedia (2019), "Godfather's Pizza," Wikipedia.org, accessed September 26, 2019.
https://en.wikipedia.org/wiki/Godfather%27s_Pizza.
80. Thorn, Jesse (2020), "Lamb Chopped: The Story Behind Brooks Brothers' Bankruptcy," Dieworkwear.com, July 17, 2020, accessed July 26, 2020.
https://dieworkwear.com/2020/07/17/lamb-chopped-the-story-behind-brooks-brothers-bankruptcy/.
81. Clausen, Todd (2017), "Kodak Turns First Annual Profit Since Bankruptcy," DemocratandChronicle.com, March 7, 2017, accessed September 26, 2019.
https://www.democratandchronicle.com/story/money/business/2017/03/07/kodak-16-revenues-were-off-10-percent/98851926/.
82. Spence, Ewan (2016), "BlackBerry Admits Defeat and Exits Smartphone Manufacturing Business," Forbes.com, September 28, 2016, accessed September 26, 2019.
https://www.forbes.com/sites/ewanspence/2016/09/28/blackberry-exits-smartphone-manufacturing/#3044c58969b7.
83. Crunchbase (2019), "Number of Acquisitions," Crunchbase.com, accessed September 28, 2019. https://www.crunchbase.com/organization/anheuser-busch/acquisitions/acquisitions_list.

3

How Industries Evolve, Mature, and Revitalize

What does the anatomy of a competitive industry look like? Our research and consulting practice involving analysis of hundreds of industries and products have revealed a typical pattern for industry evolution. All industries evolve in pursuit of two objectives: growth and efficiency; growth comes from expanding markets and expanding to new markets; efficiency through increased productivity, automation, or lowering costs. We have discovered that in their quest for efficiency and growth, most industries go through a similar evolutionary process. This life cycle consisting of start-up, growth, maturity, and aging is depicted in Fig. 1.3. Next, we discuss each phase.

Start-up Phase

Start-up industries struggle for efficiency. Growth is spectacular, but firms are inefficient due to lack of organization and scale. Thus, the first challenge is to answer how to organize and then execute. This was true in the old days of the oil industry when many refineries were dumping by-products such as gasoline in rivers after simply extracting kerosene. Meanwhile, Rockefeller's Standard Oil had figured out how to use gasoline to run its machines and also invested in other commercial uses for the by-products of oil (e.g., petroleum jelly most known for the brand Vaseline).[1]

This struggle was also true for the manufacturing of durable goods such as automatic washing machines, refrigerators, watches, and automobiles. Expertise, capital, and regulation are typical barriers to entry. Even so, as we have observed before, there were hundreds of auto manufacturers in the

© The Author(s) 2020
J. Sheth et al., *The Global Rule of Three*, https://doi.org/10.1007/978-3-030-57473-4_3

U.S. in the 1900s. These days there is less regulation and it is much easier to develop expertise and gain access to capital; thus, it is no wonder that thousands of app developers are fighting for the eyeballs of consumers in the digital age. As digital markets consolidate, the role of shakeouts and mergers will be even greater than it was during the industrial age.

Surprisingly, economies of scale are not achieved primarily through production but through procurement. For a new industry, growth is a given and what is lacking is efficiency/productivity. Thus, in the early stages of the evolution of an industry, the emphasis shifts toward efficiency. The challenge is gaining scale and those that do the best job in scaling up rapidly become the winners. The same principle also applies to the new markets being created based on the concept of shared economy today.

Growth Phase

In the growth phase, the industry is productive, doing well, and creating abundant cash flow (not only inflow but also outflow), which is reinvested in the business. It also needs to expand through new markets and product lines. Increasing volume is not challenging, but increasing market share can be. It is imperative for aspiring generalists to avoid a myopic focus on building share in a single product market. Instead, the primary objective for the generalist must be to become a full-line generalist by creating a one-stop-shop—whether it is a manufacturer, distributor, or retailer.

As generalists grow and build their market share, the Rule of Three begins to emerge. A main strategic shift occurs from fighting for market share of a focal product around which an industry is formed to adding more products and services and fighting for "share of wallet." Alternatively (or in addition), they can expand internationally from the domestic market. Figure 3.1 provides a typology of the focal options during the growth phase based on the Ansoff matrix.[2]

While retailers can often increase their scope by both product and market expansion, manufacturers are often limited to geographic expansion, and distributors usually grow by product expansion. Firms that try to create exceptions to the above convention usually fail. For example, Ford and General Motors (GM) used to be in the appliance business and both attempts failed. (Exceptions to this are conglomerates such as Hitachi and Mitsubishi which organize their business and service units as stand-alone subsidiaries.)

Market penetration: This implies selling more to the same customers/market and represents an underrated strategy. In search of growth, most

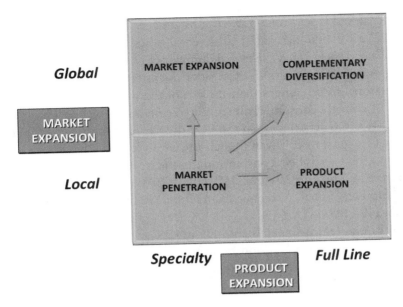

Fig. 3.1 A typology of strategic options. (Source: Adapted from "The Global Rule of Three" presentation by Jagdish N. Sheth, 2017)

companies give up on their core business too soon and focus on new markets or new products. Conquest of new markets can be appealing; managers arguably mature even before their markets do. There is significant upside potential in most markets. Worldwide penetration of smartphones stood only at about 41.5% in 2019.[3] Even in the U.S., smartphone penetration barely exceeds 70%.[4] There is room to grow because of the quick use-cycles of the phones. The smartphone upgrade cycle is well under two years for the U.S., Great Britain, France, Germany, Italy, and Spain, as well as urban China.[5] Just as with watches, even pre-teens will start to own smartphones.

Product expansion: This implies selling new products/categories and is relatively easy for retailers to pursue. For example, Wal-Mart is not only the category leader for cell phones, consumer electronics, and small kitchen appliances ahead of Amazon and Best Buy,[6] but also #1 in jewelry retail with close to $3 billion sales ahead of Sterling, Zale, or Tiffany.[7] In financial services, U.S. banks quickly expanded their offerings to include investment products after the repeal of the Glass-Steagall Act in 1999.

Market expansion: This implies selling offerings in new markets including new geographic markets. As emerging markets become the growth engines of the world, their importance for market expansion cannot be overstated. As stated above, smartphones have truly become a global market. Only 20% of the unit sales of Coca-Cola, 37% of GM, and 39% of 3M come from North America.[8] Fifty-eight percent of Unilever's business stems from emerging markets.[9] We had mentioned the global dominance of China in the steel industry among our opening examples. Consider this: not only does China produce (2.4 gigatons) more cement than the rest of the world combined (1.73 gigatons),[10] it actually consumed much more cement over a three-year period of 2011–2013 (6.6 gigatons) than the U.S. did throughout the entire twentieth century (4.5 gigatons)![11] Even though the world knows the Chinese to be tea drinkers, it also leads beer consumption in the world by far (45.7 billion liters consumed in China in 2016 vs. 24.1 billion in the U.S. which is the #2 market).[12] Similarly, tobacco revenue from China ($215 billion) dwarfs that from #2 U.S. ($97 billion).[13]

Despite the recent setbacks and talk around tariffs and trade wars among governments, market expansion by firms has never been easier than the last decade as many emerging countries continue to invite investment and encourage global players to compete in their domestic markets. BMW already announced its "In China For China" initiative and is set to become the first foreign company to take over its joint venture (JV) partner in China.[14] It also partnered with Baidu's "Internet of Vehicles" initiative for home-to-vehicle integration.[15]

Complementary diversification: This implies expanding both products/services and markets simultaneously. A straightforward path to achieving this can be through organizing distributors in an industry (e.g., Graybar, Grainger, Aero Electronics, and Ingram Micro). Similarly, the wireless telecom industry expanded its offerings and geographic scope simultaneously moving from pagers to personal digital assistants to smartphones. Daimler tried to implement this strategy with its merger with Chrysler by expanding its offerings and serving the mass market but failed. However, this approach has played a major role in the rise of Amazon to global dominance in e-commerce today.

Maturity/Aging Phase

In the maturity stage, diversification is already completed. Scale and productivity are high and it is increasingly hard to squeeze more. Meanwhile, there is struggle to revitalize. The industry (or its technology or platform) often does not survive unless it repositions itself. Thus, many incumbents in aging industries typically die because they fail to switch to new technologies before it is too late, due to their legacy investments. For example, the Swiss dominated watchmaking as a low volume, labor-intensive craft for centuries.

Watches were treated and marketed as jewelry. In the U.S., there were 14 watchmakers clustered in/around Chicago. For example, Elgin National Watch Company's plant in Elgin, Illinois was the largest watchmaking plant in the world, and half of U.S. watch production during the first half of the last century has been attributed to it.[16] However, Timex went to mass production with its pin lever jewel movement and became number one, seemingly out of nowhere. By 1962, it had become the largest watch manufacturer in the world.[17] Then it was time for the Japanese to take over with the new quartz technology, and the Rule of Three was set with Seiko, Citizen, and Casio. Interestingly, the largest watchmaker may soon hail from India—Tata's Titan Company already dominates its home market and is eyeing expansion and can eventually go mass as well as upmarket globally in partnership with Tanishq jewelry.

Similarly, while Europeans invented photography and the automobile, it was Americans that built the mass market for them. Germans once used to dominate the camera market with brands such as Leica. Kodak eventually became the leader and even invented the disposable camera, but the transformation to digital disrupted its business and it became a casualty. From the PC to the evolution of the TV market, business annals are ripe with stories of consumer and industrial products where the incumbents had to vacate the markets that they pioneered.

In an aging industry, what is peripheral becomes core, and what is core becomes peripheral—essentially a niche market. The general market becomes a specialty market. For example, being made redundant by mobile phones, communication landlines are fast becoming a past-time in most households. Iridium (satellite-based phones) once promoted as the future of global communication is now confined to narrow specialty applications. In retailing, the dominant paradigm that was brick-and-mortar has moved online, and what was once niche has become the dominant paradigm in many retail categories (e.g., books and music). The pioneers who are unable to make the transition struggle to survive as exemplified by Microsoft's acquisition of Nokia. Nokia was a long-time leader in voice but was unable to make the transition to data, and has become a niche player for the enterprise market.

The process to achieve efficiency through scale is more complex than what is typically discussed in academia or practice, where the competition-centric view of industries predominantly emphasizes shakeouts and mergers. Instead, the biggest way industries get organized for efficiency is through public policy. Both government policy and market mechanisms can create scale and efficiency. However, in many instances, government policy is more efficient than market process. Government is not always a liability as the perception seems to be in the U.S., it can also be an asset. Arguably, the U.S. has lost many markets it invented due to lax government stance/policy. As illustrated in Fig. 3.2, scale typically results as an outcome of the following four scenarios:

1. Government Mandate: In some cases, the government mandates consumption, and a market is created. In this case, setting up the supply chain rather than marketing is the real challenge. For example, when safety-related regulations, environmental policy, and so forth require mandatory use, the market immediately takes off. In contrast, the infrastructure was permitted to be handled by private companies in evolution of the railroads in the U.K. and the U.S., and consequently huge standard wars ensued. Due to the multiplicity of standards, the industry did not get organized into an efficient platform. Similarly, in the U.S. television industry, each manufacturer wanted its suppliers' business to heavily rely on its orders, which led to the proliferation of multiple chassis standards. The result was lack of scale efficiency even though the market was very large. This problem could have been avoided had the government mandated a standard. Meanwhile, the Japanese manufacturers and Phillips went with solid-state technology and made the tube-based businesses irrelevant. Similarly, as mentioned earlier, the U.S. government did not weigh in on a wireless communication format and decided to let the markets decide.

Consequently, AMPS, TDMA, GSM, and CDMA standards fragmented the U.S. market and prevented economies of scale, whereas Europe embraced

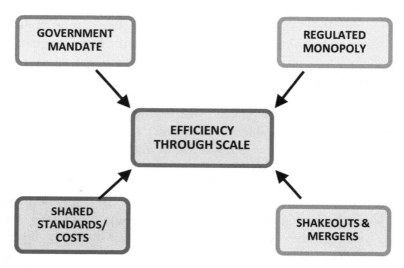

Fig. 3.2 Market pathways to scale and efficiency. (Source: Adapted from "The Global Rule of Three" presentation by Jagdish N. Sheth, 2017)

cellular technology even though they did not invent it. They were quick to adopt cellular technologies since most public phone companies were government-owned and did not have the resources to invest further in land-line infrastructure. By the time British telecom was privatized, less than half of their public phones were operational. Massive investments were needed just to maintain the copper wires. Therefore, Europe, unlike the U.S., adopted GSM as a single standard and enabled Nokia to become #1 rather than Motorola, which had invented the technology. Considering examples such as seat belts and airbags that were previously mentioned, the role of government mandates in making markets cannot be overstated. Making consumption legal through fiat, public policy, or regulation can also influence consumption, as was the case with over-the-counter drugs, with herbal medicines, and, more recently, with state-level legislation of marijuana consumption.

2. *Regulated Monopolies*: Municipality services, public highways, public health, and welfare programs (e.g., Medicare and Medicaid), airlines (before deregulation), wired telecom, and gas and electric utilities companies of today thrive or get curtailed at the hands of policy-makers. Consumers do not have multiple alternatives when it comes to utilities such as water, garbage collection, and sewage in many cases. The underlying assumption here is that the free market process can be highly evolutionary and wasteful, leading to bubbles, busts, and failed enterprises whereas established regulated monopolies can be more efficient and enable achieving scale relatively quickly. Such an approach may especially be suitable for emerging economies where access to capital is often problematic.

3. *Shared Standards/Costs*: The use of shared standards/costs can also boost licensing, contract manufacturing (outsourcing), and the creation of platforms and ecosystems (Android, Windows OS). The resounding victory of the consortia of VHS format manufacturers over Sony's Betamax format is illustrative of the advantage of shared standards. As mentioned earlier, the bulk of the cost of operation in the information/digital age is fixed. Companies such as Texas Instruments or Hughes Electronics can innovate a new communication protocol, such as DirecTV, license the technology, and watch a stand-alone industry emerge through contract manufacturing.

Similarly, Qualcomm, which invented CDMA, realized that manufacturing, selling, and maintaining products is a very slow cycle, and that it was better off licensing CDMA to all and that it could make more money from royalties than making products. Many companies are deciding if they are a technology company (Qualcomm, Apple) or a manufacturing company and they are breaking up their vertical integration. Meanwhile, Sony got stuck in the middle between devices and content, and Samsung eventually has to make a decision between leading in technology and manufacturing.

4. Shakeouts and Mergers: As hundreds of automakers tried to adapt to the moving assembly line revolution triggered by Henry Ford, an evitable shake-out occurred. In the end, the big three survivors were Ford, GM, and Chrysler. Specialists like Checkers and Studebaker also survived initially. The same pattern happened with Internet Service Providers (ISPs) where initially there were thousands of providers. Among cable providers, Comcast has over 40% share of broadband internet subscriptions, Charter is #2 and the others are in the process of consolidation for a third to emerge.[18] A similar shakeout is happening with pharmaceutical firms, and the health care industry is also restructuring, whereas the banking sector went through restructuring during the last great recession (2007–2009).

In general, markets plateau and need to revitalize, and if they fail to do so, they succumb to the aging industry phase.

Table 3.1 depicts the differences in industries from emerging to maturity stage. Eventually, the industry becomes more efficient; however, the time and resources to get there vary based on the path chosen. In general, a government mandate is the least costly process, followed by shared standards, and finally a shakeout.

Finally, it is worth remembering that barriers to entry in many sectors are substantially lower in the information/digital age which increases the number of new entrants, building up of excess capacity, and the intensity of ensuing shakeouts.

Table 3.1 Evolution of markets across stages

Emerging	Shakeout	Mature
Many small firms	Smaller number of large firms	Shopping mall Rule of Three structure
No technical standards	Multiple standards	De facto standards
Fast growth	Faster growth	Slower growth
Ease of entry and exit	Entry and exit barriers	Mobility barriers
High specialization	High specialization	Standardization and specialization
Excess capacity	Rationalized capacity	Renews capacity
Local focus	National focus	Global focus
Many local and regional brands	National brands	Megabrands and niche brands

Source: Adapted from "Competitive Positioning: The Rule of Three" presentation by Jagdish N. Sheth, 2017

Box 3.1 When Scale Is Not Enough: Economies of Scale, Scope, and the Minimum Efficient Scale

In this section, we attempt to explain why we observe such a large performance differential for firms where both the specialists and generalists can maintain double the performance of those stuck in the middle and how extant theory of business can be augmented.

Costs are broadly categorized as fixed or variable. Fixed cost includes the cost of labor, capital, and management (a.k.a. factors of production). Cost of labor tends to be roughly 10% globally, and even less in the U.S. (around 8–9%), and under 4% in PC manufacturing. Cost of capital also used to be around 10%, but it has decreased globally (due to deflationary forces) and it even used to be zero in Japan (a condition that currently also applies to most EU countries and the U.S. due to the ongoing efforts to contain the economic damage caused by the Covid-19 pandemic). Not counting R&D expenses, management costs also tended to be about 10–11% but is now down to 8–9%, due to downsizing, outsourcing, and so on.

Thus, all in all, these sources of costs only represent about 30% of all cost. Thus, the real source of reduction in costs comes from procurement. In general, economies of scale benefit the procurement function more so than manufacturing. Generalists stand to extract benefits from their suppliers based on their scale. Alas, most firms are not good buyers, and they do not know how to procure well unless they are a retailer like Wal-Mart. For example, 11–12% of the value-add in PCs is from manufacturing and 88% is from procurement! Consequently, Microsoft and Intel have been able to make money as suppliers much more so than PC manufacturers such as HP. Until recently, the supply chain management area was very nascent, and businesses have only recently started taking full advantage of economies of procurement.

It is widely accepted by economists that there is a minimum efficient scale (MES) of operation for firms where long-run average total cost is minimized. Firms operating below MES are considered to be at a significant disadvantage against their competitors operating above MES (though the extent of the disadvantage depends on the scale parameters of the industry). The MES for fixed-cost-intensive (i.e., high operating leverage) industries is significantly higher than those of variable-cost-intensive sectors.

One of the standing puzzles in industrial economics is why high economies of scale fails to deter new entrants and also why those new entrants opt to operate below MES: "[T]he observed size of most new firms is sufficiently small to ensure that the bulk of new firms will be operating at a suboptimal scale of output. Why would an entrepreneur start a new firm that would immediately be confronted by scale disadvantages?"[19] We argue that two factors can help explain this phenomenon. First, we posit that the metrics typically used to measure MES are biased and lead to an exaggerated view of generalists entering and operating under MES. For example, the most widely used measure of MES simply assumes that 50% of industry output is generated by firms that operate at less than MES.[20]

Second, the MES metric (as currently defined by economists), while critical for generalists, is not a major factor for the success of specialists. It is unfortunate that previous studies on new entrants have largely failed to distinguish between

(continued)

Box 3.1 (continued)

strategic groups of the entrants, since doing so could have revealed a different notion about generalist entry at sub-optimal scale. Many specialists are able to charge premiums (by "providing unique benefits that more than offset a higher price")[21] with superior service and perceived quality in a way that renders cost-based pricing obsolete. Hence, in a differentiated market, price premiums can sustain specialists at levels well-below MES. "Benefits of scale and scope are limited in differentiated (i.e., most branded) markets."[22] Specialists by definition have to be concerned with effectiveness where they serve a well-defined segment of customers well, rather than meeting MES requirements. In fact, a specialist preoccupied with achieving MES for a generalist will likely be bound with ever-increasing inventory (and lower profitability) when its marketing can no more stimulate demand to justify higher output levels. Increasing share/sales beyond the tipping point may quickly lead to decreased customer satisfaction and/or decay the appeal of brand exclusivity.[23]

To sum, we posit that the reason why we observe a performance jump around 10% market share is that it may correspond to a general proxy for minimum efficient scale. That is, 10% market share is a better benchmark than the plant size corresponding to 50th percentile of output across industries for MES. Generalists improve their profitability significantly when they achieve MES and subsequently continue to gradually improve with more market share.

How Do Industries Revitalize?

How does an industry organize once it achieves scale efficiency and scope capabilities? The evolution is not complete even after the organization stage as the industry still needs to grow beyond its traditional scope. Academics typically do not go beyond scale and scope in their explanations. However, most industries do not die; they evolve and get transformed. The industry can take a stand to not die of chronic illness, and reincarnate. We begin by offering a few key observations:

1. *Mature industries don't die—they get redefined and "dematured"*

Ultimately, generalists in mature markets need to take a critical look at how they define their markets in order to overcome the marketing myopia that may have crept in after years of success. Such soul searching may lead to reconceiving and repositioning a business from soft drinks to non-alcoholic beverages, or an auto manufacturer as a mobility company. Currently, the worlds of media and entertainment are colliding when considered broadly.[24] With a narrow focus, the danger is that competition may come seemingly out of nowhere. Incumbents tend to underestimate new entrants, and they then pay for this mistake dearly. Currently, a 150-year-old product, the electric car, is being reinvented by Tesla to redefine the automobile industry. Vinyl has made a comeback for collectors and DJs. In this sense, it is more appropriate to talk about repositioning and revitalization of industries rather than their death.

2. *The inevitability of the death of an industry is an exaggeration*

The old theory of industry life cycle does not have a Hollywood ending. However, as mentioned above, empirical evidence suggests that broadly reconceived industries can stage a comeback. For example, in a world where most consumers own smartphones with accurate time-telling capabilities (auto-adjust to time zone changes and daylight savings) that are more accurate than most watches, the watchmaking industry should have died unceremoniously, but it is coming back in an interesting way with smartwatches. Even though the functional purpose to wear a simple watch does not exist anymore, Japanese firms Citizen, Seiko, and Casio lead the global market for watches, while the Swiss have retreated to a niche market with high margins even as the industry is being disrupted. Currently, Fitbit, Apple, and Samsung are shaking up the watch industry by defining it and serving new unmet needs (e.g., health/GPS/information).

Similarly, General Foods' own projections for the U.S. coffee market were showing a declining trajectory, but then Starbucks came along and revitalized the industry through redefining it as an affordable luxury with friendly service. The focal point of coffee consumption now takes place at a café (or take-out from a café) rather than at home. Uber has redefined local transportation and Airbnb has done the same for the hospitality sector. We think that even commodity industries such as steel and oil will be redefined and be subject to significant transformation in the next decade.

3. *The theory of vacating markets is real*

Based on Ricardian economics, a nation can give up a market deliberately without a fight. One major wave has been from the U.S. to Japan. The U.S. gave up televisions, watches, steel production, and many more sectors to Japan. In turn, Japan has given up several sectors to Korea. For example, the U.S. (Raytheon) invented and commercialized the microwave and then outsourced to the Japanese, production then went to the Koreans, and now it is primarily done by the Chinese. Similarly, the Japanese surrendered PC

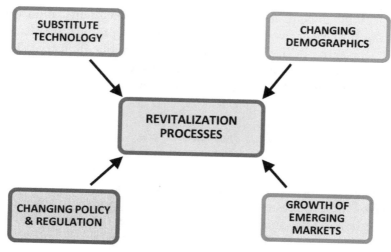

Fig. 3.3 Drivers of market revitalization. (Source: Adapted from "The Global Rule of Three" presentation by Jagdish N. Sheth, 2017)

manufacturing, and it is only a matter of time before the American companies exit voluntarily or collapse. Both Dell and HP seem to be preparing for such an outcome by gradually shifting their focus on business-to-business (B2B) from business-to-consumer (B2C) businesses. Vacating early for healthy returns is much better than being surrounded and forced to surrender.

4. *Disruptive innovation of process change comes as much from within an industry as from outside*

While it is true that radical product innovations typically come from outside, process change/innovations can arise from within, and this can also revitalize the industry. For example, the airlines have improved their processes for booking orders, advance payment, and online boarding through automation, while the product has essentially remained the same over the last four decades.

Next, we elaborate on four key drivers for revitalizing a market which are illustrated in Fig. 3.3.

Substitute Technologies

These can involve both discontinuous/disruptive or continuous improvements. For example, television sales were predicted to stagnate due to the maturity of the market, since most households already owned multiple screens and TVs remained functional for a long time. Then the industry made those TVs obsolete by introducing larger flat screens. Sales were again supposed to stagnate due to PCs and the increasing prevalence of smaller/mobile screen formats, but TV manufacturers have been doing well with larger screens, HDTV, 3D, Full HD, Ultra HD, 4K, smart, augmented reality TV, and so on. The industry has continued to evolve and remain at the convergence of technologies.

Meanwhile, the integration of digital cameras into phones has boosted the business of lens makers. Similarly, as the focal use of the internet shifted to mobile devices, cellular phones became smartphones and thrived. The idea is that new technology makes the installed base obsolete and revitalizes the industry. IBM in its heyday used to do this very well in B2B server business. Many markets were revitalized by the internet and e-commerce and now the same process is recurring with mobile commerce and AI. Aadhaar biometric database in India already includes 1.2 billion identities and has replaced the traditional identification process for more than 90% of the population.[25] Even advanced countries do not possess such a database. In summary, a tsunami of change enabled by digital is on the horizon.

Changing Demographics

It is important to constantly seek for and recognize megatrends, disrupted patterns, and opportunities based on changes in society, knowledge, culture, industry, or macro-economics.[26] By all means, the aging population is such a key demographic fact(or): "the dominant factor in the next society will be…the rapid growth of the older population and the rapid shrinking of the younger generation…will cause an even greater upheaval…because nothing like this happened since the dying centuries of the Roman Empire."[27] Global health care spending is expected to reach $10.06 trillion by 2022 and the increasing prevalence of chronic diseases will certainly have long-term repercussions.[28] Meanwhile, the spending remains uneven—health care spending per person in 2022 is expected to exceed $11,000 for the U.S. versus merely $54 for Pakistan.[29]

Trends based on demographic factors include the focus on health foods and beverages. This trend has revitalized the respective producers as well as groceries; the premiums charged for low carb foods and healthy drinks are higher and the consumption of water and natural juice is increasing at the expense of soda drinks. It is very common for the majority to adopt minority consumption behavior and tastes, especially in the U.S. (e.g., Jazz, R&B, and rap music). As such, salsa overtook ketchup consumption in the U.S. in the 1990s.[30] Thus, the peripheral is becoming the core. This transformation will only accelerate in the next few decades as minorities collectively become the majority in the U.S. Consolidators will emerge to create and serve the mass market for each ethnic minority.

Another key area for revitalizing markets is via offering luxury for the masses. Golf used to be confined to country club memberships, but has now become a mass-market sport and growing rapidly in global markets. As the number of affluent people continues to swell around the world, the profiles of the consumers of luxury products are starting to look very different from traditional buyers. "Masstige" is the term coined by L'Oréal to market prestige to the masses: New segments of buyers are able to afford everyday luxury (e.g., designer fragrances, Starbucks, and imported beers), affordable luxury (e.g., designer eyewear and Coach), and even accessible core luxury goods (e.g., Gucci and Prada) around the world. Making luxury affordable for the masses revitalizes an industry as well. For example, Leo Chen became the youngest CEO of any company traded on the New York Stock Exchange (NYSE) with Jumei, by focusing on flash sales of brand-name cosmetics in China.[31] Luxury car makers are also getting into masstige thinking by introducing more affordable versions such as the Porsche Boxster, Porsche Macan, and Maserati Levante.

Other key demographic indicators include working women and dual-income households, increasing ethnic cultural diversity, the decline of the middle class in all advanced countries, and the rise of the middle class in emerging markets. Overall, demographics are crucial drivers and make change predictable. They can become enablers to revitalize the industry (provided the industry does its research and listens to emerging market signals). Some of the global implications of the future that has already happened include immigration explosion[32] and the abandonment of fixed retirement age.[33]

Changing Policy and Regulation

Orchestrating regulatory changes represents a straightforward way of revitalizing an industry. The biggest changes often happen through regulation, and smart marketers have figured out how to use the government to bring about changes. Back in the days of the New Deal, phone and electric monopolies were created based on the idea of natural monopolies out of hundreds of contenders, which then accelerated growth as well as usage.

Since markets were not growing fast enough organically, the consensus after the first energy crisis in the 1980s was that international trade could stimulate growth. Thus, free trade agreements such as NAFTA, ASEAN, European Union, or bilateral trade agreements such as the one between Chile and the U.S. or the Caribbean Islands and the U.S. were put in place, enabling the countries to become buyers and sellers of each other's offerings. Under this arrangement, the advanced economy offers what the emerging market does not have (e.g., defense; military equipment) and the emerging market can offer agricultural products or raw materials that the advanced economy does not have. Similarly, the WTO redefined and revitalized whole sectors when it was founded back in 1995. Mandatory consumption and health care reforms continue to impact health care delivery, equipment, and the pharmaceutical industry, which together make a $2 trillion industry in the U.S.

Similarly, Fed-mandated consistently low interest rates (cheap capital) caused a boom and ultimately a bubble in the housing market (which then led to a great recession). However, lower interest rates also help the B2B sector as firms can invest in machinery and equipment easier. Naturally, businesses also lobby with federal, state, and local governments for tax rebates and cuts to improve their financial outlook.

Growth of Emerging Markets

Even though the West usually takes the benefits of the industrial revolution for granted, there are many places in the world where it still has not made much difference. The largest opportunities may still be in front of us. The economic development of emerging markets represents a win-win, encouraged and supported by the governments of both developed and developing countries. C.K. Prahalad powerfully argued that it is possible and crucial to serve the bottom of the pyramid profitably but it will take a new mindset to do so.[34] There are 4 billion underserved or unserved people that survive with less than $1500 a year and many live under $2 a day. Yet these are also consumers; the private sector plays a critical role in alleviating poverty and it can do so profitably. "Democratization of commerce is based on everyone having the right to exercise their roles as micro consumers, micro producers, micro entrepreneurs, micro investors, and micro innovators."[35] For example, Kiva. org enables micro-investors from around the world to view business plans of micro-entrepreneurs from the base of the pyramid and invest as little as $25. While the marketing function cannot create purchasing power, it can make products and services more affordable and help convert latent demand into actual demand, and serve as a vital source of entrepreneurial opportunities.[36]

Speaking of opportunities for entrepreneurs, the base of the pyramid actually represents $5 trillion in Purchasing Power Parity! However, the market is extremely diverse in terms of literacy, geography, income, culture, religion, and so forth. As such, no universal model can capture the entire opportunity, and market segmentation is necessary. For example, consider the following consumers:

A slum owner lives without clean drinking water and sewage but with kitchen appliances, cell phone, and color television...
A poor single mother invests in her son's education through private tuition as she struggles to put food on the table...
A farmer invests in new cattle before fixing his family's house...[37]

Ultimately, creating self-sustaining economic development will also be key for these segments. Accelerating global trade and prosperity requires innovations not only in terms of product development but also in business models. Large firms must work together with civil society organizations and local governments. Millions of local entrepreneurs are emerging to serve these opportunities. "In the 'underdeveloped' countries of the world, the more 'glamorous' fields such as manufacturing or construction are generally highlighted while marketing is treated with neglect...Yet marketing holds a key position in these countries...Marketing is also the most effective engine of economic development."[38]

Current opportunities in emerging markets include retailing, fast-moving consumer goods, micro-finance, telecom, and agri-business. Emerging opportunities are in computing, health, and wellness-oriented food, health care, education, pharmaceuticals, and energy. Future opportunities will include affordable and modern housing, water, and transportation. Taking advantage of these opportunities will require an innovation sandbox approach (new product development with constraints), emphasizing scalability (e.g., Amul and Nestle milk processing), price-based costing (i.e., designing with ultimate price in mind), modern technology (to decrease variable cost), global standards (quality, safety, and sustainability). For example, GE successfully used a reverse innovation approach to develop a $1000 handheld electrocardiogram and a portable ultrasound machine for emerging markets, which it was then also able to market in developed markets as well.[39]

Building an ecosystem consisting of large firms, small- and medium-sized enterprises, micro-entrepreneurs, civil society organizations, and the public sector is also critical. Finally, it is important to recognize that value is and must be co-created[40] (e.g., BP biomass stove) based on a satisfactory balance between global versus local, lean organization, and local marketing research.

The demand unlocking that Wal-Mart applied at the population level also applies at the income level where the new demand comes from the slums and other underdeveloped, underserved markets. For example, the best-selling denomination of shampoo in India is the single-use pouch which is much more affordable than a bottle. Not only is there room for three largest players to serve the base of the pyramid it is also their social responsibility. As we will discuss in Chap. 4, growing the pie is not only a profitable strategy for the #1 player in order to revitalize a mature industry, it is also socially desirable and necessary to serve the base of the pyramid.

The Middle of the Pyramid: In addition to the base of the pyramid, there is an aspiring middle class of around three billion people globally, which is increasing in number. They are already brand-conscious and have modest but increasing amounts of discretionary income for education, health, energy, transportation, and personal care. The rise of the brand-conscious middle class around the world is causing mind-boggling change. The move from unbranded to branded, unregulated to organized, is considered to be a $10 trillion market in India ($3.5 trillion) and China ($6.5 trillion) alone. The Chinese version of the American Dream goes along the following lines: "I want two houses—a house in the city and a house in the country. I want two children. And I want to send them to school in America. I want beautiful clothes, a handsome, educated husband, and time to enjoy it all."[41]

In 2020, the upper-middle-class is estimated at some 320 million households made up of 1 billion consumers in China and India.[42] Deep understanding of region, city, rural community, and gender roles is crucial to serving this emerging middle class. In some ways, e-commerce is even more important in rural areas because large supermarket stores may not exist and e-commerce enables much-needed access. Providing good value for low cost will be critical. Offerings will need to be customized. Thinking of big vast possibilities becomes the new reality with an accelerator mindset. As the new middle class begins to consume more, there will be a significant shift from consumption of unbranded products to branded ones.

However, policy-makers need to make sure that everyone has opportunities and not let income inequality get extreme.[43] The number of billionaires in China was 373 in 2018 (as opposed to 123 in Germany) and that number continues to grow around the globe.[44]

The lingering question is what happens when we add another four billion people to those two billion that are already producing and consuming in a systematic manner. First, the pyramid will start looking more like a diamond, and as the new middle class consumes more, the aggregate demand will start putting pressure on scarce resources, causing the prices of commodities to fluctuate.[45] As the new middle class begins to consume more, there will be major supply-constraints and price volatility.

Furthermore, sustainability will become a major driver of product development. P&G is already producing shampoo bottles produced from beach plastic.[46] Adidas produced and sold one million shoes made out of ocean plastic in 2017 and has committed to using only recycled plastic in all of its products, offices, outlets, centers, and warehouses by 2024.[47] Meanwhile, those with $2 daily income continue to represent a $5 trillion market based on purchasing power parity. Thus, advanced economy consumer brands such as Unilever, Nestle, and P&G will increasingly be more active in emerging markets and many innovations from emerging markets will be adapted to developed economies.

In summary, industries are not born by innovation and entrepreneurship alone; they are subject to several other key influences. While theory offers the alignment of strategy and structure or emphasizes the prominent role of shakeouts for industry organization, the real key is neither strategy nor structure but access to capital. Smart entrepreneurs actually succeed by aligning closely with capital more so than technology or customers! Thus, financiers serve as market makers through capital flows (e.g., Singapore sovereign fund) and whoever gets the blessing of private equity or venture capitalists is well on the way to success. In the old days, this function was served by kings and other wealthy people. John Rockefeller knew how to access capital and JP Morgan was a great market maker because he knew to provide capital to the right industries. So we must reiterate that capital is vital in organizing an industry. However, once an industry is organized and it is growing well, it needs scale and efficiency. Scale can come through public policy, government mandate, de facto standards, or shakeout and mergers. Then the industry begins to struggle for growth. Firms in mature markets can grow through market share gains but this approach gets tough quickly and is subject to the law of diminishing returns, so the main path at this stage is through diversification. Thus, the large players offer more product lines and become a one-stop-shop. The point of diversification is not to become a conglomerate but rather to identify a common core of unity through technology, process, or customers. For example, an insurance company can go from offering life insurance to property, casualty, for car, motorcycle, boat, home, and really anything with asset value, and become a full-line generalist. The next step is to go global.

Before we focus on specific strategies based on firm typology, it is important to recall again that the structure for a mature industry is like a shopping mall center where the full-line generalists (three anchor stores) compete on value and price and numerous niche companies compete on differentiation and service, including support services. The industry has now become efficient but is not growing. The firms need to ask themselves "What business we are in? What business we should be in?" and revitalize themselves through restructuring. In essence, it is the struggle for growth that gets an industry revitalized. Sony is a good example of a company that is going through this process (see Box 3.2).

Box 3.2   Sony's Soul-Searching

With consecutive net losses in recent years, Sony is certainly in need of some soul searching. In particular, the company has stated that "it will no longer look to pursue growth in business areas where intense competition puts it at a disadvantage." After selling its Vaio PC business to a private-equity fund in 2014, and spinning off its television sets, and audio and video divisions, the company envisioned itself in three categories:[48]

Growth drivers: Game and network services, pictures, and music. Sony wants to invest in these lines further to increase sales and return on investment (ROI). R&D will be utilized to develop applications for smartphones as well as health care. It will also focus on expanding the user base with the PlayStation gaming platform and will focus on growth areas such as streaming.

Stable profit generators: Imaging product and solutions for video and sound. Here, the generation of steady profit and positive cash flow will be emphasized.

Volatility management: TV and mobile communications. Sony wants to be more selective in this area and become profitable by limiting investment. Considered options include spin-offs and alliances.[49]

In other words, Sony is focusing on Sony Pictures, PlayStation, and making image sensors for Apple gadgets. Growth drivers, stable profit generators, and volatility management sound curiously like stars, cash cows, and question marks, based on Boston Consulting Group's (BCG's) famed growth-share matrix. Refocusing by pruning and being a content aggregator should serve Sony well at this juncture. It could focus on fast-growing developing markets where the competition is less entrenched. It can also use its R&D muscle to launch affordable but beautiful products designed specifically for developing markets.

The Sony brand still carries a lot of cachet around the world. One approach would be to offer more products along the price-quality continuum, but in fewer categories, so they can fully utilize this brand equity. They need to be competitive in segments beyond the high-end. This would require redesigning the low-end of the line for developing markets rather than outsourcing it to generic manufacturers which pump out me-too products for Sony as well as many other brands that dilute the brand image.

Sony would be well served by regaining one of its original strengths: creating great low-cost products for the emerging market. Historically, it began with the transistor radio which was a revolutionary product; it was cheaper and more versatile than the traditional vacuum-tube radios it replaced. One idea would be to follow the likes of HP and Phillips and create a separate venture arm and launch a sub-brand that focuses on affordable technology and products and services. Essentially, the company's DNA is based on technology-enabled affordable products, and soul-searching may necessitate Sony to go back to its roots to revitalize.

In the next chapter, we discuss the ten ways to innovate and revitalize industries for growth.

Key Takeaways

- All industries evolve in pursuit of two objectives: growth and efficiency; growth comes from expanding markets and expanding to new markets; efficiency through increased productivity, automation, or lowering costs.
- All industries go through start-up, growth, maturity, and aging phases.
- *Start-up Phase*: For a new industry, growth is a given and what is lacking is efficiency/productivity. Thus, in the early stages of the evolution of an industry, the emphasis shifts toward efficiency.
- *Growth Phase*: It is imperative for aspiring generalists to avoid a myopic focus on building share in a single product market. Instead, the primary objective for the generalist must be to become a full-line generalist by creating a one-stop-shop—whether it is a manufacturer, distributor, or retailer.
- During the growth phase, these are the strategic following options: market expansion, market penetration, complementary diversification, and product expansion.

(continued)

(continued)

- Manufacturers are often limited to geographic expansion, and distributors usually grow by product expansion.
- *Maturity and Aging Phase*: Here, diversification becomes complete, and the struggle is revitalization of the industry. In order for the industry and its players to survive, they must reposition and switch to new technologies. An aging industry essentially becomes a specialty industry.
- Both government policy and market mechanisms can create scale and efficiency.
- Efficiency through scale typically results from the following scenarios: shakeouts and mergers, shared standards and costs, government mandate, and regulated monopolies.
- The use of shared standards/costs can also boost licensing, contract manufacturing, and the creation of platforms and ecosystems.
- It is worth remembering that barriers to entry in many sectors are substantially lower in the information/digital age which increases the number of new entrants, building up of excess capacity, and the intensity of ensuing shakeouts.
- In general, economies of scale benefit the procurement function more so than manufacturing.
- After an industry achieves scale efficiency and scope capabilities, they can evolve to be redefined. Industries that were expected to die can make a comeback.
- The theory of vacating markets is real; one major wave has been from the U.S. to Japan. Vacating early for healthy returns is much better than being surrounded and forced to surrender.
- While it is true that radical product innovations typically come from outside, process change/innovations can arise from within, and this can also revitalize the industry.
- The four key drivers of market revitalization are substitute technologies, changing demographics, changing policy and regulation, and the growth of emerging markets.
- Many markets were revitalized by the internet and e-commerce and now the same process is recurring with mobile commerce and AI.
- The aging population is a key demographic shift. Other key demographic indicators include working women and dual-income households, increasing ethnic cultural diversity, the decline of the middle

(continued)

(continued)

class in all advanced countries, and the rise of the middle class in emerging markets.

- The rise of the brand-conscious middle class around the world is causing incredible economic change, especially in countries like China and India. Deep understanding of region, city, rural community, and gender roles is crucial to serving this emerging middle class. Providing good value for low cost will be critical.
- Sustainability will become a major driver of product development.
- The firms need to continuously ask themselves "What business are we in? What business should we be in?" and revitalize themselves.

Notes

1. Wikipedia (2019), "Standard Oil," Wikipedia.org, accessed September 27, 2019. https://en.wikipedia.org/wiki/Standard_Oil.
2. Ansoff, Igor H. (1957), "Strategies for Diversification," *Harvard Business Review*, 35 (5), 113–124.
3. O'Dea, S. (2020), "Smartphone Penetration Worldwide as Share of Global Population 2016–2020," accessed June 24, 2020. https://www.statista.com/statistics/203734/global-smartphone-penetration-per-capita-since-2005/#:~:text=For%202019%20the%20global%20smartphone,penetration%20has%20reached%2041.5%20percent.
4. Holst, Arne (2019), "Smartphone Penetration Rate as Share of the Population in the United States from 2010 to 2021," Statista.com, August 21, 2019, accessed September 27, 2019. https://www-statista-com.proxy.libraries.rutgers.edu/statistics/201183/forecast-of-smartphone-penetration-in-the-us/.
5. Armstrong, Martin (2017), "Smartphone Life Cycles Are Changing," Statista.com, March 2, 2017, accessed September 27, 2019. https://www-statista-com.proxy.libraries.rutgers.edu/chart/8348/smartphone-life-cycles-are-changing/.
6. Market Watch (2018), "Walmart Dominates Amazon and Best Buy in Market Share for Key Categories," Marketwatch.com, February 14, 2018, accessed September 27, 2019. https://www.marketwatch.com/press-release/walmart-dominates-amazon-and-best-buy-in-market-share-for-key-categories-2018-02-14.
7. Gaille, Brandon (2017), "14 Jewelry Industry Statistics and Trends," BrandonGaille.com, May 22, 2017, accessed September 27, 2019. https://brandongaille.com/14-jewelry-industry-statistics-and-trends/

8. Conway, Jan (2019), "Unit Sales Volume Share of the Coca-Cola Company Worldwide in 2017, by Region," Statista.com, May 6, 2019, accessed September 27, 2019. https://www-statista-com.proxy.libraries.rutgers.edu/statistics/725027/coca-cola-unit-sales-volume-worldwide-region/.

Wagner, I. (2019), "Vehicle Sales by General Motors in FY 2018, by Region (in 1,000 units)," Statista.com, February 7, 2019, accessed September 27, 2019. https://www-statista-com.proxy.libraries.rutgers.edu/statistics/304392/vehicle-sales-of-general-motors-by-region/.

Garside, M. (2019), "Net Sales of 3M in 2018, by Region (in million U.S. dollars)," Statista.com, February 15, 2019, accessed September 27, 2019. https://www-statista-com.proxy.libraries.rutgers.edu/statistics/736264/3m-net-sales-by-region/

9. Buss, Dale (2018), "Unilever's Sustainable Living Brands: Why Doing Good Is Good for Business," BrandChannel.com, May 10, 2018, accessed September 27, 2019. https://www.brandchannel.com/2018/05/10/unilever_sustainable_living_brands_good_business/.

10. McCarthy, Niall (2018), "China Makes More Cement Than the Rest of The World," Statista.com, July 9, 2018, accessed September 27, 2019. https://www-statista-com.proxy.libraries.rutgers.edu/chart/14595/china-makes-more-cement-than-the-rest-of-the-world/

11. Swanson, Ana (2015), "How China used More Cement in 3 Years Than the U.S. Did in the Entire 20th Century," *The Washington Post*, March 24, 2015, accessed September 27, 2019. https://www.washingtonpost.com/news/wonk/wp/2015/03/24/how-china-used-more-cement-in-3-years-than-the-u-s-did-in-the-entire-20th-century/?utm_term=.5c225760d38b

12. Conway, Jan (2018), "Annual Consumption of Beer Worldwide in 2016, by Country (in Billion Liters)," Statista.com, March 1, 2018, accessed September 27, 2019. https://www-statista-com.proxy.libraries.rutgers.edu/statistics/706163/global-consumption-of-beer-by-country/.

13. Sapun, Petar (2019), "Revenue of the Tobacco Products Market Worldwide by Country in 2018 (in million U.S. dollars)," Statista.com, June 6, 2019, accessed September 27, 2019. https://www-statista-com.proxy.libraries.rutgers.edu/forecasts/758622/revenue-of-the-tobacco-products-market-worldwide-by-country.

14. Bloomberg News (2018), "BMW Set to Be First Foreign Automaker to Control China JV," Bloomberg.com, July 12, 2018, accessed September 27, 2019. https://www.bloomberg.com/news/articles/2018-07-12/bmw-is-said-to-raise-stake-in-china-venture-with-brilliance.

15. BMW Group (2018), "BMW Connected Joins Forces with Baidu Internet of Vehicles on Home-to-Vehicle Cooperation," BMWGroup.com, June 14, 2018, accessed September 27, 2019. https://www.press.bmwgroup.com/global/article/detail/T0282113EN/bmw-connected-joins-forces-with-baidu-internet-of-vehicles-on-home-to-vehicle-cooperation?language=en.

16. Wikipedia (2019), "Elgin National Watch Company," Wikipedia. com, accessed September 27, 2019. https://en.wikipedia.org/wiki/Elgin_National_Watch_Company.

17. TIME (1963), "Corporations: Watches for an Impulse," Time.com, March 15, 1963, accessed September 27, 2019. http://content.time.com/time/magazine/article/0,9171,870225,00.html.

18. Holst, Arne (2019), "Number of Broadband Internet Subscribers in the United States from 2011 to 2019, by Cable Provider (in 1,000s)," Statista. com, August 16, 2019, accessed September 27, 2019. https://www.statista.com/statistics/217348/us-broadband-internet-susbcribers-by-cable-provider/.

19. D. B. Audretsch (1997), "Technological Regimes, Industrial Demography and the Evolution of Industrial Structures," *Industrial and Corporate Change*, 6 (1), 49–82 (pp. 71–72).

20. Not only most of the minimum efficient scale (MES) studies to date actually explain the effect of market concentration instead of MES, but they also use a rather aggressive benchmark for sub-optimality when doing so. Therefore, an attempt at establishing an alternative and pragmatic proxy for MES is warranted.

    L. W. Weiss (1963), "Factors in Changing Concentration," *The Review of Economics and Statistics*, 45, 70–77.

    W. S. Comanor, T.A. Wilson (1967), "Advertising, Market Structure and Performance," *The Review of Economics and Statistics* 49, 423–440.

    S. W. Davies (1980), "Minimum Efficient Size and Seller Concentration: An Empirical Problem," *Journal of Industrial Economics*, 38 (March), 287–301.

    M. Bhattacharya, J.R. Chen (2009), "Market Dynamics and Dichotomy: Evidence from Taiwanese Manufacturing," *Applied Economics*, 41, 2169–2179.

21. M. E. Porter (1985), *Competitive Advantage*, New York: The Free Press, p. 3.

22. Uslay, Can, Z. Ayca Altintig, and Robert D. Winsor (2010), "An Empirical Examination of the "Rule of Three": Strategy Implications for Top Management, Marketers, and Investors," *Journal of Marketing*, 74 (March), 20–39.

23. E. W. Anderson, C. Fornell, and D. R. Lehmann (1994), "Customer Satisfaction, Market Share, and Profitability: Findings from Sweden," *Journal of Marketing* 58 (July), 53–66.

24. Marketing myopia refers to the idea that managers of mature businesses tend to define their business too narrowly. For example, railroads would be better off by considering themselves in the transportation business, and Hollywood film-makers would have been better off had they conceived themselves to be in the entertainment business. Instead, most went out of business when TV became popular. The concept of marketing myopia is attributed to Professor Theodore Levitt due to his seminal article in the *Harvard Business Review* (HBR) in 1960 (which remains one of the most reprinted articles of all time

for HBR). The marketing myopia concept is widely considered as the most influential marketing idea of the past century. Interestingly, it was Drucker (1949) who questioned the existing business definitions much earlier than Levitt:

"[I]t is the business of a railroad to provide transportation…even the development of competing forms of transportation, such as air services, waterways, and highway transportation, would contribute directly to the economic performance and profitability of the railroad" (Drucker 1949, p. 205). Levitt (1975) conceded that marketing myopia was not a novel idea and that he was heavily influenced by Drucker (1946, 1954) in developing his manifesto.

Drucker, P. F. (1946), *Concept of the Corporation*, New York: John Day.

Drucker, P. F. (1949), *The New Society*, New York: Harper & Brothers.

Drucker, P. F. (1954), *The Practice of Management*, New York: Harper Business.

Levitt, T. (1960), "Marketing myopia," *Harvard Business Review*, 38 (4), 45–56.

Levitt, T. (1975). "Marketing Myopia: With Retrospective Commentary," *Harvard Business Review*, 53 (5), 26–48.

Uslay, Can, Robert E. Morgan and Jagdish N. Sheth (2009), "Peter Drucker on Marketing: An Exploration of Five Tenets," *Journal of the Academy of Marketing Science*, 37 (1), 47–60.

25. Srivastava, Abhaya and Isha Badoniya (2018), "India's Billion-Strong Biometric Database," PHYS.org, September 26, 2018, accessed September 27, 2019. https://phys.org/news/2018-09-india-billion-strong-biometric-database.html.

26. Drucker, P. F. (1993). *Post-Capitalist Society*, New York: Harper Collins, pp. 450–451.

Drucker, P. F. (1992). *The Ecological Vision: Reflections on the American condition*, New York: Transaction Books, pp. 173–174.

27. Drucker, P. F. (2002). *Managing in the Next Society*, New York: Truman Talley Books, pp. 235–236.

28. Deloitte (2019), "2019 Global Health Care Outlook," accessed October 1, 2019. https://www2.deloitte.com/us/en/pages/life-sciences-and-health-care/articles/us-and-global-health-care-industry-trends-outlook.html?id=us:2pm:3em:hcoutlook:awa:lshc:030419:smartbrief:ad2.

29. Deloitte (2019), "2019 Global Health Care Outlook," accessed October 1, 2019. https://www2.deloitte.com/us/en/pages/life-sciences-and-health-care/articles/us-and-global-health-care-industry-trends-outlook.html?id=us:2pm:3em:hcoutlook:awa:lshc:030419:smartbrief:ad2.

30. Wald, Alex Seitz (2013), "Actually, Salsa Dethroned Ketchup 20 Years Ago," *The Atlantic*, October 17, 2013, accessed September 27, 2019. https://www.theatlantic.com/national/archive/2013/10/actually-salsa-dethroned-ketchup-20-years-ago/309844/.

31. Wang, Mingan and Can Uslay (2018), "Jumei: China's Top Online Cosmetics Retailer and the Quest to Become the Top E-Commerce Hub for Women," *Emerald Emerging Markets Case Studies*, 8 (3), 1–21.
32. Drucker, P. F. (1999), *Management Challenges for the 21st Century*, New York: Harper Collins.
33. Drucker, P. F. (1993), *Post-Capitalist Society*, New York: Harper Collins.
34. Prahalad, C.K. (2004), *The Fortune at The Bottom of The Pyramid: Eradicating Poverty Through Profits*, Upper Saddle River, NJ: Prentice Hall.
35. Prahalad, C.K. (2004), *The Fortune at The Bottom of The Pyramid: Eradicating Poverty Through Profits*, Upper Saddle River, NJ: Prentice Hall, p. 22.
36. Drucker, P.F. (1958), "Marketing and Economic Development," *Journal of Marketing*, (January), 252–259, p. 256.
37. Prahalad, C.K. (2004), *The Fortune at The Bottom of The Pyramid: Eradicating Poverty Through Profits*, Upper Saddle River, NJ: Prentice Hall.
38. Drucker, P. F. (1958). Marketing and Economic Development. *Journal of Marketing*, 252–259 (January), 252.
39. Sheth, J. N. (2011), "Impact of Emerging Markets on Marketing: Rethinking Existing Perspectives and Practices." *Journal of Marketing, 75* (July), 166–182.
    Immelt, J., Govindrajan, V., & Trimble, C. (2009), "How GE is Disrupting Itself," *Harvard Business Review*, 87 (October), 56–65.
40. Sheth, Jagdish N. and Can Uslay (2007), "Implications of the Revised Definition of Marketing: From Exchange to Value Creation," *Journal of Public Policy & Marketing*, 22 (2), 302–307.
41. Silverstein, Michael, Abheek Singhi, Carol Liao, David Michael, and Simon Targett (2012), "Captivating the Newly Affluent in China and India," BCG. com, September 4, 2012, accessed September 27, 2019. https://www.bcgperspectives.com/content/articles/captivating_newly_affluent_in_china_and_india/.
42. Silverstein, Michael J., Abheek Singhi, Carol Liao, and David Michael (2012), *The $10 Trillion Prize: Captivating the Newly Affluent in China and India*, Boston, MA: Harvard Business Press.
43. Silverstein, Michael J., Abheek Singhi, Carol Liao, and David Michael (2012), *The $10 Trillion Prize: Captivating the Newly Affluent in China and India*, Boston, MA: Harvard Business Press.
44. Moynihan, Ruqayyah and Thomas Chenel (2018), "These are the 19 Countries with the Most Billionaires in the World," Business Insider, December 17, accessed October 12, 2019. https://www.businessinsider.com/these-are-the-19-countries-with-the-most-billionaires-in-the-world-2018-10.
45. Sheth, J. N. (2011), *Chindia Rising: How China and India will Benefit Your Business*, 2nd ed. Tata-McGraw Hill India.
46. Shayon, Sheila (2017), "P&G Makes First Recyclable Shampoo Bottle from Beach Plastic," Brandchannel.com, January 25, 2017, accessed September 27,

2019. http://www.brandchannel.com/2017/01/25/pg-recyclable-shampoo-bottle-012517/?utm_campaign=170125-pg-bottles&utm_source=newsletter&utm_medium=email.

47. Kharpal, Arjun (2018), "Adidas Sold 1 Million Shoes Made out of Ocean Plastic in 2017," CNBC.com, March 14, 2018, accessed September 27, 2019. https://www.cnbc.com/2018/03/14/adidas-sold-1-million-shoes-made-out-of-ocean-plastic-in-2017.html.

   Kottasova, Ivana (2018), "Adidas Joins the Fight Against Plastic," CNN.com, July 16, 2018, accessed September 27, 2019. https://money.cnn.com/2018/07/16/news/adidas-using-recycled-plastic-only/index.html.

48. Patel, Nilay (2015), "Sony is No Longer an Electronics Company," TheVerge.com, February 18, 2015, accessed September 27, 2019. http://www.theverge.com/2015/2/18/8063269/sony-electronics-future-selling-off-pc-smartphone-tv.

49. The Economist (2015), "Here's Sony's New Business Strategy," *BusinessInsider.com*, February 21, 2015, accessed September 27, 2019. http://www.businessinsider.com/heres-sonys-new-business-strategy-2015-2.

4

Ten Ways to Innovate and Revitalize Industries

As we alluded to previously, despite the existence of several theories of the firm, the literature on industry evolution and life cycles is relatively scant.[1] In this chapter, we address vital questions such as: How are industries born? How do they grow, plateau, and get revitalized? How do they get creatively destroyed?

Joseph Schumpeter famously argued for a path of creative destruction naming it "the essential fact about capitalism."[2] Interestingly, disruptive technologies or business models typically emerge from outside of the industry and revolutionize it.[3] Indeed, "[a]t least half of the important new technologies that have transformed an industry in the past fifty years came from outside the industry itself."[4] Examples include the zipper and fiberglass. However, most of the extant theories are neither articulated well nor validated sufficiently. While the traditional product life cycle (i.e., introduction, growth, maturity, and decline) or the notion of birth, growth, and inevitable death trilogy may be partially relevant, these by themselves are not sufficient to explain the evolutionary path of industries (see Fig. 4.1). Hence, there is a need for a broader explanation to explain birth, growth, plateau, and repositioning, and hopefully revitalization stages (also see Box 4.1 "The Diffusion of Innovations and Crossing the Chasm") before we discuss the rise of the Global Rule of Three.

Throughout the history of industrial organizations, firms have constantly struggled to balance their efficiency and growth. Their real challenge has been to achieve scale surprisingly not through stimulating demand but through savvy procurement. When an industry eventually matures and stabilizes, the structure that emerges is different than and contrary to what we have been

© The Author(s) 2020
J. Sheth et al., *The Global Rule of Three*, https://doi.org/10.1007/978-3-030-57473-4_4

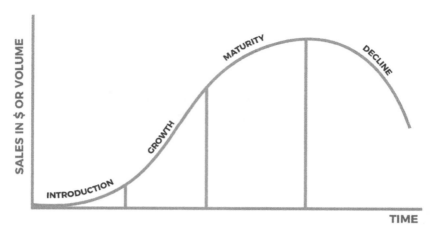

Fig. 4.1 Industry life cycle. (Source: Authors' creation based on Ted Levitt's seminal article. Levitt, Theodore (1965), "Exploit the Product Life Cycle," *Harvard Business Review*, November, (43), 81–94)

taught in economics. The prevailing neoclassical view that industries with many competitors would naturally be perfectly competitive was debunked subsequently (e.g., after studying the pharmaceutical industry, among others) by the realization that differentiated firms within the same industry may not only be numerous but also very profitable.

In reality, the prevailing industry structure is neither one of oligopoly nor of monopolistic competition. It is always both! Therefore, the neoclassical way of categorizing industries is not relevant for mature and competitive industries. Meanwhile, the dynamics of competitive evolution between specialists versus generalists are vital for understanding the organizational ecology of any industry. An industry that is composed of an excessive number of specialists ends up producing full-line generalists through shakeouts. On the other hand, when an industry is dominated by full-line generalists, specialists grow and proliferate in its neglected or underserved corners (e.g., soft drink and beer industries). Hence, industries exist in a dynamic balance between monopolistic competition (characterized by high rent, sub-monopolies, and many differentiated small players that are margin driven) and oligopoly (characterized by a focus on building scale, and one-stop-shop/full-line offerings). When an industry moves away too far from monopolistic competition toward a highly oligopolistic structure, the counterforces come into play and it begins to shift back toward monopolistic competition.[5]

All industries are part oligopoly and part monopolistic competition and shift between these two prevailing structures in the long run. Furthermore, monopolies can be differentiated (as was the case of the telecom industry) or undifferentiated (the case of most utilities such as electricity and water). Similarly, oligopolies can be differentiated (pharmaceuticals) or undifferentiated (oil, steel, and copper). There are very few sectors (if any) that are governed by perfect competition or pure monopolies. Figure 4.2 captures this taxonomy of industry structures.

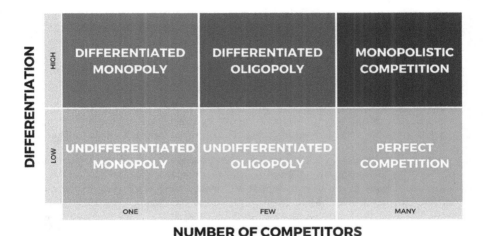

Fig. 4.2 A taxonomy of industry structures. (Source: Adapted from "Competitive Positioning: The Rule of Three" presentation by Jagdish N. Sheth, 2017)

Box 4.1   The Diffusion of Innovations and Crossing the Chasm

Stages of the traditional industry life cycle include:

Introduction: The product or service is brought to the marketplace. The cost of communicating with and acquiring customers is high. Sales and sales growth are usually slow. The product or service typically loses money. The objective at this stage is to build product/brand awareness and generate trial. By definition, the market pioneer possesses 100% share and monopolizes the market, if only for a little while. Seeing proof of concept, other players jump in and the combined market share held by the top three players soon falls under 30% and in many cases barely exceeds 10%.[6] At this stage, it is critical to emphasize sales growth more than profitability if the firm is to utilize its first/early-mover advantage and remain viable. Uber and Airbnb have recently gone through this phase using sharing economy business models.

(continued)

Box 4.1 (continued)

Growth: The industry begins to take off and sales start growing rapidly. Higher unit sales result in lower average cost per unit sold, and the product/service starts to become profitable. The objective for leading companies at this stage is to gain market share and make their offering the standard of the category. This typically means scaling up through mergers and acquisitions (M&A). The top three players' combined market share rises to 15–45%. Integrating merged entities skillfully becomes essential due to the high volume of merger activity in this phase.

Even as firms absorb other organizations and try to keep the best employees, they must not lose sight of maintaining the essence of their culture. "Companies jockeying to reach stage 3 must be among the first players in the industry to capture their major competitors in the most important markets and should expand their global reach."[7] For example, Microsoft, Amazon, Facebook, and Google sacrificed profitability early on in order to grow, establish dominance, and become global leaders in their categories. Historically, automobile, agricultural equipment, and PC manufacturers have all been through this journey of consolidation.

Maturity: Sales peak. Most consumers already have the product while some are rebuying or upgrading. Production costs tend to be low, so those with high market share can still make good profits. The objective at this stage is to emphasize making a profit while defending market share. Customer acquisition is typically at the expense of competitors. Modifying the market (targeting new segments or increasing usage among current customers), product (delivering an improved version to get new or repeat business), or the marketing mix (adding services, cutting prices, changing distribution, or promotion) can be useful at this stage. Initially, the top three firms assume 35–70% of the market, and through mergers, they can eventually claim as much as 70–90% market share. This is where we finally observe the Rule of Three structure if it has not already emerged. Examples of this category include appliances, microwave ovens, frozen dinners, aircraft, and television manufacturers.

Decline: Sales fall. For durables, since most of the market has already purchased the product/service, they do not need to buy the product anymore except for the occasional replacement. Unit sales and prices also fall, so it becomes difficult to remain profitable despite low production costs. Some niche products may do well when competitors exit the market. The objective at this stage is to reduce costs to stay profitable, to milk the product, and invest elsewhere. If possible, marketers can revitalize the Product Life Cycle (PLC); otherwise, they may look for a way out. Examples include analog cameras and now digital cameras.

Geoffrey Moore in his bestseller, *Crossing the Chasm*, argued that most start-ups fail to make the transition from selling to innovators, technology enthusiasts, and early adopters to early majority/pragmatists and die in the process. Whereas the former look for technology and performance, the latter group wants solutions and convenience. Early adopters and the early majority are essentially two very different consumer segments with different expectations, and marketing approaches must be designed accordingly.[8]

We begin the quest to understand the evolution of industries by making two observations:

1. Industry evolution and inertia are primarily driven by two factors that are often at odds with each other: the need for efficiency and growth.
2. Contrary to conventional wisdom, industries are born due to many reasons besides new technological breakthroughs.

In fact, *most new industries are born based on or building upon existing knowledge.* For example, Uber and Airbnb have come to characterize the broad sharing economy. However, car-sharing was actually launched for the first time in Zurich in 1948.[9] Similarly, childcare has become a multibillion-dollar industry without a breakthrough concept or invention over the last 100 years. Even the PageRank algorithm that has propelled Google/Alphabet to over $1 trillion market capitalization can be traced back to the early 1940s.[10]

Usually, the role of innovation and entrepreneurship are emphasized, whereas the role of marketing is downplayed when explaining industry/market creation.[11] Instead of breakthrough innovations, most industries succeed due to exceptional marketing or operational excellence displayed by their pioneers. Thus, the secret to success often lies with execution rather than invention. Similarly, Schumpeter's idea of creative destruction is perhaps given too much credit with regard to industry evolution.[12] Schumpeter was of a similar belief to that of Karl Marx in that capital (and wealth) concentrated in the hands of a few was unsustainable and would ultimately self-destruct and lead to revolution. In other words, the working class would revolt against the wealthy few and that would bring in change. Schumpeter thought that capitalism would mutate itself through creative destruction and adapt rather than self-destruct.

In 2019, we saw several signs of this, as the Business Roundtable (consisting of over 180 of the largest companies in the U.S.) revised its statement of business purpose to include value creation for all stakeholders, and the World Economic Forum issued its "Davos Declaration" calling for stakeholder capitalism to replace traditional financially focused short-term capitalism. These shifts are in line with what the Conscious Capitalism movement (and others like it, such as B Corps, the B Team, Coalition for Inclusive Capitalism, and Just Capital) has been calling for since 2008.

Interestingly, it may be more fitting to characterize the industry birth phenomena as creative duplication rather than creative destruction. Once someone has a viable idea and proves the concept, others imitate and generate lift for the entire sector. For example, the notion behind the sharing economy is utilizing idle capacity and this idea is currently being vigorously replicated across industries and geographies. The rental economy (utilization of durable assets) is picking up for rooms, cars, houses, and even palaces and islands. Even Mercedes-Benz recently jumped on the bandwagon by launching a peer-to-peer app called Croove that lets its users rent out their vehicles (not necessarily a Benz) when they are not using it.[13] The very same principles also allow for sharing of services and sharing of productive assets and building social connections.[14]

The current stage of the sharing economy evolution calls for extension to services. Consider TaskRabbit which lets consumers with general home maintenance needs, such as furniture assembly or organizing a garage, book a reliable handyman. Recognizing the potential, the largest furniture retailer in the world, IKEA, acquired TaskRabbit in September 2017.[15] Similarly, Zaarly takes the same concept and extends it to housecleaning and lawn and garden maintenance.

Nevertheless, the sharing economy is still utilitarian in nature. The future wave will increasingly involve sharing productive assets (including time) and enabling social connections. There are several examples of this already happening: MamaBake (with its recipes and cooking club) enables women to make batch meals and share them with each other to give them the gift of time to spend with their loved ones. Eatwith enables its customers to socialize with strangers while dining in the home of vetted chef. The service is favored by tourists who want to experience the authentic local culture. The decade-old-company serves tourists who want to experience the local culture, and others interested in meeting new people in an authentic setting, in dozens of major cities around the world such as Brisbane, Budapest, Cape Town, Rio, Hong Kong, and Florence.[16]

Finally, the success of subscription-based services such as Spotify and Apple Music has also led to a surge in online streaming (which grew 69% in 2016 alone which led to the biggest sales growth of the U.S. music industry since 1998, and its highest sales figures since 2009).[17]

Production sharing has long been considered to be the hope of the developing world in an increasingly global economy,[18] which has to come to life in the form of contract manufacturing (e.g., Foxconn). Historically, the cellular phone industry grew the same way. The competitive mechanism took place at the manufacturer level whereby scores of manufacturers worked simultaneously and lifted the industry in the process. Although management guru Peter Drucker is well known as a champion of innovation and entrepreneurship,[19] he also recognized the primacy of marketing execution: "Marketing is the distinguishing, unique function of the business…Any organization in which marketing is either absent or incidental is not a business and should never be managed as if it were one. The economic revolution of the American economy since 1900 has in large part been a marketing revolution."[20]

Everett Rogers discussed the diffusion of innovations as a process that begins with innovators (opinion-makers) and then moves on to the mass market segments (early adopters, early majority, late majority, and laggards).[21] However, we find that most industries are actually created by the supply side and not the demand side. Before Henry Ford came in with the moving assembly line and Model T, there were roughly 500 automakers in the U.S. Similarly, there were more than 200 competitors making tractors and agriculture equipment for farmers in the U.S. as modernization took place. Thus, we argue that the process of industry birth is more about creating (creative) duplication than one of destruction.

Based on our extensive research and synthesis of how industries come about, we have identified ten pathways through which new industries are born. Interestingly, the vast majority of these categories have nothing to do with technological innovation or even traditionally conceived notions of entrepreneurship. Next, we describe each of these.

How Are Industries Born?

1. Transformation from Manual to Automation

Historically, the transformation from manual toward automation has been the most significant impetus for industry formation. The industrial revolution was based on the need to decrease the extensive cycle of manual production, primarily for textiles as well as other goods, and increase capacity. The challenge and the opportunity at the time was to convert limited workshop production and home-grown cottage operations to factories and manufacturing plants. Gradually, but surely, power-based looms and machinery replaced centuries-old practices such as manual cotton spinning.

When Henry Ford adopted the moving assembly line in 1913, he was able to cut the assembly time for a car from 12 hours to roughly one and a half hours. By 1927, Ford was able to build a Model T every 24 seconds! He was also able to profitably drop the price from $900 to $260 in the process.[22]

The industrial age which ignited the transformation from manual to automation also highlighted the concepts of scale and scope and the need for capital investments. In the preceding agricultural era, most of the total cost had to do with labor (variable costs), with little to no overhead. One could not even buy land in feudal Europe; it had to be granted by the king to a noble or feudal lord, hence the term landlord. Industrial revolution modernized production by transforming low-cost workshops into capital-intensive factories.

Since then, a digital revolution has also taken place, further automating support functions and intensifying the need for capital investments. Secretaries that were required to learn short-hand (stenograph) are long gone; most have been replaced by self-use of word processors. Even the jobs of many white-collar professionals such as lawyers, doctors, or professors are getting more and more automated and/or moving online.

In the information age, it can cost Microsoft billions of dollars to develop a new version of Windows, or hundreds of thousands of dollars in studio time and sound engineering for a band to create an album so it can be downloaded for the first time. But how much does it really cost Microsoft or iTunes to facilitate the second or third download after that? In the information age then, in a total reversal from the agricultural era, most of the cost is fixed. (This also implies that the profit-maximizing price converges to zero in the information age, since it should be set at the point where marginal revenue (Price) is equal to marginal cost; thus, the only countervailing force against the commoditization of goods in the information age appears to be brand equity, further reinforcing our previous point about the enduring value and importance of marketing).

European airline RyanAir with its £9.99 continental flights is illustrative of both points. Using the razor and blade analogy, the airline minimizes the cost of the airfare (and there have even been times when they promoted zero fares) but then charges for sandwiches, drinks, and checked bags or even carry-ons while also assisting with car rentals and vacation packages. In the fiscal year ending March 2020, the airline netted over one billion euros (almost $1.1 billion) in profits.[23]

While embracing e-commerce can facilitate automation, creation of a truly demand-driven supply chain appears to be the current frontier for many sectors which have under-invested in infrastructure for decades. The underlying economics further reinforces the importance of fixed capital investments across sectors.

Overall, we reiterate that automation has been the biggest driver of modern industry by far. The next frontier in automation will be the automation of consumption where the personal digital assistants will automatically remind and even advise the consumers regarding what is in their best interest to consume. Smartwatches are already asking their owners to stand up and move; given the prediction for affordable and smart technologies for all, this future may not be too far on the horizon. Similarly, automated fleets of trucks carrying goods are right around the corner, and start-ups are already experimenting with delivery and food service by drones and robots.[24] In fact, we are on the cusp of another wave of automation, this time moving from human intelligence to artificial intelligence which will redefine most jobs and make many obsolete in the coming decade.[25]

2. Outsourcing

The origins of outsourcing can be traced to the separation of production from selling which enabled the era of merchants, and eventually merchant nations. Global trade has gradually increased over the centuries except for periods of interruptions due to wars and ideological differences. Outsourcing has univocally been a major driver for new business creation. When businesses outsource functions such as legal, IT, or accounting, these services become stand-alone industries.

The major shift toward outsourcing came about after the first energy crisis. The underlying traditional thinking was that the firms needed to be wholly integrated for maximum profitability. At one point, Ford even owned a sheep farm so that they could use the wool for car seats! Once the old theory was discredited and the prevailing thinking advocated focusing on core competencies,[26] outsourcing took off. Consequently, managers focused on value-producing functions or components such as engine innovations in order to improve the productivity of their resources in their quest to generate competitive advantages. This approach enabled management to excel in critical stock keeping units (SKUs)/functions and outsource the rest to other business who made it their business to excel in these respective categories (e.g., steering wheels). Availability of support service businesses also took off and outsourcing of auxiliary functions further enhanced the focus of the organization. "When the managers became free to focus on the core competency and processes of their businesses, productivity also soared. Outsourcing made business sense and was a boon for all. It not only created a growth economy but was also fueled by it."[27] For example, IT service in India has become a multi-billion-dollar industry and even IBM is thriving with its services there.

Many industries are the result of a make-or-buy decision. These days, the biggest impetus for outsourcing comes from the family. Ironically, when a chore or even a production activity is conducted inside the household, it is not accounted for in GDP calculations. The drive of women to become bread-winners led many household services such as cooking, cleaning, and childcare to boom. The time-crunched current generation is not as competent on how to cook, clean, or deal with childcare and is not keen on learning. Meanwhile, cooking (dining out, carry out, and even delivery has now given way to peer-to-peer delivery of home-made dishes), cleaning, and childcare have each become multi-billion-dollar industries. Many of the service providers are mom-and-pop businesses and not yet organized at this point. However, as mentioned in Chap. 1, we can already observe the emergence of the Rule of Three with GrubHub, DoorDash, and UberEats in delivery platforms.

3. Reducing Friction in Commerce and Consumption (Accessibility)

Frictionless or at least *less-friction* business models also commonly lead to new industries. The type of friction referred to typically exists between the buyers and sellers. The friction (or pain point) can be financial, in the payment process, in shipping/logistics, really anywhere along the value chain; however, accessibility often plays a major role. For example, Hanes Corporation's L'eggs was able to combine convenience and availability by frequently replenishing its simplified product line in supermarkets and drug stores. Netflix initially benefited from the stringent return policy of the incumbent Blockbuster. It offered flexibility in returns via its mail-order DVD service. Later on, it removed another layer of friction by rendering the need to mail and handle DVDs obsolete via its streaming service, which has subsequently become its main business.

As such, improving accessibility by matching buyers and suppliers has been crucial for the fast rise of e-commerce and online marketplaces. The greatest e-commerce companies (e.g., Amazon, eBay, iTunes, Uber, and Airbnb) have simply identified a friction (e.g., accessibility, fulfillment, and consumption) and focused on removing it. For example, Zappos (started in 1999 and acquired by Amazon in 2009 for $940 million) offers affordable shoes but, more importantly, a greater number of brands, variety, and sizes than all conventional retailers.

With the "uberization" of life, one can go to most major cities, take a cab and not worry about the wait-time, carrying cash or foreign currency, optimal route or haggling with the driver, and pay through a single account today. Once a service becomes so convenient, it becomes an addictive necessity.

Today, brick-and-mortar operations such as airlines also sell tickets directly to improve accessibility. There was a time when passengers were forced to book through travel agents and incur commissions even for domestic flights.

Southwest Airlines became an industry leader by serving smaller airports with its point-to-point service, embracing direct selling through phone, ticketless travel, and was quick to move to internet sales (even though Alaska Airlines retains the honor of selling the first domestic airline ticket online in 1995).[28]

Similarly, Google's mission happens to be "to organize the world's information and make it *universally accessible* and useful"[29] (emphasis added). Apple's app store, Google's YouTube, and Netflix have become consumer staples based on aggregating apps, videos, and movies respectively, and making them conveniently accessible.

4. Tap into Unmet Needs (Affordability)

When it comes to creating business opportunities, this is a relatively traditional category. When needs are unmet it is usually because consumers cannot afford it. Needs may not be met in an enterprise, university, governmental organization because of budgetary restraints. Even nations suffer from budgetary problems; the U.S. and the EU (Greece, Ireland), for example, routinely have to face their fiscal budget realities and the need to restructure.

Therefore, there is an opportunity for manufacturing and marketing products and services in more affordable ways. Historically, the U.S. has been a pioneer in making products more affordable through competition as well as innovation. For example, we already discussed the impact of Ford's moving assembly line on price reductions over time, but this also includes business model innovations focusing on affordability. For example, General Motors Acceptance Corporation (GMAC) was launched in 1919, and the availability of financing by manufacturers became a major catalyst in democratizing the automobile.[30]

A related development was the emergence of leasing, which enabled businesses to utilize equipment and resources without incurring the full capital expense of ownership and associated costs of maintenance, insurance, and tax. Interestingly, the concept of leasing is thousands of years old. The earliest example points to the city of Ur in Sumeria in 2010 BC, where the records show that farmers leased agricultural tools provided to them by the priests.

Leasing in the U.S. can be traced to the beginning of the eighteenth century where first horses and buggies, and later wagons, barges, railroad cars, and locomotives have been subject to lease agreements. Rent-a-Car (1918) started the age of car rentals; however, long-term leasing of vehicle fleets can be widely credited to Zollie Frank (1941).[31] Subsequently, vehicles became the gateway for equipment leasing by business owners. Nevertheless, equipment leasing remained a novelty for businesses except for non-transportation firms until the 1970s. Global leasing contract volume fluctuates based on regulatory and macro-economic conditions and currently hovers at around $1 trillion per year.[32] Most office copy-machines are leased. Most airlines lease their planes rather than buy them outright. It even seems the Rule of Three is beginning to take shape in aircraft leasing.[33]

The next stage in the evolution of leasing will surely involve B2C markets. Subscription-based business models have been gaining ground. The underlying principle of the sharing economy is utilizing idle capacity more effectively, making it affordable to businesses, and increasingly consumers. In a more traditional example, Timex offered good quality but affordable watches to shake up the watchmaking industry. They were able to accomplish this by automating watchmaking and became a large player. Subsequently, the Japanese took over with the quartz movement innovation and essentially commoditized the mass market through further manufacturing automation (also see Box 4.2 "Quartz Watches").

Data storage cost has gone down 650 times over the last decade. If the automotive sector had kept up with Moore's Law, the cost of a Lexus would be roughly one dollar, it would go the speed of sound, range 600 miles for a drop of gasoline—but unfortunately, also be the size of a postage stamp![34]

Box 4.2   Quartz Watches

The history of the quartz watch provides a good illustration of the effects of autonomy and internal competition on radical innovation. The first quartz watch was commercialized by Hattori-Seiko in 1969 (a limited edition that cost as much as a Toyota Corolla). This product was the result of a technology contest between two divisions. The two divisions maintained separate research, design, and manufacturing facilities whereby the HQ informed both divisions of its anticipated product needs. These divisions then independently developed prototypes from which production models were chosen.[35]

All Japanese watchmakers adopted quartz, led by Seiko. Seiko continuously invested in perfecting the quartz movement and LCD displays, even when their salespeople and retailers begged them for LED watches. It had determined that LEDs were not a good long-term bet. It also produced both analog and digital quartz watches. While American manufacturers ignored analog and the Swiss manufacturers ignored the digital watches, the world market was divided evenly between the two. Seiko was correct in its assessment and became the largest watch company in the world in 1977, followed by Timex, and SSIH (of Switzerland, known for Omega). While the Swiss eventually bounced back to the top (Swatch Group, Richemont, and Rolex are the top three wrist-watch manufacturers globally with 18.3%, 15.7%, and 11.2% value market share respectively),[36] the impact of the quartz movement has been enduring. Of the 1.46 billion watches produced in 2015, 1.42 billion were quartz.[37]

5. Convert Wants into Needs

Many of us cannot even imagine a life without a smartphone or a cell phone, whereas most of our parents lived without one most of their lives. And our parents may not be able to imagine a world without refrigerators, dishwashers, or credit cards, but the chances are our grandparents lived without those for most of their lives. Automobiles were once a luxury item, but have become a daily necessity for many. It is conceivable that self-driving cars will become the norm for our children, and they will not be able to live without them since they may not even know how to drive! And they may not even need to use credit cards or cash due to the convenience of mobile payments (e.g., PayPal, Venmo, and Alipay).

The overwhelming consumer demand for broadband internet and mobile access has generated major opportunities. More than half of the population of China (census-estimated at 1.42 billion in 2019) already uses smartphones, and more than 60% are predicted to use one by 2023.[38] India is lagging behind with about 30% of its population using smartphones in 2019, predicted to increase to 36% by 2022.[39] In contrast, some 95% of South Koreans have smartphones. The rest of the world has some catching up to do.[40] Overall, there are already over 3.3 billion active smartphones in the world[41] and the day when most of the world population will have wireless access to affordable broadband is not in the far future. In general, when wants become needs, it is natural for new industries to spring.

6. Unbranded to Branded Products and Services

How do you brand the unbranded and create new industries? Branding practice is rooted deep in human history. A primary rationale of branding is to build and convey trust to customers. For example, back in the seventeenth century, the Mitsukoshi department store was one of the first examples of modern marketing.[42] The Mitsui family of Japan was effectively operating the first department store by 1650. They saw themselves as the buyer for their customers, felt responsible for designing the right products for them and for developing sources for the production of such designs. They offered money-back guarantee with no questions asked. Their unique idea was to offer a large assortment of quality goods based on retail brand trust rather than specialize in a product category and build trust the old-fashioned way. The result was overwhelming customer loyalty with the Mitsukoshi brand which eventually became a chain and the largest retailer in Japan and the core of one of its largest Zaibatsu. We will discuss the topic of branding further in Chap. 7.

7. Leverage Platforms and Infrastructure

The pathway from infrastructure to commerce is rather obvious. Trade and commercial growth have historically relied on infrastructure around ports, trading posts, railroads, and highways. These days we can increasingly talk about opportunities to utilize and leverage existing platforms. For example, the cumulative number of apps downloaded from the millions of options available from Apple and Android app stores exceeded a mind-boggling 204 billion downloads in 2019.[43] Similarly, eBay platform reached 179 million active users (buyers, sellers, or both) in the fourth quarter of 2018.[44] Given the cloud infrastructure and server farms, the cost of going global has become very affordable. Similarly, supply chains have become much more efficient. While the telephone took 75 years, the radio 38 years, and the TV took 13 years to reach 50 million consumers, the internet took only 4 years, Facebook 3.5 years, iPod 3 years, AOL 2.5 years, and *Angry Birds* video game merely 35 days to do so![45]

8. Government Policy

As it turns out, many industries are created, transformed, and sometimes destroyed through government policy, by the stroke of a pen. Thus, the power of legislation can be even greater than the power of capitalism. Several instances of safety regulations illustrate this point. For example, the first U.S. patent for a seat belt was issued in 1885,[46] and they were being offered by car manufacturers as early as the 1940s (Ford famously began marketing them as an option in 1955). However, seat belts did not take off as an option until they were mandated through regulation (New York was the first state to require wearing them in 1984).[47] Similarly, airbags were invented in 1968 but did not take off until they were made mandatory some 30 years later in 1998.[48] Lead-free gasoline and no-indoor smoking both have come about by regulation.

Education, health care, defense, and even telecommunications industries are examples of sectors heavily shaped by regulation. In addition, all regulated monopoly industries fall under this category. Economists define natural monopolies where one firm can operate more efficiently then multiple firms competing in the same market. For example, utility companies have been geographically organized this way and are allowed and regulated to exist. Even the next big thing, blockchain technology, originally designed for making anonymous digital currency transactions to overcome the influence of large institutions and government, appears destined to make breakthrough impact of unimaginable magnitude following its governmental adoption and regulation.[49]

9. Invent Here, Market There

This pathway does not usually represent a top-of-the-mind consideration for managers, but it indeed represents a major opportunity. Even though knowledge has typically flowed from developed to emerging markets, the opportunity actually goes both ways. Emerging market technologies based on mobile platforms can be marketed in developed economies as well. In Kenya, transactions equivalent to more than 40% of GDP are conducted over cell phones thanks to M-Pesa,[50] and more than 60% of Kenyans are active mobile money users.[51] Similar services could be offered in advanced economies where the consumers might be willing to pay even more for the convenience.

In some ways, the emerging markets of Africa have bypassed the PC revolution with smartphones, and the bank credit/debit card revolution through new mobile payment systems. Inventions coming from advanced economies tend to encounter entrenched competition and market barriers (incumbents with infrastructure to defend) which typically do not exist in emerging markets. Initially, texting was much more important around the world than in the U.S., and texting applications developed in the U.S. were predominantly marketed elsewhere. For example, Air2Web was a wireless application service provider based in Atlanta, but also served the Indian market with over 100 million text messages for airlines and banks.[52]

10. Eureka!

This category refers to accidental inventions, some of which are easy to confuse with urban legends. The seminal example is the Post-It notes by 3M where the inventor was trying to identify a powerful adhesive. In 1968, he failed miserably in achieving that objective but in the process discovered something that can stick and unstick. 3M had not considered that there would be a market for such a product. All of a sudden, 3M had a huge hit in its hands but still did not know it. It took six years and another colleague to identify the problem this weak glue would solve.[53] Even the choice of the distinguishing yellow color was accidental; the lab next door had only yellow scrap paper available![54] Other accidental discoveries that came about from playing in and around a laboratory include the microwave, penicillin, corn flakes, plastics, saccharine, and the pacemaker.[55]

Accidental success is not limited to inventions of course. Drucker notes that new ventures find success more often than not in markets "[o]ther than the one it was originally intended to serve, with products or services not quite those with which it had set out, bought...by customers it did not think of...and used for a host of purposes besides the ones for which the products were designed."[56] Thus, businesses must be market-oriented, and they must be prepared to anticipate and be organized to capitalize on the unexpected and unseen opportunities.

Overall, new industries are born as much by exceptional marketing and operations (execution) as by innovation and entrepreneurship. For example, both FedEx and UPS grew because of exceptional execution as well as marketing. We should give due credit to marketing and operations as we do to innovation and entrepreneurship.

The above section was about how industries are born. In the next section, we focus on how industries grow and organize.

How Are Industries Organized?

Just like the birth patterns of product markets, the paths through which businesses grow and organize into industries are varied yet quite predictable. The process of creative duplication discussed earlier usually attracts numerous competitors which results in excess capacity which then needs to be rationalized. Beginning with numerous small mom-and-pop operations, the industry goes through a shake-out period and gets standardized.[57] Next, we discuss seven points that drive this industry organization process.

1. *Industries are organized by access to capital rather than by competition*

Organization is heavily influenced by access to capital rather than the alignment of strategy and structure. Similarly, the centralization-decentralization dichotomy represents the old way of thinking about organizations. Access to capital (or lack thereof) can be even more critical. Historically, we have observed that those with access to capital become market makers and organize their industries. For example, JP Morgan organized the steel, railroad, and electric power industries.

However, the era of industry titans such JP Morgan, Andrew Carnegie, John D. Rockefeller is over, and their organizational role as market makers today is assumed by private equity firms such as Warren Buffet's Berkshire Hathaway, Blackstone, or Temasek from Singapore.

While a previous generation of private equity firms may have raided firms at a steep discount, stripped the assets, and got rid of the rest, the current generation acquires corporations whose public equity values have collapsed and restructures them with an eye on long-term growth. The well-documented case of the hostile takeover of RJR Nabisco by KKR is one example that went wrong; however, KKR's takeover of Duracell Batteries had a favorable ending.[58]

Today, renowned venture capital firms in Silicon Valley fund multiple companies in the same space, get seats on their boards, and organize them into industries. Not surprisingly, they often encourage horizontal mergers and acquisitions as well. However, their deal-making finesse is dwarfed when compared to their Far Eastern counterparts. Softbank of Japan runs the $100 billion Vision Fund, the largest venture capital fund for technology in the world, and owns significant stakes in household names such as Uber, Alibaba, Yahoo, and WeWork. It has recently announced that it will launch another $100 billion fund.[59] Meanwhile, the reach of Alibaba and Tencent in China is unmatched. The duo collectively accounts for 40–50% of all venture capital flows in mainland China. In contrast, big technology groups of Silicon Valley account for less than 5% of the venture capital flows in the U.S.[60]

Finally, we must stress the rising prominence of sovereign funds, in particular, those from China. For example, China Investment Corporation was established in 2007 with roughly $200 billion under management.[61] It currently has over $940 billion under management and will increasingly play a bigger role for market-making in today's global markets. In fact, among the top dozen sovereign funds in the world based on assets, China has three more (as of February 2019): Hong Kong Monetary Authority Investment Portfolio ($523 billion), SAFE Investment Company ($441 billion), and National Social Security Fund ($295 billion).[62]

2. Access to capital is the real competitive advantage of entrepreneurs

In today's market-driven competitive landscape, it is more or less considered a given that a primary purpose of a business is to create and serve customers and that a business must be customer-centric.[63] One cannot succeed without it.

On the other hand, given that most competitive firms of today strive to serve their customers well, the notion of customer-centricity has lost much of its value as a differentiator or a source of competitive advantage. Historically, as well as today, access to capital remains a true and tested source of competitive advantage for entrepreneurs and market makers alike. For example, Christopher Columbus was not the first to dream of sailing west, but he was the first one to be able to raise capital for this voyage from the King and Queen of Spain (who deliberated for six years before agreeing to finance the maiden voyage).[64] Similarly, John D. Rockefeller who was an accounting clerk became the richest man in the modern world by turning a $4000 investment in an oil refinery business into a large stake in the Standard Oil Company. He borrowed heavily and acquired other refineries as fast as he could (the fact that his father-in-law was a prosperous and connected merchant certainly helped). Standard Oil at its height had cornered some 90% of the U.S. oil market. By 1914, John Rockefeller accounted for about 2% of the U.S. GDP, a wealth that is estimated to be worth over $318 billion in today's dollars, or three times as rich as Bill Gates![65]

3. *Shakeouts and mergers occur more due to capital shortage than differentiation and competition*

In some cases, what capital markets do to you can be even more important than what you do. Our research and consulting practices indicate that industry shakeouts, and the wave of mergers that follow, occur more so because firms have run out of capital. Why is that the case? As stated earlier, industries build excess capacity in the heat of competition and subsequently run out of cash to be able to sustain their operations. Thus, industry shakeouts also have more to do with access to capital than with lack of differentiation.

More and more studies have been pointing out that the so-called first-mover advantage is actually an incumbent's curse. Pioneers typically disappoint, disappear, or get acquired, whereas the second round of organizers makes money. Thus, it is fair to say that pioneers have an evaporating rather than enduring advantage. They mostly fail to generate positive cash flows or maintain disappointing long-term market share and rarely remain leaders in their markets.[66]

For example, Atari and Intellivision have died, whereas late entrants Sony and Microsoft thrive in the video game console market. Kodak owned most of the digital technology patents and yet went under when digital photography exploded.[67] The first commercial e-reader was not Amazon's Kindle but NuvoMedia's Rocket eBook that predated it by nine years.[68] Sony also developed an MP3 player before Apple's iPod; Research in Motion had a smartphone before Apple iPhone, and even HP had an e-reader before Apple's iPad.[69] Interestingly, Apple which pioneered personal computers almost went under itself in 1997 and might not have been around today if it had not been revived by a hefty cash infusion by Microsoft.[70] Apple also failed with the first personal digital assistant (Newton). Since then it has learned to be very careful not to be first to market. But when it enters, it does so with better design, user interface, and marketing power. When it comes to market leadership then, it is a marathon rather than a 100-meter dash.

4. *De jure as well as de facto standards are equally important in industry organization*

The most common path for organization is to become the *de facto* standard and then protect the position by enforcing intellectual property rights or trade secrets (e.g., Coca-Cola's secret formula). For example, Alphabet has organized smartphone manufacturers around its Android platform.

De jure or standards by law are also very consequential. For example, the cellular phone was invented and commercialized in the U.S. first, but then the U.S. lost the global market because it never picked a standard. A capitalistic (survival of the fittest) approach was used, which led to the proliferation of many competing standards such as AMPS, CDMA, TDMA, and GSM. Meanwhile, the European Union decided there should be one standard, GSM. Their *de jure* eventually became *de facto* globally, and the rest is history.

Another classic case anchors around the fact that Apple favored a closed system for personal computers, whereas IBM allowed clones and became the *de facto* standard for the PC industry. History repeated itself when Apple chose to keep iOS proprietary, whereas Alphabet made its Android operating system available to other manufacturers. Even though Android was launched 14 months later, as of June 2020, its global market share stood at 74% versus Apple's 25%.[71]

5. *Alfred Chandler's decentralized structure (business units) and centralized strategy is rapidly becoming obsolete, as strategy is becoming more dynamic and volatile*

The renowned business historian Alfred Chandler examined four U.S. conglomerates—DuPont, General Motors (GM), Standard Oil of New Jersey, and Sears Roebuck—and famously argued for the "structure follows strategy" paradigm. As such, an organizational structure needed to be designed to fit the strategy. Since no singular structure was optimal to meet all strategic objectives and market conditions, the suggestion for conglomerates was to have a centralized holding company with decentralized business units. It was the holding company's responsibility to provide access to capital and manage the broader portfolio of strategic business units. Many corporations such as

General Motors thrived over the last century using this organizational structure.

However, as large firms such as IBM and Microsoft have painfully realized, strategy can no longer be crafted for the long term for most businesses.[72] In many cases, strategy is even more volatile than budgeting. Every quarter, CEOs struggle to figure out what to do next. Winning is not about one long pass play to save the game as it gloriously used to be. Instead, one must scramble, scramble, and then scramble some more.[73]

Strategy can change, but what doesn't change nearly as often is a company's stated purpose—its reason for being—and the core values it lives by. For a long time, the default purpose was simply profit and/or shareholder value maximization. That is now changing, and purpose and core values provide a North Star for companies in times of turmoil in their environment.

6. *One cannot re-organize all the time*

With such a dynamic landscape as described above, it is just not possible for most firms to restructure continuously and at some point, they collapse and go out of business or get bought. As mentioned in our opening chapter, the U.S. has been witnessing rigorous M&A activity. This record would also be matched by the European Union as well if it was doing better economically. So why do good companies fail?

Regulatory change, technology, globalization, competition, and customers are the largest sources of external change. When the external environment is changing dramatically and a company is either unable or unwilling to change, it fails. Research points out to seven main reasons: denial, arrogance, complacency, incumbency, myopia, obsession of volume, and the territorial impulse.[74]

The curse of incumbency alluded to earlier is related to many of these reasons. In many cases, success breeds complacency and reinforces the old way of doing things as opposed to seeking the new. For example, Ken Olsen, the co-founder of Digital Equipment Corporation, ignored the threat posed by personal computers to his mainframe business for years and even famously said, "the personal computer will fall flat on its face in business," and "there is no reason for any individual to have a computer in his home," only to later see his company acquired by the PC upstart Compaq in 1998.[75] In contrast, DuPont invented Nylon but then assigned key employees to work on projects to make it obsolete.[76]

Success can also breed arrogance: our research indicates that more than 65% of businesses have succeeded by accident. Intel was primarily doing semiconductors for video games. IBM needed a low-end chip for PCs but did not want to develop one or use IBM-branded chips in low-end PCs. Similarly, it outsourced the operating system software to Microsoft. It is fair to say that neither Intel nor Microsoft would have become what they are today without the support of IBM. As of this writing, IBM's market capitalization is $103 billion and Intel's is $250 billion. Microsoft's market capitalization is an astounding $1.5 *trillion*!

A company that is arrogant and complacent is self-destructive. It believes that the future is predictable for the most part and that its scale will protect it in case of a setback. For example, telecom companies did not buy into the reality that wireless would replace phone lines until it had actually happened. Currently, the same phenomenon is repeating with organic foods. Traditional supermarket chains thought it was a fad, which enabled Whole Foods Market to become a dominant player.

Meanwhile, the average life-expectancy of large enterprises has been steadily declining. Companies in the S&P 500 can only enjoy a life span that is merely a fifth of the 65+ years they could expect a hundred years ago.[77] Thus, let alone its strategy and structure, the very survival of the corporation is in jeopardy. The organizational structure theories may have been on point at the time, but they are just not consistent with the business realities of today.

Even the once formidable retailer Sears which served a full line of products, and even offered houses, financing, repair, and maintenance has succumbed to this reality. It has been on life support for much of the decade, propped up by private equity. One glimmer of hope for Sears would have been to sell through multiple channels and liberate its private brands that have potential. That vision has been partially realized, as one can now buy Craftsman tools at Lowe's. However, it is not Sears that made it happen. Sears chose to sell its iconic Craftsman brand to Stanley Black & Decker in 2017 further depleting its options for recovery.[78] The future only promises more pain and downsizing for Sears.

Similarly, GM is in trouble. It still follows its traditional structure so the question is whether it can survive with one central headquarters and decentralized brand name business units such as Chevrolet, Pontiac, Buick, and Cadillac. Successful companies need to break down organizational silos and overcome marketing myopia and political resistance to change. Perhaps GM should be asking it if is in the automobile business or some other business altogether, such as mobility.

7. *The breakup value is often greater than the original corporation value*

The collapse of public equity generates double damage. When the stock market is out of favor, there is a tendency to preserve cash and generate reserves. Collapsed equity value also implies higher leverage for firms. They struggle even more if they were aggressively borrowing.

We can observe this pattern with the Great Depression, the restructuring after the first energy crisis of 1973–1974, the great recession of 2007–2009, and we expect it to hold post-Covid-19 too. There was a period in the 1980s where the stock market collapsed and values of the majority of conglomerates were less than the value of their parts combined. Thus, diversified holding companies fell out of favor. The inefficiencies were addressed through re-engineering, downsizing, and outsourcing. (Survival and preventing hostile takeovers by private equity companies were such a primary concern that many states wrote new legislation and enacted poison pills to protect their corporations from hostile takeovers.) The same pattern was observed after the 2007–2009 recession. Overall, the breakup value for many corporations was much higher as the stocks collapsed. In 2012, Kraft Foods changed its name to Mondelez International and completed the spin-off of Kraft Foods making it a separate company.[79] Long-time rivals Dow Chemical and DuPont are planning to merge with a $122 billion deal but only with the intention to break up into three companies based on business lines (plastics and chemicals, agricultural seeds and pesticides, and specialty chemicals such as food ingredients and safety equipment).[80] The spin-off and divestments trend can be seen in pharmaceutical companies as well (e.g., Novartis spin-off of Alcon)[81] and will likely maintain its current pace in the rest of this decade, as discussed in Chap. 1.

In the next chapter, we discuss the implications and the evolution of the Rule of Three at the global level.

Box 4.3   Line Pruning and Divestments

While many firms tie up their resources unnecessarily to keep struggling divisions or product lines alive, systematic abandonment and product line pruning are indeed necessary to sustain healthy growth. Maintaining an old declining product, service, market, or process at the expense of new and growing products, services, markets, or processes is a significant mistake that one may never recover from. Even as secondary business concerns, these take time, resources, and energy from priority projects. The ideal time to get rid of a product may be when the consensus is that it still has five more good years in it. Yet most divestment decisions are postponed until it is too late due to the legacy status of these products within the organization and its key managers. Overcoming this requires systematic questioning of the status quo: "[a]bandonment/divestment is the right action if…the product still has a few years of life; it is fully written off, and the current product causes neglect of new and growing product, service or process."[82] In light of this, Coca-Cola's recent announcement to eliminate its zombie brands makes sense. Over half of its roughly 400 master brands are country-specific brands that have little scale and provide below average growth.[83]

Key Takeaways

- Disruptive technologies or business models typically emerge from outside of the industry and revolutionize it.
- The prevailing industry structure is neither one of oligopoly nor of monopolistic competition. It is always both! Industries exist in a dynamic balance between monopolistic competition (characterized by high rent, sub-monopolies, and many differentiated small players that are margin driven) and oligopoly (characterized by a focus on building scale, and one-stop-shop/full-line offerings).
- When an industry moves too far away from monopolistic competition toward a highly oligopolistic structure, the counterforces come into play and it begins to shift back toward monopolistic competition.
- Stages of the traditional industry life cycle include introduction, growth, maturity, and decline.
- Industry evolution and inertia are primarily driven by two factors that are often at odds with each other: the need for efficiency and growth.
- Contrary to conventional wisdom, industries are born due to many reasons besides new technological breakthroughs. In fact, most new industries are born based on or building upon existing knowledge.
- Industries are born by:
  - Transformation from manual to automation
  - Outsourcing
  - Reducing friction in commerce and consumption (accessibility)
  - Tapping into unmet needs (affordability)
  - Converting wants into needs
  - Moving from unbranded to branded products and services
  - Leveraging platforms and infrastructure
  - Government policy
  - Inventing here, marketing there
  - Eureka!
- Industries are organized by access to capital. Access to capital is the real competitive advantage of entrepreneurs.
- Shakeouts and mergers occur more due to capital shortage than differentiation and competition.
- *De jure* as well as *de facto* standards are equally important in industry organization.
- Decentralized structure (business units) and centralized strategy is rapidly becoming obsolete, as strategy is becoming more dynamic and volatile.
- One cannot re-organize all the time; the breakup value is often greater than the original corporation value.

Notes

1. For example, Pulitzer history prize recipient Alfred D. Chandler (1918–2007) at Harvard Business School, Ronald Coase (1910–2013) at the University of Chicago, and Nobel memorial prize recipient Oliver E. Williamson (1932–2020) at University of California Berkeley all made seminal contributions to the theory of the firm. In terms of strategy, Kenneth R. Andrews (1916–2005) of Harvard Business School, H. Igor Ansoff (1918–2002) (pioneer of the widely used product-market growth matrix), and especially Edward Chamberlin (1899–1967) (known for the concepts of product differentiation and monopolistic competition) and Joan Robinson (1903–1983) at Cambridge University (who coined the term monopsony) are widely cited for making structure-conduct-performance paradigm mainstream, whereas Edith Penrose (1914–1996) is credited for pioneering today's academically dominant resource-based view of the firm.

   The early pioneers such as Adam Smith (1776) advanced some systematically related statements about separation of firm ownership and control; however, it took more than 150 years for Coase (1937) and more than 200 years for Williamson (1979) to develop an empirically testable theory of the firm in the form of transaction cost theory, and Chandler to author three seminal books—*Strategy and Structure* (1962), *The Visible Hand* (1977), and *Scale and Scope* (1990) on the subject. Nevertheless, extant research is mostly unsatisfactory when it comes to a comprehensive treatise of industry life cycle or market evolution.

   For a sample of seminal works in this domain, see:

   Smith, Adam (1776), *An Inquiry into the Nature and Causes of the Wealth of Nations*, London: W. Strahan.

   Robinson, Joan V. (1933), *The Economics of Imperfect Competition*, Macmillan. 2nd ed., 1969. Londres.

   Coase, Ronald (1937), "The Nature of the Firm," *Economica*, 4, 386–405.

   Penrose, Edith (1959), *The Theory of the Growth of the Firm*, New York: John Wiley and Sons.

   Jensen, M.C., and W.H. Meckling (1976), "Theory of the Firm: Managerial Behavior, Agency Costs and Ownership Structure," *Journal of Financial Economics*, October, 3 (4), 305–360.

   Chandler, Alfred D. Jr. (1977), *The Visible Hand: The Managerial Revolution in American Business*, Boston: MA, The Belknap Press of Harvard University Press.

   Williamson, Oliver (1979), "Transaction-Cost Economics: The Governance of Contractual Relations," *Journal of Law and Economics*, 22, 233–261.

   Fama, E.F., (1980), "Agency Problems and the Theory of the Firm," *The Journal of Political Economy*, 88 (2), 288–307.

Demsetz, H. (1988), "The Theory of the Firm Revisited," *Journal of Law, Economics and Organization*, 4, 141–161.

Millon, D. (1990), "Theories of the Corporation," *Duke Law Journal*, 201–262.

2. Schumpeter, J. (1942), *Capitalism, Socialism, and Democracy*, New York: Harper & Bros.
3. Von Hippel Eric (1988), *The Sources of Innovation*, Oxford University Press. https://books.google.com/books/about/The_Sources_of_Innovation.html?id=QQQmT2-j2zQC.
4. Drucker, P. F. (1999), *Management Challenges for the 21st Century*, New York: Harper Collins, pp. 121–122.
5. Alas, we still lack in our understanding of when and why these shifts occur. The ecological resource partitioning theory (Carroll 1985, 1997) examines the competitive dynamics between the generalists and specialists and provides further empirical support for the gradual convergence toward a few generalists and *the Rule of Three* theory. In summary, abundant and varying types of resources early on in an industry's life cycle causes generalists to proliferate. In turn, these generalists validate market potential and attract numerous specialists that position themselves in peripheral niches (Carroll 1985). However, the resources available to each organization begin to get scarce during this evolutionary process. The increasing degree of product line overlap between the generalists causes them to compete directly, which increases the casualty rate among them.

   Meanwhile, the specialists tend to thrive. They do not compete as directly or as intensively as generalists do due to their differentiation and focus in niche markets (Swaminathan 2001). Consequently, the resource partitioning theory predicts that as markets mature and get more concentrated, the birth rate of generalists will decrease (and the casualty rate will increase), and the birth rate of specialists will increase (and casualty rate will decrease) (Carroll 1985; Carroll, Dobrev, and Swaminathan 2002; Swaminathan 2001).

   Several research studies from varying industries have reported empirical evidence for the above predictions (Mezias and Mezias 2000). The resource partitioning model (Carroll 1985) and *the Rule of Three* theory are well-aligned in their characterization of the basic market evolution. However, *the Rule of Three* extends these predictions to observe the convergence to three generalists and specifies market share ranges which enable optimal performance for each strategic group. Nevertheless, our understanding of the evolutionary process and each steady-state in a dynamic industry structure equilibrium remains relatively basic.

   Carroll, Glenn R. (1985), "Concentration and Specialization: Dynamics of Niche Width in Populations of Organizations," *American Journal of Sociology*, 90 (6), 1261–1283.

Carroll, Glenn R. (1997), "Long-Term Evolutionary Change in Organizational Populations: Theory, Models and Empirical Findings in Industrial Demography," *Industrial and Corporate Change*, 6 (1), 119–143.

Mezias, John M. and Stephen J. Mezias (2000), "Resource Partitioning, the Founding of Specialist Firms, and Innovation: The American Feature Film Industry, 1912–1929," *Organization Science*, 11 (3), 306–322.

Swaminathan, Anand (2001), "Partitioning and the Evolution of Specialist Organizations: The Role of Location and Identity in the U.S. Wine Industry," *Academy of Management Journal*, 44 (6), 1169–1185.

Carroll, Glenn R, S.D. Dobrev, and A. Swaminathan (2002), "Organizational Processes of Resource Partitioning," in *Research in Organizational Behavior*, Vol. 24, R.I. Sutton and B.M. Staw, eds. Greenwich, CT: JAI Press, 1–40.

6. Deans, Graeme K., Fritz Kroeger, and Stefan Zeisel (2002), "The Consolidation Curve," *Harvard Business Review*, December 2002, accessed July 12, 2020. https://hbr.org/2002/12/the-consolidation-curve#comment-section.

7. Deans, Graeme K., Fritz Kroeger, and Stefan Zeisel (2002), "The Consolidation Curve," *Harvard Business Review*, December 2002, accessed July 12, 2020. https://hbr.org/2002/12/the-consolidation-curve#comment-section.

8. Moore, Geoffrey (1991), *Crossing the Chasm: Marketing and Selling Disruptive Products to Mainstream Customers*, New York: HarperCollins.

9. Shaheen, S., Sperling, D., & Wagner, C. (1999), "A Short History of Carsharing in the 90's," *The Journal of World Transport Policy and Practice*, 5 (3), 18–40.

10. Wassily Leontief, an economist from Harvard University, published a paper on this subject in 1941 and won the Nobel Prize in economics in 1973 for developing an iterative method of valuing sectors based on the importance of the sectors that supply them.

     https://www.technologyreview.com/s/417529/scientist-finds-pagerank-type-algorithm-from-the-1940s/.

11. The emerging specialty domain of entrepreneurial marketing attempts to remedy this drawback by pointing out the tremendous value of marketing for entrepreneurs and the effectiveness of non-conventional marketing for corporate marketers. The rise of entrepreneurial marketing can be traced back to Jay Conrad Levinson at UC Berkeley. His students engaged with start-ups were questioning him on how they could compete with the large corporation with huge marketing budgets. Levinson (1984) examined addressing marketing opportunities with little or no budget and published the first guerilla marketing book in 1984. The guerilla marketing book series became the most successful marketing book series of all time. The series now has close to 40 original volumes, has been translated to 62 languages, and sold well over 20 million copies.

Levinson defines guerilla marketing as "achieving conventional goals, such as profits and joy, with unconventional methods, such as investing energy instead of money." A key reason why entrepreneurial marketing tends to be extremely effective is that it can capture the element of surprise through the use of novel marketing campaigns (Uslay 2002). This is different than saying the product is novel (it would help but does not automatically guarantee that buzz marketing will take over). Rather the approach to marketing the product is novel. Social Media platforms such as YouTube, Twitter, and Facebook can also be used to generate buzz effect through referrals and positive word of mouth.

Also see:

Alqahtani, Nasser and Can Uslay (2020), "Entrepreneurial Marketing and Firm Performance: Synthesis and Conceptual Development," *Journal of Business Research*, 113 (May), 62–71.

Levinson, Conrad (1984), *Guerilla Marketing: Easy and Inexpensive Strategies for Making Big Profits from Your Small Business*, New York: Houghton Mifflin Harcourt.

Uslay, Can (2017), "The Good, Bad, and Ugly Side of Entrepreneurial Marketing: Is Your Social Media Campaign Unveiled, Incognito, or Exposed?" *Rutgers Business Review*, 2 (3), 338–349.

Whalen, Peter, Can Uslay, Vincent J. Pascal, Glenn Omura, Andrew McAuley, Chickery J. Kasouf, Rosalind Jones, Claes M. Hultman, Gerald E. Hills, David J. Hansen, Audrey Gilmore, Joe Giglierano, Fabian Eggers, and Jonathan Deacon (2016), "Anatomy of Competitive Advantage: Towards a Contingency Theory of Entrepreneurial Marketing," *Journal of Strategic Marketing*, 24 (1), 5–19.

Uslay, Can (2002) "Buzz Marketing: Secrets They Don't Teach You at the Business School," *Glokal*, Spring, 38–41.

12. Schumpeter, Joseph (1942), *Capitalism, Socialism, and Democracy*, New York: Harper & Bros.

13. Buss, Dale (2016), "On Verge of US Sales Crown, Mercedes Unveils Croove Car-Renting App," BrandChannel.com, December 22, 2016, accessed September 27, 2019. http://www.brandchannel.com/2016/12/22/mercedes-benz-croove-122216/.

14. Codagnone, Cristiano and Bertin Martens (2016), "Scoping the Sharing Economy: Origins, Definitions, Impact and Regulatory Issues," Institute for Prospective Technological Studies Digital Economy Working Paper 2016/01. JRC100369, European Commission.

15. IKEA Group (2017), "IKEA Group Signs Agreement to Acquire TaskRabbit," Cision PR Newswire, September 27, 2017, accessed July 12, 2020. https://www.prnewswire.com/news-releases/ikea-group-signs-agreement-to-acquire-taskrabbit-300527686.html.

16. Malhotra, Naresh K. and Can Uslay (2018), "Make, Buy, Borrow or Crowdsource? The Evolution and Future of Outsourcing," *Journal of Business Strategy*, 39 (5), 14–21.

17. Sisario, B. (2017), "Streaming Drives U.S. Music Sales Up 11% in 2016," March 30, 2017, accessed May 13, 2017. https://www.nytimes.com/2017/03/30/business/media/digital-music-spotify-apple-record-labels.html.

18. Drucker, P. F. (1980), *Managing in Turbulent Times*, New York: Harper & Row.
    Drucker, P. F. (1982), *The Changing World of the Executive*, New York: Times Books.

19. Uslay, Can, Robert E. Morgan, and Jagdish N. Sheth (2009), "Peter Drucker on Marketing: An Exploration of Five Tenets," *Journal of the Academy of Marketing Science*, 37 (1), 47–60.

20. Drucker, P. F. (1973). *Management: Tasks, Responsibilities, Practices*, New York: Harper & Row, pp. 61–62 (italics in original).

21. Rogers, Everett M. (2003) *Diffusion of Innovations*, 5th ed., New York: The Free Press.

22. Ford (2019), "100 Years of the Moving Assembly Line," Ford.com, accessed September 27, 2019. http://corporate.ford.com/innovation/100-years-moving-assembly-line.html.
    Priddle, Alisa (2013), "Ford Marks Assembly Line Anniversary with New Goals," USA Today, October 7, accessed September 28, 2019. https://www.usatoday.com/story/money/business/2013/10/07/ford-100th-anniversary-assembly-line/2939649/.

23. Statista (2020), "New Profit of RyanAir from 2011 to 2020," accessed July 12, 2020. https://www.statista.com/statistics/756093/ryanair-net-profit/#:~:text=Between%202010%2F11%20and%202017,again%20to%20one%20billion%20euros.

24. Buss, Dale (2017), "Don't Tip (Over) Your Server: Robots Fill Food Service Roles," BrandChannel.com, January 25, 2017, accessed September 27, 2019. http://www.brandchannel.com/2017/01/25/robots-fill-food-service-roles-012517/?utm_campaign=170125-robots-food&utm_source=newsletter&utm_medium=email.

25. For example, see the Special Issue on Artificial Intelligence of the *California Management Review*, Volume 61, Issue 4, 2019.

26. Prahalad, C. K., and G. Hamel (1990), "The Core Competence of the Corporation," *Harvard Business Review*, 68 (May/June), 79–91.

27. Malhotra, Naresh K. and Can Uslay (2018), "Make, Buy, Borrow or Crowdsource? The Evolution and Future of Outsourcing," *Journal of Business Strategy*, 39 (5), 14–21, p. 14.

28. Reed, Dan (2005), "Airlines try to make Internet Work for Them," *USA Today*, October 31, 2005, accessed September 27, 2019. http://usatoday30.usatoday.com/travel/2005-10-31-airlines-web_x.htm.

Also see Sheth, Jagdish N., Fred C. Allvine, Can Uslay, and Ashutosh Dixit (2007), *Deregulation and Competition: Lessons from the Airline Industry*, Thousand Oaks, CA: Sage Publications.

29. Thompson, Andrew (2019), "Google's Mission Statement and Vision Statement (An Analysis)," Panmore.com, February 13, 2019, accessed September 27, 2019. http://panmore.com/google-vision-statement-mission-statement.

30. Interestingly, the Federal Reserve issued a warning to banks in 1920 asking them not to offer financing for automobiles used for pleasure.
    Autobytel (2019), "Automotive Financing and the Pursuit of Happiness," Autobytel.com, accessed September 27, 2019. http://www.autobytel.com/auto-news/features/automotive-financing-and-the-pursuit-of-happiness-117436/2/.
    Wikipedia (2019), "Ally Financial," Wikipedia.com, accessed September 27, 2019. https://en.wikipedia.org/wiki/Ally_Financial

31. Crutcher, K. (July 1986), "A Short History of Leasing," available at http://www.automotive-fleet.com/article/story/1986/07/a-short-history-of-leasing.aspx (accessed 4 May 2017).

32. Malhotra, Naresh K. and Can Uslay (2018), "Make, Buy, Borrow or Crowdsource? The Evolution and Future of Outsourcing," *Journal of Business Strategy*, 39 (5), 14–21.

33. CAPA (2017), "State of the Market; Global Aircraft Leasing Continues its International Shift from West to East," Centreforaviation.com, April 23, 2017, accessed September 27, 2019. https://centreforaviation.com/analysis/airline-leader/state-of-the-market-global-aircraft-leasing-continues-its-international-shift-from-west-to-east-340080.
    Wikipedia (2019), "Aircraft lease," Wikipedia.com, accessed September 27, 2019. https://en.wikipedia.org/wiki/Aircraft_lease.

34. Rutgers Business School (2018), "Dan Schulman, PayPal CEO Keynote Address," YouTube.com, April 26, 2019, accessed September 27, 2019. https://www.youtube.com/watch?v=iqv18iuz3V0&feature=youtu.be.

35. Hoff, Edward J. (1985), "Hattori-Seiko and the World Watch Industry in 1980," Case # 9-385-300, Harvard Business School.

36. Statistic Brain Research Institute, "Wrist Watch Market Industry Analysis," accessed June 16, 2019. https://www.statisticbrain.com/wrist-watch-industry-statistics/.

37. Thompson, Joe (2017), "A Concise History of the Quartz Watch Revolution," Bloomberg.com, November 16, 2017, accessed September 27, 2019. https://www.bloomberg.com/news/articles/2017-11-16/a-concise-history-of-the-quartz-watch-revolution.

38. Statista (2019), "Smartphone Penetration Rate in China from 2015 to 2023," Statista.com, September 23, 2019, accessed September 27, 2019. https://www.statista.com/statistics/321482/smartphone-user-penetration-in-china/.

39. Statista (2019), "Share of Mobile Phone Users that Use a Smartphone in India from 2014 to 2022," Statista.com, September 23, 2019, accessed September 27, 2019. https://www.statista.com/statistics/257048/ smartphone-user-penetration-in-india/.

40. Telecompaper (2019), "South Korea Reaches 95% Smartphone Penetration—Study," Telecompaper.com, February 7, 2019, accessed September 27, 2019. https://www.telecompaper.com/news/south-korea-reaches-95-smartphone-penetration-study%2D%2D1279476.

41. Takahashi, Dean (2018), "Newzoo: Smartphone Users will Top 3 Billion in 2018, Hit 3.8 Billion by 2021," VentureBeat.com, September 11, 2018, accessed September 27, 2019. https://venturebeat.com/2018/09/11/ newzoo-smartphone-users-will-top-3-billion-in-2018-hit-3-8-billion-by-2021/.

42. Drucker, P. F. (1973). *Management: Tasks, Responsibilities, Practices*, New York: Harper & Row, pp. 62–63.

43. Clement, J. (2019), "Number of Mobile Active Downloads Worldwide from 2016 to 2019 (in Billions)" Statista.com, January 17, 2020, accessed June 30, 2020. https://www.statista.com/statistics/271644/worldwide-free-and-paid-mobile-app-store-downloads/.

44. Clement, J. (2019), "Number of eBay's Active Users from 1st Quarter 2010 to 2nd Quarter 2019 (in millions)," Statista.com, July 26, 2019, accessed September 27, 2019. https://www.statista.com/statistics/242235/number-of-ebays-total-active-users/.

45. Annan, G. Kofi (2019), "Reaching 50 Million users," Visual.ly, accessed September 27, 2019. https://visual.ly/community/infographic/technology/ reaching-50-million-users.

46. Bellis, Mary (2019), "History of Seat Belts," ThoughtCo.com, February 15, 2019, accessed September 27, 2019. http://inventors.about.com/od/ sstartinventions/a/History-Of-Seat-Belts.htm.

47. Wikipedia (2019), "Seat Belt," Wikipedia.com, accessed September 27, 2019. https://en.wikipedia.org/wiki/Seat_belt#Risk_compensation.
    Wikipedia (2019), "Seat Belt Laws in the United States," Wikipedia. com, accessed September 27, 2019. https://en.wikipedia.org/wiki/Seat_belt_ legislation_in_the_United_States.

48. Bellis, Mary (2019), "The History of Airbags," August 9, 2019. Accessed September 28, 2019. https://www.thoughtco.com/history-of-airbags-1991232.

49. Gupta, Vinay (2017), "A Brief History of Blockchain," HBR.com, February 28, 2017, accessed September 27, 2019. https://hbr.org/2017/02/a-brief-history-of-blockchain.

50. Wainaina, Eric (2015), "42% of Kenya GDP Transacted on M-pesa and 9 Takeaways from Safaricom Results," TechWeez.com, May 7, 2015, accessed September 27, 2019. http://www.techweez.com/2015/05/07/ten-takeaways-safaricom-2015-results/.

51. McKay, Claudia and Rafe Mazer (2014), "10 Myths About M-PESA: 2014 Update," CGAP.org, October 1, 2014, accessed September 27, 2019. http://www.cgap.org/blog/10-myths-about-m-pesa-2014-update.

52. Kats, Rimma (2019), "Velti pays $19M for Air2Web to further mobile marketing efforts," MobileMarketer.com, accessed September 27, 2019. http://www.mobilemarketer.com/cms/news/advertising/11044.html.

53. Silver, Spencer (2010), "We Invented the Post-It Note," *Financial Times*, December 3, 2010, accessed July 12, 2020. https://www.ft.com/content/f08e8a9a-fcd7-11df-ae2d-00144feab49a.

54. Zambonini, Dan (2010), "Why Are Post-It Notes Yellow?" TheJanuarist.com, February 25, 2010, accessed September 27, 2019. http://www.thejanuarist.com/why-are-post-it-notes-yellow/.

55. Donnelly, Tim (2012), "9 Brilliant Inventions Made by Mistake," INC.com, August 5, 2012, accessed September 27, 2019. http://www.inc.com/tim-donnelly/brilliant-failures/9-inventions-made-by-mistake.html.

56. Drucker, P. F. (1985). *Innovation and Entrepreneurship*, New York: Harper & Row, pp. 189–190.

57. Nelson, Richard R., and Sidney G. Winter (1982), *An Evolutionary Theory of Economic Change*, Cambridge, MA: Harvard University Press.

    Klepper, Steven and Elizabeth Graddy (1990), "The Evolution of New Industries and the Determinants of Market Structure," *Rand Journal of Economics*, 21 (1), 27–44.

    Klepper, Steven (1996), "Entry, Exit, Growth, and Innovation Over the Product Life Cycle," *American Economic Review*, 86 (3), 562–583.

    Klepper, Steven and Kenneth L. Simons, 2000. "The Making of an Oligopoly: Firm Survival and Technological Change in the Evolution of the U.S. Tire Industry," *Journal of Political Economy*, 108 (4), 728–760.

58. Burrough, Bryan and John Helyar (1990), *Barbarians at the Gate: The Fall of RJR Nabisco*, New York, NY: Harper.

    Norris, Floyd (2004), "Fund Books Loss on RJR after 15 Years: A Long Chapter Ends for Kohlberg Kravis," New York Times, July 9, 2004, accessed July 12, 2020. http://www.nytimes.com/2004/07/09/business/worldbusiness/fund-books-loss-on-rjr-after-15-years-a-long-chapter.html.

59. Fitzgerald, Maggie and Deirdre Bosa (2019), "SoftBank is launching a second version of its $100 billion fund driving Silicon Valley valuations," CNBC.com, May 9, 2019, accessed September 27, 2019. https://www.cnbc.com/2019/05/09/softbank-is-launching-a-second-version-of-its-100-billion-fund-driving-silicon-valley-valuations.html.

60. Sender, Henny (2018), "How Alibaba and Tencent became Asia's Biggest Dealmakers," Financial Times, March 26, 2018, accessed July 12, 2020. https://www.ft.com/content/38a54804-2238-11e8-9a70-08f715791301.

61. Wikipedia (2019), "China Investment Corporation," Wikipedia.com, accessed September 27, 2019. https://en.wikipedia.org/wiki/China_Investment_Corporation.

62. SWFI (2019), "Top 82 Largest Sovereign Wealth Fund Rankings by Total Assets," SWFInstitute.org, accessed September 27, 2019. http://www.swfinstitute.org/sovereign-wealth-fund-rankings/.

63. Drucker, P. F. (1973), *Management: Tasks, Responsibilities, Practices*, New York: Harper & Row, p. 63.

   Sheth, Jagdish N., Rajendra S. Sisodia and Arun Sharma (2000), "The Antecedents and Consequences of Customer-Centric Marketing," *Journal of the Academy of Marketing Science*, 28 (1), 55–66.

64. Satava, David (2007), "Columbus First Voyage: Profit or Loss from a Historical Accountant's Perspective," *The Journal of Applied Business Research*, 23 (4), 1–16.

65. Hylton, Richard D. (1992), "Rockefeller Family Tries to Keep A Vast Fortune From Dissipating," NYTimes.com, February 16, 1992, accessed September 27, 2019. http://www.nytimes.com/1992/02/16/us/rockefeller-family-tries-to-keep-a-vast-fortune-from-dissipating.html?pagewanted=all.

   O'Reilly, Sean (2016), "How Rich is the Rockefeller Family Today?" FoxBusiness, accessed June 30, 2020. https://www.foxbusiness.com/markets/how-rich-is-the-rockefeller-family-today.

   History (2019), "John D. Rockefeller," History.com, April 9, 2010, accessed September 27, 2019. http://www.history.com/topics/john-d-rockefeller.

   Segall, Grant (2001), *John D. Rockefeller: Anointed With Oil*, Oxford University Press.

66. Golder, Peter N., and Gerard J. Tellis (1993), "Pioneer Advantage: Marketing Logic or Marketing Legend?" *Journal of Marketing Research*, 30 (May), 158–170.

   Tellis, Gerard J. and Peter N. Golder (1996), "First to Market, First to Fail? Real Causes of Enduring Market Leadership," *Sloan Management Review*, (Winter), 65–75.

   Tellis, Gerard J. and Peter N. Golder (2001), *Will and Vision: How Latecomers Grow to Dominate Markets*, New York: NY, McGraw-Hill.

   Tellis, Gerard J. (2013), *Unrelenting Innovation: How to Create a Culture for Market Dominance*, San Francisco: CA: Jossey Bass-Wiley.

67. Incumbent companies such as Kodak may be locked into their invested capital. They have manufacturing plants or supply-chain arrangements that are based on traditional models, and the whole deck gets reshuffled in the digital age. Writing off all the assets and starting afresh is very difficult. The challenge is to transition from one technology to another and the chemical engineers populating a film company cannot come up with a digital product, so you have to recruit talented people from elsewhere and also engage in cultural transformation. Thus, what was a competency became a trap and liability for Kodak. Incumbents can be in a state of denial especially about competition from emerging market multinationals.

68. Kozlowski, Michael (2010), "A Brief History of eBooks," GoodeReader.com, May 17, 2010, accessed September 27, 2019. https://goodereader.com/blog/electronic-readers/a-brief-history-of-ebooks.

Lebert, Marie (2011), "eBooks: 1998—The First ebook Readers," GutenbergNews.org, July 11, 2011, accessed September 27, 2019. http://www.gutenbergnews.org/20110716/ebooks-1998-the-first-ebook-readers/.

69. Tellis, Gerard J. (2013), "Are You Cursed By Your Own Success?" CNBC.com, March 6, 2013, accessed September 27, 2019. http://www.cnbc.com/id/100450295.

70. Kawamoto, Dawn (2009), "Microsoft to Invest $150 Million in Apple," CNet.com, January 6, 2009, accessed September 27, 2019. https://www.cnet.com/news/microsoft-to-invest-150-million-in-apple/.

71. StatCounter (2020), "Mobile Operating System Market Share Worldwide," June 2020, accessed July 26, 2020. https://gs.statcounter.com/os-market-share/mobile/worldwide.

72. Reeves, Martin and Deimler, M.S. (2012), *Adaptive Advantage: Winning Strategies for Uncertain Times*, New York: The Boston Consulting Group Press.

73. Reeves, Martin, Knut Haanes, and Janmejaya Sinha (2015), *Your Strategy Needs a Strategy: How to Choose and Execute the Right Approach*, Boston: MA: Harvard Business Review Press.

74. Sheth, Jagdish N. (2007), *The Self-Destructive Habits of Good Companies*, Upper Saddle River: NJ: Wharton School Publishing.

75. Scholfield, Jack (2011), "Ken Olsen Obituary," *The Guardian*, February 9, 2011, accessed September 27, 2019. https://www.theguardian.com/technology/2011/feb/09/ken-olsen-obituary.

76. Drucker, P. F. (1992), *The Ecological Vision: Reflections on the American Condition*, New York: Transaction Books, pp. 281–282.

77. Gittleson, Kim (2012), "Can a Company Live Forever?", BBC.com, January 19, 2012, accessed September 27, 2019. https://www.bbc.com/news/business-16611040.

78. Thomas, Lauren (2017), "Lowe's to Sell Craftsman Tools, Broadening Distribution beyond Sears," CNBC.com, October 24, 2017, accessed September 27, 2019. https://www.cnbc.com/2017/10/24/stanley-black-and-decker-taps-lowes-to-sell-the-craftsman-tool-brand.html.

79. Mondelez International (2019), "Spin-Off Information," MondelezInternational.com, accessed September 27, 2019. http://www.mondelezinternational.com/investors/stock-information/spin-off-information.

80. Gandel, Stephen (2018), "DuPont's Former CEO Just Took a Major Swipe at Dow Chemical Deal," Fortune.com, October 18, 2016, accessed September 27, 2019. http://fortune.com/2016/10/18/ellen-kullman-dupont-dow-deal/.

Bunge, Jacob (2016), "DuPont CEO Says Merger With Dow Still on Track," WSJ.com, July 26, 2016, accessed September 27, 2019. http://www.wsj.com/articles/dupont-profit-beats-as-costs-decline-1469529581.

81. Liu, Angus (2019), "Alcon will Officially Leave Novartis on April 9 After an 8-Year Run. What's Next?", FiercePharma.com, March 22, 2019, accessed September 27, 2019. https://www.fiercepharma.com/pharma/after-8-year-run-alcon-to-officially-leave-novartis-april-9.

82. Drucker, P. F. (1999), *Management Challenges for the 21st Century*, New York: Harper Collins, p. 75.

83. Fleming, Molly (2020), "Coca-Cola to Cut 'Zombie Brands' as it Looks to 'Weed Out' the Poor Performers," *MarketingWeek*, July 21, 2020, accessed July 26, 2020. https://www.marketingweek.com/coca-cola-cut-zombie-brands/.

5

Evolving to the Global Rule of Three

More than three decades after the first mobile phone call made by Martin Cooper of Motorola to rival Joel Engel at Bell Labs,[1] Nokia of Finland stood proud with more than 50% global market share during 2007 Q4, followed by Motorola and Samsung of South Korea to make the global big three. However, thanks to Apple's iPhone, the deck was reshuffled in that same quarter and in just five years Nokia's global market share had slipped to merely 3.1%.[2] It was acquired by Microsoft for $7.9 billion in 2014 ($7.6 billion of which would be written off within less than two years).[3] As of 2019, Samsung, Apple, and China's Huawei rounded up the global three for smartphone manufacturers with Samsung in the lead with 20.4% and the other two vying for #2 spot, each with 14.4% global market share.[4]

At the outset of the last century, the U.S. had already surpassed England to become the largest and lowest-cost producer of steel globally. U.S. Steel Corporation alone accounted for two-thirds of the U.S. and almost 30% of world production, eventually followed by Bethlehem Steel, and Republic Steel to make the big three (unable to compete with low-cost competitors, both would go bankrupt in 2001). The U.S. produced more than 70% world steel by the end of World War II (WWII).[5] Eventually, Nippon Steel of Japan and Posco of South Korea rose to prominence. Today, U.S. firms are nowhere to be found among the list of top ten leading global steel manufacturers which consists exclusively of Asian firms. The global leader in steel is ArcelorMittal (of India, headquartered in Luxembourg), followed by China Baowu Group and HBIS Group (also from China). Indeed, Chinese firms produced more than ten times the steel produced by the U.S. in 2016.[6]

© The Author(s) 2020
J. Sheth et al., *The Global Rule of Three*, https://doi.org/10.1007/978-3-030-57473-4_5

As the birthplace of the TV and home to more than 220 manufacturers in its heyday, the U.S. had every reason to be on the leading edge of the smart and HDTV market today.[7] However, it never even had the chance. After going through its days of glory with brands such as RCA, Motorola, Westinghouse, and GE, when the last standing U.S. manufacturer Zenith was acquired by LG (of South Korea) in 1995, it was merely the #3 player in the U.S. with under 10% share. The leader was Thomson of France with more than 20% share followed by Phillips (of the Netherlands) with 15% share. The deal propelled LG from 2% share in the U.S. to the top three.[8] The same year the first flat-screen plasma TVs were introduced, and Japanese brands such as Sony, Sharp, Matsushita, and Toshiba began to shine. Yet today, even the Japanese have had to vacate the leaderboard. Samsung wrested global leadership from Sony in 2006 and has not looked back.[9] It is currently the global LCD leader with over 20% share, followed by LG with 12% share and TCL (of China) with 11% of the market.[10]

The globalization of the home appliances market can be traced back to then-world leader Electrolux's acquisition of U.S. #3 player White Consolidated in the U.S. in 1986. Whirlpool retaliated by purchasing KitchenAid (in its home market) and Phillips' appliance division to become #2 in Europe over Bosch-Siemens and Merloni. Whirlpool also acquired Maytag after a bidding war with Haier for $1.7 billion in 2006 to solidify its U.S. position. However, Haier declared its intention to be #1 globally, and building upon the strength of its domestic market, would not be denied for long. It initially started with smaller appliances and wiped out its Italian competitors. Haier then became a full-line appliance company competing successfully against global leaders Whirlpool and Electrolux. It finally became the global leader in 2009 and has further solidified its leadership with its acquisition of GE's appliance division for $5.6 billion in 2016.[11] Today, the chances are your new microwave oven which was likely to be made in Japan in the earlier days and subsequently in South Korea was actually made in China.

At first glance, all seems to be in order in the world of PC manufacturing. Based on 2018 figures, Lenovo (of China, formerly known as Legend) has the lead with 22.5% global market share, followed by HP 21.7% and Dell with 16.2%.[12] However, this apparent order does not alleviate the ongoing intensive competition between HP and Lenovo, and the pressure on Dell's position. In the next decade, it is possible for HP and Dell to not only fall out of contention for leadership but also become #3 and ditch players, respectively. Apple, which arguably pioneered personal computers, has become a specialist, and its archrival IBM long ago exited the PC manufacturing business.

In 1995, the year Amazon.com launched, Wal-Mart was already a well-entrenched incumbent with $89 billion in revenues.[13] In all, the e-commerce industry is less than three decades old; however, global e-retail sales volume was expected to rise to $3.9 trillion in 2020.[14] And despite the predictions of the early skeptics, there is no end in sight to the boom. Also, 17.5% of total global retail sales in 2021 are predicted to be online, still leaving ample room for future growth.[15] The online retail *sector has already globalized with Alibaba (31%; Taobao.com, Tmall.com), Amazon (15%), and Tencent (10%; JD.com, VIP.com, Yihaodian) taking the lead based on gross merchandise volume. Can you imagine a world where Walmart is not a global generalist? Its global share of online retail stood merely at 1% in 2019.[16]*

As Drucker observed in his usual penetrating style: "[t]he multinational corporation is both the response to the emergence of a common world market and its symbol…The multinational business is in every case a marketing business."[17] Meanwhile, we live in an era of unprecedented and disruptive change. Business leaders around the world are struggling to adapt, much less anticipate where the next wave of disruption will hit them. One cannot help but notice the winds of change. Who would've imagined that the innovators and captains of industry in the above examples would be global leaders no more?

The birthplace and home domain for marketing—distribution and retailing—have not fared much better when it comes to avoiding disruption. The market capitalization of leading retailers has been annihilated over the past decade. For example, Macy's was down 55%, Kohl's was down 64%, and JC Penney stock decreased 86% between 2006 and 2016, while Toys"R"Us and Sears are already bankrupt. Meanwhile, Amazon stock sat under $30 a share in August 2006. During the summer of 2020, it traded at over $2750 implying a return exceeding 9000%![18] In fact, when Amazon announced that it was buying Whole Foods for $13.7 billion cash in June 2017, its stock market capitalization appreciated by $15.6 billion; arguably, it acquired the company for free and pocketed $1.9 billion in the process![19]

The average life span of an S&P 500 firm has gone down from 90 years in 1935 to under 18 years today[20] and is decreasing fast.[21] Ninety percent of Fortune 500 firms in 1955 (the inaugural year the list was announced), despite their might and vast resources are no longer in the list any more.[22] Typical of the pace of the information age, early search firms of the tech era (Excite, Alta Vista, Netscape), online service providers (Prodigy, CompuServe, AOL), and PC manufacturers (Tandy, Commodore, IBM) are either out of manufacturing or out of business altogether.[23]

In our increasingly digital, mobile, and global world, the existing theories of business and economics have lost much of their relevance with the phenomenal rise of China and India,[24] the phenomenon of Brexit, and the seismic shifting of the global economic center of gravity from West to East. The traditional thinking that a developed country, often the U.S., will come up with the next major innovation, launch at home first, and then take it to other markets does not ring true anymore. Over 3.5 billion smartphones are already in use globally, and with a wide variety of smartphones currently sold for less than \$25,[25] it is not hard to imagine a day when everyone will be able to connect, experience, and become global consumers alike. This will revolutionize business as well as society.

As mentioned earlier, this book is based on empirical analyses of hundreds of markets and industries in the U.S. and globally. Competitive markets evolve in a predictable fashion across industries and geographies, where every industry goes through a similar life cycle from beginning to end (or revitalizes itself). The pattern is so consistent that it represents a natural market structure at every level from local to regional to national and ultimately global, a structure that is not only common but one that also provides the highest levels of profitability and stakeholder well-being for the entire industry!

Academics have produced a number of theories that explain organizations and competitive strategy but there are few seminal theories of industry life cycle and evolution. In this book, we describe how markets/industries evolve systematically and attempt to put forth a coherent explanation to fill this void. We rely on our own analyses as well as extant research and anecdotal evidence to develop more convincing arguments. In particular, organizational ecology and industrial organization literatures provide further support to our claims, with empirical studies from film, newspapers, telecommunications, wineries, semiconductor manufacturers, and more.[26] Even experimental research supports our main thesis of three major players and optimal profitability. Indeed, after conducting a meta-analysis of the literature and conducting a series of oligopoly experiments of their own, three experimental researchers concluded: "[t]wo are few and four are many."[27]

Finally, our own empirical analyses of hundreds of markets as well as project collaboration with the Boston Consulting Group support the foundational premises of the Global Rule of Three.[28] The world has changed so much, yet the Global Rule of Three prevails. So what exactly is the *Global* Rule of Three?

The Rule of Three and Globalization

Artificial market structures outside Europe and North America are also giving way to the "natural" market structure represented by the Rule of Three. For example, the great trading houses of Japan (such as Mitsubishi, Mitsui, and Sumitomo) have long participated in numerous business sectors, supporting weaker businesses through interlocking shareholdings (the "keiretsu" system, which creates a closed market within the overall free market). This shielded many poor performing companies from market forces, and as a result kept too many weak companies afloat in the market. In recent times, however, this system has finally started to break down. The discipline of a truly market-driven economy is forcing weak companies to exit or get acquired, often by global competitors.

In South Korea, the huge diversified "chaebol" such as Hyundai, Daewoo, Samsung, and LG have traditionally used their enormous clout with the government to maintain their leadership in virtually every major economic sector. The Asian economic crisis of 1997 and the conditions of the subsequent International Monetary Fund (IMF) bailout of South Korea started the process of breaking down this cozy relationship and brought market forces to bear to a greater extent.

In India, most major industries have been dominated by the large industrial houses, many of them family-controlled. Two decades ago, foreign companies faced stringent restrictions on their ability to participate in the Indian economy. Capacity rationalization was nearly impossible to achieve as a result of licensing and the inability to "downsize" (reduce the labor force) when market conditions so dictated. All of this has changed, as economic liberalization and the demise of isolationist economic thinking have triggered a shift toward competitive markets.

The important and ongoing shift toward global markets leads to a significant corollary of the Rule of Three: *no matter how large the market, the Rule of Three prevails.* In other words, when the scope of a market expands—whether from local to regional, regional to national, or national to global—the Rule of Three prevails, and further consolidation and industry restructuring become inevitable. Many nationally or regionally dominant companies find themselves trailing badly once the market globalizes.

For example, though U.S. banks are still prohibited from true, no-holds-barred interstate banking, they are working around those restrictions with holding company structures making *de facto* regional banking increasingly the norm. Consolidation through mergers and acquisitions is proceeding apace toward a Rule of Three market structure. Such a structure already exists in Germany and Switzerland. Likewise, the U.S. airline market has moved from a regional to national scope, and the process of sorting out full-line players from geographic specialists has been underway. The survivors are American, United, and Delta. Cable TV franchises, once the most local type of business, have consolidated into large regional players, with national and international consolidation following close behind.

Because local or regional markets are relatively rare (and are usually maintained only through regulatory mandate), the most important transition is when a market organized on a country-by-country basis moves toward becoming truly global. A distinct pattern emerges when markets move to this level, offering some of the most powerful evidence for the Rule of Three.

When the market globalizes, many full-line generalists that were previously viable as such in their secure home markets are unable to repeat that success in a global context. When this happens, we usually find that there are three survivors globally—typically, but not necessarily, one from each of the three major economic zones of the world: North America, Western Europe, and the Asia-Pacific region (also see Chap. 6 on the New Global Triad). To survive as a *global* full-line generalist, a company has to be strong in at least two of the three legs of this triad.

If a country has a large stake in an industry, it may be home to two or even all three full-line players. This was true in the aerospace market in the U.S., where the Defense Department essentially bankrolled the industry's technological superiority. Japan targeted industries such as consumer electronics, steel, shipbuilding, and several others. In the long run, however, political considerations make it unlikely that one country could dominate a significant market globally. Thus, in the aerospace market, the historical dominance by U.S. companies led several European governments to boost Airbus to a position of global prominence.

With globalization, the #1 company in each of the three triad markets is best positioned to survive as a global full-line generalist. Other players either go through mergers as a consequence of global consolidation or selectively exit certain businesses to become product or market specialists, often by geographic region.

However, in the U.S. consumer electronics market, where not a single U.S. generalist has survived, a fierce fight for market share is taking place where the Koreans (Samsung/LG) have pushed aside the Japanese (Matsushita/Panasonic and Sony). This battle will determine which players survive as global full-line generalists. The U.S. presents an ideal battleground because there is no company with a "home court advantage"; since there is no major domestic consumer electronics player, there is little danger of government intervention. Ultimately, however, the Chinese may take over the U.S. market from the Koreans.

In the airline market, globalization is proceeding simultaneously with the market's evolution toward national competition after deregulation. Given the numerous restrictions on foreign ownership of airlines, and in the absence of true "open skies" competition, the global industry is organizing into three big alliances: Star Alliance (Air Canada, Lufthansa, SAS, Turkish, United Airlines, and several others; 24% share), SkyTeam (Delta, Air France, Aeromexico, Alitalia, CSA Czech Airlines, and Korean Air Lines; 21% share), and Oneworld

(Aer Lingus, American Airlines, British Airways, Cathay Pacific, Finnair, Iberia, LanChile, and Qantas; 18% share).[29]

From local to regional to national markets, the last stop in the evolution of industries and markets is going global, where three players eventually emerge globally and become dominant. "Globalization cannot be stopped, and there will be winners and losers in the transformation to a global marketplace."[30] A national market leader must have a strong foothold in at least two out of the three largest markets to become a global leader. As powerfully argued by Kenichi Ohmae in his seminal work on Triad Power, these three major markets were North America, Europe, and Japan historically.[31]

If the competitive process has already enabled the Rule of Three to apply in each of the three largest markets, then one player may rise as a global Rule of Three player from each market. We observe this most clearly in the global tire industry. The historical order in the U.S. was Goodyear, Firestone, and BF Goodrich (with Uniroyal and General Tire as specialists); Michelin, Dunlop, and Pirelli in Europe (and Continental since the EU had still not integrated, thus regulation allowed for the persistence of a fourth player); and Bridgestone, Toyo, and Yokohama in Japan. Then the world market became standardized through radial tires. Currently, Bridgestone, Michelin, and Goodyear make the top three players in the world and the Rule of Three has prevailed globally as well.

On the other hand, a great deal of change is taking place and the global leaderboards are far from immune. Indeed, a new triad power has emerged, making it increasingly unlikely that one player from North America, Europe, and Japan each will continue to prevail as global leaders. On the contrary, the global leaders of the twenty-first century will increasingly arise from emerging markets. For example, Apple, once the disrupter and global leader of smartphones, vacated the #1 position to Samsung and was then surpassed by Huawei from China.[32]

Similarly, global PC manufacturing incumbent HP has been surpassed by Lenovo. And if you guessed the global leader in a legacy industry such as the tobacco market is Philip Morris or British-American Tobacco, you'd be wrong. China National Tobacco Corporation is the global leader with a 32% global market share that dwarfs Philip Morris' 15% and British-American Tobacco's 16%, respectively.[33] Finally, *all three* of the most valuable banks in the world (namely ICBC, China Construction Bank, and Agricultural Bank of China) hail from China measured by brand value or assets.[34] The center of gravity is clearly shifting from the West to the East, from the Atlantic to the Pacific Ocean. Why and how did we get here?

In many ways, the notion of shifting economic powers and the commensurate rise of nations is nothing new. For example, South Korea took leadership in a number of industries such as steel, appliances, and telecom. Before South Korea, the economic miracle story was Japan, whose firms took leadership from their European and American counterparts in a number of industries such as automobiles, robotics, and consumer electronics. And even before then, Americans were aggressively conquering markets from European incumbents. Thus, the European Century (nineteenth) gave way to the American Century (twentieth) and now the twenty-first century clearly seems to belong to Asia. And China and, as we will discuss in Chap. 6, India are taking full advantage.

Liberal policies tend to bring prosperity and accelerate the transfer of wealth, whereas protectionist policies try hard but fail to stop it. Taking a historical view, it is important to recognize that openness and increasing trade permeated across the globe during the late nineteenth century. Unfortunately, the rise of nationalism and two World Wars prevented the natural evolution of free trade until the second half of the twentieth century. Subsequent to World War II, there was a period of time where several world leaders emphasized self-sufficiency through tariff and non-tariff barriers rather than building comparative advantages based upon the natural as well as human resources of their countries. However, protectionism threatened the affluence of both developed and developing nations.[35] When it became all too obvious that these approaches did not work, globalization resumed its inevitable path to prominence.[36] The volume of trade between and among the NAFTA countries, EU, and ASEAN has been increasing since the 1980s as a result of trade liberalization. After the collapse of communism, economic pragmatism became prevalent; privatization unlocked value for consumers and investors and accelerated this process. Tariffs were decreased. New innovations in communication, increased travel, internet, and advertising also led to a higher acceptance of foreign-origin products and services. "Consumers came to appreciate diversity and variety in the marketplace. Turkish doner became the most consumed fast-food in Germany, Indian curry became the flavor of choice in England. Salsa sells more than ketchup in the US…."[37]

Globalization also has cultural, social, and humane implications. Cultural diversity is our human heritage. Arguably, the single most important source of economic as well as scientific development has been based on trade between nations (with varying resource advantages). "However, nations do not trade, merchants do. These merchants not only generated financial wealth, but also served as a bridge for new inventions, social innovations, and culture. For example, pasta as well as gunpowder found their way to Europe through trade…Merchants of today are increasingly global corporations,"[38] and the world is a "global shopping center" with an autonomous economy which is more than the sum of national economies.[39] In this context, global competitiveness is the new institutional imperative for corporations.[40]

It is fair to say that whereas the twentieth-century business was based primarily on ideology, politics, and advanced nations, the twenty-first century will be primarily based on markets and resources of emerging nations.[41] Akin to the emergence of three players in each cycle from local to regional to national, the convergence to the Global Rule of Three is also economics driven. To the extent that deregulation (open competition) accelerates the national Rule of Three, low barriers to trade and free markets accelerate the convergence to the Global Rule of Three. Our position is that the reach of globalization is irrevocable. Hence, no matter how much protectionist policies get in the way of progress, a global convergence is also ultimately inevitable. And when the industry globalizes, there is no room for more than three players, in the long run, no matter how big the companies.

In the next section, we trace the evolution of global markets and examine which multinational corporations might emerge as the top players.

First, let's take a look at the big picture and identify the nations of the new triad power. An examination of the IMF Purchasing Power Parity (PPP) Index shows that half of the top ten and two of the top three spots are already occupied by developing nations with China and India in secure spots as #1 and #3 nations respectively (see Table 5.1). Thus, just like the traditional European economic powers (Germany, France, and the U.K.) were replaced by the

Table 5.1 2019 GDP indexed to purchasing power parity (PPP)

China	$27.31 trillion
U.S.	$21.43 trillion
India	$11.04 trillion
Japan	$5.71 trillion
Germany	$4.44 trillion
Russia	$4.39 trillion
Indonesia	$3.74 trillion
Brazil	$3.48 trillion
U.K.	$3.16 trillion
France	$3.06 trillion

Source: IMF World Economic Outlook "Gross Domestic Product Based on Purchasing-Power-Parity in Current Prices," Knoema, April 2020, accessed July 26, 2020. https://knoema.com/atlas/ranks/GDP-based-onPPP#:~:text=The%20top%205%20countries%20(others,billion%20international%20dollars%20in%202019. https://knoema.com/IMFWEO2020Apr/imf-world-economic-outlook-weo-april-2020

U.S. in the twentieth century, the trade triad of the previous century (North America/EU/Japan) has already been replaced (China/U.S./India).[42]

In a global economy, multinational corporations play a significant role in the transfer of wealth between regions and nations. Margin expectations at the stock exchanges of advanced economies lead the incumbents to divest or vacate commoditized segments and businesses. This trend has favored Asian firms. As markets are vacated by incumbents, we expect to see China become #1 or #2 globally in an increasing number of industries. In that sense, the center of gravity of the Global Rule of Three is shifting from the U.S. and Europe to Asia, and from Japan and Korea to China and India. There will inevitably be more consolidation as well as newly emerging players in the global arena. For example, Japan has already conceded the shipbuilding sector to South Korea. Meanwhile, Hanjin Shipping Company, South Korea's largest shipping line, and one of the largest container carriers in the world went bankrupt in February 2017.[43] We predict that the Chinese shipping firms will rise to further prominence to challenge Danish shipping giant Maersk in the future.

Transition from Local to Regional to Continental to Global

Businesses that used to compete locally can become regional with government blessing. For example, the U.S. banking sector used to be local within each State. Consolidation followed gradual deregulation and the Rule of Three became prevalent at the regional level on both East and West Coasts. Currently, Bank of America, JP Morgan Chase, and Wells Fargo all have more than 10% share and are jockeying for position.[44] Meanwhile, regional banks are trying to scale up as evidenced by the recent merger of BB&T and SunTrust valued at $66 billion.[45] While Uber and Airbnb both started as local operations in San Francisco and have become global network empires, most hospital groups, universities, and colleges are still local, and many utilities are still run as local monopolies.

Open markets lead to rationalization and a continental Rule of Three structure. Currently, the airline industry is transitioning from national to regional/continental, and regional economies such as the EU and ASEAN facilitate this transition. Despite the potential impact of Brexit, German, French, or Italian markets cannot be conceived independently of another.

Meanwhile, some of the most fascinating journeys take place when industries transition from regional/continental to global. This transition to global markets can be attributed to the following factors:

New market opportunities: Globalization of markets can come about based on new market opportunities. For example, U.S. companies became increasingly global after WWII to revitalize the destroyed infrastructure and economies of Japan and Europe through the Marshall plan "which was geared to build a market for U.S. goods and private sector open to U.S. investment...."[46] U.S. businesses were motivated by the government to enter these foreign markets and invest; the rest is history. IBM, Coca-Cola, Boeing, McDonnell-Douglas, Lockheed, and Johnson Controls all became dominant players globally, beginning with the Japanese market.

Liberalization of trade: The old model used to be about starting and getting established domestically first, and subsequently using the cash flow from domestic operations to fund/subsidize gradual international expansion. The typical evolution took place through joint ventures because foreign acquisitions were blocked through formal and informal mechanisms. For example, Xerox had joint ventures with Fuji (Japan), and Rank (U.K.). However, the energy crisis and the subsequent sluggish economic conditions in the 1970s gave way to rise of free markets in the 1980s and 1990s. Western economies were not growing domestically while emerging markets needed machinery and capital, so foreign trade and operations were encouraged. Globalization accelerated as large emerging economies came to the realization that they could not survive on their ideologies alone; be it communism in the Soviet Bloc, socialism in India, or China where a doctrinaire communist regime proved unsustainable and needed to be reformed. Latin America went through a similar process. Thus, the European Union was founded (1993), NAFTA was signed (1994), the GATT was folded into the WTO (1995), and the ASEAN bloc was expanded—all in the 1990s. It was thanks to this liberalization of trade that the multinational corporations of the West were eventually allowed to buy out the stakes of their joint venture partners, and integrate their foreign subsidiaries with their domestic operations.

Private sector participation: Nowadays, governments around the world permit and even encourage the private sector to participate in new market opportunities. For example, the richest person in Latin America (and fifth in the world) is Carlos Slim, thanks primarily to his telecom empire enabled by the Mexican government (a consortium led by Slim's Grupo Carso bought Telmex, the old government monopoly, when it was privatized in 1990 and made big bets in wireless telecommunications).[47] Similarly, almost 100 Russian oligarchs accumulated a wealth of more than $1 billion each following the privatization that took place after the collapse of communism.[48] Billionaires came out of nowhere in emerging markets such as China, India, Brazil, Mexico, and Turkey, and formed conglomerates. And then as a natural next step, these conglomerates from emerging markets also started going global (also see Chap. 7).

Globally conceived tech firms: Globalization has also been accelerated by born-global technology companies who think about global leadership from day one. The classic example of this phenomenon is Microsoft whose operating system became dominant globally well-within a decade of the company's inception in 1975. Indeed, its first international office, Microsoft Japan (named ASCII Microsoft at the time) was founded in 1978, two years before the company's famous deal to develop the operating system for the IBM PC.[49] Similarly, Apple (founded in 1976) had its first authorized dealer in Japan in 1977[50] and always capitalized on the potential of global markets for each of its products from then on. Google search engine was designed to serve consumers globally from the get-go, and Facebook with its 2.7 billion users is also clearly a global player.[51] Naturally, the revenues of these global tech giants are also commensurate with the size and number of the markets served. Silicon Valley is full of start-ups with global aspirations. The new breed of tech firms (e.g., Snapchat and Twitter) was all born global. For example, Airbnb had over 4 million listings in some 65,000 cities across 191 countries in 2018.[52]

However, the born-global business is not unique to the U.S. In fact, born-global firms are more likely to come out of countries with limited home market potential such as Estonia (population 1.33 million; Skype), Sweden (pop. 10.23 million; IKEA), Finland (pop. 5.52 million; Nokia), or Israel (pop. 8.88 million; M-Systems) which ranks #1 for R&D intensity in the world and has also been dubbed the Startup Nation.[53]

Based on the above factors which underline and fuel globalization, several consequences are to be expected:

Domestic Consolidation: The influx of new competitors further necessitates the need to build efficiency and cause within-border mergers of equals. Historically, we have witnessed intensive consolidation among the airlines following deregulation (and the entry of new low-cost carriers). GE's acquisition of RCA and the HP-Compaq merger are additional examples of this phenomenon. Current examples can be found in the financial (e.g., SunTrust-BB&T merger) and pharmaceutical sectors (e.g., BMS Celgene acquisition).

Global Consolidation: As companies expand globally, they tend to enjoy scale and scope which comes from adding multiple product lines, and adding new geographies. However, as markets grow from local to regional, regional to national, national to continental, and ultimately global, industries consolidate further. The evolution in consumer electronics is reflective of this. For example, top PC manufacturers have already become global, and we predict no survivors from the U.S. in the future. Lenovo will be #1, and Acer will likely become global #2. Perennial leader IBM years ago exited the business by selling to Lenovo, and the future for other household names such as HP and Dell does not look bright. A similar pattern is taking place in the world of television; U.S. companies exited during the early 1980s because they could not compete with Japanese, and the Japanese now find it hard to compete with the Koreans, who will not be able to compete against the Chinese! The same pattern also applies to IT infrastructure manufacturers in the evolution to a global structure. The Alcatel-Lucent merger (2006) and Nokia's acquisition of Alcatel-Lucent (2016) are further examples of this enormous surge in global M&A with no end in sight.

Restructuring of Survivors: If a generalist is strong in all three triad markets, it will survive. In fact, strength in only two of the three markets is frequently sufficient for survival. Since Asia is proving a challenge for global telecom giants, they have been trying their hands in the relatively neutral U.S. While Deutsche Telecom has held onto its 3# position in the U.S. with T-Mobile, Vodafone, the second-largest mobile operator in the world, was bought out of its 45% stake in Verizon Wireless for $130 billion in 2013.[54] In the final analysis, there is only room for three global players, and some leaders will either be acquired or must give up their generalist status, abandon certain markets, and become niche players. For example, recall the example of The Great Atlantic & Pacific Tea Company a.k.a. A&P discussed previously. Once a leading supermarket chain, A&P had to change its business model, abandon markets, and become a niche company in order to exit the ditch.

Major Investment in Emerging Markets: In most cases, these investments already have to be completed in order to remain ahead of the curve. Arguably, General Motors (GM) is surviving today because of its early foray into the Chinese market. Even though GM exited China in 1949 and re-entered with a joint venture in 1994, its presence dates back almost a century. In fact, there was a Chevy dealer in Shanghai as early as the 1920s, and Sun Yatsen, who is recognized as the father of Chinese democracy, the first premier Zhou Enlai, and the last emperor Puyi all owned Buicks. Reportedly, over 15% of the cars in China in the 1930s were Buicks. Not surprisingly, Buick continues to do well in China.[55]

Similarly, Volkswagen started initial negotiations for entering China in the 1970s and has had a presence for almost four decades.[56] L'Oréal, with over 20 years of experience in China, also boasts a headquarters, R&D center, two plants, and four business divisions there and has clearly benefited from the tremendous growth of its economy over the last two decades.[57] The future of L'Oréal and many luxury brands increasingly lies with China, and it is increasingly apparent that beauty can even overcome trade wars, as sales of Lancôme and Yves Saint Laurent Beauté continue to rise regardless of the economic sub-text.[58]

Box 5.1   Owner-Managed Businesses: The Case of Professional Services

Most accounting, law, and consultancy firms are private. They are based on a partnership structure where owners are also the managers, whereas ownership in public firms is divorced from management. Nevertheless, the journey to Rule of Three commences whenever the partnership structure is abandoned. For example, advertising agencies were historically founder-driven. Subsequently, leading agencies such as Ogilvy, Leo Burnett, and Young & Rubicam decided to divest ownership and create groups. Hundreds of agencies have consolidated, and a big four (Omnicom, WPP, Publicis, and Interpublic) have emerged globally.[59] Indeed, if the 2014 Publicis Omnicom merger deal had not collapsed, we would have already observed the Rule of Three in this historically fragmented industry.

The journey for accounting firms has been somewhat different. There used to be eight large accounting firms which have since consolidated into the big four (Deloitte, PricewaterhouseCoopers or PwC, Ernst & Young or EY, KPMG). Smaller accounting firms such as BDO, Grant Thornton, and CliftonLarsonAllen continue to consolidate further. However, as long as they remain partnerships, the Rule of Three structure may not be realized. Interestingly, their primary competitors in IT consulting, such as IBM and EDS, were already publicly traded. Thus, the big four decided that traditional accounting such as audit, advisory, restructuring, and tax could remain partner-driven whereas the consulting side could be divested or publicly traded. For example, EY sold its IT consulting to Capgemini and PwC sold it to IBM, both of which are publicly traded. Deloitte and KPMG may similarly decide to divest. Interestingly, there were internal fights within Andersen as to which group would keep the Andersen name which ironically became a liability following the Enron scandal; thus, the consulting practice was rebranded as Accenture. The main reason for this structural transformation is that partnerships are unable to utilize stock options the way they are utilized by publicly traded firms to reward employees. This creates a competitive disadvantage. Typically, the Rule of Three goes in tandem with going public. Indeed, it is rare for private firms to prevail as global contenders.

If a global player somehow misses the boat, it is compelled to make major acquisitions in emerging markets in order to survive as a global player. Besides China, which now boasts many global brands such as Haier, many emerging nations have developed their own dominant brands. Investing in emerging markets represents both an offensive and defensive play: multinational corporations from emerging markets are rising to prominence globally; hence, the incumbent multinationals must scramble to equalize.

For example, Uber (which recently bought Middle Eastern start-up Careem for $3.1 billion),[60] is competing with Didi from China rather than Lyft from the U.S. for global dominance.

Similarly, Starbucks has been in China for two decades with over 4000 outlets in 140 cities, but now finds itself in competition with Luckin Coffee which is three years old but has already surpassed Starbucks with over 4500 locations across China. In response, Starbucks plans to expand to 6000 locations by 2022.[61] Similar battles have played out in India as well. For example, after Coca-Cola was forced out of India in the 1970s, local soda brands such as Thums Up, Campa Cola, and Limca thrived. When Coca-Cola returned to India in the 1990s, it found that Thums Up did better than the original Coke and wisely decided to keep the brand they purchased. Today, Thums Up is the #2 selling soda brand in India after Sprite.[62]

Besides China and India, the key emerging markets that require presence by all global players differ based on sector. For example, Brazil is key for agriculture, industrial raw materials, and construction equipment. For global players with foresight (e.g., Huawei), African nations represent the current frontier for infrastructure investments.

The anticipated Rule of Three (R3) pattern has materialized in the U.S. first, followed by Europe and Japan. Currently, the R3 structures are emerging in many markets in China, India (and Korea and elsewhere). As depicted in Fig. 5.1, the typically observed R3 pattern in the largest three markets used to be as follows:

U.S.: three big players + niche players

Europe: three Players (primarily Western Europe), one German, one French, one Italian/Dutch/British, and so on + niche players.

Japan: three big players (Japan used to be second-largest economy, now is the fourth) + niche players

Mega-mergers such as AOL-Time Warner and now AT&T and Time Warner continue to increase in size and frequency, delighting investment bankers. However, beyond 40% domestic market share, the incremental value generated by the market leader starts to diminish and there are greater incentives to engaging in international market development. Yet no matter how big the market, there is simply not enough room for nine top players globally. Thus, another round of consolidation takes place, this time in the form of cross-border M&A, until the leading player assumes a viable share of the global market. The mergers that have been taking place are not only within countries but between regions. For example, there is tremendous activity in

The Global Rule of Three

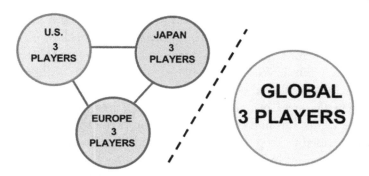

Fig. 5.1 The Global Rule of Three circa 2000. (Source: Adapted from "The Global Rule of Three" presentation by Jagdish N. Sheth, 2017)

global M&A and exits in the steel industry, carbon black, aluminum, cellular phones, and so forth. In the end, we fully expect to see the emergence of the Global Rule of Three in each of these sectors.[63]

We proceed now with additional examples of global industries and then discuss the evolution in greater depth.

The Case of the Tire Industry

Consider the global automotive tire industry. As you may recall, this is an example of a structure where the large players are balanced among the three markets. That is, there are established incumbents in each of the key markets. Interestingly, when there are three established players in each key market, one (usually #1) out of each market becomes a global leader, and #3 players become the first casualties as industries become global. As foreign firms enter, competition becomes too intense and the #3 firm collapses trying to fight for market share. For example, Dunlop was acquired by Goodyear under distress, and BF Goodrich sold to Michelin. (There was no #2 or #3 at the time in Japan.)

The industry started globalizing in the 1970s. Michelin capitalized on the success of its radial tires and opened a manufacturing plant in the U.S. in 1975. As the U.S. manufacturers were trying to catch up or exiting, Michelin was acquiring companies in the U.S., Poland, Hungary, and Colombia in the

1980s and eventually became the global leader. However, Bridgestone of Japan also had leadership aspirations. It outbid Pirelli to acquire Firestone (then the #2 player in the U.S., which also had a European presence) in 1988 and subsequently became the global leader. Finally, Goodyear was not able to hold onto its market leadership in the U.S. and is currently the #3 player globally. Thus, the global big three consists of #1 Bridgestone, #2 Michelin, and #3 Goodyear.

Amidst the intense competition, specialists such as Cooper Tire and Rubber, and Kumho remained profitable.[64] However, as we will discuss in Chap. 7 in detail, a Chinese company such as ZC Rubber or an Indian manufacturer such as Apollo could put pressure and dethrone one of the global three players (likely Goodyear) over time, utilizing domestic scale advantages for car or truck tires. Italian heritage brand Pirelli has already been acquired by ChemChina in 2015 for $7.7 billion and there is further M&A (likely involving Continental or one of the Japanese brands) on the horizon as Bridgestone and Michelin continue to fight for global leadership.[65]

U.S.:   Goodyear-Firestone-BF Goodrich (see Box 5.2 on BF Goodrich for an illustrative example of dealing with an intensively competitive market structure).

Japan: Bridgestone (it was the only player historically but now has three more competitors, Sumitomo, Yokohama, and Toyo).

Europe: Michelin-Continental-Pirelli

Figure 5.2 illustrates the global competition in the passenger car tire market.

The Case of the Automobile Industry

The evolution of the U.S. automobile industry is illustrative of the predictive power of the Rule of Three. During its early days, the industry's facilities consisted of workshops. By 1914, over 300, mostly small, automakers had set up shop. By the 1940s, however, the maturing industry was consolidating to three front-runners, GM, Ford, and Chrysler, alongside small specialists such as American Motors Corporation (AMC) and Studebaker. The structure provided stability over the next couple of decades. However, the industry was disrupted by the Japanese market entry with smaller reliable cars, and subsequently the fuel crisis. Toyota (and for a while Honda) became strong competitors. Consequently, when the competition for market share between GM and Ford intensified, the number three incumbent Chrysler succumbed to

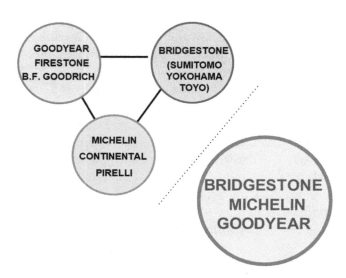

Fig. 5.2 Global passenger car tires. (Source: Adapted from "The Global Rule of Three" presentation by Jagdish N. Sheth, 2017)

the ditch at the end of the 1970s. Its revival required not only CEO Lee Iacocca's exemplary leadership but also the biggest government bailout to date in 1979. When the government's shot-in-the-arm subsided, Chrysler once again attempted to exit the ditch by purchasing AMC in 1987.

AMC was another ditch dweller which had downsized to a specialist and acquired earlier in the decade by Renault. However, the structural problem in the market (i.e., Japanese competition) persisted, so struggling Chrysler tried a third time to get out of the ditch by merging with Daimler in 1998. This, in light of the Rule of Three, was bound to fail yet again because Daimler is a specialist in the U.S., and the combined shares of the two still left the Daimler-Chrysler combo stuck in the ditch with the wrong size. Moreover, differences in corporate culture between the two companies proved too much to bear. Finally, facing a global financial crisis, and once again rising fuel prices, the U.S. automobile industry experienced peril in the new millennium. In 2008, both Chrysler and GM had to be bailed out by the government.

Left to market forces, Toyota, Ford, and a nimble, restructured, and divested GM would likely have prevailed as the new big three in America. With cash infusion from Fiat, Chrysler temporarily overcame the ditch hurdle by improving its share from 8.9% to 11.5%.[66] Whether the new products and technology from Fiat's platforms will succeed in keeping them on the right side of the fence remains to be seen. Historically, Chrysler had, and still has, the option to survive as a specialist or get acquired by one of the top three. It appears that every ten years or so, structural problems surface and something has to give in the U.S. automobile industry.

Globally, the question remains as to who will be the #3 player behind Volkswagen and Toyota. Superniche players like Ferrari and Lamborghini will remain. In fact, Ferrari's annual volume of roughly 10,000 sports cars gave it a market cap of $29.8 billion in May 2020 which exceeded that of GM, Ford, or Fiat Chrysler.[67] However, volume-driven players will have problems, and casualties are expected to occur in Europe and Japan. What will happen to smaller players such as Honda, Nissan, and BMW? One can speculate that downsizing and specializing would be more suitable for BMW than Honda. Thus, Honda could become casualty, yet it has traditional pockets of strength for building engines for other applications to fall back on. Nissan, which has already been bailed out by Renault previously could be headed for bigger trouble.

Meanwhile, the entire deck is being reshuffled with Germany vowing to stop production of internal combustion engines by 2030![68] Who will dominate the electric cars in the new world order? Tesla is very innovative yet remains undercapitalized and its stock is among the most shorted in history.[69]

And do not count out latecomers such as China's Geely, which sold more than 1.5 million vehicles in 2018.[70] Another shakeout appears to be on the horizon and we will surely see more M&A activity in this space in the next decade. When there are two global players, a third one emerges sooner or later, usually through M&A or alliances. No wonder Fiat Chrysler CEO Sergio Marchionne has been trying to talk GM into a merger for years.[71] As the reported aspirations of Peugeot to buy Fiat Chrysler, and the plans of Renault to buy both Nissan and then Fiat Chrysler demonstrates, the push for global consolidation will remain quite strong in the automotive industry.[72] Meanwhile, Ford is focusing on trucks to boost its profitability and may even exit the four-door sedan market one day.

Our prediction is for Volkswagen to be #1 globally, #2 Toyota, and #3 to emerge among GM, Fiat, or Ford via mergers. A move by BMW-Honda while controversial would not be inconceivable. The race is on as GM is trying to establish itself in China to remain a significant global player, while Ford is specializing in trucks. Figure 5.3 illustrates the competition in the auto industry.

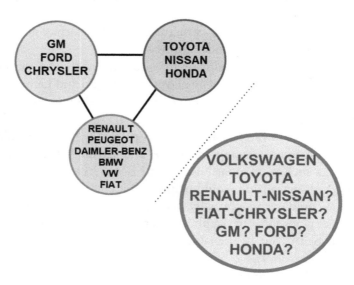

Fig. 5.3 Global auto manufacturers. (Source: Adapted from "The Global Rule of Three" presentation by Jagdish N. Sheth, 2017)

U.S.:   GM-Ford-Chrysler
Japan: Toyota-Nissan-Honda
Europe: Volkswagen-Renault-Fiat-Daimler Benz-BMW

The Case of Aircraft Manufacturing

There was a time when the U.S. had a complete monopoly over aircraft manufacturing following the Wright brothers' successful flight at Kitty Hawk. The old-world order used to be Boeing, McDonnell Douglas, and Lockheed. However, Lockheed lost billions in its transatlantic partnership with Rolls-Royce over a decade and its wide-body jet business collapsed in the early 1980s, so it decided to focus on military aircraft where margins were healthier.[75]

Europe's joint Airbus consortium effort (supported by several governments) capitalized on the gap and became #2, effectively creating a global triad between Boeing, Airbus, and McDonnell Douglas. During an intensely

Box 5.2   The Case of BF Goodrich[73]

While you may be familiar with Goodyear, Bridgestone, or Michelin, you are probably not as familiar with BF Goodrich, unless you are an auto enthusiast. It may also come as a surprise that BF Goodrich is the oldest and arguably the most innovative tire manufacturer in the U.S. It is illuminating to review its storied history.

BF Goodrich was founded by Dr. Benjamin Franklin Goodrich in 1870 in Akron, Ohio, a city that would come be to known as the rubber capital of the U.S. (Goodyear as well as several other tire manufacturers would be later based there). Its first products included fire-hoses covered with cotton and later on bicycle tires. The company quickly thrived and became one of the largest rubber and tire manufacturers in the world.

BF Goodrich was decidedly innovative from the start. It established a rubber research laboratory in 1895, the first of its kind in the U.S. The company also became one of the earliest suppliers of tires and other equipment to airplanes. BF Goodrich was proud to let the public know that the winner of the inaugural international flying race in 1909, as well as Charles Lindbergh when he flew solo from New York to Paris for the first time in 1927, had BF Goodrich tires on their airplanes. The R&D engine of BF Goodrich churned out one great invention after another. For example, the rubber reclamation process that BF Goodrich developed was widely adopted by the industry and utilized for decades.

More important, BF Goodrich invented the PVC (polyvinyl chloride) in 1926. PVC went on to have a number of very successful applications such as floor covering, electrical insulation, garden hoses, and luggage. Charles Lindbergh had commented that ice was the biggest danger he faced on his historic flight across the Atlantic. BF Goodrich developed and introduced the first aircraft de-icing mechanism in 1932 to address the problem.

The company focused on two areas of specialty to build upon its expertise in rubber manufacturing—specialty chemicals and aerospace. The specialty chemicals focus was in part based upon the need to improve the characteristics of rubber products, which the customers demanded. Similarly, the focus on aerospace was initially limited to supplying tires and rubber products to planes but consequently expanded to military applications.

In 1938, and just in time for World War II, BF Goodrich invented synthetic rubber and scaled-up production. This invention turned out to be critical for the U.S. war effort since as much as 95% of the production relied on the natural rubber supplies from the Far East. Since Japan controlled the trading routes, the U.S. would have lost much of its mobility without BF Goodrich's synthetic rubber.

In 1946, BF Goodrich invented the tubeless tire which represented another breakthrough innovation for the industry. Whereas tires with tubes were more likely to blow out due to friction, the new tubeless tires had airtight seals, resulting in significantly better tire safety.

After World War II, BF Goodrich developed a new strategy for a peace-time economy. It began to diversify and expand its presence in the aircraft industry via acquisitions. Aerospace became an independent division within the organization in 1956. The fuel controls of the first jet airliners were provided by none other than BF Goodrich. Even astronauts are familiar with the brand BF Goodrich. To develop its first spacesuit, NASA commissioned the company in 1961. During

(continued)

Box 5.1 (continued)

the cold war era, BF Goodrich continued its investments in emerging technologies such as surveillance, reconnaissance, space, and aviation technologies.

Tire Industry Evolution

The bread-and-butter tire business which accounted for 60% of BF Goodrich's revenues was getting more and more competitive. The company was struggling to remain among the top three players and prevent succumbing to the ditch. Many of the new innovations (such as tubeless tires) served to extend the usable life of the tires which meant fewer replacement tire sales and more intense competition for the original equipment manufacturer (OEM) tire business (i.e., tires installed on new cars by their makers). This point was brought home by William O'Neil Sr., who founded General Tire: "Detroit wants tires that are round, black, and cheap-and it don't care whether they are round and black."[74] In the 1960s, while the replacement tire market profit margin ranged between 5% and 8%, it was merely 3–5% for the OEM market.

In 1979, BF Goodrich's world market share was about 4% against 23% for Goodyear, 16% for Michelin, 14% for Firestone, 7% for Bridgestone, and 6% for Pirelli. The historical focus of BF Goodrich was the replacement tire market which represented about three-quarters of the tires sold. Again, about three-quarters of these tires were typically bought for passenger cars. For example, in 1987, of the 205 million tires sold, 152 million were replacement tires and 53 million were OEM tires.

Worldwide production exceeded 800 million tires in the late 1980s. The market was more or less divided between North America (30%), Asia (30%), and Europe (25%). Benefiting from the success of their steel belt radial tires, Michelin from France became the largest manufacturer, followed by Goodyear (U.S.), and Bridgestone (Japan).

The Move to Radial Tires

Radial tires were commercially introduced by Michelin in 1948 and made popular in Europe. Nevertheless, they were not immediately successful in the U.S. By 1970, 97% of tires sold in France, and 80% of tires sold in Italy were radial, whereas they represented merely 2% of sales in the U.S. Radial tires required automobiles to have an updated suspension system. They also cost about 35% more to produce and resulted in a harder ride. In 1971, the CEO of General Motors declared that "[y]ou won't see a changeover to radial tires as original equipment on Detroit's new cars in the near future." And yet radial OEM orders started to come in by Fall 1972.

Goodyear initially questioned the new technology but subsequently introduced its own all-season radial tire five years later in 1977. The incumbents also made efforts to upgrade to advanced bias ply with steel belts (belted bias ply). Among these, Firestone made significant investments but failed to merge radials to existing bias-ply system and maintain product quality. Subsequently, they agreed to a voluntary recall of 8.7 million tires in 1978 at a cost of $150 million, which amounted to the largest product recall in U.S. history at the time.

The new radial technology provided longer product life, increased safety, handling, and economy than even the most expensive bias tires. For example, radial tires last three to four times longer than ply tires. However, producing radial tires required U.S. manufacturers to get new equipment such as tire building machines, fabric and wire bias-cutters, new or modified curing, slacking, and

(continued)

handling systems. Once again, it was BF Goodrich that first produced and sold radial tires to the American public in 1965. They also launched the "Radial Age" advertising campaign.

Michelin began making inroads to the U.S. market through its private branding deal with Sears and was selling one million tires annually. The tire industry was going global. Globalization required more R&D which was only sensible if the significant sum could be allocated over a larger number of units. For example, when Honda entered the U.S. market, Bridgestone brand tires followed them. As the fourth largest tire manufacturer in the U.S., BF Goodrich experienced some market share gains but was increasingly seeing its profit margins shrink.

The Aftermath

BF Goodrich recognized the structural problems, the inherently intensive competition, and the thin margins in the tire manufacturing business, and decided that their core competency of specialty chemicals was better deployed elsewhere, namely in the aerospace industry. First, their solution to the structural problem was to spin-off their tire division and strengthen it with a merger with Uniroyal 1986. Alas, the Uniroyal Goodrich generated close to $2 billion in revenue but merely $35 million in profits in 1987. Thus, it was welcome news when Michelin offered to buy the company in 1988 and completed the buyout for roughly $1.5 billion in 1990. The shrewd strategic move away from tires paid off, and BF Goodrich never looked back. In 2001, it divested its specialty chemicals division to focus on aerospace and related markets and changed its name to Goodrich Corporation. Eventually, it became the largest pure-play aerospace company in the world. In 2012, United Technologies acquired Goodrich in an $18.4 billion deal (additionally assuming another $1.9 billion in Goodrich debt obligations). Meanwhile, Goodyear which was the perennial market leader when Goodrich exited the tire business in 1990 had a market capitalization of merely $3.28 billion in 2012, just a fraction of what United Technologies paid for the Goodrich deal.

competitive period between Boeing and Airbus during the 1990s, McDonnell Douglas found itself in the ditch. Airbus made its foray into the U.S. by leasing planes to failing airlines such as Continental, and Air Canada. Eventually, even American Airlines also bought from them, breaking the Boeing monopoly. After McDonnell Douglas' efforts to create an alliance with Taiwan Aerospace were blocked by the U.S. government, it merged with Boeing in a $13.3 billion deal in 1997.[76]

The global competition rages on. Currently, there is a conspicuous absence of a third player (presumably due to the tremendous capital investment needed and high risk of R&D) which we suspect will ultimately emerge from China. Indeed, the share of the Asia-Pacific in aircraft fleets is expected to exceed 40% (from 31%) in the next couple of decades,[77] and Commercial

Aviation Corporation of China (COMAC) could emerge as the third global generalist. Meanwhile, others such as Bombardier and Embraer will remain viable narrow-body specialists. Figure 5.4 illustrates the competition in aircraft manufacturing.

Post the United Technologies-Raytheon mega-merger, a wave of M&A appears to be on the horizon for the aerospace and defense industry in the next few years. We expect some players to act soon. Boeing needs to counterbalance its commercial market domination and 737 Max woes, and engine-maker GE Aviation could be the likely target. Lockheed Martin, General Dynamics, and to a lesser extent, Northrop Grumman will all suffer financially and get acquired if they do not actively seek mergers. Private equity has an increasingly large role to play in consolidating industries that are quickly becoming global (also see Box 8.1 "Why More Mergers Are Inevitable in Aerospace and Defense" in Chap. 8).

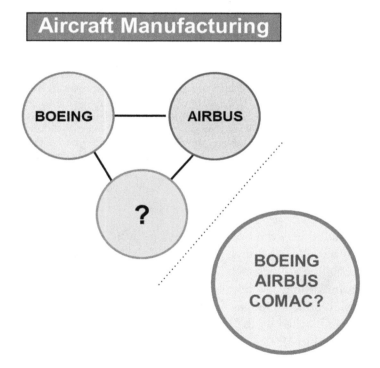

Fig. 5.4 Global aircraft manufacturers. (Source: Adapted from "The Global Rule of Three" presentation by Jagdish N. Sheth, 2017)

The Case of the Airline Industry/Alliances

The U.S. airline industry went through big-bang deregulation in 1978.[78] The Civil Aeronautics Board was abolished, and regional franchises and price-controls were abandoned. Nearly 70 airlines collapsed in the race to grow and become national. For example, Allegheny (which was later renamed US Airways) bought Lake Central, Mohawk, Pacific Southwest, Piedmont, Trump Shuttle, Metrojet, and America West, and finally merged with American Airlines in 2015. Northwest and Continental both succumbed to the ditch and were acquired by Delta and United respectively. At the end of the journey, American, United, and Delta emerged as legacy carriers, until Southwest decided to become a national airline and disrupt the Rule of Three. Southwest is currently competing with American Airlines head-to-head for domestic market leadership. Meanwhile, Delta took advantage of its rival's customer service woes and public relations blunders to dislodge United and become the #2 legacy carrier (#3 overall).[79] A similar journey is still taking place in Europe. In fact, since October 2018, five European airlines have collapsed (Wow Air, Primera Air, Cobalt Airways, Germania, British Midland).[80] Further consolidation looms large to the extent that antitrust policy permits it. And when it doesn't, new alliances are forged.

Certain industries such as postal services, telecom, electric utilities, and airlines are subject to heavy government rules and regulations. Because of public sector ownership or antitrust concerns, companies may not be able to merge. Thus, they form alliances to which the Rule of Three also applies.

For example, the airline industry is still regulated globally, however, we expect to see more transformation as it becomes more and more deregulated, and government-owned airlines get privatized/divested. In the meantime, consolidation comes in the form of airline alliances and operational efficiencies via code sharing. Swissair was the first to start a European alliance, which was toppled by American Airlines, British Airways, and Qantas alliance (One World), which was then toppled by a consortium of 13 airlines including United, Lufthansa (Star Alliance), and Delta leads the SkyTeam alliance. Figure 5.5 illustrates the competition in the airline industry.

U.S.:	American-Delta-United[81]
Note:	Southwest Airlines has the lead in domestic passengers but is not interested in global expansion.
Far East:	All Nippon-Singapore Air-Qantas
Europe:	Lufthansa-British Airways-Air France
Global Consortia:	Star Alliance-One World-SkyTeam

Fig. 5.5 Global airline industry and alliances. (Source: Adapted from "The Global Rule of Three" presentation by Jagdish N. Sheth, 2017)

However, once again the global order is likely about to change. China, having observed the aftermath of the big-bang deregulation experience of the U.S. and seeing dozens of airlines go out of business decided to consolidate their airline operations and allow for only three major carriers (China Southern, China Eastern, and Air China) to exist in the first place. This enabled them to avoid the loss of capital, jobs, and turmoil of consolidation.[82] Meanwhile, India followed in the footsteps of the U.S. deregulation approach and still has room for further consolidation currently with four carriers with more than 10% domestic market share and a couple in the ditch. Nevertheless, domestic travel is booming in both India and China. For example, China Southern (already the sixth-largest airline globally) plans to grow its fleet by a full one-third in just two years.[83]

Due to their domestic market scale, Chinese and Indian carriers are bound to make it to the global leaderboards eventually. Even others such as Etihad, Emirates, Qatar, and Turkish airlines can become viable regional players or even global players through investment and alliances. Meanwhile, Covid-19 reshuffled the deck for the industry and propelled Zoom Communications' market cap to over $48 billion, more than the market value of the top seven airlines combined (just over $46 billion, led by#1 Southwest Airlines [$14.04 billion] and rounded up by #7 Air France [$2.14 billion])! In all, the largest seven carriers lost 62% of their value between January and May of 2020.[84]

When an industry is dominated by firms from the same country (e.g., the U.S. in aerospace after WWII, soft drinks), then all three players race across continents to form the Global Rule of Three from one geography. Japan experienced this, and at one time, the largest watchmakers as well as TV manufacturers were all Japanese firms. In investment banking, JP Morgan, Goldman Sachs, and Morgan Stanley are emerging as global players and even after extending the list to include Bank of America (BofA) Securities and Citi that round up the global top five, all are notably based out of the U.S.[85] We will see many more examples of this with China and India dominating entire sectors globally in the future.

In order to survive as a global player, you have to be strong in all three triad markets, or at least in two of them. If a company is strong in only one market, and the industry globalizes, it may only remain a regional player (market specialist) in the long run, and will ultimately be bought out by one of the global players. The axioms of the Global Rule of Three can be summarized as follows:

Global Rule of Three Generalizations

When the market globalizes, many full-line generalists that were previously viable as such in their secure home markets are unable to repeat that success in a global context. When this happens, we usually find that there are three survivors globally; typically, but not necessarily, one from each of the three major economic zones of the world: North America, Western Europe, and the Asia-Pacific region. To survive as a *global* full-line generalist, a company has to be strong in at least two of the three legs of this triad.

The path to global dominance relies on aligning procurement/supply chain/finance while staying on top also requires strategic marketing proficiency.

Firms with global aspirations have to conquer their home markets first. A weak domestic base becomes a hindrance during global expansion.

Global consolidation continues until a clear leader emerges and the top three players all command a minimum critical share (i.e., 10%) of the global market each.

Firms with global aspirations need to craft the right attack strategy. A good product at a lower price penetrates the markets faster than a great product at a premium price.

Timing is important. Expansion is easier if an industry is going through (de)regulation or shakeout.

Attack as a pack: Your traditional suppliers, distributors, and even competitors may consider entering at the same time. There are synergies and it may even trigger a paradigm shift in how the new players are perceived. (Koreans did this with LG, Daewoo, Hyundai, and Samsung entering markets within a short period of time.)

Much of the discussion up to this point has focused on generalists. Yet by definition, there can at most be a handful of generalists in each market which eventually consolidate in the convergence to the big three. Meanwhile, there are hundreds of viable specialists globally. Niche companies/specialists in a globalizing market have four options: (a) they can expand internationally and become a global niche player, (b) they can remain domestic as a superniche company, (c) they can launch new specialist businesses, or (d) they can let themselves be acquired at a premium. Many specialists will experience at least two of these options, if not more, in the coming decades.

Online specialists are advised to think locally and act globally—create supply diversity by organizing peer-to-peer networks and connecting them globally. Then take the best of these products and look for ways to scale them and make them global.

One cannot be loyal to a channel as a global generalist, while this may still be possible for a specialist. For example, Pizza Hut refused to engage in delivery for a long time and lost market share to Papa John's and others in the process. Starbucks, in addition to expanding the number of its locations, also began to sell through supermarkets. This is also consistent with Amazon's recent foray into brick and mortar, its Whole Foods acquisition, and plans to operate more physical stores soon.[86]

We observe that three global players have already emerged in several narrowly defined product markets: cellular baseband processor vendors (Qualcomm, MediaTek, Samsung), cigarette vendors (CNTC, PMI, BAT), cloud IT infrastructure vendors (ODM Direct, Dell, HPE/H3C), credit card processing (UnionPay, Visa, Mastercard), CRM vendors (Salesforce.com, SAP, Oracle), DRAM chip vendors (Samsung, SK Hynix, Micron), external enterprise storage systems vendors (Dell, NetApp, HPE/H3C), graphics chip vendors (Intel, Nvidia, AMD), hard copy peripherals vendors (HP, Canon,

Box 5.3 Beyond Global: The Universal Rule of Three

There is something special about the number three in so many contexts that it is worthwhile reflecting. For example, as a writing principle, Rule of Three implies that a trio of events or characters is more effective for engaging the reader, for example, The Three Musketeers, Three Little Pigs. As a presentation technique, in advertising slogans, and journalism, the Rule of Three also comes up consistently since audiences tend to remember three things: "A Mars a day helps you work, rest and play." Rule of Three can convert an ordinary speech to a moving one, for example, "Veni, Vidi, Vici" (Julius Caesar), "Friends, Romans, Countrymen" (Shakespeare in Julius Caesar), "Blood, Sweat and Tears" (General Patton), "Government of the people, by the people, for the people" (Gettysburg Address), "the Good, the Bad and the Ugly." The Rule of Three in Finance refers to trading patterns and expectations of traders regarding three successive trading outcomes. In Statistics, The Rule of Three means that "3/n is an upper 95% confidence bound for binomial probability p when n independent trials no events occur."[87] In other words, let's say you read the first 200 pages of this book and found no typos. We can all hope that the rest of the book is typo-free but the statistical Rule of Three would imply that the probability of your finding a page with a typo in the rest of the book would be under 1.5% (3/200).[88] In history, triumvirate (troika in Russian) refers to three individuals sharing political power for administration (Caesar, Crassus, Pompey; Anthony, Lepidus, Octavian). In perception, a third dimension adds sufficient complexity. In physics, a tripod is more stable than a square-shaped object. In government, the balance of power is maintained through legislative, executive, and judicial bodies. Finally, the trinity principle which contrasts with the duality (either/or thinking) in the Western cultures is commonplace in religion (Father, Son, and the Holy Spirit). Religious affiliations in the world are led by three religions with Christianity 31%, Islam 24%, and Hinduism 15% "market share."[89] In the U.S., Christian denominations are divided into three large groups: Evangelical Protestantism, Mainline Protestantism, and the Catholic Church[90] The third dimension is critical and usually strategically different than the first two: for example, body, mind, and soul.[91] Hence, three appears to represent a universal structure for balancing the phenomena, whatever it may be.

Epson), mobile internet browsers (Chrome, Safari, UC Browser), LCD TV vendors (Samsung, Sony, LG), security appliance vendors (Cisco, Palo Alto Networks, Fortinet), smart speaker vendors (Amazon, Google, Baidu), server system vendors (HPE, ODM, Dell), storage hardware vendors (EMC, NetApp, IBM), tablet vendors (Apple, Samsung, Huawei), and vaccine companies (GSK, Merck, Pfizer). (Please refer to the Appendix for many more global markets and our projections for 2030.)

Next, we discuss the new triad power and its impact on global markets, resources, geopolitical alignment.

Key Takeaways
- The Rule of Three emerges locally, nationally, regionally, and ultimately globally.
- The average life-span of an S&P 500 firm went down from 90 years in 1935 to under 18 years today, and 90% of Fortune 500 firms from 1955 are no longer on the list.
- Competitive markets evolve in a predictable fashion across industries and go through similar life cycles. There is a common structure that provides the highest levels of profitability and stakeholder well-being for the entire industry.
- The market-driven economy is causing weak companies to exit, get acquired by global competitors, or become specialists, often based on geographic region.
- No matter how large the market, the Rule of Three prevails.
- Many generalists that are dominant in their countries or regions are unable to have the same success when the market globalizes. When this happens, there is generally one global survivor from each of the three major economic zones.
- For a company to survive and succeed as a global, full-line generalist, they must be prominent in at least two of the three legs of the global triad.
- If a country has a large stake in an industry, it may be home to two or even all three full-line players.
- The path to global dominance relies on aligning procurement, supply chain, finance while staying on top also requires strategic marketing proficiency.
- Firms with global aspirations have to conquer their home markets first. A weak domestic base becomes a hindrance during global expansion.
- Global consolidation continues until a clear leader emerges and the top three players all command a minimum critical share of the global market each.
- Firms with global aspirations need to craft the right attack strategy. A good product at a lower price penetrates the markets faster than a great product at a premium price.
- Timing is important. Expansion is easier if an industry is going through (de) regulation or shakeout.
- Attack as a Pack: Your traditional suppliers, distributors, and even competitors may consider entering at the same time. There are synergies and it may even trigger a paradigm shift in how the new players are perceived.
- One cannot be loyal to a channel as a global generalist, while this may still be possible for a specialist.
- Specialists in a globalizing market have four options: (a) they can expand internationally and become a global niche player, (b) they can remain domestic as a superniche company, (c) they can launch new specialist businesses, or (d) they can let themselves be acquired at a premium. Many specialists will experience at least two of these options, if not more, in the coming decades.
- Online specialists are advised to think locally and act globally—create supply diversity by organizing peer-to-peer networks and connecting them globally. Then take the best of these products and look for ways to scale them and make them global.

Notes

1. Fox News (2013), "The First Mobile Phone Call was Placed 40 Years Ago Today," FoxNews.com, April 3, 2013, accessed September 26, 2019. http://www.foxnews.com/tech/2013/04/03/first-mobile-phone-call-was-placed-40-years-ago-today.html.

2. Statista (2013), "Global Market Share Held by Nokia Smartphones Q1 2007–Q2 2013," Statista.com, July 25, 2013, accessed September 26, 2019. https://www.statista.com/statistics/263438/market-share-held-by-nokia-smartphones-since-2007/.

3. Keizer, Gregg (2015), "Microsoft Writes off $7.6B, Admits Failure of Nokia Acquisition," Computerworld.com, July 8, 2015, accessed September 26, 2019. https://www.computerworld.com/article/2945371/smartphones/microsoft-writes-off-76b-admits-failure-of-nokia-acquisition.html.

4. Holst, Arne (2019), "Smartphone/Mobile Phone Market Share Worldwide by Vendor 2009–2019," Statista.com, August 2, 2019, accessed September 26, 2019. https://www.statista.com/statistics/271496/global-market-share-held-by-smartphone-vendors-since-4th-quarter-2009/.

5. Wikipedia (2019) "History of the Iron and Steel Industry in the United States," Wikipedia.org, accessed September 26, 2019. https://en.wikipedia.org/wiki/History_of_the_iron_and_steel_industry_in_the_United_States.
   Wikipedia (2019), "History of the Steel Industry (1850–1970)," Wikipedia.com, accessed September 26, 2019. https://en.wikipedia.org/wiki/History_of_the_steel_industry_(1850%E2%80%931970).

6. World Steel Association (2017), "World Steel in Figures 2017," accessed on September 28, 2019. https://www.worldsteel.org/en/dam/jcr:0474d208-9108-4927-ace8-4ac5445c5df8/World+Steel+in+Figures+2017.pdf.

7. TV History (2019), "Television Manufacturers in USA Marketplace," TVHisotry.tv, accessed September 26, 2019. http://www.tvhistory.tv/1960-2000-TVManufacturers.htm.

8. Feder, Barnaby J. (1995), "Last U.S. TV Maker Will Sell Control to Koreans," NYTimes.com, July 18, 1995, accessed September 27, 2019. http://www.nytimes.com/1995/07/18/us/last-us-tv-maker-will-sell-control-to-koreans.html.

9. Larsen, Rasmus (2016), "Samsung dominates global TV market for 10th straight year," Flatpanelshd.com, March 15, 2016, accessed September 27, 2019. https://www.flatpanelshd.com/news.php?subaction=showfull&id=1458017308.

10. Liu, Shanhong (2019), "Global Market Shipment Share Held by LCD Manufacturers from 2008 to 2019," Statista.com, August 12, 2019, accessed September 27, 2019. https://www.statista.com/statistics/267095/global-market-share-of-lcd-tv-manufacturers/.

Business Wire (2018), "TCL TV Sustains 3rd Position in Global TV Market: Emerges as the Fastest Growing TV Brand in India," TheHinduBusinessLine.com, January 11, 2018, accessed September 27, 2019. http://www.thehindubusinessline.com/business-wire/tcl-tv-sustains-3rd-position-in-global-tv-market-emerges-as-the-fastest-growing-tv-brand-in-india/article9794754.ece.

11. CBS News (2016), "GE Selling Home Appliance Business to Chinese Company," CBSNews.com, January 15, 2016, accessed July 26, 2020. http://www.cbsnews.com/news/general-electric-co-selling-ge-appliance-chinese-haier-group-china/.

   Thompson, Ashlee Clark (2016), "It's Official: GE Appliances Belongs to Haier," CNet.com, June 6, 2016, accessed July 26, 2020. https://www.cnet.com/news/its-official-ge-appliances-belongs-to-haier/.

12. Holst, Arne (2019), "Market Share Held by the Leading Personal Computer Vendors Worldwide in 2018," Statista.com, August 30, 2019, accessed September 27, 2019. https://www.statista.com/statistics/267018/global-market-share-held-by-pc-vendors/.

13. Vinsnji, Margaret (2019), "Amazon vs Walmart Revenues and Profits 1995–2014," RevenuesandProfits.com, January 22, 2019, accessed September 27, 2019. https://revenuesandprofits.com/amazon-vs-walmart-revenues-and-profits-1995-2014/.

14. Cramer-Flood, Ethan (2020), "Global Ecommerce 2020," eMarketer, June 22, 2020, accessed July 12, 2020. https://www.emarketer.com/content/global-ecommerce-2020.

15. Clement, J. (2019), "E-commerce Share of Total Global Retail Sales from 2015 to 2023," Statista.com, August 30, 2019, accessed September 27, 2019. https://www-statista-com.proxy.libraries.rutgers.edu/statistics/534123/e-commerce-share-of-retail-sales-worldwide/.

16. Clement, J. (2019), "E-commerce Market Share of Leading e-Retailers Worldwide in 2017, Based on GMV," Statista.com, September 6, 2019, accessed September 27, 2019. https://www-statista-com.proxy.libraries.rutgers.edu/statistics/664814/global-e-commerce-market-share/.

17. Drucker, P.F. (1973), *Management: Tasks, Responsibilities, Practices*, New York: Harper & Row, pp. 736–738.

18. Yahoo Finance (2020), "Amazon.com, Inc," accessed June 30, 2020. https://finance.yahoo.com/quote/AMZN/.

19. Pisani, Bob (2017), "After its Stock Pop, Amazon will Get Whole Foods Essentially for Free," CNBC.com, June 16, 2017, accessed September 27, 2019. https://www.cnbc.com/2017/06/16/after-its-stock-pop-amazon-will-get-whole-foods-essentially-for-free.html.

20. Borpuzari, Pranbihanga (2016), "Lifespan of Companies Shrinking to 18 Years: McKinsey's Dominic Barton," IndiaTimes.com, January 29, 2016, accessed September 27, 2019. https://economictimes.indiatimes.com/small-

biz/hr-leadership/lifespan-of-companies-shrinking-to-18-years-mckinseys-dominic-barton/articleshow/50775384.cms.

21. Anthony, Scott D., S. Patrick Viguerie, Evan I. Schwartz and John Van Landeghem (2018), "2018 Corporate Longevity Forecast: Creative Destruction is Accelerating," Innosight.com, accessed September 27, 2019. https://www.innosight.com/insight/creative-destruction/.

22. Perry, Mark J. (2017), "Fortune 500 firms 1955 v. 2017: Only 60 Remain, Thanks to the Creative Destruction that Fuels Economic Prosperity," accessed June 27, 2018, [http://www.aei.org/publication/fortune-500-firms-1955-v-2017-only-12-remain-thanks-to-the-creative-destruction-that-fuels-economic-prosperity/].

23. This paragraph is drawn from a phenomenal keynote speech by PayPal CEO, Dan Schulman, given at the Innovations at Undergraduate Business Education Conference organized by the Rutgers Business School in October 2017, available at https://www.youtube.com/watch?v=iqv18iuz3V0&feature=youtu.be.

24. Sheth, Jagdish N. (2011), *Chindia Rising: How China and India Will Benefit Your Business*, 2nd ed. Tata-McGraw Hill India.

25. Carter, Jamie (2017), "The Land of the $20 Smartphone," Techradar.com, March 11, 2017, accessed September 27, 2019. https://www.techradar.com/news/the-land-of-the-20-smartphone.

26. See, for example: Porter, Michael, E. (1980), *Competitive Strategy*. New York: The Free Press.

    Carroll, Glenn R. (1985), "Concentration and Specialization: Dynamics of Niche Width in Populations of Organizations," *American Journal of Sociology*, 90 (6), 1261–1283.

    Scherer, Frederic M. and David Ross (1990), *Industrial Market Structure and Economic Performance*, 3rd ed. Boston: Houghton Mifflin.

    Carroll, Glenn R. (1997), "Long-Term Evolutionary Change in Organizational Populations: Theory, Models and Empirical Findings in Industrial Demography," *Industrial and Corporate Change*, 6(1), 119–143.

    Carroll, Glenn R. and Michael T. Hannan (2000), *The Demography of Corporations and Industries*. Princeton, NJ: Princeton University Press.

    Carroll, Glenn R, S.D. Dobrev, and A. Swaminathan (2002), "Organizational Processes of Resource Partitioning," in *Research in Organizational Behavior*, Vol. 24, R.I. Sutton and B.M. Staw, eds. Greenwich, CT: JAI Press, pp. 1–40.

27. Huck, Steffen, Hans-Theo Normann, and Jorg Oechssler (2004), "Two Are Few and Four Are Many: Number Effects in Experimental Oligopolies," *Journal of Economic Behavior & Organization*, 53 (4), 435–446.

28. Uslay, Can, Z. Ayca Altintig, and Robert D. Winsor (2010), "An Empirical Examination of the "Rule of Three": Strategy Implications for Top Management, Marketers, and Investors," *Journal of Marketing*, 74 (March), 20–39.

Uslay, Can, Ekaterina Karniouchina, Ayca Altintig, and Martin Reeves (2017), "Do Businesses Get Stuck in the Middle? The Peril of Intermediate Market Share," September 28, 2017, accessed July 11, 2020. https://papers.ssrn.com/sol3/papers.cfm?abstract_id=3043330.

29. Boon, Tom (2018), "The 3 Major Airline Alliances: Star Alliance, One World and SkyTeam – Why Are They Good?" Simple Flying, October 20, 2018, accessed July 12, 2020. https://simpleflying.com/the-3-major-airline-alliances-star-alliance-oneworld-and-skyteam-why-are-they-good/.

30. Sheth, Jagdish N. (1986), "Global Markets or Global Competition?" *Journal of Consumer Marketing,* 3 (2), 9–12.

Sheth, Jagdish N., Can Uslay, and Rajendra S. Sisodia (2008), "The Globalization of Markets and the Rule of Three," in *Marketing Metaphors and Metamorphosis*, Philip J. Kitchen, Ed. London: UK, Palgrave Macmillan, pp. 26–41.

Uslay, Can, Sengun Yeniyurt, and Olivia F. Lee (2013), "Globalization of Markets: Implications for the Entrepreneurial Firm in the 21st Century," in *Entrepreneurial Marketing: A Global Perspective*, Z. Sethna, R. Jones, and P. Harrigan Eds., Emerald Publishing, pp. 111–126.

31. Ohmae, Kenichi (1985), *Triad Power*, MacMillan-Free Press.

Sheth, Jagdish N. and Rajendra S. Sisodia (2006), *Tectonic Shift: The Geoeconomic Realignment of Globalizing Markets*, Thousand Oaks: Response.

32. Su, Jeb (2018), "Huawei Fortifies #2 Spot In Global Smartphone Market, Beating Apple Again," Forbes.com, November 2, 2018, accessed September 27, 2019. https://www.forbes.com/sites/jeanbaptiste/2018/11/02/huawei-fortifies-2-spot-in-global-smartphone-market-beating-apple-again/#689d76e51305.

33. Irigoyen, Santiago (2019), "Global Cigarette & Tobacco Manufacturing," IBISWorld, November 2019, accessed July 12, 2020. https://my-ibisworld-com.proxy.libraries.rutgers.edu/gl/en/industry/c1131-gl/major-companies.

34. Brand value was measured as "value of the trade mark and associated marketing IP within the branded business."

Desjardins, Jeff (2019), "The World's Most Valuable Bank Brands," VisualCapitalist.com, February 8, 2019, accessed September 27, 2019. https://www.visualcapitalist.com/worlds-most-valuable-bank-brands/.

Statista (2020), "Largest Banks Globally as of December 2018, by Assets," accessed July 12, 2020. https://www-statista-com.proxy.libraries.rutgers.edu/statistics/269845/largest-banks-in-the-world-by-total-assets/.

35. Drucker, P.F. (1958), "Marketing and Economic Development," *Journal of Marketing* (January), 252–259.

36. Globalization has been defined by Merriam-Webster dictionary as "the development of an increasingly integrated global economy marked especially by free trade, free flow of capital, and the tapping of cheaper foreign labor markets."

37. Sheth, Jagdish N., Can Uslay, and Rajendra S. Sisodia (2008), "The Globalization of Markets and the Rule of Three," in *Marketing Metaphors and Metamorphosis*, Philip J. Kitchen, Ed. London: UK, Palgrave Macmillan, pp. 26–41, 30–31.

38. Sheth, Jagdish N., Can Uslay, and Rajendra S. Sisodia (2008), "The Globalization of Markets and the Rule of Three," in *Marketing Metaphors and Metamorphosis*, Philip J. Kitchen, Ed. London: UK, Palgrave Macmillan, pp. 26–41, 30.

39. Drucker, P.F. (1969a), *The Age of Discontinuity*. New York: Harper & Row.

40. Drucker, P.F. (1973), *Management: Tasks, Responsibilities, Practices*. New York: Harper & Row.

41. Sheth, Jagdish N. (2011), Chindia Rising: *How China and India Will Benefit Your Business*, 2nd ed. Tata-McGraw Hill India.

42. Sheth, Jagdish N. (2011), *Chindia Rising: How China and India Will Benefit Your Business*, 2nd ed. Tata-McGraw Hill India.

43. DW (2017), "South Korea's Hanjin Shipping Declared Bankrupt," DW.com, February 17, 2017, accessed September 27, 2019. http://www.dw.com/en/south-koreas-hanjin-shipping-declared-bankrupt/a-37593429.

44. Szmigiera, M. (2019), "Market Share of Leading Banks in the United States in 2018, by Value of Domestic Deposits," Statista.com, June 14, 2019, accessed September 27, 2019. https://www-statista-com.proxy.libraries.rutgers.edu/statistics/727546/market-share-of-leading-banks-usa-domestic-deposits/.

45. CNBC (2019), "BB&T to Buy SunTrust in All-Stock Deal Worth $66 Billion That Will Create the Sixth-Largest US bank," CNBC.com, February 7, 2019, accessed September 27, 2019. https://www.cnbc.com/2019/02/07/bbt-and-suntrust-to-combine-in-an-all-stock-merger-of-66-billion.html.

46. Webb, Susan (2002), "Marshall Plan: A Cover for Corporations," PeoplesWorld.org, May 3, 2002, accessed September 27, 2019. https://www.peoplesworld.org/article/marshall-plan-a-cover-for-corporations/.

47. Reference for Business (2019), "Carlos Slim, 1940–," ReferenceforBusiness.com, accessed September 27, 2019. https://www.referenceforbusiness.com/biography/S-Z/Slim-Carlos-1940.html.
    Emspak, Jesse (2019), "How Carlos Slim Built His Fortune," Investopedia.com, June 25, 2019, accessed September 27, 2019. https://www.investopedia.com/articles/investing/103114/how-carlos-slim-built-his-fortune.asp.

48. McKenzie, Sheena, Nicole Gaouette and Donna Borak (2018), "The Full 'Putin list' of Russian Oligarchs and Political Figures Released by the US Treasury," CNN.com, January 30, 2018, accessed September 27, 2019. https://www.cnn.com/2018/01/30/politics/full-us-list-of-russian-oligarchs-with-putin-ties-intl/index.html.

49. Wikipedia (2019), "Timeline of Microsoft," Wikipedia.com, accessed September 27, 2019. https://en.wikipedia.org/wiki/Timeline_of_Microsoft.

50. Wikipedia (2019), "History of Apple Inc.," Wikipedia.com, accessed September 27, 2019. https://en.wikipedia.org/wiki/History_of_Apple_Inc.

51. Clement, J. (2019), "Number of Monthly Active Facebook Users Worldwide as of 2nd Quarter 2019 (in millions)," Statista.com, August 9, 2019, accessed September 27, 2019. https://www.statista.com/statistics/264810/number-of-monthly-active-facebook-users-worldwide/.

52. Dickinson, Greg (2018), "How the World is Going to War with Airbnb," Telegraph.co.uk, June 8, 2018, accessed September 27, 2019. https://www.telegraph.co.uk/travel/news/where-is-airbnb-banned-illegal/.

53. Bridgwater, Adrian (2020), "How Israel Became a Technology Startup Nation," *Forbes*, February 21, 2020, accessed July 12, 2020. https://www.forbes.com/sites/adrianbridgwater/2020/02/21/how-israel-became-a-technology-startup-nation/#46c494ae780e.

54. Holton, Kate and Sinead Carew (2013), "Verizon, Vodafone Agree to $130 Billion Wireless Deal," Reuters.com, September 2, 2013, accessed September 27, 2019. https://www.reuters.com/article/us-vodafone-verizon/verizon-vodafone-agree-to-130-billion-wireless-deal-idUSBRE97S08C20130903.

55. Nelson, Christina (2011), "General Motors Races Ahead in the China Market," ChinaBusinessReview.com, April 1, 2011, accessed September 27, 2019. https://www.chinabusinessreview.com/general-motors-races-ahead-in-the-china-market/.

56. Volkswagen (2019), "Volkswagen in China – A Long Lasting Friendship," Volkswagenag.com, accessed September 27, 2019. https://www.volkswagenag.com/en/news/stories/2018/04/volkswagen-in-china-a-long-lasting-friendship.html.

57. Spencer, Natasha (2017), "L'Oreal Launches Women Empowerment Fund to Celebrate 20 Years in China," CosmeticsDesign-Asia.com, February 6, 2017, accessed September 27, 2019. https://www.cosmeticsdesign-asia.com/Article/2017/02/06/L-Oreal-20-years-in-China.

58. Lubin, Matthew (2018), "China's Beauty Bubble: YSL, L'Oreal Sales Shrug Off Trade War," JingDaily.com, November 7, 2018, accessed September 27, 2019. https://jingdaily.com/chinas-beauty-bubble-ysl-loreal-shrug-off-trade-war/.

59. Seeking Alpha (2016), "'Big 4' Advertising Agencies, Part 1: Introducing the Companies and Industry," SeekingAlpha.com, April 21, 2016, accessed September 27, 2019. https://seekingalpha.com/article/3967004-big-4-advertising-agencies-part-1-introducing-companies-industry.

60. Evans, Michelle (2019), "Uber Acquires Careem for $3.1 Billion As The Middle East Startup Pushes To Become A Super App," *Forbes*, March 26, 2019, accessed September 27, 2019. https://www.forbes.com/sites/michelle-evans1/2019/03/26/meet-careem-ubers-3-1-billion-new-acquisition-in-the-middle-east/#608d1a0e1e3c.

61. Gopalan, Nisha (2018), "Starbucks, There's a Unicorn in Your China Shop," *Bloomberg*, December 3, 2018, accessed September 27, 2019. https://www.bloomberg.com/opinion/articles/2018-12-03/luckin-coffee-is-stiff-competition-for-starbucks-sbux-in-china.

Statista (2020), "Number of Starbucks Stores in China from 2005 to 2019," accessed July 12, 2020. https://www.statista.com/statistics/277795/number-of-starbucks-stores-in-china/.

Bezek, Ian (2020), "Luckin Coffee Has Rallied, But Will the Good Times Last?" InvestorPlace, June 10, 2020, accessed July 12, 2020. https://investorplace.com/2020/06/luckin-coffee-stock-rallied-but-for-how-long/.

62. Obermeier, Kylie (2019), "When India Kicked Out Coca-Cola, Local Sodas Thrived," Atlasobscura.com, February 15, 2019, accessed September 27, 2019. https://www.atlasobscura.com/articles/what-is-thums-up.

63. See, for example, Baxter-Reynolds, Matt (2013), "The 'Rule of Three' Explains the Smartphone Market Perfectly," ZDNet, August 15, 2013, accessed July 12, 2020. http://www.zdnet.com/article/the-rule-of-three-explains-the-smartphone-market-perfectly/.

64. Sheth, Jagdish N., Can Uslay, and Rajendra S. Sisodia (2008), "The Globalization of Markets and the Rule of Three," in *Marketing Metaphors and Metamorphosis*, Philip J. Kitchen, Ed. London: UK, Palgrave Macmillan, pp. 26–41.

65. Malik, Yogender (2017), "China on the Rise Tire Companies Making Waves Around the Globe," TireReview.com, September 1, 2017, accessed September 27, 2019. https://www.tirereview.com/china-rise-tire-companies-making-waves-around-globe/.

66. Halpert, Julie (2012), "Chrysler Group is Adage's Marketer of the Year," *AdAge*, Nov. 26, 2012, accessed July 12, 2020. http://adage.com/article/special-report-marketer-alist-2012/chrysler-group-ad-age-s-marketer-year/238443/.

67. Minkoff, Yoel (2020), "Ferrari Tops Detroit Three, Tesla Tops All," SeekingAlpha, May 5, 2020, accessed July 26, 2020. https://seekingalpha.com/news/3568836-ferrari-tops-detroit-three-tesla-tops-all.

68. Schmitt, Bertel (2018), "Germany's Bundesrat Resolves End of Internal Combustion Engine," Forbes.com, October 8, 2016, accessed September 27, 2019. http://www.forbes.com/sites/bertelschmitt/2016/10/08/germanys-bundesrat-resolves-end-of-internal-combustion-engine/#413ec95931d9.

69. Franck, Thomas (2018), "Tesla is the Biggest Short in the US Stock Market," CNBC.com, April 11, 2018, accessed September 27, 2019. https://www.cnbc.com/2018/04/11/tesla-is-the-biggest-short-in-the-us-stock-market.html.

70. Geely Global Media Center (2019), "Geely Auto 2018 Sales Reach 1.5 Million Units, Increasing Over 20% From Previous Year," Geely.com, January 7, 2019, accessed September 27, 2019. http://global.geely.com/media-center/news/geely-auto-2018-sales-reach-1-5-million-units-increasing-over-20-from-previous-year/.

71. BeBord, Matthew (2015), "Fiat Chrysler CEO Marchionne is really Pushing His Luck with Hopeless GM Merger Talk," BusinessInsider.com, June 9, 2015, accessed September 27, 2019. http://www.businessinsider.com/fiat-chrysler-ceo-marchionne-is-really-pushing-his-luck-with-hopeless-gm-merger-talk-2015-6.

72. Tatelbaum, Julianna (2019), "Global Automakers are Lining up to Buy Fiat Chrysler. Here's Why," CNBC.com, March 29, 2019, accessed September 27, 2019. https://www.cnbc.com/2019/03/29/peugeot-and-renault-are-both-said-to-want-to-buy-fiat-chrysler.html.

73. This mini-case is drawn from the following sources:

    BF Goodrich Tires (2020), accessed on September 27, 2019. www.bfgoodrichtires.com.

    Ohio History Connection (2008), "B.F. Goodrich Company," accessed on September 27, 2019. www.ohiohistorycentral.org.

    Wikipedia (2020), "Goodrich Corporation," accessed on September 27, 2019. https://en.wikipedia.org/wiki/Goodrich_Corporation.

    Sull, Donald N. (2000), "The Dynamics of Standing Still: Firestone Tire & Rubber and the Radial Revolution," HBS.edu, November 27, 2000, accessed September 27, 2019. https://hbswk.hbs.edu/item/the-dynamics-of-standing-still-firestone-tire-rubber-and-the-radial-revolution.

    Y Charts (2020), "Goodyear Tire & Rubber Co (GT,)" accessed on September 27, 2019. https://ycharts.com/companies/GT/market_cap.

74. Rajan, R., P. Volpin, L. Zingales (2000), "The Eclipse of the U.S. Tire Industry," in *Mergers and Productivity*, S. Kaplan ed., Chicago: IL, University of Chicago Press, pp. 51–92, 58.

75. Lindsey, Robert (1981), "Lockheed to Halt Output of Tristar," NYTimes.com, December 8, 1981, accessed September 27, 2019. https://www.nytimes.com/1981/12/08/us/lockheed-to-halt-output-of-tristar.html.

76. Knowlton, Brian (1996), "Boeing to Buy McDonnell Douglas," The New York Times, December 16, accessed September 28, 2019. https://www.nytimes.com/1996/12/16/news/boeing-to-buy-mcdonnell-douglas.html.

77. Air & Cosmos International (2018), "COMAC Sees $6 Trillion Commercial Aircraft Market," Aircomosinternational.com, November 16, 2018, accessed September 27, 2019. http://www.aircosmosinternational.com/comac-sees-6-trillion-commercial-aircraft-market-117205.

78. Sheth, Jagdish N., Fred C. Allvine, Can Uslay, and Ashutosh Dixit (2007), *Deregulation and Competition: Lessons from the Airline Industry*, Thousand Oaks, CA: Sage Publications.

79. Mazareanu, E. (2019), "Domestic Market Share of Leading U.S. Airlines from July 2018 to June 2019*," Statista.com, September 16, 2019, accessed September 27, 2019. https://www.statista.com/statistics/250577/domestic-market-share-of-leading-us-airlines/.

80. Zhang, Benjamin (2019), "No Fewer than 5 European Airlines Have Collapsed Since October. Here They Are," BusinessInsider.com, April 1, 2019, accessed September 27, 2019. https://www.businessinsider.com/airlines-shut-down-october-europe-2019-3.

81. Wikipedia (2019), "World's Largest Airlines," Wikipedia.org, accessed September 27, 2019. https://en.wikipedia.org/wiki/World's_largest_airlines.

82. Sheth, Jagdish N., Fred C. Allvine, Can Uslay, and Ashutosh Dixit (2007), *Deregulation and Competition: Lessons from the Airline Industry*, Thousand Oaks, CA: Sage Publications.

83. Reed, Dan (2018), "China's Big Three Airlines Are on A Fast Track to Overtake U.S. Big Three Within A Few Years," Forbes.com, September 20, 2018, accessed September 27, 2019. https://www.forbes.com/sites/daniel-reed/2018/09/20/chinas-big-three-airlines-are-on-a-fast-track-to-overtake-u-s-s-big-three-within-a-few-years/#5705112112234.

84. Ghosh, Iman (2020), "Zoom is Now Worth More than the World's 7 Biggest Airlines," May 15, 2020, accessed July 12, 2020. https://www.visualcapitalist.com/zoom-boom-biggest-airlines/.

85. Szmigiera, M. (2019), "Global Market Share of Revenue of Leading Investment Banks as of July 2019," Statista.com, July 10, 2019, accessed September 27, 2019. https://www.statista.com/statistics/271008/global-market-share-of-investment-banks/.

86. Kim, Eugene (2016), "Amazon is Doubling Down on Retail Stores with Plans to Have Up to 100 Pop-up Stores in US Shopping Malls," BusinessInsider.com, September 9, 2016, accessed September 27, 2019. http://www.businessinsider.com/amazon-big-expansion-retail-pop-up-stores-2016-9.

87. Jovanovic, B. D. and P. S. Levy (1997), "A Look at the Rule of Three," *The American Statistician*, 51(2), 137–139.

88. Cook, John D (2010), "Estimating the Chances of Something that Hasn't Happened Yet," accessed June 29, 2020. https://www.johndcook.com/blog/2010/03/30/statistical-rule-of-three/.

89. Hackett, Conrad and David McClendon (2017), "Christians Remain World's Largest Religious Group, but They are Declining in Europe," PewResearch.org, April 5, 2017, accessed September 27, 2019. http://www.pewresearch.org/fact-tank/2017/04/05/christians-remain-worlds-largest-religious-group-but-they-are-declining-in-europe/.

90. Wikipedia (2019), "Christianity in the United States," Wikipedia.org, accessed September 27, 2019. https://en.wikipedia.org/wiki/Christianity_in_the_United_States.

91. This section is compiled from the following sources:

Presentation Magazine (2006), "Examples of the Rule of Three," PresentationMagazine.com, August 11, 2006, accessed September 27, 2019. https://www.presentationmagazine.com/rule-of-three-836.htm.

Wikipedia (2019), "Rule of three (writing)," Wikipedia.com, accessed September 27, 2019. https://en.wikipedia.org/wiki/Rule_of_three_(writing).

Sweney, Mark (2008), "Mars revives 'Work, rest, play' slogan," The Guardian, February 28, 2008, accessed September 27, 2019. https://www.theguardian.com/media/2008/feb/28/advertising.

Wikipedia (2019), "Triumvirate," Wikipedia.org, accessed September 27, 2019. https://en.wikipedia.org/wiki/Triumvirate.

6

The New Triad Power: Impact on Global Markets, Resources, and Politics

If we examine the economic growth engines for the world, the nineteenth century can be characterized as the European century, thanks to the industrial revolution and the colonial expansion needed to run the factories of industrial revolution. That is when multinational corporations such as the East India Company emerged. The twentieth century belonged to America by most metrics, and the twenty-first century (at least the first half of it) can be characterized as the Asian century. China and India naturally have a lot to do with this, but the contributions of the ASEAN nations such as Singapore, Indonesia, Malaysia, Thailand, and Vietnam cannot be denied. Furthermore, Australia's support for the growth of Asian nations should not be overlooked.

The old triad consisted of Western Europe, North America, and Japan. Forty-five percent of world trade and 70% of the world's GDP was concentrated among the triad powers.[1] A total of 15 nations conducted and controlled much of world trade. It was as if the rest of the world did not matter. This held true for the duration of the cold war, all the way to the collapse of communism in 1991.

However, those days are in the past, and the source of economic growth has long shifted from advanced nations to emerging nations such as China, India, Brazil, and Russia.

Similar to the Japanese model following World War II, China relied on cheap labor to become a low-cost provider to the world in the 1990s. However, the undeniable economic success of Japan led to increased wages and standard of living, which coupled with an aging population, resulted in higher costs. Thus, manufacturers gave their attention and business to China next, which quickly became known as "the workshop of the world." "As in Japan, that

© The Author(s) 2020
J. Sheth et al., *The Global Rule of Three*, https://doi.org/10.1007/978-3-030-57473-4_6

strategy was very successful in China for the next two decades…But just as happened in Japan, China's economic growth has led to higher wages, an increased standard of living, and they will eventually experience lower productivity from an aging population."[2]

No need to worry however, since the entire continent of Africa is awakening to opportunities. While the last century was shaped by ideology and politics (e.g., World War I, World War II, and the Cold War), the current century is closely anchored to competitive markets and resources. Arguably, a new triad power consisting of America, China, and India has been emerging, which will reshape world policy in the twenty-first century. The global race for resources is on, and competition for a new geopolitical order of the world is fierce.

The members of the old triad need jobs and economic growth just as badly as the new one. Without job growth, politicians tend to lose their jobs. Ironically, most elections are won based on economics rather than ideology. For example, George H.W. Bush became even more popular than Ronald Reagan following the Gulf War; unlike today, America was even admired as the savior of the oppressed nation of Kuwait. However, Bush lost the 1992 election to Bill Clinton despite his popularity and incumbent advantage because of the Clinton campaign's realization (in James Carville's phrase) that "It's the economy, stupid." On the other hand, Bill Clinton from the small state of Arkansas was able to win re-election despite his personal indiscretions because the economy was doing well.

The same phenomenon occurred in the U.K. (where John Major lost the election to Tony Blair), in Germany (where unemployment rose to 10% following the East Germany integration, the people were fed up and demanded a new government), in Australia, China, India, Africa, Latin America, and so on. After the Turkish Lira became the worst-performing currency in the world,[3] even President Tayyip Erdogan may be losing his tight grip. His party surprisingly lost the municipal election in Istanbul twice (with an even wider margin the second time after the first election was canceled based on alleged foul play by Erdogan's party, AKP).[4] The mayorship of Istanbul had been in the hands of Erdogan's AKP party for over 25 years. Thus, the fact that economics trumps (pun intended) ideology is certainly not a strictly U.S. phenomenon.

There are a few forces driving the triad shift. First, the affluent advanced nations of the world are rapidly aging. For example, the Japanese population has been aging so rapidly that more adult diapers are sold there than baby diapers.[5] Its birthrate at 1.4 is significantly below the 2.1 needed to maintain the population. In fact, its population decreased by over half a million people just in 2019 and is expected to shrink from 124 million in 2018 to just 88 million in 2065. The situation in South Korea is even more dire; the fertility rate dropped to a mere 0.98 in 2018.[6] Germany, the U.K., France, Italy, Canada, and many other developed nations suffer from the same problem. With a birthrate of 1.72 (lowest in record for over three decades), the U.S. owes its population growth to immigrants but at a much slower pace than it is accustomed to.[7]

Second, economic reforms that took place in communist and socialist countries (such as China and India) have accelerated the transformation to market economies. Third, the discontinuous rise and integration of the new middle class to the industrial economy, which is completely separated from the previous generation (which largely grew up in an agricultural economy) is mind-boggling. The most drastic example of this is the transformation of China in the 1970s from an agrarian to an industrial economy. It rapidly became a manufacturing powerhouse for the world. Its young consumers have also become buyers of all sorts of branded goods, automobiles, smartphones, washing machines, and so on.

And outsourcing comes home through services. Just like their developed market counterparts,[8] young consumers from emerging markets are also significant consumers of household services. While the stereotypical example of outsourcing may be Indian IT firms, outsourcing of household services (cooking, cleaning, childcare, etc.) is actually a major driver of economic growth in emerging markets. Finally, emerging nations have enormous resource advantages. The real wealth of a nation is the wealth of its citizens and the resources of emerging countries increasingly involve human resources in addition to natural resources.

Consider the economies of China and India beyond 2020. China's economy is expected to slow down due to the one-child policy adopted in 1979. Even though the program was revised in 2015, its effects are expected to be enduring.[9] Earlier in this decade, 117 boys were born in China for every 100 girls. This imbalance has drastically increased the number of imported brides as well as human trafficking concerns.[10]

The real economic boom will come from the Indian economy, albeit later, since there is a need for massive investments in infrastructure before the potential can be realized.

Eventually, the GDP of India and China may become relatively equal as measured by Purchasing Power Parity. There is no denying that "Chindia" is rising.[11] China and India will have to learn to cooperate economically initially with trade and later with mutual investments. For example, in categories such as farming equipment and software, India may be a net exporter to China, whereas China may dominate the relationship in categories such as consumer electronics and appliances. However, the U.S., due to its genes of entrepreneurship and innovation will remain a major power alongside China and India, forming the new triad power.

Unlike the harmonious ideological, economic, and military alignments orchestrated by the U.S. in the old triad, the new triad power comes with tensions, especially between the U.S. and China. On the one extreme, America is capitalistic and heavily relies on free markets. On the other extreme, China has a communist legacy where strategic sectors are not trusted to private enterprise. India is in the middle with a semi-socialistic society. These differences will inevitably create tensions, which have already begun to mushroom with tariffs and trade renegotiations.

The advantage of a triad structure is that in case one party gets too dominant, the remaining two can always form a coalition as a counterbalance. Given the global rivalry between the U.S. and China, India will increasingly become a more strategic partner to both. Next, we consider the impact of the new triad power on global markets, resources, and politics, respectively.

Impact of the New Triad on Global Markets

The emergence of the world's largest consumer markets: Markets with sizes never seen before will emerge in China and India. Even more than a decade ago, China already produced more pigs than the next 43 top pork-producing countries combined![12] And more recently (as of 2016 and 2017), it annually consumed 59% of cement, 47% of aluminum, 56% of nickel, 50% of coal, 50% of copper, 50% of steel, 27% of gold, 14% of oil, 31% of rice, 47% of pork, 23% of corn, and 33% of cotton in the world![13] As of February 2019, there were 1.58 billion registered phone subscriptions in China,[14] whereas India is projected to have 829 million smartphone users by 2022.[15] Both of these figures dwarf the U.S. market whose current 248 million smartphone users is expected to reach 270 million in the same time frame.[16]

While America invented cellular technology and commercialized smartphones, it will lose the telecommunications market permanently. The biggest manufacturers, as well as wireless operators and consumer markets, are already all in Asia. This is essentially the same trajectory that television followed (invented in the U.S. and then lost to Asia). Tencent's sales have already caught up to that of Facebook, thanks to its dominance in China.[17] India is rapidly moving from bicycles to motorcycles and has already become the largest market in the world for them.[18] Eventually, the largest demand for housing the world has ever seen will also come from these two economies. However, the biggest growth areas will be in services ranging from banking to broadband and from household support services to education and health care.

Much of this scale will come from the growth of second, third, and fourth-tier cities, as well as rural markets. When comparing rural areas with urban markets, the demand for branded products and services is narrowing more and more. Just like the case of Wal-Mart which gave access to world-class brands to rural customers in small towns at affordable prices, rural consumers in emerging markets are also catching up to the rest of the world in their consumption patterns and tastes. In some ways, the emerging market story is more drastic.

Consider the case of a software engineer. Having studied for 15 years and still single, s/he goes to Bangalore, Delhi, or any one of the metro areas, makes about 60,000–70,000 Rupees ($900–$1000) a month and barely can save anything at the end of the month. S/he has to pay rent (15,000–20,000 Rupees). S/he is rather contemporary and wears stylish branded attire of the season, must have a smartphone and internet service to be on social media, and goes out in the evenings a lot. Eating out and night clubs are almost necessities. Alas, the expenses typically end up being much greater than the discretionary income after tax deductions.

Contrast that with the case of a crane operator in the port of Mundra. Having studied 12 years concluding with vocational training, he earns even more (about 80,000–85,000 Rupees a month). He is married to a homemaker wife. Whereas one-third of income goes to rent in urban areas, rural consumers tend to live with the expanded family and do not have to incur rent costs. Therefore, the discretionary income of the crane operator is much greater than that of the software engineer. He has buying power for discretionary items such as a motorcycle, furniture/upkeep, or a high-end smartphone, but importantly, can also invest more in the future of his children. Therefore, the rural-urban divide is getting narrower not only from a digital divide or e-commerce perspective, but also in terms of aspirations and desires which increasingly mean more branded goods and services, resulting in the world's largest consumer markets.

Rise of Chindia's global enterprises: Huawei, a name few people had heard of until a decade ago, is the largest manufacturer of telecommunications infrastructure in the world today. Its global dominance has put the U.S. government on the defensive. A more familiar name from India, Tata is a large conglomerate with stakes in many sectors. For example, Tata Consultancy Services (TCS) is the third most valued IT services brand globally (after Accenture and IBM),[19] and Tata Tea has become the #2 producer of teas in the world (right after Unilever which owns Lipton). Likewise, Hindalco (of

India) has become a major player in aluminum. Banks, appliances, e-commerce firms from China will similarly rise to global dominance. In fact, Haier from China has already become the top appliance-maker globally and Alibaba continuously beats Amazon when it comes to operating margin and earnings.[20]

R&D shifts to Chindia: This calls for a paradigm shift. R&D centers of pharmaceuticals, information, and communication technology firms of advanced nations will increasingly be located in Asia, mainly in China and India, to be closer to talent. For example, Intel developed its high-end Xeon 7400 chip in its Bangalore R&D center.[21] With over 425 foreign-invested R&D centers in Shanghai alone,[22] IBM, Microsoft, Google, Intel, and Facebook can all be expected to have R&D centers in Asia. This trend becomes inevitable as companies ranging from BASF and General Electric to Mercedes Benz realize where their future growth lies.[23]

Affordability becomes the focus of innovation: If necessity is the mother of invention, affordability is the father of innovation. Acceptable quality at affordable prices for the mass market will be a major criterion for innovation going forward. While the Tata Nano car eventually failed due to positioning blunders, it represented a breakthrough to be able to produce a car for under $2000.

The fusion of cultures: Rudyard Kipling's sentiment that "East is East and West is West and never the twain shall meet" simply does not ring true. Today, Asians are westernized (wearing jeans), while the world is becoming simultaneously easternized through music (K-pop), entertainment, arts, culture, spirituality (Buddhism, Feng Shui), and food (Indian curry). However, the transformation all surfaces as a fusion. While westernization was more of an export model, easternization is more of blending model, for example, Christian-yoga! Since western cultures are more open to innovation and external influences, easternization will take place much more rapidly than westernization ever has.

Private equity in emerging markets: Large companies are already active in Chindia. Coca-Cola believes its twenty-first-century growth will rely heavily on China (as it did very much so on India in the twentieth century). Similarly, McDonald's, KFC, Caterpillar, General Motors (GM), and Starbucks all have large-scale operations which are still growing. From education to health care, global leaders are paving their way to Asia. The only exception is likely the defense industry since they are not allowed to operate in China. KKR, Blackstone, and major private equity players cannot be left far behind. Eventually, financial markets will follow the growth as well, and Shanghai is bound to become the largest capital market in the world surpassing both London and New York (when one combines public, private equity and debt markets).

Impact of the New Triad on Global Resources

Resource-driven global expansion: Akin to a producer which might want to be close to fertile land for agriculture, IBM has decided that they need to be in India to be closer to human resources. In fact, today IBM employs more people in India than it does in the U.S.; more than one-third of its headcount hails from India.[24] Similarly, Accenture whose IT business has shown tremendous growth in recent years[25] has over 150,000 employees in India (about three times the size of its U.S.-based employees) that make up more than a third of its global workforce.[26] It might even become the largest IT employer in India one day. Accenture has also launched "a massive, first-of-its-kind innovation hub in Bengaluru. The facility is populated with talent and tools in the most happening digital areas, including AI, blockchain, security, automation, cloud, as also in a variety of areas, such as baking, telecom, and healthcare."[27] The basis of these expansions is resource-driven as opposed to market-driven, which is a key phenomenon to understand across global markets of today.

Resource-driven global mergers: In addition to organic investment and growth, the need to expand to where the resources are will continue to fuel global mergers. For example, there has been a big wave of mergers in mining, spanning Australia, Canada, Latin America, Africa, and even the Caribbean. Of the five biggest mega-merger deals exceeding $10 billion in value in mining history, four consisted of cross-border transactions. For example, Brazilian CVRD bought Inco of Canada for $13 billion in 2006 to become the #2 nickel mining company in the world. Similarly, Anglo-Austrian Rio Tinto bought Alcan of Canada for $38 billion in 2007 to become the largest producer of aluminum and bauxite minerals at the time. And more recently, Barrick Gold of Canada acquired Randgold of Mali for $18 billion in 2018 creating the world's largest gold producer.[28]

The emergence of strange bedfellows: Gulf nations have long been buying land (in Sudan, Mozambique, Tanzania, Kenya, Mali, Senegal, and Ethiopia) to ensure agricultural supplies to prepare for a future where "food security" may no longer be a given. In fact, even a decade ago 115 million acres of land (larger than the size of the U.K.) was being sold or rented to foreign investors.[29] However, the Belt and Road Initiative (BRI) of China will potentially be the most important catalyst in the race for access to global resources. It involves infrastructure investments in 65 countries spanning Asia, Europe, Africa, the Middle East, and the Americas. These countries are collectively home to 30% of global GDP, 62% of world population, and 75% of known energy reserves.[30]

The initiative has two main components: the Silk Road Economic Belt connects China to Central and South Asia onto Europe, and the New Maritime Silk Road connects China to South East Asia, the Gulf Countries, North Africa, and Europe. It is estimated that trade flows between participating countries could increase by over 4% and potentially three times more if trade reforms are adapted.[31] Furthermore, shipment times and trading costs along the BRI corridors are expected to decrease by up to 12% and 10% respectively.[32] However, not all is rosy with the project. The mega initiative (which has been estimated to involve as much as $8 trillion in investment) will also leave numerous countries in debt that they might struggle to pay back. In particular, Pakistan, Djibouti, the Maldives, Laos, Mongolia, Montenegro, Tajikistan, and Kyrgyzstan have been singled out.[33] Recall that the U.S. bought Louisiana from France for $15 million in 1803 (roughly $300 million today) and Alaska from Russia for $7.2 million in 1867 (roughly $140 million today).[34]

Considering the vast natural resources of several of the countries along the belt and road, it is not inconceivable that BRI may eventually serve the territorial expansion of China. While a direct land concession to a foreign country is not politically acceptable, debt servitude and concessions can come in the form of sales and long-term leases or other schemes that enable resource access to Chinese corporations or military. In fact, it is already happening. Burdened with debt, Sri Lanka gave control of its Hambantota port and 15,000 acres of surrounding land to state-owned China Harbor Engineering Company for 99 years in December 2018.[35] While the deal erased $1 billion in debt, the Sri Lankan burden continues as other outstanding Chinese loans still carry much higher interest rates than available from other international sources.[36] Similarly, facing burden of public debt amounting to 88% of its GDP, the government of Djibouti allowed China to build its first overseas military base.[37] Seeing the writing on the wall, Pakistan, Malaysia, Myanmar, Bangladesh, and Sierra Leone have already canceled or sought revisions to their previous commitments citing impact on national debt.[38] Just like England had invested in and built industries in America centuries ago (e.g., in steel and textile), China has already massively invested in the infrastructure of Africa and exerts significant soft power.

Rise of scarcity driven profits: Significant profits will be made at the commodity level due to unanticipated scarcities for raw materials. For example, African swine fever led to a 36% increase in pork prices in China the first week of April 2019 and was expected to lead to a 33% increase in Chinese 2019 pork imports bringing it to 2 million metric tons.[39] Prices of eggs in the U.S. jumped by more than 16% during April 2020 due to Covid-19, and other grocery categories such as bakery items, fish, meat, poultry, fruits, and vegetables were all impacted.[40] The usual expectation is for downstream activities (with higher value-add) to command higher margins. Counter-intuitively, industrial raw materials and commodities may command higher margins than finished products in the near future. For example, in the PC industry, merely a fraction of value-add comes from manufacturing in factories whereas the lion's share comes from procurement. Moreover, most of the value-add from procurement benefits Microsoft, Nvidia, and Intel, whereas Dell, Acer, and HP continue to struggle. Similar proportions also apply to consumer electronics in general. Sony and several other consumer brands have been struggling whereas the component manufacturers (especially for chips and software) have been thriving.

Shortage-driven breakthrough innovations: Breakthrough innovations will increasingly stem from efforts to replenish natural resources rather than automating manual labor. Camel, cattle, sheep, pig, deer, horses, mules, rabbits, and many more species have been cloned.[41] Advances in science may actually help us perfect Mother Nature. For example, pearl farms can produce more perfect-shaped pearls much faster and more economically (and in desired size and color and shape) than Mother Nature. Whereas physics and chemistry dominated the last century, the twenty-first century will be dominated by biomedical sciences, (nano)technologies, and machine learning.

Sustainability imperative: There are over 3090 active landfills and 10,000 old municipal landfills in the U.S. Ninety percent of solid waste does not get recycled. If only 10% of newspapers were recycled annually, 25 million trees would be saved in the U.S. alone.[42] Interestingly, the eventual restrictions to the spectacular growth of China and India will not come from lack of capital or technology but from the environment. Climate change will increasingly be top of mind for nations in the second half of the century. For example, it is expected that more than a quarter of U.S. metropolitan cities will experience over 100 days per year with over 95 degrees Fahrenheit beyond 2060 as opposed to just 1% today.[43] Similarly, heat waves caused by climate change will only worsen China's woes; the country is already suffering from over a million premature deaths a year due to air pollution.[44] Hence, the business logic will have to shift from exploiting and extracting nature to nurturing nature. Addressing sustainability will increasingly be a key imperative for China, the U.S., and India in the twenty-first century. Leading multinational corporations will also need to embrace the principles for sustainability either through their own initiatives, whereas laggards are bound to succumb to regulation as it becomes the norm. The need for conscious capitalism has never been more urgently felt.[45]

Impact of the New Triad on Geopolitics

Economics as a driver of politics: As we have discussed already, politics is heavily driven by economics. Filling the stomachs and wallets of the population enable politicians to survive regardless of whether the system is one of a full-blown parliamentary democracy, republic, single-party, or even a non-democratic dictatorship; economic well-being of citizens is key. BRICS countries (Brazil, Russia, India, China, and South Africa) have been hosting their own summits due to the realization that they need to build trade and investment among each other despite their differences. North-South trade/investment is increasingly being replaced/displaced by South-South trade.

G-8 becomes G-20: G7 historically was formed due to the need to deal with the energy crisis. Subsequently, Russia was added. Now instead of adding China and India, a larger league of 20 nations has been invited to the table to drive the world economy. The year 2019 was the 20th anniversary of the conception of G-20. The group of nations originally consisting of Canada, France, Germany, Italy, Japan, the U.S., and the U.K. now includes Argentina, Australia, Brazil, China, India, Indonesia, Mexico, Russia, Saudi Arabia, South Africa, South Korea, and Turkey as well. G-20 collectively accounts for 66% of the world population, 85% of global economic output, 75% of international trade, and 80% of global investment.[46] The influence of G-20 is bound to increase over time with the U.S., China, and India at the helm at the expense of traditional European powers.

Rise of multilateral politics: The American universal view has been replaced by multilateralism with the new triad. While it has been relatively easy for the U.S. to get its way in a post-Soviet era, Asia, Europe, and America increasingly have their own unique views on how the world should be governed. China is already increasing its influence, for example, the Philippines is already following suit of its "friend" China at the expense of its historical ally, the U.S., regarding disputes in the South China Sea.[47] China's One China Principle is destined to cause a clash with Taiwan as well as Vietnam due to the ensuing border disputes.[48] While the general trend will be gradually diminishing global influence for the U.S., the resulting political arena will be more complex yet surprisingly stable, since a triad also offers counterbalance against a leading nation's dominant whims.

Growth of Asian Sovereign Funds: By definition, sovereign funds are best suited for large scale and long-term infrastructure projects. We had mentioned the increasing role of sovereign funds for organizing industries in Chap. 4. In addition to the several large funds from China and India, others such as Temasek of Singapore, Abu Dhabi Investment Authority, and Khazanah of Malaysia play a significant role in Asia, just like the Swiss have an outsized presence in the European economy.[49] Emerging markets of China, India, and Africa need massive investments that only sovereign funds have the scope to undertake. The aforementioned $8 trillion Belt and Road infrastructure initiative involves sovereign funds. It has been estimated that the Asia-Pacific region will need $1.7 trillion additional infrastructure investment per annum for a total of $26 trillion by 2030 at current growth rates.[50] The private sector alone cannot sustain investment at such a scale and Asian sovereign funds will play a major role and actively step in.

Multiple Currency Reserves: Throughout the 1980s, most U.S. debt was bought by the Japanese. America then encouraged Japan to convert public debt into private equity. Bank of Japan made low/no interest loans to the banks of keiretsu. These banks in turn made loans to their manufacturing business units to invest and produce in the U.S. as opposed to simply exporting. Honda, Toyota, and Nissan all built their own plants in the U.S. Even when the U.S. was trying to catch up and compete with Japanese in terms of quality, the Japanese were permitted to buy equity/firms in the U.S. Hence, they bought U.S. television manufacturers and invested in real estate. The current U.S. debt rate is not sustainable in the long run.

The same evolution is expected to happen for China (and India) which will convert its mountain of debt instruments (T-bonds) into equity. In the case of India, interestingly, Western capital will be used to acquire Indian firms which may then be leveraged to buy U.S. and other Western assets. In order to diversify risk, China and other emerging market governments will also begin to hold massive reserves in multiple currencies and gold. Indeed, this is already happening: Chinese gold reserves that averaged 995 tons from 2000 until 2019 have increased to an all-time high of 1936 tons in the third quarter of 2019.[51] Similarly, gold reserves in India averaged 462 tons from 2000 until 2019 but have reached all-time high of 618 tons in the second quarter of 2019.[52] Trade wars, as prominent as they are today, will actually be augmented by currency wars in the future where the central banks will play a more active role by shifting their focus from fiscal to monetary policy.

Redefining Capitalism and Democracy: History is written by the hand of the victors, and ideology is always defined by the superpower of the era. When the British were in power, Adam Smith and David Ricardo defined the pillars of capitalism and free markets. The British defined democracy as a parliamentary government system with two primary parties, which the U.S. adopted. However, whereas in the U.K., the people choose the party and the party chooses the prime minister who can be replaced through a vote of no-confidence, the U.S. favors stability and continuity, and you have a leader for at least four years once a President is elected. The U.S. is a Republic-Democracy where the states influence Congress based on their electoral votes. Thus, popular versus electoral votes can make a major difference as the last few Presidential elections have demonstrated.

The current definition of capitalism is not sustainable when there is such a large base of the pyramid in the global society (over one billion living on less than $2 a day). Going forward, a more participatory and nurturing style of capitalism (that incorporates all stakeholders—customers, employees, suppliers, and community—rather than simply shareholders) than that defined by the West is necessary. Corporate social responsibility is not enough; the fiber of capitalism must be refreshed and a more egalitarian/equitable basis for shared value is required.[53]

Democracy allowed to its extreme of acrimony and gridlocks becomes anarchy. When individuals have the right to express themselves without any checks and balances, things can quickly get out of control due to the amplification of messages through social media (as we have seen recently with fake news). The best enforcement is self-discipline. A disciplined approach to dialogue is necessary to avoid such acrimony. Thus, the *disciplined democracy* of the future will need to balance the rights of the individual with the rights of institutions (government, education, religion, family). Autocratic nations are dominated by institutions. The highly contested issue of abortion laws in the U.S. represents a case where society/institutions currently dictate this key decision over the individual.

On the other hand, a purely democratic approach where individual rights trump organizations, institutions, or society is also not sustainable. An example of this is the gun legislation in the U.S. where the constitutional right of individuals (to bear arms) from a bygone era is being used as the ruse to prevent meaningful protection of citizens. Institutions are just as valuable to society as individuals. *The rights of the institutions and the individual must be properly balanced for a caring capitalism and disciplined democracy.* The rise of Chindia will redefine both. The center of gravity is clearly shifting from the Atlantic to the Pacific Ocean.

Next, we discuss the global expansion strategies for multinationals from emerging markets.

Key Takeaways

- The nineteenth century can be characterized as the European century, thanks to the industrial revolution and the colonial expansion. The twentieth century belonged to America by most metrics, and the twenty-first century (at least the first half of it) can be characterized as the Asian century.
- While the twentieth century was driven by ideologies and politics of advanced nations, the twenty-first century will be driven by markets, resources, and realities of emerging nations.
- Aging of affluent nations, economic reforms, the rise of the new middle class, and resource-based advantages are responsible for this mega-shift.
- A new triad power consisting of China, America, and India has emerged, replacing Western Europe, North America, and Japan. Rise of Chindia will have a global impact on resources, markets, and politics. Fostering economic growth through trade and investment between triad powers will be critical for worldwide peace and stability.
- The real economic boom will come from the Indian economy, albeit later, since there is a need for massive investments in infrastructure before the potential can be realized. Eventually, the GDP of India and China may become relatively equal as measured by Purchasing Power Parity.
- In categories such as farming equipment and software, India may be a net exporter to China, whereas China may dominate the relationship in categories such as consumer electronics and appliances. However, due to its genes of entrepreneurship and innovation, the U.S. will remain a major power alongside China and India, forming the new triad power.
- Allowing large-scale investment and trade into the triad markets by each geopolitical and economic mega-power is a better prevention mechanism than nuclear bombs ever were! The more nations become interdependent through trade and investment, the less the urge to go to war against each other. Collectively, the triad has the power and sway to deter and hold every other nation at bay.
- Demand for the world's resources will create strange bedfellows among nations, as well as resource-driven global expansion for all enterprises and nations. Major technology breakthroughs, including cloning and nanotechnology will stem from resource conservation and resource scarcity. Key drivers of innovation will be affordability and accessibility of products, technologies, and services. The world economy will decouple from the dollar denomination for trade and investment to be able to cope with volatility and speculation.
- China and India will be integrated into world political, social, and economic forums and institutions. We can already see evidence of this in world bodies such as the WTO, UN, World Bank, IMF, WHO, with many Asians in leading positions. They will be on the sidelines no more. M&A and private equity will play a significant role in the new triad power. Most M&A activity has been concentrated among the new triad economies and investment has also been flowing in the same direction. These investments will manifest in several global leaders from a wide array of sectors.

Notes

1. The reason why GDP was more concentrated than trade was that the triad powers received natural resources from their ex-colonies which somewhat diversified trade distribution.

   Also see Sheth, Jagdish N. (2011), *Chindia Rising: How China and India Will Benefit Your Business*, 2nd ed. Tata-McGraw Hill India.

2. Sheth, Jagdish N. (2011), *Chindia Rising: How China and India Will Benefit Your Business*, 2nd ed. Tata-McGraw Hill India, p. iii.

3. Ahval (2019), "Lira is World's Worst Performer and Times Could Get Harder—Bloomberg," Ahvalnews.com, January 15, 2019, accessed September 27, 2019.

   https://ahvalnews.com/turkish-lira/lira-worlds-worst-performer-and-times-could-get-harder-bloomberg.

4. Sariyuce, Isil and Ivana Kottasová (2019), "Istanbul Election Rerun Won by Opposition, in Blow to Erdogan," CNN.com, June 23, 2019, accessed September 27, 2019.

   https://www.cnn.com/2019/06/23/europe/turkey-istanbul-mayor-election-intl/index.html.

5. Herships, Sally (2016), "There are More Adult Diapers Sold in Japan than Baby Diapers," Marketplace.org, August 29, 2016, accessed September 27, 2019.

   https://www.marketplace.org/2016/08/09/world/japans-changing-culture.

6. Emiko Jozuka, Jessie Yeung and Jake Kwon (2019), "Japan's Birth Rate Hits Another Record Low in 2019," CNN.com, accessed June 27, 2020, https://www.cnn.com/2019/12/25/asia/japan-birthrate-hnk-intl/index.html.

7. Chappell, Bill (2019), "U.S. Births Fell to a 32-Year Low In 2018; CDC Says Birthrate Is In Record Slump," NPR.org, May 15, 2019, accessed September 27, 2019.

   https://www.npr.org/2019/05/15/723518379/u-s-births-fell-to-a-32-year-low-in-2018-cdc-says-birthrate-is-at-record-level.

   Google.com (2019), "Public Data: Fertility Rate," accessed September 28, 2019.

   https://www.google.com/publicdata/explore?ds=d5bncppjof8f9_&met_y=sp_dyn_tfrt_in&idim=country:USA:CHN:JPN&hl=en&dl=en.

8. Jagdish N. Sheth and Rajendra S. Sisodia (1999), "Outsourcing Comes Home," *The Wall Street Journal*, June 281,999, accessed July 12, 2020. Page A26.

9. Wee, Sui-Lee (2017), "U.S. Births Fell to a 32-Year Low In 2018; CDC Says Birthrate Is In Record Slump," NYTimes.com, January 7, 2017, accessed September 27, 2019.

https://www.nytimes.com/2017/01/07/world/asia/after-one-child-policy-outrage-at-chinas-offer-to-remove-iuds.html.

10. The Washington Post (2018), "U.S. Births Fell to a 32-Year Low In 2018; CDC Says Birthrate Is in Record Slump," FreedomUnited.org, April 18, 2018, accessed September 27, 2019.
 https://www.freedomunited.org/news/chinas-one-child-policy-rise-imported-brides/.

11. Sheth, J. N. (2011). *Chindia Rising: How China and India will Benefit your Business*, 2nd ed. Tata-McGraw Hill India.

12. Frangos, Alex and Juliet Ye (2010), "The Vital Role of China's Pork Prices," WSJ.com, April 20, 2010.
 https://blogs.wsj.com/chinarealtime/2010/04/20/the-vital-role-of-china%E2%80%99s-pork-prices/?mod=djemChinaRTR_h%23.

13. Desjardins, Jeff (2018), "U.S. Births Fell to a 32-Year Low In 2018; CDC Says Birthrate Is In Record Slump," Visual Capitalist, March 2, 2018, accessed September 27, 2019.
 https://www.visualcapitalist.com/chinas-staggering-demand-commodities/.

14. Statista (2019), "Number of Mobile Cell Phone Subscriptions in China from January 2018 to February 2019 (in millions)," September 23, 2016, accessed September 27, 2019.
 https://www.statista.com/statistics/278204/china-mobile-users-by-month/.

15. The Economic Times, (2019), "India to Have Over 800 Million Smartphone Users by 2022," accessed June 15, 2019. https://economictimes.indiatimes.com/tech/hardware/india-to-have-over-800-million-smartphone-users-by-2022-cisco-study/articleshow/66917976.cms?from=mdr.

16. IIA (2018), "Research Peek of the Week: Smartphone Users in the US Expected to Reach Over 270 Million by 2022," InternetInnovation.org, July 3, 2018, accessed September 27, 2019.
 https://internetinnovation.org/general/research-peek-of-the-week-smartphone-users-in-the-us-expected-to-reach-over-270-million-by-2020/.

17. Bhardwaj, Prachi (2018), "Tencent's Business is About as Big as Facebook's Thanks to its Stronghold in China," BusinessInsider.com, May 16, 2018, accessed September 27, 2019.
 https://www.businessinsider.com/tencent-compare-facebook-revenue-charts-2018-5.

18. Doval, Pankaj (2017), "India is Now the World's Biggest Two-Wheeler Market," TimesofIndia.com, May 7, 2017, accessed September 27, 2019.
 https://timesofindia.indiatimes.com/auto/bikes/india-is-now-worlds-biggest-2-wheeler-market/articleshow/58555735.cms.

19. The Economic Times (2019), "TCS 3rd Most-Valued IT Services Brand Globally: Brand Finance," IndiaTimes.com, January 23, 2019, accessed September 27, 2019.
    https://economictimes.indiatimes.com/tech/ites/tcs-3rd-most-valued-it-services-brand-globally-brand-finance/articleshow/67660948.cms.

20. Mourdoukoutas, Panos (2018), "Why Alibaba Is More Profitable Than Amazon," Forbes.com, May 6, 2018, accessed September 27, 2019.
    https://www.forbes.com/sites/panosmourdoukoutas/2018/05/06/why-alibaba-is-more-profitable-than-amazon/#5e6862f21678.

21. Yamado, Go (2015), "Multinationals Recognize India's Potential as Global R&D Hub," Nikkei.com, July 6, 2015, accessed September 27, 2019.
    https://asia.nikkei.com/Business/Multinationals-recognize-India-s-potential-as-global-R-D-hub.

22. The American Chamber of Commerce in Shanghai (2018), "Chasing Innovation: R&D Barriers and Incentives in China," April 2018, accessed September 27, 2019.
    https://www.amcham-shanghai.org/sites/default/files/2018-04/R%26D%20viewpoint%202018%20April%20Final%20EN_0.pdf.

23. Yamado, Go (2015), "Multinationals Recognize India's Potential as Global R&D Hub," Nikkei.com, July 6, 2015, accessed September 27, 2019.
    https://asia.nikkei.com/Business/Multinationals-recognize-India-s-potential-as-global-R-D-hub.

24. Goel, Vindu (2017), "IBM Now Has More Employees in India Than in the U.S.," NYTimes.com, September 28, 2017, accessed September 27, 2019.
    https://www.nytimes.com/2017/09/28/technology/ibm-india.html.

25. Sood, Varun (2018), "Accenture New Revenue Catches up with top Five Indian IT firms," LiveMint.com, October 9, 2018, accessed September 27, 2019.
    https://www.livemint.com/Companies/rDPAuBfOVQi8Unjp2I6UvI/Accenture-new-revenue-catches-up-with-top-five-Indian-IT-fir.html.

26. Phadnis, Shilpa (2018), "Accenture New Revenue Catches up with Top Five Indian IT firms," IndiaTimes.com, July 26, 2018, accessed September 27, 2019.
    https://timesofindia.indiatimes.com/business/india-business/accenture-says-india-employees-have-to-specialise-or-go/articleshow/65144526.cms.

27. Phadnis, Shilpa (2018), "Accenture New Revenue Catches up with Top Five Indian IT Firms," IndiaTimes.com, July 26, 2018, accessed September 27, 2019.
    https://timesofindia.indiatimes.com/business/india-business/accenture-says-india-employees-have-to-specialise-or-go/articleshow/65144526.cms.

28. Husseini, Talal (2018), "Hot Prospects: The Biggest Mining Mergers to Rock the Industry," Mining-Technology.com, October 2, 2018, accessed September 27, 2019.
https://www.mining-technology.com/features/biggest-mining-mergers/.

29. Pomroy, Matt (2014), "Why are Gulf States Buying Land in Africa?" Esquireme.com, May 21, 2014, accessed September 27, 2019.
https://www.esquireme.com/brief/business/why-are-gulf-states-buying-land-in-africa.

30. World Bank (2018), "Belt and Road Initiative," WorldBank.org, March 29, 2018, accessed September 27, 2019.
http://www.worldbank.org/en/topic/regional-integration/brief/belt-and-road-initiative.

31. World Bank (2019), "Trade Effects of the New Silk Road: A Gravity Analysis (English)," WorldBank.org, January 10, 2019, accessed September 27, 2019.
http://documents.worldbank.org/curated/en/623141547127268639/Trade-Effects-of-the-New-Silk-Road-A-Gravity-Analysis.

32. World Bank (2019), "How Much Will the Belt and Road Initiative Reduce Trade Costs? (English)," WorldBank.org, October 15, 2018, accessed September 27, 2019.
http://documents.worldbank.org/curated/en/592771539630482582/How-Much-Will-the-Belt-and-Road-Initiative-Reduce-Trade-Costs.

33. Ming, Cheang (2018), "China's Mammoth Belt and Road Initiative Could Increase Debt Risk for 8 Countries," CNBC.com, March 5, 2018, accessed September 27, 2019.
https://www.cnbc.com/2018/03/05/chinas-belt-and-road-initiative-raises-debt-risks-in-8-nations.html.

34. Global Policy Forum (2006), "US Territorial Acquisition," GlobalPolicy.org, January 2006, accessed September 27, 2019.
https://www.globalpolicy.org/component/content/article/155/25993.html.

35. Chandran, Nyshka (2017), "India and China Compete for Control of an Almost Empty Sri Lanka Airport," CNBC.com, December 13, 2017, accessed September 27, 2019.
https://www.cnbc.com/2017/12/13/india-and-china-rivals-compete-for-control-of-empty-sri-lanka-airport.html.
Chandran, Nyshka (2019), "Fears of Excessive Debt Drive More Countries to Cut Down their Belt and Road investments," CNBC.com, January 17, 2019, accessed September 27, 2019.
https://www.cnbc.com/2019/01/18/countries-are-reducing-belt-and-road-investments-over-financing-fears.html.

36. Abi-Habib, Mari (2018), "How China Got Sri Lanka to Cough Up a Port," NYTimes.com, June 25, 2018, accessed September 27, 2019.

https://www.nytimes.com/2018/06/25/world/asia/china-sri-lanka-port.html.

37. Cheng, Amy (2018), "Will Djibouti Become Latest Country to Fall Into China's Debt Trap?" ForeignPolicy.com, July 31, 2018, accessed September 27, 2019.
    https://foreignpolicy.com/2018/07/31/will-djibouti-become-latest-country-to-fall-into-chinas-debt-trap/.
    Yang, You and Li Jingyi (2019), "Djibouti: Chinese Military's First Overseas Support Base," CGTN.com, April 21, 2019, accessed September 27, 2019.
    https://news.cgtn.com/news/3d3d514d7859544d34457a6333566d54/index.html.

38. Chandran, Nyshka (2019), "Fears of Excessive Debt Drive More Countries to Cut Down their Belt and Road investments," CNBC.com, January 17, 2019, accessed September 27, 2019.
    https://www.cnbc.com/2019/01/18/countries-are-reducing-belt-and-road-investments-over-financing-fears.html.

39. Liu, Yujing and Orange Wang (2019), "China's African Swine Fever Crisis 'Very Serious' with Stocks Falling and Pork Prices Set to Hit All-Time High," SCMP.com, April 23, 2019, accessed September 27, 2019.
    https://www.scmp.com/economy/china-economy/article/3007359/chinas-african-swine-fever-crisis-very-serious-stocks-falling.

40. Cortes, Michelle Santiago (2020), "It's Not You, Grocery Prices Are Going Up," Refinery29, May 14, 2020, accessed July 12, 2020.
    https://www.refinery29.com/en-us/2020/05/9816335/grocery-prices-rising-more-expensive-coronavirus-impact.

41. Wikipedia (2019), "List of Animals That Have Been Cloned," Wikipedia.com, accessed September 27, 2019.
    https://en.wikipedia.org/wiki/List_of_animals_that_have_been_cloned.

42. Brucker, Drew (2018), "50 Recycling & Trash Statistics That Will Make You Think Twice About Your Trash," RubiconGlobal.com, November 14, 2018, accessed September 27, 2019.
    https://www.rubiconglobal.com/blog-statistics-trash-recycling/.

43. Blackrock (2019), "Getting Physical: Scenario Analysis for Assessing Climate-related Risks," April, accessed October 5, 2019. https://www.blackrock.com/ch/individual/en/literature/whitepaper/bii-physical-climate-risks-april-2019.pdf.

44. McKenna, Phil (2019), "Global Warming is Worsening China's Pollution Problems, Studies Show," (August 14), accessed October 5, 2019. https://insideclimatenews.org/news/14082019/climate-change-china-pollution-smog-soot-jet-stream-global-warming.

45. Suhas, Apte, & Jagdish N. Sheth (2016), *The Sustainability Edge: How to Drive Top-Line Growth with Triple-Bottom-Line Thinking*, Toronto, Canada, University of Toronto Press.

Mackey, John and Raj Sisodia (2013), *Conscious Capitalism: Liberating the Heroic Spirit of Business*, Boston, MA, Harvard Business Review Press.

46. Kuo, Frances (2018), "G20: The Evolution and Expansion of the International Summit," CGTN.com, November 29, 2018, accessed September 27, 2019. https://america.cgtn.com/2018/11/29/g20-the-evolution-and-expansion-of-the-international-summit.

47. Mourdoukoutas, Panos (2019), "South China Sea: Beijing Shouldn't Treat Vietnam Like The Philippines," Forbes, July 13, 2019, accessed September 27, 2019. https://www.forbes.com/sites/panosmourdoukoutas/2019/07/13/south-china-sea-beijing-shouldnt-treat-vietnam-like-the-philippines/#510ae8b35ff4.

48. Gertz, Bill (2019), "U.S. Sides with Vietnam in Maritime Dispute with China," FreeBeacon.com, July 24, 2019, accessed September 27, 2019. https://freebeacon.com/national-security/u-s-sides-with-vietnam-in-maritime-dispute-with-china/.

49. SWFI (2019), "Top 82 Largest Sovereign Wealth Fund Rankings by Total Assets," Swfinstitute.org, accessed September 27, 2019. https://www.swfinstitute.org/fund-rankings/sovereign-wealth-fund.

50. HSBC (2018), "Where is the Funding for a $26 Trillion Initiative Coming from?" CNBC.com, March 6, 2018, accessed September 27, 2019. https://www.cnbc.com/advertorial/2018/03/06/where-is-the-funding-for-a-26-trillion-initiative-coming-from.html.

51. Trading Economics (2019), "China Gold Reserves," accessed September 28, 2019. https://tradingeconomics.com/china/gold-reserves.

52. Trading Economics (2019), "India Gold Reserves," accessed September 28, 2019. https://tradingeconomics.com/india/gold-reserves.

53. Porter, Michael E. and Mark R. Kramer (2011), "Creating Shared Value," *Harvard Business Review*, January–February, 62–77.

Kramer, Mark R. and March W. Pfitzer (2016), "The Ecosystem of Shared Value," *Harvard Business Review*, October, 80–89.

7

Global Expansion Strategies for Multinationals from Emerging Markets

NYU Stern School of Business global management and strategy professor and architect of the Global Connectedness Index, Pankaj Ghemawat has observed that: "perhaps the biggest business strategy issue of our time [is] how competition between emerging market and established multinationals is likely to unfold with the big shift in many economic activities from advanced economies to emerging economies."[1] Globalization has undoubtedly generated economic prosperity on a mass scale, creating more employment, innovation, infrastructure, and trade. Despite temporary reverse headwinds that are taking the world toward trade wars and Brexit, global competitiveness remains the institutional imperative.[2]

Simultaneously, we are witnessing an inevitable shift in global economic activity from advanced to emerging markets, as what was once peripheral becomes the core.[3] For example, Brazil, Russia, India, and China have almost tripled their share of global GDP from 8% in 2001 to 22.4% in 2017.[4] The dominance of BRIC countries accelerated further with the inclusion of South Africa, and their annual summits may soon create an alternative to the old Bretton Woods geopolitical alignment of North America, the EU, and Japan.[5] Emerging markets are home to 85% of the world's population, and they collectively generated over 80% of the world's economic growth since 2008.[6] One-third of the world's largest "unicorns" (companies exceeding $1 billion in market value) hail from emerging markets.[7]

Practitioners and scholars have rightfully focused their attention on the contemporary management of business and innovation in emerging markets, as the infrastructure, regulatory, socio-economic, socio-political, technological, and cultural systems in emerging markets are drastically different.[8]

© The Author(s) 2020
J. Sheth et al., *The Global Rule of Three*, https://doi.org/10.1007/978-3-030-57473-4_7

Meanwhile, many emerging-market multinational companies (EMNCs from here on) also have global aspirations.[9] Yet, the path for global dominance is long and arduous, and conglomerates from developed markets have significantly more experience in running multinational enterprises.

Do players from emerging markets stand a chance against these corporate giants? Yes. Is there one specific strategy or country (emerging or not) that will dominate the future? Not likely. So which global expansion strategies should EMNCs employ? We assert that their business and marketing strategies have been and should be different from those of the traditional conglomerates of the world in order to succeed. One thing is for sure; the initial group of top three players is far from assured to make it into the final set of global players.

There is a multitude of extant prescriptive literature for mature global players from the advanced economies of the West, but not nearly enough for new entrants to the global arena from emerging markets.[10] We find extant theories, such as transaction cost-based explanations, to be insufficient when it comes to explaining the rise of EMNCs. In this chapter, we attempt to address this void by examining how EMNCs should go about successfully operating in other emerging and developed markets so they, too, can become global players.

Growth of Multinationals from Emerging Markets

We begin by providing some surprising facts:

1. Tata Motors acquired the iconic British brand Jaguar from Ford in 2008. Ford had a multiple luxury brand strategy (Jaguar, Volvo, Land Rover) but was struggling due to the economic downturn in 2008 during which the U.S. automobile industry was decimated. Thus, Ford put the brands up for sale and Jaguar and Land Rover were surprisingly bought by the Indian company Tata Motors for $2.3 billion.[11] Jaguar was an official car used by diplomats all over the world in the old British Empire (Cadillac used to have the same stature for U.S. diplomats). The purchase of Jaguar by a company from a former colony would have been unimaginable a couple of decades ago. Ford's remaining jewel, Volvo, was bought by another emerging market company, Geely, for $1.8 billion in 2010.[12]

2. Though the Indian IT/BPO service industry began with simple Y2K software coding projects that involved converting old systems from two to four digits, it later boomed, exceeding $160 billion annually in sales.[13] Operating in more than 45 countries, Tata Consultancy Services alone generates over $20 billion in revenue and boasts its own AI/cloud-based

neural automation platform, Ignio.[14] Infosys has also exceeded $10 billion in revenue, and Wipro and six other firms all aim to surpass the $10 billion mark. Most of the industry is export-oriented, and these players compete head-to-head with the likes of IBM, Accenture, and Capgemini. Today, they already dominate the ERP space where they install large platforms and are taking business from Oracle and SAP. In addition, these companies are capable of full systems integration and are getting into cloud-based and mobile computing services. Cumulatively, they are expected to generate $350 billion in revenues by 2025![15]

3. In 2002, SAB, the largest brewing company of South Africa, bought Miller, the #2 producer in the U.S., from Philip Morris for $5.6 billion to become SABMiller.[16] In 2004, Brazilian AmBev merged with Belgian beer company Interbrew (creating InBev) in an $11.5 billion deal to temporarily become the top producer in the world.[17] This conglomerate bought the largest U.S. producer Anheuser-Busch in 2008 for $52 billion.[18] Finally, consolidation came full circle with SAB Miller and Anheuser-Busch InBev's merger in a $106 billion mega-deal in 2015 to form AB InBev.[19]

4. The future of autonomous rides may be uncertain, but EMNCs are not taking any chances to prepare for the eventuality which is demonstrated by their ride-sharing investments. China's Tencent and JD.com were among the lead investors in the last $1 billion investment round of the Indonesian ride-hailing company Go-Jek (valued at $10 billion), while Singapore-based Grab (valued at $6 billion) acquired Uber's Southeast Asian business.[20] Didi Chuxing also owns a large stake in Grab.[21]

These are surprising anecdotes because conventional thinking would have predicted the opposite. For example, one would expect Anheuser-Busch, in its quest of globalization, to make a bid for Interbrew (or Kirin in Japan, Tiger in Singapore, or Kingfisher in India), but not the other way around. Similarly, Uber would have been expected to make a bid for Grab rather than divesting its Southeast Asian presence.

The media and the public imagination are preoccupied with exciting stories coming from Silicon Valley and firms such as Airbnb, LinkedIn, Uber, and so forth. Indeed, most of these firms are younger than 20 years; they can be considered millennium babies. However, there is an alternative reality in traditional industries such as beer, steel, automobile where EMNCs are "springboarding" to global prominence like never before, either through acquisition or greenfield expansions.[22]

The world had to wait for 700 years for the next big wave of globalization after Genghis Khan's Mongolian Empire in the twelfth century. The Ricardian theory of comparative advantage propelled trade then.[23] Ricardo proposed that nations should focus on utilizing their existing resources, and should even pay more for certain goods than domestic production would enable, as long as the domestic resources could be used more productively elsewhere. Thus, Great Britain was to buy corn, steel, and textiles from Spain, the U.S., and India and sell them machinery and higher value-added products. Consequently, Great Britain also exported technology, and effectively, the industrial revolution to its colonies. The result was a boon for trade, a win-win for Great Britain and its colonies, and a rejuvenated global economy.

By the 1850s, England was widely considered to be the "workshop of the world." Naturally, the Ricardian logic also applies to today's wave of outsourcing. If your neighbor is better in auto manufacturing than you are, you can focus on services, including car rentals, and generate higher value-add in the process.[24] In many ways, the U.S. and India both owe their heritage industries to Great Britain. Upon becoming an industrial powerhouse, the U.S. outsourced some of its manufacturing to the politically aligned Taiwan, Korea, and Japan, fueling their growth.[25]

It is no longer disputed that large emerging nations will serve as the economic growth engines of the twenty-first century. "These emerging nations are already moving away from being exporters of raw materials and inexpensive mass-produced goods, to manufacturing of high value-added goods and services by importing more machinery, equipment and know-how from their developed counterparts. Their next phase in globalization will be to create global brands."[26]

For example, the global market leader in the steel industry has surprisingly come from an emerging market. After the collapse of communism in the early 1990s, many of the Eastern European bloc countries became truly independent nations. They had stranded assets in government-owned enterprises, especially steel mills. Poland, Hungary, the Czech Republic, and Slovakia all wanted to divest. Lakshmi Mittal (of Indian origin, but based out of London for tax purposes and capital access) became the aggregator, and with subsequent acquisitions, rose to global dominance. Mittal Technologies acquired Arcelor (out of Luxembourg) in a $33 billion hostile bid, and ArcelorMittal is currently the largest steel producer in the world by far.[27] Similarly, Huawei, which has been filing an average of 5000 unique patents per year, became the largest telecom infrastructure manufacturer in the world.[28] In the process, it also overcame Lucent (which had merged with Alcatel and still failed), Ericsson, and Siemens.

Interestingly, 200 years after the last golden age of globalization, we may now be coming full circle. There are new world realities where multinationals from emerging markets have very high aspirations. In the new world order, some regions or nations may dominate entire sectors globally. For example, it is now conceivable that the steel and telecom sectors may be dominated by companies from the Far East (India, China, South Korea, or Japan) without a single European or U.S. competitor to challenge them.

Global competition from EMNCs is real and is spread across a wide variety of industries. The top two agricultural seed companies are from Mexico and India, and China and India are among the largest exporters of industrial raw materials such as iron ore and coal. Multinationals from emerging markets are active in fiber for making garments, petrochemical products, and increasingly branded consumer products and services.

China has already become a globally dominant player and competes against other super-economies such as the U.S., Japan, and Germany. It competes virtually across all sectors and will eventually become dominant across several industries in the aggregate analysis: for example, steel mills, banking, pharmaceuticals, telecom infrastructure, mobile phone manufacturing, and services. Thus, China will lead EMNCs; however, they will also come from countries such as India, Mexico, South Africa, Russia, and Brazil. This is the new global reality no matter how you look at it. Competition from other emerging countries (e.g., Vietnam, Turkey) will be much more focused and selective. Each global industry will be subject to a different configuration of competitors. As markets consolidate and converge, it is vital to comprehend where the new set of global leaders will come from and what their respective expansion strategies are.[29]

Ramamurti offered a typology for EMNCs consisting of five categories: natural-resource vertical integrator (based on special access to natural resources or home markets, e.g., Lukoil); local optimizer (serving low-income consumers via underdeveloped infrastructures, e.g., HiSense and Mahindra & Mahindra); low-cost partners (that utilize skilled low-wage workforce, e.g., Infosys and Dr. Reddy's); global consolidator (based on home-country scale advantage, e.g., Hindalco, Lenovo, and Cemex), and global first-mover (low-cost operation in new growth industry, e.g., Huawei and Embraer).[30] In Fig. 7.1, we augment previous efforts by identifying 12 strategies that are, in many ways, very different from the patterns and theories of mature MNCs from the West. We discuss each of these next.

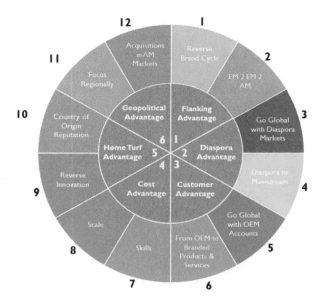

Fig. 7.1 Twelve strategies and six differential advantages of EMNCs. (Source: Jagdish N. Sheth presentation on "Global Expansion Strategies of Multinationals from Emerging Markets," 2018)

Competitive Strategies of Multinationals from Emerging Markets

Reverse Brand Life Cycle

The competition for consumer and business brands generally takes place within (as opposed to across) three segments: premium, value, and price. The premium segment is typically 15–25% of the total market whereas the price segment tends to be between 10% and 15% (larger if there is no value brand yet). The majority lies within the value segment, which usually is 50–65% of the total market. Brands also go through life cycles.[31] The prototypical brands begin with a premium image (with high margin, low volume), evolve into value brands (with low margin, high volume), and eventually degenerate into price brands (with low margin, low volume).[32] For example, the businesses that grew out of the industrial revolution such as those from Germany, France, England, and the U.S., typically began with an invention. They had a proprietary technology and/or patent protection which provided them with high margin but confined them to low volume early on. The high margin was necessary to create positive cash flow and invest in new R&D and plants. Later, their objective shifted to growing sales and becoming mainstream, so they eventually became value brands, and ultimately got commoditized with thin margins as their industries matured. This pattern applied to pharmaceuticals, steel, machinery, gun manufacturing, automobile, and certainly consumer electronics among others.

More specifically, consider again the case of Levi's which was established as a premium brand early on. Rather than remain a specialty niche brand, Levi's chose to go through volume-driven retailers such as JC Penney and Sears for the sake of growth. In the process, it became a volume brand. Volume-driven businesses enjoy good growth; however, their margins collapse. Consequently, Levi's went through vigorous cost-cutting and destroyed its brand equity in the process. The brand was no longer unique or exceptional and eventually became so mainstream that it got commoditized. The end result was the opposite of what it started out as; it became price-sensitive. Overall, such a brand life cycle is very typical and predictable.

The reverse brand cycle is not only fascinating but also very disruptive: a brand that starts out by focusing on price can develop itself into a value brand and ultimately get into the premium segment. The original impetus for the reverse brand cycle approach was sheer necessity. All global premium and value-based markets had established incumbents from developed countries. Thus, EMNCs had to resort to a reverse strategy and focused on the gap in the marketplace based on price competition.

For example, though the Chinese initially emphasized price, they subsequently improved their quality and became value brands. Specifically, Haier started with smaller appliances and wiped out Italian competitors. It then became a full-line appliance company, successfully competing against Electrolux and Whirlpool. Haier's worldwide success put pressure on and served as the impetus for GE's exit from appliances altogether by selling to Haier in a $5.6 billion deal.[33] Today, Haier is the top-selling appliance brand in the world, and Chinese-manufactured products possess the same mass-quality as everyone else. In fact, China, as the *de facto* factory of the world, can manufacture anything from the most low-end to the most premium products; for instance, both uniforms and delicate lingerie are manufactured in China sometimes under the same roof. Other examples of China's manufacturing prowess can be observed in chandeliers, smartphones, telecom equipment, steel, and pharmaceuticals.

As mentioned in an opening example to this section, Indian IT firms' capabilities began with outsourced coding, then moved up to enterprise applications (ERP), and, now, full-service system integration.[34] Similarly, Mahindra & Mahindra of India started by selling small agricultural tractors to the U.S. market (55 HP or less: cost-efficient/fuel-efficient). It emphasized affordability; the vehicles could even be operated as sit-down lawnmowers in large acreage homes. Today, it is competing with John Deere successfully in this niche market. The next stage for this company is to move up-market and become a value market player in the U.S. as John Deere further moves into premium. As an aside, John Deere wishes to host an ecosystem (i.e., MyJohnDeere) of agricultural products/services for its farmers becoming much like what Apple does with its ecosystem for its customers. (In fact, John Deere had already commercialized the first self-driving vehicles in 2004, years before Tesla or Google, and it is estimated that over a third of the crop acreage in North America is handled with such tractors.[35])

Of course, this approach is not new. In fact, this is precisely the strategy Japanese firms have followed in foreign markets. For example, Yamaha entered the U.S. market with low-end small home-use pianos but then demonstrated value and became a formidable competitor to Steinway on the high-end of the market. In the process, it also became the largest piano manufacturer in the world.[36]

Similarly, Datsun 210 was a boxy car with no frills, no A/C, not even heating/cooling on some models; later Nissan was launched as a value brand, and ultimately Infiniti as the luxury brand. Similarly, Honda entered the U.S. with Civic, which was followed by the family sedan Accord, and eventually launched Acura as its luxury brand. Toyota entered the U.S. market with Corolla, then upgraded to Camry (which became the best-selling family Sedan in the competitive mass market), and ultimately launched Lexus as their luxury brand. Today, Toyota is the top-selling auto brand in the world.[37] Korean companies like Samsung and Hyundai went through the same journey in the 1980s.

Now it is the turn for other emerging market firms such as those from Brazil, Russia, Indonesia, and South Africa. Therefore, in the reverse brand life cycle (see Fig. 7.2), brands emphasize price first and value later, and ultimately premium image which is expected to result in better financial performance for EMNCs than when they employ the traditional premium-value-price sequence.

REVERSE BRAND LIFE CYCLE

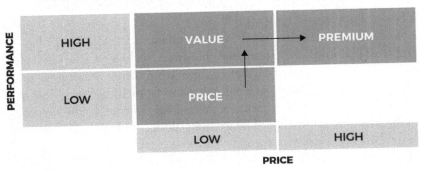

Fig. 7.2 The reverse brand life cycle, (Source: Jagdish N. Sheth presentation on "Global Expansion Strategies of Multinationals from Emerging Markets," 2018)

Emerging Market to Emerging Market to Advanced Markets

As the recent tariff wars between China and the U.S. have shown, jobs are at stake and the sentiment to protect domestic manufacturers remains alive and well even in free-market economies. Even without tariffs, established market incumbents have political clout and lobbying power in their home markets, which serve them well in slowing down new entrants despite free trade agreements in B2C and B2B markets.

Given this impediment, EMNCs have been compelled to go to other emerging markets first, build their scale and international business experience, and then enter advanced markets. This approach is already being practiced by the Chinese very well; Huawei and Xiaomi are prime examples. Huawei started by providing infrastructure for wireless carriers in China (e.g., China Mobile), and they later did the same for carriers in Africa. Once the technology was hardwired, Huawei was able to develop core engineering capabilities as well as understand and obtain experience in diverse markets, climate, and topology. With all that learning curve behind, Huawei aims to earn half of its sales from outside China by 2020 where it already successfully competes against Erickson, Siemens, and Alcatel for wireless infrastructure contracts.

Cell phone maker Xiaomi, with its online-only business model, eliminated a lot of costs initially. Like Apple, they organized an efficient supply chain for manufacturing without engaging in manufacturing themselves. Next, they entered India, broadening their distribution to offline. As Xiaomi builds on that success, it plans to become available in 14 European markets beginning with Spain, France, and Italy soon.[38]

A third case-in-point is Lenovo, which enhanced its position globally after buying IBM's ThinkPad PC franchise. However, its biggest gains in its leadership challenge to Hewlett-Packard came from other emerging markets. Similarly, Godrej is a multinational company from India operating in both B2C and B2B markets. It dominates the market for metal cabinets for home use. Godrej's core competency is not only design but also its lock systems. (Wood cabinets rot easily in Indian climate so metal cabinets are used to keep jewelry, cash, and other valuables.) Godrej is also in mosquito repellents as well as hair care businesses. From India, they went to South Asia, Africa, and Latin America where the climates are similar. In the future, they may enter the U.S. and other advanced markets and compete with leading companies such as S.C. Johnson.

Similarly, IHH of Malaysia which is the largest private health care provider of Southeast Asia also owns Acibadem Healthcare of Turkey and Parkway Pantai of Singapore, each of which also happens to be the largest private health care provider in its country. They also own Continental Hospitals of India.[39] IHH operates in 11 countries including China and the United Arab Emirates among others. Heading West, it acquired Tokuda Hospital in Bulgaria in 2016, and Acibadem launched hospitals in Macedonia and the Netherlands in 2017. After conquering its home market, Mahindra & Mahindra of India has bought a majority stake (80%) in Jiangling Tractors of China in addition to other minority investments and JV efforts. It then focused its attention to advanced markets—Mahindra currently operates five assembly and distribution centers in the U.S. and has been the top-selling manufacturer of tractors worldwide since 2010.[40]

The common denomination here is Walmart founder Sam Walton's "hit them where they ain't" approach. Walmart initially went to small towns that big retailers such as Sears and Kmart ignored.[41] In the process of moving from these rural areas into metro locations, Walmart became the largest retailer in the world.[42] The demand from low population density areas that Walmart aggregated and served can also be aggregated at the income level where the new demand comes from the slums and other underdeveloped, underserved markets. EMNCs can initially focus on less competitive markets and defer attacking the rest until they are ready. Their product and market adaptation in their home markets can provide them with competitive advantages in other emerging markets.[43]

Go Global with Diaspora Markets

EMNCs can follow the lead of their diasporas as an inexpensive way of global expansion. They can simply utilize their home-brand equity; the immigrants grew up with the brand in the home market so many still seek and cherish it in their new homes abroad as well. Examples include Inca Kola (Peru), and Thums Up soft drinks (India). This approach has been tested and holds not only for Chinese and Indian firms but also for the Brazilian, Nigerian, Turkish, and Mexican brands and products.

India has more than 30 million non-residents abroad. Many people go to Gulf countries to work (Saudi Arabia alone is home to 3 million Indians).[44] When IT professionals go to outsourcing assignments and they seek their own food, Udipi, a vegetarian restaurant, takes advantage by following them.

In Los Angeles alone, there are at least 70 communities from around the world that speak their native language, buy their native products including canned products, frozen foods, and fresh produce. Little Saigon feels like Vietnam, and on Pioneer Boulevard in Cerritos you may feel like you are in Mumbai.

The Chinese diaspora in Southeast Asia and around the world is over-whelming. Similar to the Indian diaspora, they have very large communities in San Francisco, New York, Atlanta, Europe, and Latin America. Ali Baba effectively enables Chinese merchants to sell their products anywhere in the world. Following one's diaspora makes for a great starting point in making foreign markets familiar. Kumar and Steenkamp suggest focusing primarily on affluent biculturals and ethnic affirmers based on their high level of desire to maintain home country identity and characteristics.[45]

From Diaspora to Mainstream Markets

The journey may begin with specialty stores/groceries for ethnic groups but then the multinationals can become mainstream through restaurants and supermarkets. For example, Mexican cuisine is well established in the U.S. and tortillas and salsa are in every supermarket in America. Italians have done the same with pasta, pizza, and cheese; Greeks with gyros and yogurt.

In the U.K., Tesco, Sainsbury's, or other mainstream supermarkets offer spicy Pathak pickles. The most consumed convenience food in the U.K. is no longer fish and chips; it is Indian curry (and Pathak pickles go well with it).

Inca Cola, which was started by a British ex-pat couple who moved to Peru in 1935, offers the Latin lifestyle. With its heritage, affordable price, and sweet flavor that complemented the local cuisine well, it achieved 35% market share in the 1980s against Coca-Cola's 21%.[46] Unable to compete successfully, Coca-Cola finally acquired it in 1999 and converted it into a diaspora Latin American culture brand. San Pellegrino of Italy was similarly acquired and converted to a Mediterranean mainstream brand by Nestle. Thums Up of India was bought by Coca-Cola when they re-entered the Indian market. Heineken bought Kingfisher and Tiger beers and could build both to global brands by following their diaspora followers and then going mainstream.

As an aside, the educated members of the diaspora can also become returnees to invest and/or boost innovation in their home countries.[47] There is also the case of reverse diaspora: Deep Foods started in New Jersey where there is a large Indian community. It plans to bring the brand to India for a generation that does not know how to cook. In the meantime, as a leading Indian packaged food producer, it can still go mainstream in the U.S. Several "mainstream stores began stocking frozen Indian entrees like kafta curry, palak paneer, and samosas, many bearing the Deep Foods label."[48] Its Tandoor Chef line is sold across 11,000 retail locations including those by Whole Foods, Kroger, Albertsons, Safeway, and Publix.[49] The company offers hundreds of items for Indian food lovers around the world through Amazon as well as other e-retailers, and estimates to have already captured 60% share of frozen foods across ethnic retailers in the U.S.[50]

Go Global with Key Accounts

This approach involves riding the coattails of your key accounts and expanding with them as they become global. EMNCs' best customers would prefer that their suppliers join them because of established relationships, quality, and value proposition.

For example, Surinder Kapur, the founder of Sona Group, after studying engineering in the U.S., went back to India and started making steering wheels for automobile makers. Toyota was one of Sona's key customers. Since then, Toyota has taken Sona all around the world wherever they started manufacturing. The same pattern is also common in the aerospace sector. As part of geopolitical alignment, companies such as Boeing, Airbus, and Lockheed do not buy from Chinese or Russian companies but instead source from Indian suppliers. Foxconn is similarly going global with clients such as Apple. It is worth noting that the partnership implied here goes beyond low-cost supplier status. The suppliers need to meet and exceed international quality standards to become viable global partners. Xia and colleagues provide evidence from the Chinese context that working with MNCs can help domestic firms to build their own capabilities and increase their propensity to go abroad.[51]

OEM to Branded Products and Services

Branding practice is rooted deep in human history. In thirteenth-century England, bakers, goldsmiths, and silversmiths were required to mark their goods. Papermakers have long used watermarks. Potters' marks were used in China around 1300 BC, and branding of cattle has been practiced since 2000 BC. Overall, the concept of branding may be 5000 years old, with evidence of brand advertising in Babylon dating back to 3000 BC.[52]

Branding is used for products, services, people, and even cities, destinations, and nations.[53] Meanwhile, many products and services still remain unbranded/generic around the globe. The shift in consumer preferences toward branded goods provides a major opportunity, especially for EMNCs. In a traditional bazaar of the agricultural era, offerings such as rice, lentils, and wheat had no branding. Hundreds of years later, as much as 60% of consumption in emerging markets is still through unbranded products and services and a lack of branding is still very prevalent in many emerging markets from the spice market of Istanbul to the boat vendors in Bangkok.[54] On the other hand, snacks that street vendors sell in India are increasingly becoming branded packaged goods, and in the process, markets are created based on selective demand as opposed to generic demand. Branding provides quality assurance and value, but at the same time, it typically does not require new technology; thus, success relies on mostly marketing and quality of execution.

Ultimately, brand equity can be a source of competitive advantage. (In developed economies, most products are already branded; however, the main opportunity is for branding services. For example, hair stylists—especially women's hair saloons are still primarily small store operations, and there are thousands of them. Despite regional efforts, this service remains primarily unorganized and unbranded.)

EMNCs access the market, gain economies of scale, develop a skilled workforce, and put manufacturing excellence in place initially as OEM suppliers, but later as marketers of their own global brands. For example, Global Green has a presence in over 50 countries and fulfills orders for the largest pickle manufacturers around the world. Most pickles sold in the U.S. are not made in California anymore but come from India. As a leading producer of processed vegetables and fruits, Global Green developed the brand Tify for the Indian market, and we expect it to build its brand(s) globally in the future.[55]

We also observe this pattern in the automotive sector: in India and, to a certain extent, in China, turn signals, ignition controls, and steering wheels manufacturers have been moving from OEM to branded offerings. It is also a very common strategy for garment makers. For example, OEM manufacturers from China, Bangladesh, and Caribbean Islands make garments for Manhattan, Van Heusen men's shirts, Arrow shirts, or private store brands. Over time, they can create their own brands and go to market directly.

Finally, moving from OEM to new global branding is also very common in engineering and professional services (e.g., Wipro IT services, SCIS aerospace security services). In particular, we single out EMNC branding based on sustainability position as a potential differentiator in emerging markets, as environmental constraints become more prominent.[56] Being lulled into the comfort of OEM is a mistake if the firm has global aspirations, especially since the relative value-add of manufacturing activities has been decreasing.[57] For example, Taiwanese firms have been criticized for not having the strategic vision to invest in branding and marketing capabilities to complement their early know-how and manufacturing competencies.[58] Therefore, EMNCs that transform themselves from OEM/unbranded offerings to branded products and services perform better than those that do not.

Leverage Skill Advantage

This approach goes back to the Ricardian model of comparative advantage.[59] As discussed earlier, a country or region that has unique skills or resource advantages should put them to use. The Resource-Based View of the firm that has dominated management literature over the last three decades proffers that the resources in question go beyond capital, and must be imperfectly mobile, rare, and hard to imitate at scale.[60] Examples include carpet-making in the Middle East (expert rug-makers), Indian IT services (based on a very large pool of software engineers), and the Philippines (business process outsourcing).

Leveraging its unique local talent, India has become the leading center for diamond cutting in the world, especially for small-size high-volume pieces. Raymond Diamond Tools are respected even in advanced markets. Meanwhile, the cutters located in New York or Antwerp are now specializing in niche markets (larger diamonds). Turkey has utilized its creative talent to become #2 exporter of TV series in the world after the U.S.[61]

Leverage Country-of-Origin Reputation

There is a long lineage of research regarding the country-of-origin effect.[62] To be fair, country-of-origin matters less in a global world where ownership, design, and manufacturing of a product can each reside in different continents around the world. The shirt you buy from a leading U.S. retailer may be contracted to a third party based in Hong Kong, manufactured in Singapore with fabric from Pakistan and buttons and zippers from Japan. Consumers do not even recognize the country of origin of many household brands as in the case of Haagen-Dazs or Haier. Nevertheless, country-of-origin still remains an important factor in many product categories such as Caribbean rum, (French) Champagne, Russian vodka, Mexican beers, Swiss chocolate or watches, Egyptian cotton, Cuban cigars, or Turkish tobacco. To the extent that a country of origin advantage is applicable, it represents a form of resource that can be utilized by EMNCs.[63] Japan, for example, was able to overcome its quality gap in consumer goods following World War II under the leaders such as Akio Morita (Sony) and Kiichiro Toyoda (Toyota). Today, "Made in Japan" is perceived favorably worldwide unequivocally, especially for electronics. The importance of country-of-origin can also vary by market. For example, Russian consumers are known to put considerable weight on the country-of-origin over the brand name for their purchases.[64]

Leverage Domestic Scale Advantage

With this approach, the EMNC dominates its home market first and then goes global. Country-specific resource advantages are assumed to be available to all firms operating in a given country. In reality, EMNCs enjoy advantages in their home countries that other MNCs do not due to protectionism, brand equity, or customer-centricity.[65] For example, the largest tobacco company in the world is China National Tobacco Corporation which is responsible for a third of global production. While it focused on its enormous domestic market for much of its history, it is currently expanding into select foreign markets.[66]

Reliance which started out as a modest polyester producer in 1966, was renamed Reliance Industries in 1973, later diversifying into financial services, refining, and energy. It has recently surpassed ExxonMobil to become #2 most valuable energy firm in the world second only to Saudi Aramco.[67]

Additional examples include telecommunications and flour:

Telecom: China Mobile is the largest cellular network operator in the world, even bigger than Vodafone. It is now expanding outside of China to Southeast Asia (e.g., Vietnam, Cambodia, Thailand, and Indonesia). Airtel of India is also going global.

Flour: Grupo Bimbo, the world's largest baking company, began as a small bakery in Mexico City in 1945. After dominating the home market until the 1980s, the company began exporting to the U.S. in 1984. It eventually became the largest flour maker in the U.S. through acquisitions.[68]

Home-country location advantages (such as scale enabled by market size) can be critical for the success of EMNCs.[69]

Reverse Innovation

The R&D engines of MNCs have traditionally been geared toward high quality/margin innovations. Reverse innovation changes this traditional focus of innovation from the developed markets, superior performance, and convenience, to emerging markets, affordability, and accessibility.[70]

Despite the enormous latent demand, consumers in emerging markets cannot afford the products/services or access them through the existing distribution infrastructure. Thus, it is imperative for EMNCs to invent for the local market with acceptable quality using "business models that provide truly beneficial products and services to the poor at prices they can afford."[71]

Consider the case of battery-operated medical instruments. These days companies like HP, GE, Siemens, or Phillips move their R&D to India or China to learn how to make more affordable (in some cases by a factor of 10) but profitable products.[72] These MNCs can then take the invention and offer the same product in rural, small-town hospitals in developed markets such as those in the U.S. These are patients who cannot afford expensive products that are designed for a system where the cost is covered by insurance.

There is an untapped opportunity to serve disadvantaged consumer markets even in advanced economies.[73] Consider the startling statistic that nearly two-thirds of Americans live paycheck-to-paycheck and approximately 40% have less than $400 in the bank for emergency expenses.[74]

There is a large opportunity for EMNCs to come up with significant innovations to serve the base of the pyramid. Most already have the domestic market scale advantage; it is only a matter of time for them to combine scale with speed, and serve these customers affordably. This advantage led to the birth of Japanese conglomerates historically; now EMNCs can follow a similar approach. Consumers in emerging markets may skip stages in adopting e-commerce due to necessity, and they are even ahead of developed markets in adoption in some cases, which further boosts the accessibility of new products/services.[75] M-Pesa from Kenya mentioned earlier is an example of this.

Interestingly, price-led costing that reverse innovation is based on "is an American invention...GE's turbines and transformers...designed from the price the customer could pay and was willing to pay; and so the customer could and did buy them."[76] "Under price-led costing, the entire economic framework focuses upon creating value for the customer and meeting cost targets while earning the necessary rate of return on investment."[77] Drastic cost reductions, hybrid solutions, scalable and transportable solutions, eco-friendly products, radical redesign, process innovation, de-skilled work/services, customer education in product usage, adaptability to extreme environments, adaptable user interfaces, and a broad architecture that enables quick changes are some of the pathways through which reverse innovations can be realized.[78]

For example, Reliance Jio (a subsidiary of Reliance Industries) has disrupted the mobile telecom market in India in just a few years. Jio bypassed the obsolete 2G and 3G technologies and invested in an Long Term Evolution (LTE) network that covers all of the urban population and 85% of the population of India overall. "The result is a high-quality mobile network that has gained about 15% market share and carries some 1.7 billion gigabytes of data traffic every month (the highest rate in the world) at the lowest prices in the world: 0.05 rupees/MB."[79] When it launched in 2016, the company also offered free trials and plans for under $1 per month.[80] (One U.S. dollar is about 75 Indian Rupees as of July 2020.)

EMNCs have become dominant players for generic drugs and are able to sell their products in advanced markets as well. Governments and insurance companies are promoting the prescription and use of generic drugs due to their affordability.

Focus Regionally

If an EMNC does not have sufficient resources to expand globally via major acquisitions, then they can expand regionally through greenfield investments. For example, Turkey, hopeful of ultimately integrating to the EU one day, has traditionally focused on the European markets where it also has a large diaspora. Vestel Electronics captured a quarter of the European television market by producing on an OEM basis for a large number of distributors.[81] Historically, Russia has also been a large customer of Turkish branded products.

Likewise, South Africa has made similar forays in Africa, and Brazil has done the same in Latin America. The link to the chosen region can be based on geographic, cultural, socio-economic, or socio-political proximity or other market-based characteristics for specializing EMNCs. Therefore, resource-constrained EMNCs that focus regionally are expected to perform better than those that do not.

Focus and Make Acquisitions in Advanced and Mature Markets

Hindalco, India's largest aluminum producer, acquired Novelis for $6 billion in 2007.[82] Novelis, headquartered in Atlanta, Georgia, was the global leader in beverage can recycling and a leading producer of rolled aluminum. It was spun off from Alcan of Canada, whose stature was akin to Alcoa in the U.S. (the Canadian Government mandated that Alcan break up for antitrust reasons, and a separate company, Novelis, was formed in 2005). Aditya Birla Group, which owns Hindalco, also bought Columbian Chemicals and became the largest producer of carbon black (a widely used industrial raw material) in the world based on the combined market sizes of India and the U.S.[83]

Heinz and Kraft were bought by a partnership between Brazil's 3G Capital and Warren Buffet's Berkshire Hathaway and then merged together in 2015. This global merger created the third-largest food and beverage company in North America and the fifth-largest food and beverage company in the world. Heinz-Kraft might go after Campbell, General Mills, Kellogg, or ironically even Mondelez (a previous spin-off of Kraft) next.[84]

SAB's acquisition of Miller and InBev's original bid for Anheuser-Busch can be considered in this category. Turkish Yildiz Group acquired Godiva Chocolate in 2007. Similarly, Grupo Bimbo of Mexico made acquisitions in the U.S. to reinforce and solidify their flour business, and Raymond from India has bought garment design houses in France and Spain.

Some shareholders, as well as scholars, have been puzzled that EMNCs make large acquisitions in areas where they lack competitive advantages and legitimacy.[85]

It has been suggested that EMNCs use acquisitions to catch-up with MNCs on technology.[86] We believe that the reason for the surge in acquisitions[87] is more basic: EMNCs seek access to global markets, and these legacy businesses tend to be available at reasonable prices. EMNCs are typically encouraged by their governments to become global and the urgency to show progress usually manifests itself in large acquisitions instead of painstaking organic entry and growth.[88] Upon acquisition, EMNCs leverage their combined resources and infuse their entrepreneurial spirit into these mature sectors.[89] (We observe that MNCs will be challenged to replicate this EMNC entrepreneurial spirit at scale.) If Uber, Tesla, or Netflix were up for sale at reasonable P/E multiples and the government did not object, EMNCs would be buyers of them too.

EMNCs also invest in advanced complementary capabilities when possible. For example, Jain Irrigation (India) acquired Observant (Australia) for its farm information management platforms; Midea Group (China) acquired KUKA (Germany) which manufactures robots and Servotronix (Israel) for its AI-based automation systems; Zoomlion (China) acquired m-tec (Germany) for its accelerated building processes; Tianqi Lithium (China) acquired a controlling stake in Windfield, which is parent to Talison Lithium, the world's largest lithium producer.[90] Roughly 20% of the $200 billion that Chinese firms spent in global acquisitions in 2016 were spent on technology firms.[91]

More typically, however, acquisitions in mature markets involve acquiring established companies with great brands, human resources, technology assets, in low growth, low margin, commoditized industries with typically depressed asset prices. The original owners want to divest, and EMNCs are happy to oblige; essentially, this relationship is an example of Ricardo's comparative advantage theory (which we also refer to as a theory of vacating markets) in practice.

Competitive Advantages of EMNCs in Executing Identified Strategies

In sum, competition from EMNCs is real and is not limited to China. The strategies we have outlined are not mutually exclusive. There is no single model of global expansion but rather a wide range of options from flanking to domestic scale/skill advantages to leveraging key customers and diaspora ecosystems. The two strategies that provide the most sustainable futures for EMNCs are acquisitions in mature legacy industries where advanced market multinationals have already exited or are seeking to exit (a sunset mindset exists for incumbents in many mature industries in the U.S., Japan, Scandinavia, and Germany), and the reverse brand life cycle.

While the most common pattern will be one globally dominant player from each of the largest markets of China, India, and the U.S., it is possible for one nation to dominate an entire sector if it has a distinct operand (knowledge and skills) and operant resource (tangible factors of production such as land and equipment) advantage. Brand equity and/or concentration of capital in a sector can also lead to a similar outcome.

For example, the U.S. historically dominated the soft drinks and mainframe computer markets, and China may soon dominate telecom manufacturing. Of course, this does not mean that this outcome is inevitable and multinationals elsewhere should give up on building resource advantages. Australia can take the lead in pockets of mining with further global investment. The delicate balance between free trade and protectionism will surely preserve ample space for multinationals from emerging markets in the coming decades. In Table 7.1, we recap the *differential* advantages of EMNCs.

Meanwhile, many EMNCs such as those from Mexico, Brazil, China, and India are still ethnocentric. Successfully transitioning to a transnational culture represents the key challenge to their long-term success. Many of the EMNCs are rooted in trading and favor push over pull strategies, and intuition over marketing research.[92] This mentality must change to prevail in higher-margin sectors.

Table 7.1 Differential advantages of EMNCs

Differential advantages
Flanking advantage: EMNCs foray into advanced markets and flank competition using the reverse brand lifecycle.
Diaspora advantage: The greater the diaspora, the greater the advantage for the EMNCs to eventually go mainstream.
Customer advantage: EMNCs can benefit from the patronage of their key customer(s). They can go global with their key accounts, eventually, learn how to market and distribute globally themselves, and offer their own branded products and services.
Cost advantage: EMNCs have access to skilled workforce at reasonable cost. Some also benefit from the scale of their domestic markets.
Home turf advantage: EMNCs can engage in reverse innovation since they know the realities of their consumer markets better than foreign MNCs and utilize country-of-origin reputation.
Geopolitical advantage: The importance of this factor cannot be overstated. Markets are shaped as much by country relationships as they are by free markets; for example, India has a significant advantage over China for access to the U.S. Geopolitics enables certain firms to easily obtain a beachhead, and subsequently, EMNCs can follow up with investments by buying out mature companies. Governments also encourage their firms to engage where geopolitical alignments are favorable.

Source: Jagdish N. Sheth presentation on "Global Expansion Strategies of Multinationals from Emerging Markets," 2018

The Ultimate Prize: Consolidate Resources to Prevail as a Global Leader

An appropriate constellation of resources is critical for recognizing opportunities and entrepreneurial action[93] and is vital for any type of firm to become dominant. As mentioned above, operant resources (knowledge and skills) and operand resources (tangible factors of production such as land and equipment) can both be sources of differentiation and competitive advantage.[94] However, in certain sectors such as mining, it is not possible to become a global player without tangible resources. Furthermore, due to unprecedented demand from emerging markets and increasing sustainability concerns, there will be natural resource shortages, and commodity prices are likely to fluctuate in the twenty-first century.[95] Hence, we posit that MNCs will need to aggregate both operant and operand (natural) resources in order to prevail as global leaders in the long run. For example, Apple is not likely to remain a global generalist by relying solely on its vast operant resources, as operand resource-rich EMNCs from China and India build their own operant resources and close in. Apple is destined to become a very profitable global specialist unless it changes its strategy. Even sharing economy players proudly devoid of physical assets (such as Airbnb and Uber) will need to operate their own locations/fleets in key markets to keep up with demand, competition, or regulation. However, these are "first-world" problems.

For EMNCs, it is imperative to gather operant resources quickly to succeed as global leaders. Success in developed markets necessitates the use of indirect learning more than direct learning.[96] In the short run, EMNCs' dominance will be most apparent in sectors where operand resources are dominant (e.g., mining and palm oil). Over time, EMNCs will challenge global leadership sectors where both operand and operant resources are critical (automobiles, high-end consumer electronics). In these sectors, we may see global leadership shared between MNCs and EMNCs. The last frontier will be sectors where primarily operant resources are sufficient (AI); these sectors may be where MNCs have the best chance of holding on to their turfs. However, even here we expect the emergence of global players from EMNCs within the next decade. EMNCs that aggregate operand *and* operant resources the fastest will emerge as global leaders. By the end of the century, EMNCs from today's emerging markets will tend to occupy two (and in some cases all top three) leadership spots across all global markets.

"In the 'underdeveloped' countries of the world, the more 'glamorous' fields such as manufacturing or construction are generally highlighted while marketing is treated with neglect … Yet marketing holds a key position in these countries … Marketing is also the most effective engine of economic development."[97] Drucker's words ring true today as much as they did six decades ago.

Opportunities for EMNCs include retail, fast-moving consumer goods, micro-finance, telecom, affordable housing, and agri-business, and will increasingly involve artificial intelligence, health- and wellness-oriented foods, health care, education, pharmaceuticals, energy, and transportation. Taking advantage of these opportunities will require an innovation sandbox approach (new product development with constraints), emphasis on scalability, price-based costing, modern technology, and global standards (quality, safety, as well as sustainability).[98] Resource scarcity will drive major technology breakthroughs, such as cloning and nanotechnologies, where key drivers of innovation will be affordability and accessibility of products, technologies, and services. Policy-makers need to ensure that there is access to opportunities and not let wealth inequality get extreme. Once again, we think EMNCs may be the solution to the world's challenges.

Key Takeaways
- Globalization has generated economic prosperity on a mass scale, creating more employment, innovation, infrastructure, and trade.
- Emerging markets are home to 85% of the world's population, and they collectively generated over 80% of the world's economic growth since 2008. One-third of the world's largest "unicorns" (companies exceeding $1 billion in market value) hail from emerging markets.
- The infrastructure, regulatory, socio-economic, socio-political, technological, and cultural systems in emerging markets are drastically different. We assert that their business and marketing strategies have been and should be different from those of the traditional conglomerates of the world in order to succeed.
- The Ricardian logic also applies to today's wave of outsourcing.
- The competitive strategies of multinationals from emerging markets include:

  – Reverse brand cycle
  – Emerging market to emerging market to advanced markets

(continued)

(continued)

- Going global with diaspora markets, from diaspora to mainstream markets
- Going global with key accounts
- OEM to branded products and services, leveraging skill advantages
- Leveraging country-of-origin reputation
- Leveraging domestic scale advantage
- Reverse innovation
- Focusing regionally
- Focusing and making acquisitions in advanced and mature markets

- Differential Advantages of EMNCs include:

  - Flanking Advantage
  - Diaspora Advantage
  - Customer Advantage
  - Cost Advantage
  - Home Turf Advantage
  - Geopolitical Advantage

- Competition from EMNCs is real and is not limited to China. There is no single model of global expansion but rather a wide range of options. The two strategies that provide the most sustainable futures for EMNCs are acquisitions in mature legacy industries where advanced market multinationals have already exited or are seeking to exit, and the reverse brand lifecycle.
- In the short run, EMNCs' dominance will be most apparent in sectors where operand resources are dominant (e.g., mining and palm oil). Over time, EMNCs will challenge global leadership sectors where both operand and operant resources are critical (automobiles, high-end consumer electronics). In these sectors, we may see global leadership shared between MNCs and EMNCs. The last frontier will be sectors where primarily operant resources are sufficient (AI); these sectors may be where MNCs have the best chance of holding on to their turfs. However, even here, we expect the emergence of global players from EMNCs within the next decade.

Notes

1. Pankaj Ghemawat (in Cuervo-Cazurra and Ramamurti 2014).
   Cuervo-Cazurra, A. & Ramamurti, R. (2014), *Understanding Multinationals from Emerging Markets*. Cambridge University Press.
2. Drucker, P. F. (2001), "The next society," *The Economist*, (November 3), 3–20.
   Ghemawat, P. & Altman, S. A. (2016). DHL global connectedness index 2016: The state of globalization in an age of ambiguity. http://www.dhl.com/en/about_us/logistics_insights/studies_research/global_connectedness_index/global_connectedness_index.html#.VFff5MkpXuM.
3. Cavusgil, S. Tamer & Cavusgil, Erin (2012), "Reflections on International Marketing: Destructive Regeneration and Multinational Firms," *Journal of the Academy of Marketing Science*, 40, 202–217.
   Sheth, Jagdish N. (2011), "Impact of Emerging Markets on Marketing: Rethinking Existing Perspectives and Practices." *Journal of Marketing*, 75 (July), 166–182.
4. Vazquez, K. C (2018), "Can the BRICS Propose a New Development Paradigm?", July 25, 2018, accessed on September 27, 2019. https://www.aljazeera.com/indepth/opinion/brics-propose-development-para-digm-180718121646771.html.
5. Sheth, Jagdish N. and Rajendra S. Sisodia (2006), *Tectonic Shift: The Geoeconomic Realignment of Globalizing Markets*. Thousand Oaks: Sage.
6. Lagarde, C. (2016), "The Role of Emerging Markets in a New Global Partnership for Growth," IMF.org, February 4, 2016, accessed July 26, 2020. https://www.imf.org/en/News/Articles/2015/09/28/04/53/sp020416.
7. BCG Global Challengers (2018), "Digital Leapfrogs," accessed September 28, 2019. https://www.bcg.com/publications/collections/2018-global-chal-lengers-digital-leapfrogs.aspx.
8. Achrol, R. S. and Kotler, P. (2012), "Frontiers of the Marketing Paradigm in the Third Millennium," *Journal of the Academy of Marketing Science*, 40, 35–52.
   Pels, J. & Sheth J. N. (2017), "Business Models to Serve Low-Income Consumers in Emerging Markets," *Marketing Theory*, 17(3), 373–391.
9. Cuervo-Cazurra, A. and Ramamurti, R. (2014). *Understanding Multinationals from Emerging Markets*. Cambridge University Press.
   Ramamurti, R. & Singh, J. V. (2009). *Emerging Multinationals in Emerging Markets*. Cambridge University Press.
10. Banerjee, S., Prabhu, J. C., & Chandy, R.K. (2015), "Indirect Learning: How Emerging Market Firms Grow in Developed Markets," *Journal of Marketing*, 79(1), 10–28.
    Ancarani, F., Frels, J. K., Miller, J., Saibene, C, & Barberio, M. (2014), "Winning in Rural Emerging Markets: General Electric's Research Study on MNCs," *California Management Review*, 56(4), 31–52.
    Tsai, H-T & Eisingerich, A. B. (2010), "Internationalization Strategies of Emerging Markets Firms," *California Management Review*, 53(1), 114–135.

11. Spector, M. & Bellman, E. (2008), "Tata and Ford Reach Deal for Land Rover, Jaguar," *The Wall Street Journal*, March 27, 2008, accessed July 26, 2020. https://www.wsj.com/articles/SB120652768989365191.
12. Klesty, V. (2010), "Geely Signs $1.8 Billion Deal for Ford's Volvo Car Unit," Reuters, March 28, 2010, accessed July 26, 2020. https://www.reuters.com/article/us-volvo-geely/geely-signs-1-8-billion-deal-for-fords-volvo-car-unit-idUSTRE62Q1F520100328.
13. Kurmanath, KV (2018), "Nasscom Pegs Growth Rate for 2018–19 at 7–9%" February 20, 2018, accessed July 12, 2020. https://www.thehindubusinessline.com/info-tech/nasscom-pegs-growth-for-2018-19-at-7-9/article22804578.ece.
14. BCG Global Challengers (2018), "Digital Leapfrogs," accessed September 28, 2019. https://www.bcg.com/publications/collections/2018-global-challengers-digital-leapfrogs.aspx.
    Tata Consultancy Services (2019), "TCS Q4 FY 2018–19 Financial Results," April 12, 2019, accessed on September 29, 2019. https://www.tcs.com/tcs-financial-results-q4-fy-2019.
15. India Brand Equity Foundation (2019), "IT & ITeS," IBEF.org, April 2019, accessed July 12, 2020. https://www.ibef.org/download/it-ites-apr-2019.pdf.
16. CNNMoney (2002), "SAB Buys Miller brewing," CNNMoney, May 30, 2002, accessed July 26, 2020. http://money.cnn.com/2002/05/30/news/deals/miller_sab/.
17. The Boston Globe (2004), "Beer Firms Interbrew, Ambev Merge," The Boston Globe, March 4, 2004, accessed July 26, 2020. http://archive.boston.com/business/articles/2004/03/04/beer_firms_interbrew_ambev_merge/.
18. De la Merced, M. J. (2008), "Anheuser-Busch Agrees to be Sold to InBev," *New York Times*, July 14, 2008, accessed July 26, 2020. https://www.nytimes.com/2008/07/14/business/worldbusiness/14beer.html.
19. Snider, M. (2016), "DOJ Approves Anheuser-Busch InBev's $107 Billion Deal for SABMiller," *USA Today*, July 20, 2016, accessed July 26, 2020. https://www.usatoday.com/story/money/business/2016/07/20/report-doj-ok-ab-inbev-sabmiller-deal/87347546/.
20. Reuters (2019), "Go-Jek raises $1 billion in round led by Google, Tencent, JD," February 1, accessed September 28, 2019. https://www.reuters.com/article/us-go-jek-indonesia-fundraising/go-jek-raises-1-billion-in-round-led-by-google-tencent-jd-idUSKCN1PQ4BY.
    Ghoshal, Abhimanyu (2018), "Uber's Southeast Asia Operations Acquired by Grab," March 26, accessed September 2019. https://thenextweb.com/asia/2018/03/26/ubers-southeast-asia-operations-acquired-by-grab/.
21. Russell, Jon (2018), "Grab Picks up $2 Billion More To Fuel Growth in Post-Uber Southeast Asia," August 1, 2018, accessed September 28, 2019. https://techcrunch.com/2018/08/01/grab-picks-up-2-billion/.

22. Luo, Y., & Tung, R.L. (2007), "International Expansion of Emerging Market Enterprises: A Springboard Perspective," *Journal of International Business Studies, 38*(4), 481–498.

   Fey, C. F., Nayak, A. K. J. R., Wu, C., & Zhou, A J. (2016), "Internationalization Strategies of Emerging Market Multinationals," *Journal of Leadership & Organizational Studies, 23*(2), 128–143.

23. Ricardo, D. (1821). *On the Principles of Political Economy and Taxation.* Third ed. John Murray, Albemarle-Street, London.

24. Sheth, J. N., & Sisodia, R. S. (2006). *Tectonic shift: The Geoeconomic Realignment of Globalizing Markets,* Thousand Oaks: Sage.

25. Sheth, J. N. (2004), "Making India Globally Competitive," *Vikalpa, 29*(4), 2 (October–December).

26. Sheth, Jagdish N., Can Uslay, and Rajendra S. Sisodia (2008), "The Globalization of Markets and the Rule of Three," in *Marketing Metaphors and Metamorphosis,* Philip J. Kitchen, Ed. London, UK: Palgrave Macmillan, 26–41, pp. 30–31.

27. Sun Journal (2006), "Mittal Bids $33B on Arcelor," Sun Journal, June 26, 2006, accessed July 12, 2020. http://www.sunjournal.com/mittal-bids-33b-arcelor/.

28. Tao, T., De Cremer, D., & Chunbo, W. (2018), *Huawei: Leadership, Culture, and Connectivity.* Sage Publications.

   BCG Global Challengers (2018), "Digital Leapfrogs," accessed September 28, 2019. https://www.bcg.com/publications/collections/2018-global-challengers-digital-leapfrogs.aspx.

29. Sinkovics, R. R., Yamin, M., Nadvi, K., Zhang, Y. (2014), "Rising Powers from Emerging Markets—the Changing Face of International Business," *International Business Review, 23*(4), 675–679.

30. Ramamurti, R. (2009), "The Theoretical Value of Studying Indian Multinationals," *Indian Journal of Industrial Relations, 45*(1), 101–114.

31. Bivainiene, L. (2010), "Brand Life Cycle: Theoretical Discourses," *Journal of Economics & Management. 15*, 408–414.

32. Tellis, G. J. (1988), "The Price Elasticity of Selective Demand: A Meta-Analysis of Econometric Models of Sales," *Journal of Marketing Research,* 25 (November), 331–341.

33. CBSNews (2016), "GE Selling Home Appliance Business to Chinese Company," CBSNews, January 15, 2016, accessed July 12, 2020. http://www.cbsnews.com/news/general-electric-co-selling-ge-appliance-chinese-haier-group-china/.

34. Gopalkrishnan, R. I, Sheth, J. N. & Sharma, A. (2012), "The Resurgence of India: Triumph of Institutions over Infrastructure?" *Journal of Macromarketing, 32*(3), 309–318.

35. Peterson, Andrea (2015), "Google Didn't Lead the Self-Driving Vehicle Revolution. John Deere Did," *The Washington Post,* June 22, 2015, accessed

September 28, 2019. https://www.washingtonpost.com/news/the-switch/wp/2015/06/22/google-didnt-lead-the-self-driving-vehicle-revolution-john-deere-did/.

NASA (2018), "How NASA and John Deere Helped Tractors Drive Themselves," April 18, accessed September 28, 2019. https://www.nasa.gov/feature/directorates/spacetech/spinoff/john_deere.

36. Yu, Howard (2018), *Leap: How to Thrive in a World Where Everything Can be Copied*, New York, PublicAffairs.

37. Braithwaite-Smith, G. (2018), "Revealed: The Biggest Car Brands in the World 2017," MotoringResearch, February 21, 2018, accessed July 26, 2020. https://www.motoringresearch.com/car-news/features/biggest-car-brands-2017/.

38. Russell, J. (2018), "Xiaomi Goes After Global Markets with Two New Android One Phones," TechCrunch, July 24, 2018, accessed July 26, 2020. https://techcrunch.com/2018/07/24/xiaomi-mi-a2-mi-a2-lite/.

39. BCG Global Challengers (2018), "Digital Leapfrogs," accessed September 28, 2019. https://www.bcg.com/publications/collections/2018-global-challengers-digital-leapfrogs.aspx.

40. Wikipedia (2019), "Mahindra Tractors," accessed on September 28, 2019. https://en.wikipedia.org/wiki/Mahindra_Tractors.

41. Rumelt, R. (2011), *Good Strategy, Bad Strategy*, New York: NY, Random House.

42. However, now Walmart may have to leave the crown to Amazon because it has a legacy-oriented IT architecture and is falling behind. In the banking and financial service industries, the banks are falling behind their online lending counterparts. Similarly, Airbnb and Uber have gained advantage over the incumbents in a very short period of time.

43. Cuervo-Cazurra, & Ramamurti, R. (2017), "Home Country Underdevelopment and Internationalization: Innovation-based and Escape-based Internationalization," *Competitiveness Review: An International Business Journal, 27* (3), 217–230.

44. Bagchi, I. (2017), "Number of Indians Heading to Gulf Countries Falls, Remittances Dip," *Times of India*, July 24, 2017, accessed July 26, 2020. https://timesofindia.indiatimes.com/india/number-of-indians-heading-to-gulf-countries-falls-remittances-dip/articleshow/59729926.cms.

45. Kumar, N. & Steenkamp, J-B, E. M. (2013), "Diaspora Marketing," *Harvard Business Review*. 127–131 (October).

46. Knowledge@Wharton (2012), "Branding Lessons from Inca Kola, the Peruvian Soda that bested Coca-Cola," October 3, 2012, accessed July 26, 2020. http://knowledge.wharton.upenn.edu/article/branding-lessons-from-inca-kola-the-peruvian-soda-that-bested-coca-cola/.

47. Gillespie, K., Riddle, L., Sayre, E. & Sturges, D., (1999), "Diaspora Interest in Homeland Investment," *Journal of International Business Studies, 30*(3), 623–634.

Li, H., Zhang, Y., Li, Y., Zhou, L, & Zhang, W. (2012). Returnees versus Locals: Who Perform Better in China's Technology Entrepreneurship? *Strategic Entrepreneurship Journal, 6*(3), 257–272.

48. Nathan, Joan (2003), "From a Deep-Fryer in a Garage to an Indian Food Empire," The New York Times, April 23, accessed September 28, 2019. https://www.nytimes.com/2003/04/23/dining/from-a-deep-fryer-in-a-garage-to-an-indian-food-empire.html?pagewanted=all&src=pm.

49. Ortenberg, Carol (2019), "40 Years In, Deep Plans for the Next Decade," Nosh.com, May 16, accessed September 28, 2019. https://www.nosh.com/news/2019/40-years-in-deep-plans-for-the-next-decade.

50. Ortenberg, Carol (2019), "40 Years In, Deep Plans for the Next Decade," Nosh.com, May 16, accessed September 28, 2019. https://www.nosh.com/news/2019/40-years-in-deep-plans-for-the-next-decade.

51. Xia, J., Ma, X., Lu, J.W., & Yiu D.W. (2013), "Outward Foreign Direct Investment by Emerging Market Firms: A Resource Dependence Logic," *Strategic Management Journal, 35*(9), 1343–1363.

52. VanAuken, B. (2006). History of Branding, August 14. http://www.brandingstrategyinsider.com/2006/08/history_of_bran.html.

53. Bayraktar, Ahmet and Can Uslay (2016), *Strategic Place Branding Methodologies and Theory for Tourist Attraction,* edited book, Hershey, PA: IGI Global, 326 pages.

    Bayraktar, Ahmet and Can Uslay (2016), *Global Place Branding Campaigns across Cities, Regions, and Nations*, edited book, Hershey, PA: IGI Global, 346 pages.

    Cicek, Mesut, Sevincgul Ulu, and Can Uslay (2019), "The Impact of the Slow City Movement on Place Authenticity, Entrepreneurial Opportunity, and Economic Development," *Journal of Macromarketing,* 39 (4), 400–414.

54. Sheth, J. N. (2011a), "Impact of Emerging Markets on Marketing: Rethinking Existing Perspectives and Practices," *Journal of Marketing,* 75 (July), 166–182.

55. The Global Green Company (2019), "Our Story," accessed July 26, 2020. https://globalgreengroup.com/our-story/.

56. Sheth, J. N. & Sinha, M. (2015), "B2B Branding in Emerging Markets: A Sustainability Perspective," *Industrial Marketing Management, 51,* 79–88.

57. Birnik, A., Birnik, A-K., and Sheth, J. N. (2010), "The Branding Challenges of Asian Manufacturing Firms," *Business Horizons,* 53, 523–532.

58. Yu, H. N. & Shih, W. C. (2014), "Taiwan's PC Industry, 1976–2010: The Evolution of Organizational Capabilities," *Business History Review.* 88(2), 329–357.

59. Maneschi, A. (1998). *Comparative Advantage in International Trade: A Historical Perspective*. Cheltenham, Elgar.

    Cuervo-Cazurra, Luo, Y., Ramamurti, R., & Ang, S. H. (2018), "The Impact of the Home Country on Internationalization," *Journal of World Business, 53*(5), 593–604.

60. Kozlenkova, I.V., Samaha, S. A., & Palmatier R.W. (2014), "Resource-based Theory in Marketing," *Journal of the Academy of Marketing Science, 42*, 1–21 (April).

Barney, J. B. (1996), "The Resource-Based Theory of the Firm," *Organization Science*, 7, 469.

Hunt, S. D., & Morgan, R. M. (1996), "The Resource-Advantage Theory of Competition: Dynamics, Path Dependencies, and Evolutionary Dimensions," *Journal of Marketing*, 60, 107–114.

Barney, J. B. (1991), "Firm Resources and Sustained Competitive Advantage," *Journal of Management*, 17, 99–120.

61. Avundukluoglu, E. (2017), "Turkey Ranks Second in TV Series Exports," Anadolu Agency, November 17, 2017, accessed July 12, 2020. https://www.aa.com.tr/en/culture-and-art/turkey-ranks-second-in-tv-series-exports-minister/967731.

62. Balabanis, G., & Diamantopoulos, A. (2004), "Domestic Country Bias, Country-of-Origin Effects, and Consumer Ethnocentrism: A Multidimensional Unfolding Approach," *Journal of the Academy of Marketing Science*, 32(1), 80–95.

Maier, R. & Wilken, R. (2017), "Broad and Narrow Country-of-Origin Effects and the Domestic Country Bias," *Journal of Global Marketing*, 30(4), 256–274.

63. Cuervo-Cazurra, Luo, Y., Ramamurti, R., & Ang, S. H. (2018), "The Impact of the Home Country on Internationalization," *Journal of World Business*, 53(5), 593–604.

64. Prema, Nakra (2015), "Should You Care about Country of Origin Impact," August 24, accessed September 28, 2019. https://www.shippingsolutions.com/blog/should-you-care-about-country-of-origin-impact.

65. Hennart, J-F. (2012), "Emerging Market Multinationals and the Theory of the Multinational Enterprise," *Global Strategy Journal*, 2(3), 168–187.

66. Fang, J., Lee, K., & Sejpal, N. (2017). The China National Tobacco Corporation: From domestic to global dragon? *Global Public Health*. 12(3), 315–334.

67. Livemint (2020), "RIL is World's 2nd Most Valuable Energy Firm," Livemint, July 24, 2020, accessed July 25, 2020. https://www.livemint.com/companies/news/reliance-breaks-into-top-50-most-valued-companies-globally-ranks-48-11595506817920.html.

68. Caruso-Cabrera, M. (2013). Grupo Bimbo: Meet the Mexican CEO who made your English muffin. CNBC.com, https://www.cnbc.com/id/100798699.

69. Narula, R. & Santagelo, G. D. (2012), "Location and Collocation Advantages in International Innovation," *Multinational Business Review*, 20(1), 6–25.

Ramamurti, R. (2009), "The Theoretical Value of Studying Indian Multinationals," *Indian Journal of Industrial Relations*, 45(1), 101–114.

70. Immelt, J., Govindrajan, V., & Trimble, C. (2009), "How GE is disrupting itself," *Harvard Business Review*, 87, 56–65 (October).
71. Karnani, A. (2011). *Fighting Poverty Together*. New York, Palgrave Macmillan p. 17.
72. Ramamurti, R. & Govindarajan, V. (2018). *Reverse Innovation in Health Care: How to Make Value-Based Delivery Work*. Harvard Business School Press.
73. Ramamurti, R. & Govindarajan, V. (2018). *Reverse Innovation in Health Care: How to Make Value-Based Delivery Work*. Harvard Business School Press.
74. Soo Youn (2019), "40% of Americans Don't Have $400 in the Bank for Emergency Expenses: Federal Reserve," ABC News, May 24, 2019, accessed June 27, 2020. https://abcnews.go.com/US/10-americans-struggle-cover-400-emergency-expense-federal/story?id=63253846.
75. Rajaretnam, J. & Sheth, J. N. (2017), "A Multi-Stage Model of Adoption of Online Buying in India," *Journal of Global Marketing*, *31*(2), 60–72.
76. Drucker, P.F. (1995). *Managing in a Time of Great Change*. Truman Talley/E.P. Dutton, pp. 47–48.
77. Drucker, P.F. (1999). *Management Challenges for the 21st Century*. New York: Harper Collins, p. 115.
78. Prahalad, C. K. (2004). *Fortune at the Bottom of the Pyramid: Eradicating Poverty through Profits*. Upper Saddle River, NJ: Prentice Hall.
79. BCG Global Challengers (2018), "Digital Leapfrogs," accessed September 28, 2019.
    https://www.bcg.com/publications/collections/2018-global-challengers-digital-leapfrogs.aspx, p. 17.
80. Ang, Carmen (2020), "What Does 1GB of Mobile Data Cost in Every Country?" Visual Capitalist, July 3, 2020, accessed July 12, 2020. https://www.visualcapitalist.com/cost-of-mobile-data-worldwide/.
81. Kuser, M. (2006), "The Unknown TV giant," Bloomberg Businessweek, https://web.archive.org/web/20120130164354/http://www.businessweek.com/globalbiz/content/jun2006/gb20060609_371863.htm.
82. David, R. (2007), "Hindalco to buy Novelis for $6 Billion," *Forbes*, Feb 11, http://www.forbes.com/2007/02/11/mergers-acquisitions-aluminum-biz-cx_0211hindalco.html.
83. Stephan, D. (2011), "Aditya Birla Completes Acquisition of Columbian Chemicals, Becoming Largest Carbon Black Producer," Process Worldwide, June 24, 2011, accessed July 12, 2020. http://www.process-worldwide.com/aditya-birla-completes-acquisition-of-columbian-chemicals-becoming-largest-carbon-black-producer-a-320784/.
84. Business Wire (2015), "The Kraft Heinz Company Announces Successful Completion of the Merger between Kraft Foods Group and H. J. Heinz Holding Corporation." http://news.kraftheinzcompany.com/press-release/finance/kraft-heinz-company-announces-successful-completion-merger-between-kraft-foods.

85. Nadhok, A. & Kayhani, M. (2012), "Acquisitions as Entrepreneurship: Asymmetries, Opportunities, and the Internationalization of Multinationals from Emerging Markets," *Global Strategy Journal*, 2, 26–40.
    Zhang, H., Young, M. N., Tan, J., & Sun, W. (2018), "How Chinese Companies Deal with a Legitimacy Imbalance When Acquiring Firms from Developed Economies," *Journal of World Business*, 53, 752–767.
86. Awate, S., Larsen, M. M., & Mudambi, R. (2012), "EMNE Catch-up Strategies in the Wind Turbine Industry: Is There a Trade-off Between Output and Innovation capabilities?" *Global Strategy Journal*, 2(3), 205–223.
87. Boateng, A., Du, M., Wang, Y., Wang, C., & Ahammad, M. F. (2017), "Explaining the Surge in M&A as an Entry Mode: Home Country and Cultural Influences," *International Marketing Review*, 34(1), 87–108.
88. Peng, M. W. (2012), "The Global Strategy of Emerging Multinationals from China," *Global Strategy Journal*. 2(2), 97–107.
    Yan, Z. J., Zhu, J. C., Fan, D., & Kalfadellis, P. (2018), "An Institutional Work View Toward the Internationalization of Emerging Market Firms," *Journal of World Business*, 53, 682–694.
89. Sarasvathy, Saras D. (2001), "Causation and Effectuation: Toward a Theoretical Shift from Economic Inevitability to Entrepreneurial Contingency," *Academy of Management Review*, 26, 243–263.
    Read, S., Dew, N., Sarasvathy, S. D., Song, M., & Wiltbank, R. (2009), "Marketing Under Uncertainty: The Logic of an Effectual Approach," *Journal of Marketing*, 73(3), 1–18.
90. BCG Global Challengers (2018), "Digital Leapfrogs," accessed September 28, 2019. https://www.bcg.com/publications/collections/2018-global-challengers-digital-leapfrogs.aspx.
91. 2017 M&A Report: The Technology Take-Over, BCG Report, June 2017.
92. Birnik, A., A-K. Birnik, and Jagdish N. Sheth (2010), "The Branding Challenges of Asian Manufacturing Firms," *Business Horizons*, 53, 523–532.
93. Whalen, Peter, Can Uslay, Vincent J. Pascal, Glenn Omura, Andrew McAuley, Chickery J. Kasouf, Rosalind Jones, Claes M. Hultman, Gerald E. Hills, David J. Hansen, Audrey Gilmore, Joe Giglierano, Fabian Eggers, Jonathan Deacon (2016), "Anatomy of Competitive Advantage: Towards a Contingency Theory of Entrepreneurial Marketing," *Journal of Strategic Marketing*, 24 (1), 5–19.
94. Vargo, S. L., and R. F. Lusch (2004), "Evolving to a New Dominant Logic for Marketing," *Journal of Marketing*, 68(1), 1–17.
    Vargo, Steve L., and R.F. Lusch (2008), "Service-Dominant Logic: Continuing the Evolution," *Journal of the Academy of Marketing Science*, 36(1), 1–10.
95. Sheth, Jagdish N. (2011). *Chindia Rising: How China and India will Benefit your Business*, 2nd ed. Tata-McGraw Hill India.

96. Banerjee, S., J.C. Prabhu, and R.K. Chandy (2015), "Indirect Learning: How Emerging Market Firms Grow in Developed Markets," *Journal of Marketing*, *79*(1), 10–28.
97. Drucker, Peter F. (1958), "Marketing and Economic Development," *Journal of Marketing*, *22*(3), 252–259, p. 252.
98. Prahalad, C.K. (2012), "Bottom of the Pyramid as a Source of Breakthrough Innovations," *Journal of Product Innovation & Management*, *29*(1), 6–12.

8

Epilogue: What Does the Global Future Hold?

The first industrial revolution used water and steam, the second used electricity, and the third used electronics and information technology to streamline, generate, and automate mass production respectively. As World Economic Forum Executive Chairman Klaus Schwab astutely observes, "[n]ow a Fourth Industrial Revolution is building on the Third, the digital revolution....It is characterized by a fusion of technologies that is blurring the lines between the physical, digital, and biological spheres."[1]

This final chapter has three sections. First, we go over macro-level trends and underline entrepreneurship as the prevailing force for economic development in the twenty-first century. Second, we provide four key observations for business success in a global arena. We conclude by reiterating the underlying principles and summarizing the key takeaways from the Global Rule of Three (also see Appendix for our projections for a variety of global markets).

The Past, Present, and Future Locus of Power, Economic Development, and Geopolitical Alignments

Any credible projection into the future has to begin with a look at the past. A retrospective look at the history of civilizations reveals a distinct evolution in the locus of power. It is fair to state that authority lay primarily with military leaders first; even the earliest tribes had warlords, and rulers like Alexander the Great, Attila the Hun, and Genghis Khan defined power.

© The Author(s) 2020
J. Sheth et al., *The Global Rule of Three*, https://doi.org/10.1007/978-3-030-57473-4_8

Gradually but surely, religious leaders rose to prominence, and even the nobles and the Kings wanted to align themselves with the clergy. Popes began to call the shots, orchestrating eight crusades and literally moving European armies as if they were chess pieces. One may wonder how the Ottoman Empire was able to flourish, extend over Asia, Africa, and Europe for close to six centuries in the same era. It had military might, but it is important to remember that the Sultan also assumed the role of Caliph (protector of the world of Islam) since the fifteenth century. That is a key reason why the Ottomans were able to cope with so many fronts simultaneously and expand to the West with few conflicts from their Eastern flank. Western expansion and conquests were made in the name of Islam, and Suleiman (the Magnificent) called himself the "Caliph of the World."[2] So arguably, the supremacy of the Ottoman realm had as much to do with religious authority as it did with military might.

Alas, selling passes to heaven, burning witches, and suppressing scientific and social development to concentrate and protect power inevitably led to the decline of the clergy. It was time for political leaders such as Gandhi, and Churchill (and unfortunately Hitler), to rise to power and define the twentieth century, for better and worse.

Meanwhile, economics was always in the subtext. Early on, wealth was accumulated through loot, pillage, and tribute, and later on through donations, rent, or taxes. However, economics gained ground fast at the expense of politics and religion, beginning with the industrial revolution. Trade gave way to colonization of the new and third worlds for resources and finally to globalization.

As such, it is business leaders, instead of military, religious, or political figures, that will define the twenty-first century. Davos takes precedence over the Vatican, and businessman Trump trumped numerous political figures to rise to power. And just as the locus of power has been shifting, the focus of business has been evolving as well.

The most important function of a business leading up to and in the first half of the twentieth century was manufacturing. In an era further prolonged by two world wars, mass-market demand outstripped supply for industrial and consumer goods. However, soon after World War II, aggregate capacity caught up with and exceeded demand, and sales (1950s), and eventually marketing (1960s) became the point of emphases. Corporations needed capital to expand further and enter international markets and also needed to invest the profits that marketing enabled, which led to the rise of finance (1970s and 1980s). Finally, after they grew to significant size and scale and diminishing returns to scale kicked in, corporations sought to diversify, and strategy (where to compete) came to prominence over the last two decades of the last century.

However, a new emphasis has emerged over the first two decades of this century: entrepreneurship. We strongly believe that innovation and entrepreneurship will define the twenty-first century. Entrepreneurs such as Bill Gates, Richard Branson, Warren Buffet, Steve Jobs, Jack Ma, Elon Musk, Mark Zuckerberg, and Sergey Brin have exerted, and will continue to exert, more power than political figures. During the reign of politics, top minds used to work for the government (e.g., NASA) and the public sector (universities). In the current era, top minds working on developing cutting-edge technologies such as AI, blockchain, and cryptocurrency are most likely to be found in start-ups (striving to become the next unicorn) and in private enterprises, many of which did not exist 25 years ago.

Therefore, the future of a global world will surprisingly have more to do with entrepreneurship than it does with capitalism or open markets. Yet, we often associate or confuse entrepreneurship with capitalism. This is due to its linkage with wealth creation by Adam Smith, the father of modern capitalism. Adam Smith emphasized land, labor, capital, and entrepreneurship for creating wealth in his magnum opus "The Wealth of Nations."[3]

Entrepreneurship has been around since the dawn of civilization. And civilization has often survived through entrepreneurial activities. It is based on survival instinct, innovation, and change. In Adam Smith's characterization, "the invisible hand" of capitalism is all about market governance through competitive market forces and price mechanisms: leave the markets alone, don't interfere; so the collective wisdom of participants, owner-managers, and self-interest will serve as a self-correcting mechanism, and price will be the governing factor.

Entrepreneurship, on the other hand, is all about market development and disruption. As discussed in Chap. 3, Joseph Schumpeter coined the phrase "creative destruction" and argued powerfully for it. Throughout the history of civilization, entrepreneurs have served as catalysts (with or without radical innovation) to bring about change and revitalize stagnating businesses and industries. We do not think this process will be any different in the twenty-first century. In many ways, entrepreneurship is a much broader and more powerful force than capitalism.

Efficient and prominent public stock exchanges are typically viewed as a sign of a functioning capitalistic society; however, there is a growing tension between new entrepreneurial ventures and public listings. For example, the number of U.S. companies listed on public exchanges decreased by more than half over the last two decades (7500+ in 1997 vs. 3618 in 2016).[4] However, while the longevity of Fortune 500 firms has been decreasing steadily, the average age of *publicly listed firms* has increased from 12 years in 1997 to 20 years in 2016 further demonstrating a lack of newcomers to the stock exchanges.[5] All types of firms, but especially smaller firms with fewer than 5000 employees, appear to avoid listing on the stock exchanges more and more.[6] "It is not possible to put the entire blame on crowdfunding for this systemic problem [of decreasing number of publicly listed firms]; this is a serious issue that requires a thoughtful response, as the future of capitalism may be at stake."[7]

Next, we outline why the global future will rely on entrepreneurship more than on capitalism:

Entrepreneurship is more universal than capitalism. It extends beyond business into non-business sectors such as education, health, fine arts as well as social and political issues. Many social activists, musicians are also great entrepreneurs. Just like typical business entrepreneurs, they are obsessed about what they want to do, and they know how to organize, which is the key principle of entrepreneurship.

Entrepreneurship is more inclusive than capitalism. Anyone can be an entrepreneur irrespective of age, gender, literacy, or faith. All faiths have had their entrepreneurs. Women are often better entrepreneurs than men. Illiterate people are as good or sometimes better entrepreneurs than educated people. Most successful entrepreneurs of our age are college dropouts such as Bill Gates and Mark Zuckerberg, and if they were legally allowed, they might have been high-school dropouts. Young people can be entrepreneurs, as evidenced by Silicon Valley start-ups over and over; however, older entrepreneurs such as Colonel Sanders and Ray Croc can also find success.

Entrepreneurship is more trusted than capitalism. Entrepreneurs such as Richard Branson, Elon Musk, and Jack Ma are respected for their exploration, ingenuity, and passion. Meanwhile capitalists and "too big to fail" businesses are mistrusted as exploiters of society.

Entrepreneurship is more egalitarian than capitalism. Entrepreneurship is admired and cheered especially among those who struggle and survive. On the other hand, capitalism is perceived as elitist and manifested in gated communities and country clubs. What a contrast these two images provide between a business capitalist and an entrepreneur, especially a social entrepreneur.

Entrepreneurship is more innovative than capitalism. Entrepreneurs by definition challenge the prevailing wisdom in all spheres of life. On the other hand, capitalism strives toward equilibrium and provides stability. It is inherently biased toward the status quo and legacy. That is why many industries and firms do not survive in the long term, whereas entrepreneurship survives. The body and the mind may go away but the innovative spirit and soul survives.

Entrepreneurship is more future positive than capitalism. By definition, entrepreneurship is about a hopeful future and encourages the human spirit to embrace uncertainty in times of turbulence. Challenging the status quo represents a great opportunity for entrepreneurship.[8] Change, social and political movements have come out of challenges. Entrepreneurs thrive under conditions of uncertainty and chaos.

Entrepreneurship is the great equalizer. Entrepreneurs are like David, against the Goliaths governing dynamics such as the entrenched institutions. They are the underdogs who prevail over the incumbents against all odds. They are admired over privileged legacy businesses.

Entrepreneurship helps realize human potential. Entrepreneurship enables humans to realize their own potential. It makes ordinary people extraordinary. If you take a grain of wheat, the value added is about three times. If you take a rough diamond and polish it, a good diamond cutter will enhance the value by 15–20 times. However, if you take a human being, you can polish, educate, and mentor him/her, you can develop vast potential. The value of mentoring a human being is infinite.

Entrepreneurship gives back. It is not just about creating wealth; it is equally about giving back. If you think back historically during the times of monarchy, the contributions of business to society has been relatively limited. On the other hand, entrepreneurs, especially when they come from humble beginnings, feel grateful to the society that has enabled them to accomplish so much and they have a sense of giving back. Immigrant entrepreneurs give back even more. Hundreds of billionaires have signed the Giving Pledge promising to give back at least half of their wealth.[9]

Entrepreneurship is a nation's real competitive advantage. It is the recipe that knows how to blend a nation's agricultural, human, and capital resources. Great nations with great natural resources have floundered. The real competitive advantage of a nation is its entrepreneurship DNA. A society that recognizes, nurtures, and respects entrepreneurs has a significant advantage over those that don't. Entrepreneurship trumps education, faith, or natural resources in creating competitive advantage. Entrepreneurship rather than capitalism unlocks the potential of societal resources, especially human talent. That is why China (encouraging entrepreneurship by policy), India (using a grassroots approach), and other nations such as those in Africa will increasingly play a bigger role in the global markets of the twenty-first century.

It is worth noting that the ongoing digital revolution has also democratized the spirit of entrepreneurship. What used to take millions of dollars of investment for IBM was transformed by a few thousand dollars by Apple in a garage. And now anyone with a few hundred dollars may write an app and cash in or build it into the next unicorn in a few short years. Just like it happened during the gold rush in the U.S., those who can organize sectors are profiting the most (app store platforms and private equity). However, we are currently in the middle of building a digital technology bubble. Capital is cheap and flowing abundantly into tech start-ups. Bending the outcomes to look good to investors is expected or even encouraged.[10] This "fake it till you make it" attitude will inevitably burst and the capital flow will temporarily dwindle, similar to the dot.com bubble in 2000. Many of the start-ups will succumb and consolidate just like the automobile industry did over 100 years ago.

In the meantime, how should a brand manager defend herself from the onslaught of the likes of Amazon/Alibaba when their private labels capture significant share in category after category? In fact, Amazon's share of private labels was a mind-boggling 48% in clothing, shoes, and jewelry, according to a March 2019 study by Marketplace Pulse.[11] It "grabbed nearly a third of the online market for batteries, outselling both Energizer and Duracell on its site."[12] Meanwhile, Salesforce reported that 68% of consumer goods leaders they surveyed "believed that consumers were more loyal to Amazon than their own brands."[13]

As we hope you are convinced by now, the world of business is moving at a breakneck pace. One sector after another is being upended; market definitions change and new companies using new business models emerge. Blockchain anyone? Entertainment, trucking, retail, automotive, insurance, and financial services will all see more turbulence over the next decade than they have seen over the last 30 or in some cases even 100 years.

With all this turbulence and even more ahead, how can one even predict the future? Amidst trade and tariff wars and the anticipated challenges of a post-Brexit world, it is easy for one to lose sight of the big picture. We would like to make four important observations:

Mega-trends prevail no matter the turbulence. We have discussed what Drucker astutely referred to as "the future that has already happened" earlier in this book. Science fiction writer William Gibson expressed a similar idea: "The future is already here. It's just not evenly distributed yet." For one, we are certain that emerging markets will redefine competition. New competitors will arise from countries that incumbents never expected to compete against. Previously, this competition was from Japan and Korea. Now it is from China and India. However, the rise of Chinese and Indian corporations will follow different trajectories. Chinese corporations (with the exception of the few propped up by the Chinese government early on for global domination) will grow by primarily serving their domestic market first. These corporations will then grow very large globally, and they will do so initially through natural resource-driven investments and acquisitions. In contrast, many Indian corporations will go global via acquisitions even before fully developing their domestic market. More and more R&D and high-end jobs will be concentrated in China and India. Margins from upstream activities will remain healthy due to the enormous demand from emerging economies. Meanwhile, advanced countries will continue to exit commoditized industries. Markets vacated by the U.S., France, Japan, Korea, and the like are being taken over by China or India, but soon others hailing from emerging markets such as Brazil, Indonesia, Malaysia, Nigeria, Russia, Saudi Arabia, South Africa, and Turkey will join the ranks.

Emerging markets will also redefine marketing. More (frugal) innovations that impact most of the world's population (base of the pyramid) will come from these markets. Emerging markets will also greatly impact the environment; and will be impacted by it the most; as the growth of emerging markets will be restricted by the environment more so than by capital or technology. Commodity prices will fluctuate and enable large fortunes. The focus of innovation will increasingly be on affordability and sustainability, and new technologies to cope with scarcity. As such, sustainability and mindful consumption will prove increasingly important, and purpose-driven marketing (a higher-level purpose) will be a key differentiator.[14] China is already the largest economy in the world, but it will slow down (due to its former one-child policy and aging population similar to Japan).

Governing dynamics of the Global Rule of Three persist and overcome the test of time. In the aggregate analysis, it is worthwhile remembering that even two world-wars proved to be temporary hiccups in the globalization journey. Markets are evolving and evolving fast, yet the competitive dynamics we outlined in this book held true hundreds of years ago, and they continue to do so and create very predictable outcomes today. For example, while we were not sure who would acquire upstart Harry's in razors and shaving or who would merge with whom to produce the Rule of Three structure in the aerospace and defense sector when we began to write this book, we were keenly expecting new deals in these spaces, just as predicted by the Rule of Three theory (see Box 8.1 on aerospace and defense). Strategy is as much about what not to pursue as it is about what to do. Managers would be well advised to prioritize, prune, and narrowly focus their resources into becoming leaders in select global markets guided by the Global Rule of Three principles rather than diversifying the business too thinly to become easy pickings for others.

Heed and Master the Five Forces of Collaboration: Michael Porter put his stamp on the world of corporate strategy with his work on Five Forces of Competition. Bargaining power of buyers and suppliers, the threat of substitutes and new entrants, and competitive rivalry became staples for analyzing competitive industry structure. While the framework has rightfully earned its place in MBA programs and corporate boardrooms, it does not recognize that there are also five forces that govern coopetition.[15] For example, what happens to the five forces as competition intensifies and becomes hyper, which by and large happens to be the case across markets as ever-decreasing margins demonstrate? The traditional response may be that collaboration is inversely related to competition and that it may disappear as extreme competition takes over. We disagree. Excessive competition can hurt industry profitability and the reaction is usually more collaborative behavior. There is actually a U-shaped relationship between competition and collaboration as illustrated in Fig. 8.1.

When the competitive intensity (x-axis) is low and most firms are profitable, there is initially a higher tendency to collaborate (y-axis). This tendency quickly disappears as the markets get competitive (bottom of the curve). As the competition intensifies and becomes cut-throat, collaboration also rises as the antidote, and competition causes existing firms to form coalitions. At that level, firms must simply collaborate in order to survive! Partnership opportunities loom large in procurement: how to better partner with suppliers.

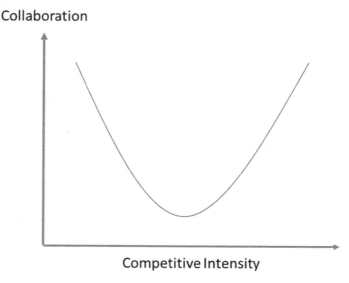

Fig. 8.1 The relationship between collaboration and competitive intensity. (Source: Authors' creation)

Box 8.1 Why More Mergers Are Inevitable in Aerospace and Defense

In the biggest deal ever in aerospace and defense, United Technologies (UT) and Raytheon announced a "merger-of-equals" during June 2019. A mega-merger indeed. The market cap of the two corporations put together is almost $166 billion! However, there is no equality based on sales—UT had revenues of $66.5 billion against Raytheon's $27.05 billion in 2018. The united entity (pun intended) has chosen to adopt the name Raytheon Technologies.

Was that a "masterstroke of dealmaking" for UT CEO Greg Hayes (who also orchestrated the acquisition of Rockwell Collins for $30 billion in 2015 and was CFO during the 2012 Goodrich acquisition) as a columnist has praised? Or does the deal have "no strategic logic" as activist Bill Ackman claimed? We think it is simply the latest example of governing industry dynamics at play. Let us explain.

As we have argued throughout this book, the principles of the Global Rule of Three apply here as well: we find that aerospace and defense industry is predictably evolving toward a structure where three large players (generalists that are volume-driven) collectively dominate. Think AT&T, Verizon, T-Mobile Sprint in telecom services or GE Aviation (given its stake in CFM), Pratt & Whitney (owned by UT), and Rolls-Royce in jet engines. Meanwhile, numerous super-specialists (smaller, focused firms that are margin driven) also thrive. The remaining players get stuck in the ditch, in the middle with 5–10% market share. They have neither the scale and scope of their larger competitors nor the margin advantage of their super-specialist counterparts. Thus, they underperform financially and become casualties unless they downsize and focus, grow organically into higher-margin products/services or merge. Since downsizing is painful and organic growth often proves elusive, the most feasible and straightforward path out of the ditch is via M&A. We have already seen this pattern play out with Lockheed first and subsequently McDonnell Douglas in commercial aviation.

This "rule of three" consolidation process is often accelerated when an industry transitions from domestic to global, as exemplified by appliances and the automobile sectors. For example, the domestic dominance of Whirlpool, GE, and Maytag, and GM, Ford, and Chrysler was disrupted by globalization. Haier, Electrolux, and Whirlpool in appliances and Volkswagen (VW), Toyota, and arguably GM in automobiles emerged as global leaders. Despite the dampening impact of aerospace and defense regulation that limits the usual number of suitors, more M&A is on the horizon toward a Global Rule of Three, and the industry turbulence is not likely to stabilize until the share of the leader approaches 40%.

As illustrated in Table 8.1, based on their respective 2018 revenues, UT + Raytheon would achieve $93.55 billion in global revenue which would bring its share of the largest nine corporations to 20.18%, breathing down the neck of Boeing's 21.81%. However, this is not a pattern that usually persists; a distinct market share order emerges in most sectors (think Amazon Web Services, Microsoft Azure, Google Cloud) where the number one company reaches 40% share, the number two company 20%, and the number three company 10–15% share.

Raytheon Technologies will reportedly begin to generate $1 billion in savings in a few years due to reduced overhead and economies of procurement. Many other firms need to scale up to become legitimate contractors rather than remain

(continued)

Box 8.1   (continued)

Table 8.1 Revenue and share of the top ten firms in the aerospace and defense industry (2018)

Post-merger standing	2018 global revenue (in billions)	2018 share of top ten revenues
Boeing (U.S.)	$101.12	21.81%
UT + Raytheon (U.S.)	$93.55	20.18%
Airbus (EU)	$72.86	15.72%
Lockheed Martin (U.S.)	$53.76	11.60%
General Dynamics (U.S.)	$36.19	7.81%
GE aviation (U.S.)	$30.56	6.59%
Northrop Grumman (U.S.)	$30.09	6.49%
Safran (France)	$24.07	5.19%
BAE (U.K.)	$21.34	4.60%

Source: Table compiled by the authors based on data from army-technology.com; https://www.army-technology.com/features/top-aerospace-and-defence-companies/, accessed July 25, 2020. Shares calculated based on total revenues of the top ten firms

primarily sub-contractors. The leading players that used to sell to one branch of the military (Airforce, Navy, Army, or Marines) will increasingly need to develop differentiated product lines to become full-line generalists. Problems that continue to plague the Marine Corps and Navy variants of the F-35 stealth fighter demonstrate the limitations of one-size-fits-all design thinking.

The new world geopolitical realignment where the U.S., China, and India eventually replace the old triad of the U.S., the EU, and Japan, will also necessitate further consolidation. Therefore, we expect to see several more continental as well as transcontinental deals in the next few years. Boeing might strike back with a deal even sooner via a private equity partnership. For example, GE Aviation would provide competitive counterbalance to Pratt & Whitney engines owned by UT. In a post-Brexit world, where Britain is expected to reinforce its alliances with the U.S. more so than the EU, BAE will also be itching for more acquisitions in the U.S. through private equity. Meanwhile, Airbus will be safe in the near-term thanks to its sheltered EU markets and lucrative contracts from China, which unsurprisingly prefers Airbus over Boeing. However, Airbus is not likely to sit still either as airlines continue to consolidate, share procurement through alliances, and put further pressure on their vendors. In an industry with so much room to further consolidate, it will be fascinating to observe the journey. Given the necessity to avoid 5–10% stuck in the middle share range, General Dynamics, Lockheed Martin, and to a lesser degree Northrop Grumman may urgently need to explore their M&A options, and not necessarily with only each other.

A final caveat is that one cannot count out the Chinese; we fully expect COMAC to emerge as a global player sooner rather than later. In all, there is no assurance that any of the current top three players will retain their position. What is for certain is that the three prevailing leaders must access private equity as well as excel in product development and marketing in order to thrive.

(continued)

Box 8.1 (continued)

Perhaps the number two tire manufacturer Michelin and the number two aerospace and defense leader Raytheon Technologies can learn from their shared experiences. Besides both aggressively utilizing M&A to get in contention for global market leadership in their respective sectors, they surprisingly share an innovation DNA that both have, in part, inherited from a company that arguably was the most innovative tire manufacturer in the world: BF Goodrich. As we discussed earlier, BF Goodrich which used to be one of the top three domestic tire manufacturers (alongside Goodyear and Firestone) invented the tubeless tire, synthetic rubber, PVC, and the pressured spacesuit among others. Bridgestone, in its quest for global leadership, needed to bolster its U.S. presence and bought Firestone in 1988. Failing to capitalize on its merger with Uniroyal, and recognizing the appeal of much healthier margins in aerospace over being stuck in the ditch as a tire maker, Uniroyal Goodrich agreed to sell its tire business to Michelin the same year. Goodrich Corporation went on to become the largest pureplay aerospace specialist in the world, which UT acquired in 2012 in an $18.4 billion deal. Meanwhile, at the time of this writing during July 2020, the sole remaining U.S. tire manufacturer Goodyear's market capitalization hovered around $2 billion.

Our analysis serves as a reminder that outstanding results can occur when strategic logic is aligned with industry dynamics as opposed to trying to withstand it. Despite his reservations about the UT-Raytheon deal, we trust Bill Ackman would agree that more M&A activity in this sector is inevitable.

However, the extent of collaboration has no boundaries and extends to all five forces.

For example, it is not hard to imagine that the remaining retailers will collaborate to create buying groups from the same suppliers (as already practiced by the automotive industry) or share a drone distribution network to counter the onslaught by Amazon (to mitigate seller power and rivalry). Partnerships with foreign competitors are also on the rise. It is already common practice for incumbents to invest in upstarts with an eye on acquiring them later (to mitigate threat of new entrants). Facebook, Amazon, Netflix, and Google (FANG) have deeper understanding of consumers than the brand managers of most businesses. Wary of losing further ground to FANG and their current and future private labels, many marketers will have to partner with other technology firms as algorithms increasingly take over services and manufacturing processes (to mitigate threat of substitutes). This can also be observed in the biogenetics investments of pharma firms. Finally, collaborations with buyers that were already commonplace in B2B markets (e.g., P&G and Walmart) are now being extended to B2C markets via crowdfunding platforms such as Kickstarter. These are only some of the immediate examples that come to mind as there are many more ways to collaborate than ways to compete. Collaboration is the only way firms can survive the tsunami of hyper-competition on the horizon.

Finally, it is important to reiterate that collaboration is, in part, the reason why the Global Rule of Three exists: three large players in a market or a triad power in the world simply offers the most stability. The (potential for an) alliance between #2 and #3 prevents #1 from becoming too dominant or an oppressive force. Facing pressure from the likes of Perrigo, GSK and Pfizer have recently joined forces in a joint venture (JV) to create the world's largest supplier of over-the-counter (OTC) medications. The result was a combined portfolio of leading OTC brands such as Sensodyne, Flonase, Tums, Advil, Centrum, and Caltrate. The JV is enjoying "category leadership positions in pain relief, respiratory, therapeutic oral health and vitamins, minerals and supplements and therapeutic oral health, according to GSK, which said the combined business will hold the No. 1 position in O-T-Cs in the United States and the No. 2 position in China."[16]

The next frontier in collaborations is via tri-sector innovations: The relationship between business and government is an interesting one. In some cases, government may be a customer, in others a competitor or a provider of substitute services; however, it is almost always omnipresent as the provider of infrastructure (e.g., regulation, highways, or the internet) on which most businesses run. And as Coinstar and WinWin Founder Jens Molbak would be the first to tell you (see Box 8.2 on Coinstar), most businesses have a private and social sector strategy (CSR and cause marketing), but not necessarily a public sector one.

The potential of tri-sector partnerships is not limited to the developed countries and is even greater in emerging markets where awareness and utilization of assets may be even lower. There is a need to adopt "mindful" business practices to improve effectiveness and sustain the quality of life.[17] For example, the United Nations has identified 17 goals for sustainable development and conservatively estimates that $5–7 trillion may be sufficient to remedy the world's most pressing issues. Meanwhile, private, public, and especially the government sector have vast and under- and unutilized assets that could be put to use in unique ways to make an outsized impact.

Jens Molbak's current venture WinWin invests in start-ups like Propel, which utilizes the tri-sector approach to serve 45 million unique food stamp users who collectively represent $70 billion in spending power in the U.S. Using a cloud-based system, the Propel app increases the spending power of its users by providing them location-specific deals, access to social services, and employment opportunities. While for-profit firms have a tendency to avoid government contact to the extent possible (except for competitive bidding for contracts), there are countless government and social programs with enormous potential for collaborations "to repurpose and realign assets" for the benefit of public, private, and government sector profitably.[18] In the face of ever-increasing competition, no one company or even sector can do it alone. The best way to win a fight is to avoid direct conflict; therefore, organizations are advised to shape industry structure and their joint future through the five forces of cooperation and coopetition.

Box 8.2 Coinstar: Unleashing the Power of Tri-Sector Collaborations[19]

Jens Molbak was a graduate student at Stanford when he wondered how his hundreds of coins filling a large jar could be turned to paper money. When he failed to identify an easy option, Coinstar was born in 1991. Coinstar installed its first exchange kiosk in San Francisco in 1992. This first kiosk was followed by the thousandth kiosk four years later and the ten-thousandth kiosk within ten years in 2002.

What Molbak did not immediately realize what that his entrepreneurial venture was also providing a significant benefit to the U.S. government. He found out that even though there are $15 billion worth of coins in circulation in the U.S., only $8 billion were actually actively exchanged whereas the rest remained idle. And since circulated coins were exchanged roughly 20 times a year on average, this implied a $140 billion business opportunity.

While the U.S. Mint was taken by surprise when the West Coast Federal Reserve canceled its future coin orders in the late 1990s, they quickly recognized the benefits Coinstar offered. By facilitating the turnaround of coins, Coinstar helped the government save over $2 billion in manufacturing and distribution costs!

Coinstar became one of the fastest-growing U.S. companies and eventually became a billion-dollar company. However, its success was also well-aligned with public purpose from the start. It partnered with leading non-profit organizations and processed over $100 million in charitable donations. At each kiosk, Coinstar customers could conveniently identify the partner-charity of their choice, donate, and leave with a tax-deductible receipt.

Due to the accountability enabled, its charity partners encouraged their volunteers to use Coinstar. The Fed was a fan too: Coinstar gained access to the U.K. market thanks to the endorsement of the Federal Reserve.

We summarize our generalizations based on the Global Rule of Three next.

Global Rule of Three: Overview, Underlying Principles, and Key Takeaways

To recap the Rule of Three theory, in the absence of excessive regulation or anti-competitive practices, any given industry is expected to evolve toward an optimal market structure in which there are three full-line generalist firms (e.g., General Motors, Ford, and Chrysler) that are volume-driven, and numerous successful small specialists (e.g., Mini Cooper, Volvo, and Porsche) that are margin-driven.[20] Moreover, the Rule of Three structure provides the highest overall industry financial performance compared to all competing market structures as measured by return on assets, return on sales, and cumulative abnormal stock market returns for both short- and long-term time horizons.[21] Even as new players and new niche players come in and emerge, the Rule of Three remains pervasive across industries (spanning consumer products, services, and B2B markets).

This convergence to three is due to several factors such as industry cost structure and shared infrastructure, government intervention or deregulation, industry consolidation, globalization, and technological processes and emerging product standards but works like clockwork.[22] Industries ranging from mobile communications, aluminum, and banking to pharmaceuticals, oil, and airlines are going through rationalization and consolidation around the world, moving closer toward what we call the Global Rule of Three.

The big three typically possess 70–90% of their contested markets with the remainder of the market shared among the rest. Generalists need at least 10% market share in order to be a viable volume-based operation. Specialist firms' performance begins to deteriorate as they outgrow their niches and approach 5% market share. In between these two types of firms are those that are stuck in the ditch with 5–10% share. These ditch-dwellers perform significantly worse than both generalists and specialists since they neither have the volume of their larger counterparts nor the customer focus or product differentiation of the specialists.

While the Rule of Three has implications for both industry performance and industry concentration, the optimal level of concentration remains heavily dependent on the extent to which fixed costs dominate the industry. For example, aerospace, automotive, and semiconductors are all capital-intensive and fixed-cost-driven industries.

Heavy fixed-cost burdens make it necessary for generalists such as Boeing, Michelin, or Coca-Cola to build market volume to be able to utilize capacity and recoup their hefty up-front investment. The benefits from economies of scale and experience apply not only to manufacturing but also to procurement, marketing/branding, and vending. After an inevitable shakeout period where the excess capacity is rationalized, only three major players tend to survive. Niche companies tend to thrive, whereas the mid-sized firms stuck in the middle tend to suffer. If the industry is substantial enough and the consumer demand is fragmented sufficiently, the market may break into subcategories in each of which the Rule of Three also applies; meanwhile in other cases, markets that used to be distinct can come together, for example, due to technological or regulatory change and their boundaries may collapse. The outcome is a new round of firms jockeying for the top three order in a new world. As such, the merging industries of information, cable TV, and telecom have caused the major players in each sector to scramble for acquisitions to maintain their standing (AT&T's $85.4 billion acquisition of Time Warner and Disney's $71.3 billion acquisition of Fox are recent examples).[23]

The Rule of Three represents a natural structure for industry profitability because the three generalists act as the tripod that can stabilize it against hyper-competition or collusion. With two generalists, each is more likely to engage in predatory competition or collusion, and either option ultimately leads to a *de facto* monopoly. With three large players in an industry, the possibility of a retaliatory alliance between two competitors which would restore the balance of power discourages predatory schemes. In other words, Rule of Three provides an optimal mix of competition, collaboration for industry profitability, and customer value in mature industries.

Conversely, industries with more than three generalists experience more intensive competition and pressure on profit margins. Additional generalists are not necessary to maintain the competitive balance in the industry, and thus become expendable when rationalizing and reorganizing for efficiency. This expectation is intuitive and would also be expected by industrial organization economics.

Somewhat counter-intuitively, the Rule of Three suggests that markets with fewer than three full-line generalists are also expected to experience lower profitability due to lower levels and variety of innovation, quality, increased complacency, and in some cases decreased economies of scale in procurement. This expectation is in line with the resource partitioning theory with the reasoning that two large firms would not be able to cover the spatial distribution of resources as effectively as three, implying lower utilization of the market potential, and hence lower overall profitability.[24] In addition, high market concentration decreases the survival rate of large firms but leads to the formation of many start-ups, both of which might depress the aggregate profitability of the industry.[25]

There is also evidence in the industrial organization economics literature that high profitability by existing players signals market attractiveness and will lure newcomers.[26] Profitable market niches are unlikely to endure for very long since they can grow to have mass appeal and attract competitors or bring pressure to cut costs.[27] Everything else being equal, high market concentration leads to market power and high profitability which attracts new entrants. In addition, the presence of fewer than three large players in an industry can signal a gap to potential new competitors. Regardless of the reason for entry, a new competitor may: (a) fail during entry phase but depress industry profitability until it exits or is acquired, (b) survive initially but fail to establish itself as a viable generalist, and subsequently depress industry profitability (refer to the discussion of "the ditch" in Chap. 2), or (c) succeed as a healthy generalist, and aid convergence to three generalists as predicted by the Rule of Three. In any case, it appears that the Rule of Three logic prevails. Key takeaways from the Rule of Three include:

In any industry, companies make money at the extremes of market share. The worst place to be is in the middle, which we refer to as the ditch. The rule of the marketplace is that whoever is closest to the ditch is very likely to go in the ditch. Hence, the smallest of the volume-driven generalists and the largest of the margin-driven specialists are most likely to fall in the ditch.

You must have a minimum of 10% market share to be a profitable volume-driven competitor. Similarly, you must not exceed 5% market share to be a market or product specialist niche competitor.

The number three is usually the most innovative generalist in any industry (e.g., T-Mobile/Sprint, Chrysler, and Keurig Dr Pepper).

The best defensive strategy for the number one company is fast follower and the best offensive strategy is to grow the total market.

The best defensive strategy for the number two company especially if you are a distant number two company is to co-exist with number one company. Once you have gained significant shares, say 20% or more, then the best offensive strategy is to challenge the market leader. (Sometimes M&A between two and three or two and four can propel them to leadership—e.g., Cingular + AT&T surpassed Verizon.)

When the industry is not growing, there is usually a market share fight between number one and number two companies. Surprisingly, in such price and trade or advertising wars, the number three company goes in the ditch (e.g., Chrysler, RC Cola, and Schlitz beer).

No matter how large the market size, the Rule of Three prevails. Therefore, when the market expands from local to regional or from regional to national or from national to global, there are usually shakeouts and mergers in the industry and only three volume-driven players survive as regional, national, or global players.

There are several exceptions to the Rule of Three. These consist of patent-based industries, regulated monopolies, owner-managed industries, and regulated economies. In all these cases, the industry is shielded from the forces of competition. However, when competition is encouraged by public policy, the industry restructures itself into three volume-driven full-line and numerous margin-driven niche players.

All industries go through life cycles. In the beginning, they grow rapidly, but have no scale of efficiency. Therefore, the industry gets organized to become scale efficient, either by market processes of shakeouts or by shared standards. It can also be made efficient by government intervention and by creating natural monopolies. Once an industry is scale efficient, it expands further by increasing its scope through product or market expansion.

Finally, the industry matures. It now needs to be revitalized for further growth. This usually occurs by technology migration, changing demographics, policy change or by reaching the emerging markets. All industries get reincarnated. This cycle of birth and rebirth is a continuous journey until it is permanently replaced by some other industry.

Ultimately, roughly two-thirds of each market will get consolidated and a global Rule of Three structure will emerge in each standardized market. This can be in the form of one generalist from each triad (e.g., automotive, insurance, and tires) or result in one triad dominating the sector globally (e.g., cruise-lines, investment banking, and shipbuilding) (see Appendix for trajectory and predictions for more than 40 global markets).

In the aggregate analysis, the growth story of the first third of the twenty-first century will belong to China, second third to India, and the final stretch will belong to Africa.[28] But that is better left for another book in another decade! We hope you enjoyed learning about the Global Rule of Three and its vast implications for the future of business.

Key Takeaways

- We are amidst a digital revolution, which will shape the rest of the twenty-first century.
- The locus of power, economic development, and geopolitical alignments will continue to shift. However, the ultimate destination is clear: from West to East and Atlantic to Pacific.
- Power used to be with military, clergy, and political leaders. Now, it is business leaders who will increasingly define the twenty-first century.
- Similarly, manufacturing, distribution, marketing, finance, and strategy organizational functions are giving way to the rise of entrepreneurship. Top minds can be regularly found working in start-ups.

(continued)

(continued)

- In many ways, entrepreneurship is a much broader and more powerful force than capitalism. The number of publicly listed firms in the U.S. stock exchanges has been decreasing.
- *Entrepreneurship is more universal* than capitalism. It extends beyond business into non-business sectors such as education, health, and fine arts, as well as social and political issues.
- *Entrepreneurship is more inclusive* than capitalism. Anyone can be an entrepreneur irrespective of age, gender, literacy, or faith.
- *Entrepreneurship is more trusted* than capitalism. Entrepreneurs such as Richard Branson, Elon Musk, and Jack Ma are respected for their exploration, ingenuity, and passion.
- *Entrepreneurship is more egalitarian* than capitalism. Entrepreneurship is admired and cheered especially among those who struggle and survive.
- *Entrepreneurship is more innovative* than capitalism. Entrepreneurs by definition challenge the prevailing wisdom in all spheres of life.
- *Entrepreneurship is more future positive* than capitalism. By definition, entrepreneurship is about a hopeful future and encourages the human spirit to embrace uncertainty in times of turbulence.
- *Entrepreneurship is the great equalizer*. Entrepreneurs are like David against the Goliaths of entrenched institutions.
- *Entrepreneurship helps realize human potential*. It makes ordinary people extraordinary.
- *Entrepreneurship gives back*. It is not just about creating wealth; it is equally about giving back.
- *Entrepreneurship is a nation's real competitive advantage*. It is the recipe that knows how to blend a nation's agricultural, human, and capital resources. The real competitive advantage of a nation is its entrepreneurship DNA.
- The ongoing digital revolution has also democratized the spirit of entrepreneurship.
- Entertainment, trucking, retail, automotive, insurance, and financial services will all see more turbulence over the next decade than they have seen over the last 30 or in some cases even 100 years.
- Mega-trends prevail no matter the turbulence.

(continued)

(continued)

- Governing dynamics such as the Five Forces and the Global Rule of Three persist and overcome the test of time.
- *The next frontier in collaborations is* via *tri-sector innovations:* Government may be a customer, competitor, or a provider of substitute services; however, it is almost always omnipresent as the provider of infrastructure (e.g., regulation, highways, or the internet) on which most businesses run.
- To recap the Rule of Three theory, in the absence of excessive regulation or anti-competitive practices, any given industry is expected to evolve toward an optimal market structure in which there are three full-line generalist firms that are volume-driven, and numerous successful small specialists that are margin-driven.
- Moreover, the Rule of Three structure provides the highest overall industry financial performance compared to all competing market structures for both short- and long-term time horizons.
- In the aggregate analysis, the growth story of the first third of the twenty-first century will belong to China, second third to India, and the final stretch will belong to Africa.

Notes

1. Schwab, Klaus (2016), "Klaus Schwab: The 4th Industrial Revolution, What It Means, How to Respond," January 17, accessed September 28, 2019. https://www.ge.com/reports/the-4th-industrial-revolution-what-it-means-how-to-respond/.
2. Daily History (2019), "How Did the Ottoman Empire Become the Third Great Islamic Caliphate," accessed September 28, 2019. https://dailyhistory.org/How_Did_the_Ottoman_Empire_Become_the_Third_Great_Islamic_Caliphate%3F.
3. Smith, Adam (1776), *An Inquiry into the Nature and Causes of the Wealth of Nations*, London: W. Strahan.
4. Guilford, Gwynn (2018), "US Startups Don't Want to Go Public Anymore: That's Bad News for Americans," *Quartz*, February 1, 2018, accessed July 12, 2020. https://qz.com/1192972/us-startups-are-shunning-ipos-thats-bad-news-for-americans/.

5. Guilford, Gwynn (2018), "US Startups Don't Want to Go Public Anymore: That's Bad News for Americans," *Quartz*, February 1, 2018, accessed July 12, 2020. https://qz.com/1192972/us-startups-are-shunning-ipos-thats-bad-news-for-americans/.

6. Doidge, Craig, Kathleen M. Kahle, G. Andrew Karolyi, and Rene M. Stulz (2018), January. "Eclipse of the Public Corporation or Eclipse of the Public Markets?" NBER Working Paper No. 24265, accessed July 12, 2020. https://www.nber.org/papers/w24265.

7. Uslay, Can (2019), "The Next Frontier in Marketing: Self-Sustaining Marketing, Society, and Capitalism through Collaborative yet Disruptive Partnerships" in *Handbook of Marketing Advances in the Era of Disruptions—Essays in Honor of Jagdish N. Sheth*, A. Parvatiyar and R.S. Sisodia eds., Sage, 490–500.

8. Sheth, Jagdish N. (2007), *The Self-Destructive Habits of Good Companies*, Upper Saddle River: NJ, Wharton School Publishing.

9. Clifford, Catherine (2017), "These 14 Billionaires Just Promised to Give Away More Than Half of Their Money Like Bill Gates and Warren Buffet," CNBC.com, May 31, accessed September 28, 2019. https://www.cnbc.com/2017/05/31/14-billionaires-signed-bill-gates-and-warren-buffetts-giving-pledge.html.

10. Griffith, Erin (2016), "The Ugly, Unethical Underside of Silicon Valley," December 28, accessed September 28, 2019. http://venturebeat.com/2016/12/28/the-ugly-unethical-underside-of-silicon-valley/.

11. Droesch, Blake (2019), "Consumer Goods Brands Hope to Fend Off Amazon by Investing in D2C," June 4, accessed September 2019. https://www.emarketer.com/content/consumer-goods-brands-hope-to-fend-off-amazon-by-investing-in-d2c?ecid=NL1001.

12. Ho, Sheji (2018), "Taobao Xinxuan: Alibaba's entry into Private Label Goods?" July 4, accessed September 28, 2019. https://ecommerceiq.asia/taobao-xinxuan-alibaba-private-label/.

13. Droesch, Blake (2019), "Consumer Goods Brands Hope to Fend Off Amazon by Investing in D2C," June 4, accessed September 2019. https://www.emarketer.com/content/consumer-goods-brands-hope-to-fend-off-amazon-by-investing-in-d2c?ecid=NL1001.

14. Uslay, Can and Emine Erdogan (2014), "The Mediating Role of Mindful Entrepreneurial Marketing (MEM) Between Production and Consumption," *Journal of Research in Marketing & Entrepreneurship*, 16 (1), 47–62.

   Cicek, Mesut, Sevincgul Ulu, and Can Uslay, (2020) "The Impact of the Slow City Movement on Place Authenticity, Entrepreneurial Opportunity, and Economic Development," *Journal of Macromarketing*, 39 (4), 400–414.

   Uslay, Can (2019), "The Next Frontier in Marketing: Self-Sustaining Marketing, Society, and Capitalism through Collaborative yet Disruptive Partnerships" in *Handbook of Marketing Advances in the Era of Disruptions—*

Essays in Honor of Jagdish N. Sheth, A. Parvatiyar and R.S. Sisodia eds., Sage, 490–500.

Malhotra, Naresh K., Olivia F. Lee, and Can Uslay (2012), "Mind the Gap: The Mediating Role of Mindful Marketing Between Market and Quality Orientations, Their Interaction, and Consequences," *International Journal of Quality & Reliability Management*, 29 (6), 607–625.

Sheth, Jagdish N., N.K. Sethia, and S. Srinivas. (2011), "Mindful Consumption: A Customer-centric Approach to Sustainability," *Journal of the Academy of Marketing Science*, 3 (9), 21–39.

15. Brandenburger, Adam M. and Barry J. Nalebuff (1996), *Co-opetition*. New York: Bantam Doubleday Dell.

16. MassMarketRetailers (2019), "GlaxoSmithKline, Pfizer Close Joint Venture," MassMarket Retailers, August 1, 2019, accessed July 12, 2020. https://www.massmarketretailers.com/glaxosmithkline-pfizer-close-joint-venture/.

17. Malhotra, Naresh K., Olivia F. Lee, and Can Uslay. (2012), "Mind the Gap: The Mediating Role of Mindful Marketing between Market and Quality Orientations, Their Interaction, and Consequences," *International Journal of Quality & Reliability Management*, 29 (6), 607–625.

Uslay, Can, and Emine Erdogan (2014), "The Mediating Role of Mindful Entrepreneurial Marketing (MEM) Between Production and Consumption," *Journal of Research in Marketing & Entrepreneurship*, 16 (1), 47–62.

Sheth, Jagdish N., N.K. Sethia, and S. Srinivas. 2011. "Mindful Consumption: A Customer-centric Approach to Sustainability." *Journal of the Academy of Marketing Science*, 3 (9): 21–39.

18. Molbak, Jens (2017), "Jens Molbak: Tri-Sector Innovation, KIN Global 2017," YouTube, June 22, 2017, accessed July 12, 2020. https://www.youtube.com/watch?v=2PWPfeo2Yyo.

19. Molbak, Jens (2017), "Jens Molbak: Tri-Sector Innovation, KIN Global 2017," YouTube, June 22, 2017, accessed July 12, 2020. https://www.youtube.com/watch?v=2PWPfeo2Yyo.

Uslay, Can (2019), "The Next Frontier in Marketing: Self-Sustaining Marketing, Society, and Capitalism through Collaborative yet Disruptive Partnerships" in *Handbook of Marketing Advances in the Era of Disruptions— Essays in Honor of Jagdish N. Sheth*, A. Parvatiyar and R.S. Sisodia eds., Sage, 490–500.

20. Sheth, Jagdish N. and Rajendra S. Sisodia (2002), *The Rule of Three: Surviving and Thriving in Competitive Markets*. New York: The Free Press.

Uslay, Can (2015), "The Rule of Three: Market Share and Performance," in *Empirical Generalizations about Marketing Impact*, D. M. Hanssens ed., Cambridge, MA: Marketing Science Institute, 17–18.

21. Uslay, Can, Z. Ayca Altintig, and Robert D. Winsor (2010), "An Empirical Examination of the 'Rule of Three': Strategy Implications for Top Management, Marketers, and Investors," *Journal of Marketing*, 74 (March), 20–39.

Uslay, Can (2015), "The Rule of Three: Market Structure and Performance," in Empirical Generalizations about Marketing Impact, D. M. Hanssens ed., Cambridge, MA: Marketing Science Institute, 16.

22. The industrial organization literature offers a substantial treatment of how cost structures and government policies influence industry structure; for example, see Scherer (1980) for a review. Berger, Demsetz, and Strahan (1999) overview how industry consolidation and globalization can impact industry structure, and Klepper and Simons (1997) describe the significant role that convergence on a dominant technology or product design can have on industry structure.

Scherer, Frederic M. (1980), *Industrial Market Structure and Economic Performance*, 2nd ed. Boston: Houghton Mifflin.

Klepper, Steven and Kenneth L. Simons (1997), "Technological Extinctions of Industrial Firms: An Inquiry into Their Nature and Causes," *Industrial and Corporate Change*, 6 (2), 379–460.

Berger, Alan N., Rebecca S. Demsetz, and Philip E. Strahan (1999), "The Consolidation of the Financial Services Industry: Causes, Consequences, and Implications for the Future," *Journal of Banking and Finance*, 23 (2–4), 135–94.

23. Gold, Hadas, and Charles Riley (2017), "Disney is Buying Most of 21st Century Fox for $52.4 Billion," CNN, December 14, accessed September 28, 2019. http://money.cnn.com/2017/12/14/media/disney-fox-deal/index.html.

Wells, Sarah (2018), "New $71.3 Billion Disney Bid for Fox Tops Comcast's" Techcrunch.com, June 20, 2018, accessed September 28, 2019. https://techcrunch.com/2018/06/20/new-71-3-billion-disney-bid-for-fox-tops-comcasts/.

Vander Werrf, Emily Todd (2019), "Here's what Disney Owns After the Massive Disney/Fox Merger," Vox.com, March 20, 2019, accessed September 28, 2019. https://www.vox.com/culture/2019/3/20/18273477/disney-fox-merger-deal-details-marvel-x-men.

24. Swaminathan, Anand (2001), "Partitioning and the Evolution of Specialist Organizations: The Role of Location and Identity in the U.S. Wine Industry," *Academy of Management Journal*, 44 (6), 1169–85.

25. Carroll, Glenn R. (1985), "Concentration and Specialization: Dynamics of Niche Width in Populations of Organizations," *American Journal of Sociology*, 90 (6), 1261–83.

26. For example, see Scherer, Frederic M. (1980), *Industrial Market Structure and Economic Performance*, 2nd ed. Boston: Houghton Mifflin.

27. Drucker, P. F. (1985). *Innovation and Entrepreneurship*. New York: Harper & Row.

28. Sheth, J. N. (2011), *Chindia Rising: How China and India will Benefit your Business*, 2nd ed. Tata-McGraw Hill India.

Appendix: Past, Current, and Future Top Three Players in Global Markets

Projections into Global Markets

The Global Rule of Three powerfully predicts the number of dominant players and underlying characteristics of these firms but it does not specify companies, how long it will take them to get there, or how long they will prevail. Nevertheless, we provide our predictions in a variety of global markets to show the trajectory from the last two decades and into the next decade based on the theoretical underpinnings of the Global Rule of Three. However, please keep in mind the wise words of Nobel Prize winner Wassily Leontief: "[r]egarding the projections, the only thing I am certain about is that they are wrong."[1] In other words, as the adage goes, predictions are hard especially when they are about the future. Alas, we offer no replacement for a magic crystal ball. The boundaries between markets are blurring faster than ever. Hence, we present the following Tables to offer food for thought, notwithstanding unforeseen circumstances and Black Swan events such as the Covid-19 pandemic. Please also note that each Table is based on data from different sources and may not precisely reflect the revenue rank during the calendar years 2000 and 2020.

© The Author(s) 2020
J. Sheth et al., *The Global Rule of Three*, https://doi.org/10.1007/978-3-030-57473-4

The Global Big Three

Table A.1 Accounting/consulting firms

2000	2020	2030
Ernst & Young (U.K.)	Deloitte	PwC
Deloitte & Touche (U.S.)	PricewaterhouseCoopers (U.K.)	Deloitte
Arthur Andersen (U.S.)	Ernst & Young	KPMG (Netherlands)

Source: Gonzales, Eddie (2019), "Global Accounting Services," IBISWorld, December 2019, accessed July 25, 2020. https://my-ibisworld-com.proxy.libraries.rutgers.edu/gl/en/indU.S.try/l6713-gl/major-companies
"The 20 Top Accounting Firms in The World" (2020), *The Big 4 Accounting Firms*, accessed July 25, 2020. https://big4accountingfirms.org/the-top-accounting-firms-in-the-world/
Note: Arthur Andersen collapsed due to its mishandling of Enron audits. We think that the global anti-American headwinds will help PricewaterhouseCoopers (PwC) take the crown from Deloitte over the next couple of decades. Ironically, isolation and instability from Brexit will help KPMG edge over Ernst & Young (E&Y)

Table A.2 Advertising agencies

2000	2020	2030
Publicis Groupe (France)	WPP (U.K.)	Google (U.S.)
Omnicom Group (U.S.)	Omnicom Group	Facebook (U.S.)
Interpublic GR OF COS	Publicis	Alibaba (China)

Source: Uslay, Can (2018), "Is Advertising Stuck in the Middle? A Commentary," *Journal of Advertising Education*, 22 (2), 147–151
Note: Advertising conglomerates of today are being quickly dwarfed by tech giants who may soon take over agency work initially via programmatic advertising, followed by artificial intelligence (AI) and creative work

Table A.3 Aerospace companies

2000	2020	2030
Boeing (U.S.)	Boeing	Boeing
United Technologies (U.S.)	Raytheon Technologies (U.S.)	Airbus
Lockheed Martin (U.S.)	Airbus (EU)	COMAC (China)

Source: Jammula, Ajay Kumar Reddy (2019), "Top Aerospace and Defence Companies: Ranking the top 10 by Market Share," Army Technology, March 20, 2019, accessed July 25, 2020. https://www.army-technology.com/features/top-aerospace-and-defence-companies/
Note: As discussed in a sidebar in Chap. 8, Raytheon Technologies recently edged Airbus due to the merger between Raytheon and United Technologies. However, Airbus is expected to strike back with M&A of its own, and combined with ensuing pressure from COMAC, Raytheon may not be able to hold on to its brand identity

Table A.4 Agricultural equipment makers

2000	2020	2030
John Deere (U.S.)	John Deere	John Deere
CNH Global (Netherlands/U.K.)	CNH Global (Netherlands/U.K.)	CNH Global
AGCO (U.S.)	Kubota (Japan)	Mahindra & Mahindra (India)

Source: Statista (2020), "Selected Farm Machinery Manufacturers Worldwide in FY 2018, Based on Revenue" accessed July 25, 2020. https://www.statista.com/statistics/461428/revenue-of-major-farm-machinery-manufacturers-worldwide/
Statista (2019), "Brand Value of Mahindra in India in 2016 to 2019," accessed July 25, 2020. https://www-statista-com.proxy.libraries.rutgers.edu/statistics/748754/mahindra-brand-value-india/
Note: Mahindra & Mahindra is likely to not only utilize is domestic scale advantage but also grow globally to capture the #3 spot. Brand value of Mahindra has almost doubled in the past four years

Table A.5 Aircraft engine makers

2000	2020	2030
General Electric Aviation (U.S.)	CFM International (U.S.)	CFM International
Pratt & Whitney (U.S.)	Pratt & Whitney	General Electric Aviation
Rolls-Royce (U.K.)	Rolls-Royce	Rolls-Royce

Source: Statista (2020), "Market Share of the Leading Commercial Aircraft Engine Manufacturers Worldwide as of December 2019" accessed July 25, 2020. https://www-statista-com.proxy.libraries.rutgers.edu/statistics/1099835/global-aircraft-engine-manufacturer-market-share/
Statista (2020), "Top Aircraft Engine Manufacturers Worldwide Between 2019 and 2028, by MRO demand," accessed July 25, 2020. https://www-statista-com.proxy.libraries.rutgers.edu/statistics/1097253/world-aircraft-engine-manufacturer-mro-demand/
Note: In 2017, General Electric Aviation and Rolls-Royce were awarded major multi-year military contracts in the U.S. and China, respectively

Table A.6 Aircraft alliances

2000	2020	2030
Star Alliance	Star Alliance	SkyTeam
One World Alliance	SkyTeam	Star Alliance
SkyTeam	One World Alliance	One World Alliance

Source: Boon, Tom (2018), "The 3 Major Airline Alliances: Star Alliance, One World and SkyTeam—Why Are They Good?" Simple Flying, October 20, 2018, accessed July 12, 2020. https://simpleflying.com/the-3-major-airline-alliances-star-alliance-oneworld-and-skyteam-why-are-they-good/
Note: Due to network effects, we do not foresee a newcomer taking over any of the top three alliances. However, SkyTeam which already carries the most passengers annually is likely to challenge Star Alliance and may establish itself as the global leader based on its emerging markets presence

Table A.7 Aluminum producers

2000	2020	2030
Alcoa (U.S.)	Hongqiao Group (China)	Hongqiao Group
Pechiney (France)	Chalco (China)	Xinfa (China)
Alcan (Canada)	Rusai (Russia)	Rio Tinto (Australia)

Source: Statista (2020), "The World's Leading Primary Aluminum Producing Companies in 2019, based on Production Output," accessed July 25, 2020. https://www.statista.com/statistics/280920/largest-aluminum-companies-worldwide/

Table A.8 Apparel companies

2000	2020	2030
Levi Strauss (U.S.)	VF Corporation	PVH
VF Corporation (U.S.)	PVH (U.S.)	VF Corporation
Jones Apparel Group Inc. (U.S.)	Hanes (U.S.)	Hanes

Source: Statista (2020), "Largest Apparel Companies by Revenue Worldwide in 2019," accessed July 25, 2020. https://www-statista-com.proxy.libraries.rutgers.edu/statistics/831185/revenues-of-the-largest-global-apparel-companies/
Statista (2019), "Market Share of Global Apparel Demand from 2005 to 2020, by region," accessed July 25, 2020. https://www-statista-com.proxy.libraries.rutgers.edu/statistics/821457/demand-share-of-global-apparel-market-by-region/
Note: The demand for apparel is increasing in the Asia-Pacific region and in women and children's segments. PVH is focusing on global markets and leads in these high-growth segments

Table A.9 Appliance makers

2000	2020	2030
GE (U.S.)	Haier Group (China)	Midea Group (China)
Whirlpool (U.S.)	LG (South Korea)	Gree Electric Appliances (China)
Electrolux (Sweden)	Samsung (South Korea)	Haier Group

Source: Statista (2018), "Global Sales Volume Share of the Major Household Appliances in 2017, by Brand," accessed July 25, 2020. https://www-statista-com.proxy.libraries.rutgers.edu/statistics/912276/household-appliance-global-sales-volume-brand-share/
Statista (2019), "Sales of the Leading Household Appliance Companies Worldwide in 2019," accessed July 25, 2020. https://www-statista-com.proxy.libraries.rutgers.edu/statistics/257968/sales-of-the-leading-household-appliance-companies-worldwide/
Statista (2020), "Electrolux's Total Revenue from 2001 to 2019 (in billion U.S. dollars)*," accessed July 25, 2020. https://www-statista-com.proxy.libraries.rutgers.edu/statistics/220819/electroluxs-total-revenue-since-2011/
Statista (2020), "Electrolux's Revenue in the U.S. from 2001 to 2019," accessed July 25, 2020. https://www-statista-com.proxy.libraries.rutgers.edu/statistics/220830/electroluxs-revenue-in-U.S.-since-2001/
Note: Electrolux may eventually be acquired as its global revenues continue to decrease

Table A.10 Athletic apparel companies

2000	2020	2030
Nike (U.S.)	Nike	Nike
Adidas (Germany)	Adidas	Adidas
Reebok (U.K.)	Puma (Germany)	Under Armour (U.S.)

Source: Statista (2019), "Leading Athletic Apparel, Accessories and Footwear Companies Worldwide in 2019, by sales," accessed July 25, 2020. https://www.statista.com/statistics/900271/leading-sportswear-and-performance-wear-companies-by-sales-worldwide/
Note: Adidas acquired Reebok for $3.1 billion in 2006. Lululemon and Columbia can thrive as specialists

Table A.11 Banks (custodial)

2000	2020	2030
Bank of New York (U.S.)	Bank of New York Mellon (U.S.)	Bank of New York Mellon
Chase Manhattan (U.S.)	State Street Bank and Trust (U.S.)	JP Morgan Chase
State Street (U.S.)	Bank of America (U.S.)	Bitmain (China)

Source: Butler, Brenna (2020), "Custody, Asset & Securities Services in the US," IBISWorld, February 2020, accessed July 25, 2020. https://my-ibisworld-com.proxy.libraries.rutgers.edu/us/en/industry/52399/major-companies
Statista (2019), "Leading Blockchain Companies with the Most Amount of Total Equity Funding Raised in China as of 1st Quarter 2019," accessed July 25, 2020. https://www-statista-com.proxy.libraries.rutgers.edu/statistics/1041221/china-companies-with-the-most-equity-funding/
Note: Cryptocurrencies enabled by the blockchain are expected to make headway over the next decade

Table A.12 Banks (full service)

2000	2020	2030
Citigroup (U.S.)	ICBC (China)	ICBC
Bank of America (U.S.)	China Construction Bank	China Construction Bank
HSBC Holdings (U.K.)	Agricultural Bank of China	Agricultural Bank of China

Source: Khan, Yusuf (2019), "These Are the 10 Biggest Banks in the World in 2019," Markets Insider, July 4, accessed July 25, 2020. https://markets.businessinsider.com/news/stocks/top-10-banks-in-the-world-2019-2019-7-1028330545#3-agricultural-bank-of-china-china-243-billion8
Bagnall, Elinor (2019), "Top 1000 World Banks 2019," The Banker, January 7, accessed July 25, 2020. https://www.thebanker.com/Top-1000-World-Banks/Top-1000-World-Banks-2019-The-Banker-International-Press-Release-for-immediate-release
Statista (2020), "Largest Banks Globally as of December 2018, by Assets," accessed July 25, 2020. https://www-statista-com.proxy.libraries.rutgers.edu/statistics/269845/largest-banks-in-the-world-by-total-assets/
The Banker Database (2020), "Top 5 Banks," accessed July 25, 2020. https://www.thebankerdatabase.com/

Table A.13 Banks (investment)

2000	2020	2030
Morgan Stanley (U.S.)	JPMorgan (U.S.)	Goldman Sachs
Merrill Lynch (U.S.)	Goldman Sachs	JPMorgan
Goldman Sachs (U.S.)	Morgan Stanley	Morgan Stanley

Source: Macrotrends (2020), "JPMorgan Chase Revenue 2006–2020," accessed July 25, 2020. https://www.macrotrends.net/stocks/charts/JPM/jpmorgan-chase/revenue
Macrotrends (2020), "Goldman Sachs Revenue 2006–2020," accessed July 25, 2020. https://www.macrotrends.net/stocks/charts/GS/goldman-sachs/revenue
Macrotrends (2020), "Morgan Stanley Revenue 2006–2020," accessed July 25, 2020. https://www.macrotrends.net/stocks/charts/MS/morgan-stanley/revenue
Statista (2019), "Global Market Share of Revenue of Leading Investment Banks as of December 2019," accessed July 25, 2020. https://www.statista.com/statistics/271008/global-market-share-of-investment-banks/
Note: Blackstone and BlackRock are emerging as highly profitable specialists

Table A.14 Beer producers (sub-category of alcoholic beverages)

2000	2020	2030
Anheuser-Busch (U.S.)	Anheuser-Busch InBev (Belgium)	Anheuser-Busch InBev
SABMiller (U.K.)	Heineken (Netherlands)	Heineken
Coors (U.S.)	Molson Coors (Canada)	Asahi (Japan)

Source: Irigoyen, Santiago (2019), "Global Beer Manufacturing," IBISWorld, July 2020, accessed July 25, 2020. https://my-ibisworld-com.proxy.libraries.rutgers.edu/gl/en/industry/c1121-gl/major-companies

Table A.15 Beverage companies (alcoholic)

2000	2020	2030
InBev (Belgium)	Anheuser-Busch InBev (Belgium)	Anheuser-Busch InBev
SABMiller (U.K.)	Heineken (Netherlands)	Heineken
Diageo (U.K.)	Diageo (U.K.)	Diageo

Source: Statista (2019), "Sales of the Leading Beer Companies Worldwide in 2019," accessed July 25, 2020. https://www-statista-com.proxy.libraries.rutgers.edu/statistics/257670/sales-of-the-leading-beer-companies-worldwide/
Statista (2020), "Leading Beverage Companies Worldwide in 2019, based on sales," accessed July 25, 2020. https://www-statista-com.proxy.libraries.rutgers.edu/statistics/307963/leading-beverage-companies-worldwide-based-on-net-sales/
Statista (2019), "The World's Leading 10 Brewing Groups in 2018, Based on Production Volume," accessed July 25, 2020. https://www-statista-com.proxy.libraries.rutgers.edu/statistics/227197/leading-10-brewing-groups-worldwide-based-on-production-volume/
Jernigan, David H. (2009), "The Global Alcohol Industry: An Overview," *Addiction*, 104, 6–12. http://www.ias.org.uk/uploads/pdf/Economic%20impacts%20docs/The%20global%20alcohol%20industry%20%2D%2D%20Jernigan%20paper.pdf
Note: InBev acquired Anheuser-Busch and SABMiller. No leadership changes anticipated unless alcoholic beverage makers manage to consolidate sooner than anticipated

Table A.16 Beverage companies (non-alcoholic)

2000	2020	2030
Coca-Cola (U.S.)	Coca-Cola	Coca-Cola
PepsiCo (U.S.)	PepsiCo	PepsiCo
Cadbury Schweppes (U.K.)	Keurig Dr Pepper (U.S.)	Keurig Dr Pepper

Source: Statista (2019), "Market Share of Leading Carbonated Soft Drink (CSD) Companies in the United States from 2004 to 2018," accessed July 25, 2020. https://www-statista-com.proxy.libraries.rutgers.edu/statistics/225464/market-share-of-leading-soft-drink-companies-in-the-U.S.-since-2004/ Statista (2019), "Coca-Cola Company's Market Share in the United States from 2004 to 2018," accessed July 25, 2020. https://www-statista-com.proxy.libraries.rutgers.edu/statistics/225388/U.S.-market-share-of-the-coca-cola-company-since-2004/ Statista (2019), "PepsiCo Company's Market Share in the United States from 2004 to 2018," accessed July 25, 2020. https://www-statista-com.proxy.libraries.rutgers.edu/statistics/225419/U.S.-market-share-of-the-pepsico-company-since-2004/
Note: Cadbury Schweppes is now Keurig Dr Pepper

Table A.17 Biotechnology companies

2000	2020	2030
Monsanto (U.S.)	Amgen	Amgen
Amgen (U.S.)	Gilead Sciences (U.S.)	Novo Nordisk
Quest Diagnostics (U.S.)	Novo Nordisk (Denmark)	Jiangsu Hengrui (China)

Source: Phillipidis, Alex (2018), "Top 25 Biotech Companies of 2018," Genetic Engineering & Biotechnology News, accessed July 25, 2020. https://www.genengnews.com/a-lists/top-25-biotech-companies-of-2018/

Table A.18 Brokerage firms/wealth management

2000	2020	2030
Merrill Lynch (U.S.)	Bank of America (U.S.)	Morgan Stanley
Morgan Stanley Dean Witter (U.S.)	Morgan Stanley	Bank of America
Goldman Sachs Group (U.S.)	JP Morgan (U.S.)	JP Morgan

Source: Mieles, Carlos (2020), "Global Investment Banking & Brokerage," IBISWorld, January 2020, accessed July 25, 2020. https://my-ibisworld-com.proxy.libraries.rutgers.edu/gl/en/industry/j5521-gl/about
Jonas, Daniel (2020), "The Biggest and Best Wealth Management Firms," Investopedia, February 22, accessed July 25, 2020. https://www.investopedia.com/articles/investing/061314/best-best-wealth-management-firms.asp
Statista (2020), "Leading Wealth Managers Worldwide as of June 2020" accessed July 25, 2020. https://www-statista-com.proxy.libraries.rutgers.edu/statistics/329685/leading-wealth-managers-by-assets-under-management-usa/

Table A.19 Candy makers

2000	2020	2030
Hershey (U.S.)	Mars Wrigley	Mars Wrigley
Mars Inc. (U.S.)	Ferrero SpA (Italy)	Ferrero SpA
Nestlé (Switzerland)	Mondelez International Inc. (U.S.)	Meiji Holdings (Japan)

Source: Irigoyen, Santiago (2019), "Global Candy & Chocolate Manufacturing," IBISWorld, August 2019, accessed July 25, 2020. https://my-ibisworld-com.proxy. libraries.rutgers.edu/gl/en/industry/c1113-gl/major-companies
BNP Media (2020), "2020 Global Top 100 Candy Companies Candy Industry" accessed July 25, 2020. https://www.candyindustry.com/2020/global-top-100-candy-companies
Statista (2020), "Meiji's net sales FY 2013–2019" accessed July 25, 2020. https://www-statista-com.proxy.libraries.rutgers.edu/statistics/782257/meiji-net-sales/
Statista (2020), "Mondelez International's net revenue worldwide 2011–2019" accessed July 25, 2020. https://www-statista-com.proxy.libraries.rutgers.edu/statistics/260298/net-revenue-of-mondelez-international-worldwide/
The Washington Post (2005), "Mars INC." accessed July 25, 2020. www.washingtonpost. com/wp-srv/business/post200/2005/MARS.html
Note: Mondelez continues to lose market share, creating opportunity for Meiji to take the third global spot

Table A.20 Chemical companies

2000	2020	2030
BASF (Germany)	BASF	BASF
DuPont (U.S.)	Dow	Dow
Dow Chemical (U.S.)	LyondellBasell (U.S.)	Mitsubishi Chemical Holdings (Japan)

Source: Statista (2020), "Chemical Industry Worldwide" accessed July 25, 2020. https:// www-statista-com.proxy.libraries.rutgers.edu/study/69047/global-chemical-industry/
Statista (2020), "2020 Global List of Leading Chemical Companies Based on Revenue" accessed July 25, 2020. https://www-statista-com.proxy.libraries.rutgers.edu/ statistics/272704/top-10-chemical-companies-worldwide-based-on-revenue/
Statista (2020), "LyondellBasell's Revenue 2008–2019" accessed July 25, 2020. https:// www-statista-com.proxy.libraries.rutgers.edu/statistics/281391/revenue-of-lyondellbasell/
Note: LyondellBasell is losing market share, creating opportunity for Mitsubishi Chemical Holdings

Table A.21 Communications equipment companies

2000	2020	2030
Lucent Technologies (U.S.)	Huawei (China)	Huawei
Nortel Networks (Canada)	Cisco Systems	Cisco Systems
Cisco Systems (U.S.)	Fujitsu (Japan)	Nokia (Finland)

Source: Statista (2020), "Mobile Infrastructure Market Share Worldwide 2017–2018, by company" accessed July 25, 2020. https://www-statista-com.proxy.libraries.rutgers.edu/ statistics/526037/global-telecom-equipment-market-share/
Statista (2020), "Telecom Infrastructure Companies by Brand Value 2020" accessed July

25, 2020. https://www-statista-com.proxy.libraries.rutgers.edu/statistics/500041/telecom-infrastructure-brand-value/
Statista (2020), "Telecom Equipment Companies Worldwide Ranked by Total Revenue 2018" accessed July 25, 2020. https://www-statista-com.proxy.libraries.rutgers.edu/statistics/314657/top-10-telecom-equipment-companies-revenue/
Note: Dot.com bubble affected the communications equipment industry; Lucent Technologies had major losses and was acquired by Avaya; Nortel declared bankruptcy in 2009. Nokia or Ericsson from Europe could make a comeback

Table A.22 Computer disk drive manufacturers

2000	2020	2030
Maxtor (U.S.)	Samsung (South Korea)	Samsung
Seagate (U.S.)	Western Digital	Western Digital
Western Digital (U.S.)	Seagate	Toshiba (Japan)

Source: Farrance, Rex (2006), "Timeline: 50 Years of Hard Drives," *PCWorld*, September 12, accessed July 25, 2020. https://www.pcworld.com/article/127105/article.html
Statista (2020), "Global Disk Drive Market Share by Maker 2018–2019" accessed July 25, 2020. https://www.statista.com/statistics/915062/disk-drive-market-share-by-maker/
Note: Seagate acquired Maxtor in 2006 and Samsung's HDD unit in 2011

Table A.23 Coal companies

2000	2020	2030
Massey Energy (U.S.)	Coal India (India)	Coal India
Consol Energy (U.S.)	BHP Billiton (Australia)	Shenhua Energy Company
Arch Coal (U.S.)	Shenhua Energy Company (China)	BHP Billiton

Source: Technavio (2018), "Top 5 Largest Coal Mining Companies in the World," accessed July 25, 2020. https://blog.technavio.com/blog/top-5-largest-coal-mining-companies

Table A.24 Consumer electronics manufacturers

2000	2020	2030
Matsushita (Japan)	Samsung (South Korea)	Foxconn
Sony (Japan)	Foxconn (China)	Samsung
Philips (Netherlands)	Hitachi (Japan)	Huawei

Source: Rowe, Sam (2020), "Top 10 Electronics Manufacturers in the World," Manufacturing, June 18, accessed July 25, 2020. https://www.manufacturingglobal.com/top10/top-10-electronics-manufacturers-world
Gonzales, Eddie (2019), "Global Consumer Electronics Manufacturing," IBISWorld, August 2019, accessed on July 25, 2020. https://my-ibisworld-com.proxy.libraries.rutgers.edu/gl/en/industry/c2525-gl/major-companies
Macrotends (2020), "Hitachi Revenue 2006–2019," accessed July 25, 2020. https://www.macrotrends.net/stocks/charts/HTHIY/hitachi/revenue
Philips (2000), "Annual Report 2000: Management Report," accessed July 25, 2020. https://ddd.uab.cat/pub/infanu/33431/iaPHILIPSa2000ieng1.pdf
Statista (2020), "Huawei's Revenue by Business Segment 2012–2019" accessed July 25, 2020. https://www-statista-com.proxy.libraries.rutgers.edu/statistics/368519/revenue-of-huawei-by-business-segment/

Table A.25 Contact lens makers

2000	2020	2030
Novartis (Switzerland)	Johnson & Johnson (U.S.)	Johnson & Johnson
Bausch & Lomb (U.S.)	Novartis	Novartis
Vistakon (U.S.)	The Cooper Companies (U.S.)	Bausch Health Companies (Canada)

Source: Curran, Jack (2020), "Contact Lens Manufacturing," IBISWorld, May 2020, accessed on July 25, 2020. https://my-ibisworld-com.proxy.libraries.rutgers.edu/us/en/industry-specialized/od4155/major-companies
Note: Vistakon is now a part of Johnson & Johnson. Bausch & Lomb was acquired by Valeant Pharmaceuticals, now Bausch Health companies

Table A.26 Cosmetics companies

2000	2020	2030
Unilever (Netherlands)	L'Oréal	L'Oréal
L'Oréal (France)	Unilever	Unilever
Procter & Gamble (U.S.)	Estée Lauder (U.S.)	Estée Lauder

Source: Romanowski, Perry (2018), "The 20 Biggest Cosmetic Companies in the World," Chemists Corner, April 6, accessed July 25th, 2020. https://chemistscorner.com/the-20-biggest-cosmetic-companies-in-the-world/
Koronios, Eva (2019), "Global Cosmetics Manufacturing," IBISWorld, September 2019, accessed on July 25, 2020. https://my-ibisworld-com.proxy.libraries.rutgers.edu/gl/en/industry/c1934-gl/major-companies

Table A.27 Credit card companies

2000	2020	2030
Visa (U.S.)	Visa	Visa
Mastercard (U.S.)	Mastercard	UnionPay
American Express (U.S.)	UnionPay (China)	Mastercard

Source: Sembower, Toby (2020), "Credit Card Companies: 15 Largest Issuers (2020 List)," Card Rates.com, June 18, accessed July 25, 2020. https://www.cardrates.com/news/credit-card-companies/
Statista (2019), "Distribution of Credit Card Issuers Worldwide 2017, by purchase Transactions" accessed July 25, 2020. https://www.statista.com/statistics/278970/share-of-purchase-transactions-on-global-credit-cards/

Table A.28 Cruise lines

2000	2020	2030
Carnival (U.S.)	Carnival	Carnival
Royal Caribbean (U.S.)	Royal Caribbean	Royal Caribbean
Princess (U.S.)	Norwegian	Norwegian

Source: Cruise Market Watch (2018), "2018 Worldwide Cruise Line Market Share," accessed July 25, 2020. https://cruisemarketwatch.com/market-share/

Table A.29 Defense contractors

2000	2020	2030
Lockheed Martin (U.S.)	Lockheed Martin	Lockheed Martin
Boeing (U.S.)	Raytheon Technologies (U.S.)	Raytheon Technologies
BAE Systems (UK)	Boeing	BAE Systems (U.K.)

Source: Stebbins, Samuel & Comen, Evan (2019), "Military Spending: 20 Companies Profiting the Most from War," *USA Today*, February 21, 2019, accessed July 25, 2020. https://www.usatoday.com/story/money/2019/02/21/military-spending-defense-contractors-profiting-from-war-weapons-sales/39092315/
Note: United Technologies and Raytheon merged in 2019. Watch for more M&A in this space as the boundaries between aerospace and defense blur (see sidebar in Chap. 8)

Table A.30 Engineering and construction companies

2000	2020	2030
Bechtel (U.S.)	China Communications Construction Company (China)	PowerChina (China)
Raytheon (U.S.)	PowerChina (China)	China Communications Construction Company (China)
Stone and Webster (U.S.)	Vinci (France)	ACS (Spain)

Source: Chinn, Sela (2020), "Top 18 Biggest Construction Companies in the World and What Makes Them Great," eSUB Construction Software, accessed July 25, 2020. https://esub.com/top-18-biggest-construction-companies-in-the-world-and-what-makes-them-great/
Note: Projects in Africa can propel PowerChina to the #1 spot globally

Table A.31 Entertainment producers

2000	2020	2030
Viacom (U.S.)	Disney (U.S.)	Disney
Fox Entertainment Group (U.S.)	Warner Media (U.S.)	Amazon (U.S.)
Metro-Goldwyn-Mayer Inc. (U.S.)	NBCUniversal (U.S.)	Alphabet (U.S.)

Source: Lesemann, Mara (2019), "The World's Top 10 Entertainment Companies," *Investopedia*, May 17, accessed July 25, 2020, https://www.investopedia.com/articles/investing/020316/worlds-top-10-entertainment-companies-cmcsa-cbs.asp
Wikipedia (2020), "Major Film Studios," accessed July 25, 2020. https://en.wikipedia.org/wiki/Major_film_studio
Note: We anticipate that Alphabet and Amazon will both become mega-players here, possibly through major acquisition. Current players such as Netflix are likely acquisition targets

Table A.32 Forest products companies

2000	2020	2030
Georgia-Pacific CP (U.S.)	West Fraser Timber (Canada)	West Fraser Timber
Weyerhaeuser Co. (U.S.)	Canfor (Canada)	Canfor
Willamette Industries (U.S.)	Weyerhaeuser Co.	Interfor (Canada)

Source: Lesprom Network (2018), "13 Biggest Lumber Companies Increase Production by 2.3% to 34.2 Billion Board Feet in 2017," April 26, accessed July 25, 2020. https://www.lesprom.com/en/news/13_biggest_lumber_companies_increase_production_by_2_3_to_34_2_billion_board_feet_in_2017_82957/

Table A.33 Global retailers

2000	2020	2030
Walmart (U.S.)	Walmart (U.S.)	Amazon
Carrefour (France)	Amazon (U.S.)	Walmart
Target (U.S.)	Costco (U.S.)	JD (China)

Source: François, Jean-Marc (2020), "Amazon Vs. Walmart: The Next Decade Will Decide Which Comes Out On Top," Forbes Magazine, January 15, accessed July 25, 2020. https://www.forbes.com/sites/jeanmarcfrancois/2020/01/15/amazon-vs-walmart-the-next-decade-will-decide-which-comes-out-on-top/#2d81e6a44403
Statista (2020), "Leading 50 Retailers Worldwide in 2018, Based on Retail Revenue" accessed July 25, 2020. https://www-statista-com.proxy.libraries.rutgers.edu/statistics/266595/leading-20-retailers-worldwide-based-on-revenue/
Statista (2020), "Leading 15 Fast-Moving Consumer Goods Retailers Worldwide in 2018, Based on Revenue," accessed July 25, 2020. https://www-statista-com.proxy.libraries.rutgers.edu/statistics/192558/leading-10-consumer-goods-retailers-worldwide-in-2010-based-on-sales/
Note: Amazon is expected to overtake Walmart by 2022

Table A.34 Grain companies

2000	2020	2030
Glencore (U.K./Switzerland)	Glencore	COFCO
Cargill (U.S.)	Cargill	Glencore
ConAgra (U.S.)	COFCO (China)	Cargill

Source: Morris, Nigel (2013), "The Big Five Companies That Control the World's Grain Trade," The Independent, January 23, accessed July 25, 2020. https://www.independent.co.uk/news/uk/home-news/the-big-five-companies-that-control-the-worlds-grain-trade-8462266.html
COFCO (2017), "Base in China March onto the Global Scene," accessed July 25, 2020. http://www.cofco.com/en/AboutCOFCO/#:~:text=At%20present%2C%20COFCO%20has%20total,capacity%20of%2065%20million%20tons

Table A.35 Ground coffee companies, non-durable

2000	2020	2030
Folgers (U.S.)	Folgers (U.S.)	Folgers (U.S.)
Maxwell House (U.S.)	Maxwell House (U.S.)	Starbucks (U.S.)
Sara Lee Brands (U.S.)	Starbucks (U.S.)	Maxwell House (U.S.)

Source: Leibtag, Ephraim, Alice Nakamura, Emi Nakamura, and Dawit Zerom (2007), "Cost Pass-Through in the U.S. Coffee Industry," *SSRN Electronic Journal*. https://www.ers.usda.gov/webdocs/publications/45761/11745_err38b_1_.pdf?v=0
Statista (2020), "Market Share of Ground Coffee in the United States in 2020, by Leading Brands" accessed July 25, 2020. https://www-statista-com.proxy.libraries.rutgers.edu/statistics/451969/market-share-of-ground-coffee-in-the-us-by-leading-brand/

Table A.36 Health care insurers

2000	2020	2030
Aetna (U.S.)	Anthem (U.S.)	People's Insurance Company of China
United Health Group (U.S.)	UnitedHealthcare	Allianz (Germany)
Cigna Corp. (U.S.)	Humana (U.S.)	Cigna (U.S.)

Source: Price, Sterling (2020), "Largest Health Insurance Companies of 2020," ValuePenguin, June 4, accessed July 25, 2020, https://www.valuepenguin.com/largest-health-insurance-companies

Table A.37 Hotel chains

2000	2020	2030
Marriott (U.S.)	Marriott	Marriott
Hilton (U.S.)	Hilton	Hilton
Sheraton (U.S.)	Accor (France)	Airbnb (U.S.)

Source: Morris, James (2017) "Biggest Hotel Groups around the World," Tourism Review News, July 31, accessed July 25, 2020. https://www.tourism-review.com/biggest-hotel-groups-by-revenue-news5501
Note: Airbnb is expected to challenge and consolidate local operators and continue to grow over the next two decades

Table A.38 Insurance companies, full line

2000	2020	2030
AXA (France)	Berkshire Hathaway (U.S.)	Ping An Insurance
American International Group (U.S.)	Ping An Insurance (China)	Berkshire Hathaway
Aegon (Netherlands)	Allianz (Germany)	People's Insurance Company of China

Source: Statista (2020), "Leading Global Insurance Companies Worldwide in 2018, by Revenue" accessed July 25, 2020. https://www.statista.com/statistics/185746/revenue-of-the-leading-global-insurance-companies/

Table A.39 Insurance companies, property, and casualty

2000	2020	2030
Allstate (U.S.)	Berkshire Hathaway (U.S.)	People's Insurance Company of China
Loews Corp. (U.S.)	People's Insurance Company of China	Berkshire Hathaway
CAN Capital (U.S.)	Munich Re (Germany)	Munich Re

Source: Statista (2020), "Leading Property and Casualty (Stock) Insurance Companies Globally in 2018, by Revenue" accessed July 25, 2020. https://www.statista.com/statistics/185758/leading-global-property-and-casualty-insurance-companies-by-revenue/

Table A.40 Investment securities

2000	2020	2030
Morgan Stanley Dean Witter (U.S.)	Citigroup (U.S.)	Citigroup
Merrill Lynch (U.S.)	JP Morgan Chase & Co (U.S.)	JP Morgan Chase & Co
Goldman Sachs (U.S.)	Goldman Sachs	Morgan Stanley (U.S.)

Source: Mieles, Carlos (2020), "Global Investment Banking & Brokerage," IBISWorld, January 2020, accessed on July 25, 2020. https://my-ibisworld-com.proxy.libraries.rutgers.edu/gl/en/industry/j5521-gl/major-companies#major-players

Table A.41 Meat producers

2000	2020	2030
Cargill (U.S.)	Cargill	Cargill
JBS (Brazil)	JBS	JBS
Tyson (U.S.)	Tyson	Tyson

Source: Sharma, Shefali (2018), "Mighty Giants: Leaders of the Global Meat Complex," Institute for Agriculture and Trade Policy, April 10, accessed July 25, 2020. https://www.iatp.org/blog/leaders-global-meat-complex
Masters, Nick (2020), "Meat, Beef & Poultry Processing in the US," IBISWorld, February 2020, accessed on July 25, 2020. https://my-ibisworld-com.proxy.libraries.rutgers.edu/us/en/industry/31161/major-companies
Note: WH Group from China is expected to take longer than a decade to become a top global contender

Table A.42 Medical supply companies

2000	2020	2030
Abbott (U.S.)	Medtronic (U.S.)	Medtronic
Baxter (U.S.)	Johnson & Johnson (U.S.)	Johnson & Johnson
Becton Dickinson (U.S.)	Thermo Fisher (U.S.)	Weigao (China)

Source: Vara, Vasanthi (2019), "The Top Ten Medical Devices Companies by Market

Share in 2018," Verdict Medical Devices, March 7, accessed July 25, 2020. https://www.medicaldevice-network.com/features/top-medical-device-companies/
IBISWorld (2020), "Medical Supplies Manufacturing in China," IBISWorld, May 2020, accessed on July 25, 2020. https://my-ibisworld-com.proxy.libraries.rutgers.edu/cn/en/industry/2770/major-companies
Macrotrends (2020), "Koninklijke Philips Revenue 2006–2020" accessed July 25, 2020. https://www.macrotrends.net/stocks/charts/PHG/koninklijke-philips/revenue
Note: Medtronic is an American company headquartered in Ireland for tax purposes. Shandong Weigao Group Co., Ltd., is the main contender with almost 19% market share in China

Table A.43 Mining companies

2000	2020	2030
BHP (Australia)	Glencore (Switzerland)	Glencore
Rio Tinto (U.K.)	BHP	China Shenhua Energy Company Limited (China)
Cameco Corp. (Canada)	Rio Tinto	Yanzhou Coal Mining (China)

Source: Statista (2020), "2020 ranking of the leading global oil and gas companies based on revenue" accessed July 25, 2020. https://www.statista.com/statistics/272710/top-10-oil-and-gas-companies-worldwide-based-on-revenue/

Table A.44 Mobile phone manufacturers

2000	2020	2030
Ericsson (Sweden)	Samsung (South Korea)	Huawei
Nokia (Finland)	Apple (U.S.)	Xiaomi (China)
Motorola (U.S.)	Huawei (China)	Samsung

Source: Gadgets Now Bureau (2019), "10 Biggest Smartphone Companies of the World," February 21, accessed July 25, 2020. https://www.gadgetsnow.com/slideshows/10-biggest-smartphone-companies-of-the-world/Samsung/photolist/68097576.cms

Table A.45 Movie theater chains

2000	2020	2030
United Artists (U.S.)	AMC Theaters (U.S.)	AMC Theaters (U.S.)
Loews Cineplex (U.S.)	Cineworld (UK)	Cineworld (UK)
AMC Entertainment (U.S.)	Cinemark (U.S.)	Cinepolis (Mexico)

Source: Perlman, Elisabeth (2017), "These are Some of the Biggest Cinema Chains in the World," Verdict, December 5, accessed July 25, 2020. https://www.verdict.co.uk/biggest-cinema-chains/

Table A.46 Music publishers

2000	2020	2030
Warner EMI (U.S.)	Sony	Sony
Sony (Japan)	Universal (U.S.)	Universal
BMG (Germany)	Warner Chappell (U.S.)	Warner Chappell

Source: Ingham, Tim (2019), "Who's the Biggest Music Publisher in the World?" Music Business Worldwide, December 17, accessed July 25, 2020. https://www.musicbusinessworldwide.com/whos-the-biggest-music-publisher-in-the-world/

Table A.47 Office copier manufacturers

2000	2020	2030
Canon (Japan)	Hewlett-Packard (U.S.)	Hewlett-Packard
Xerox (U.S.)	Canon	Canon
Ikon Office Solutions (U.S.)	Epson (Japan)	Epson

Source: Statista (2020), "Market Share Held by Hardcopy Peripherals Vendors Worldwide from 2009 to 2019" accessed July 25, 2020. https://www-statista-com.proxy.libraries.rutgers.edu/statistics/272074/market-shares-held-by-hardcopy-peripheral-producers-worldwide-since-2009/

Table A.48 Office furniture manufacturers

2000	2020	2030
Steelcase (U.S.)	Steelcase	Steelcase
Haworth (U.S.)	Herman Miller	HNI (U.S.)
Herman Miller (U.S.)	Urban Office (U.K.)	Herman Miller

Source: BizVibe (2020), "Top 10 Office Furniture Manufacturers in the World 2020, Top Commercial Furniture Manufacturers," March 6, accessed July 25, 2020. https://www.bizvibe.com/blog/top-office-furniture-manufacturers/

Table A.49 Online travel agencies

2000	2020	2030
Travelocity (U.S.)	TUI Group (Germany)	Booking Holdings
Expedia (U.S.)	Booking Holdings (U.S.)	TUI Group
Preview Travel	Expedia	Expedia

Source: Couillard, Lucie (2020), "Global Travel Agency Services," IBISWorld, March 2020, accessed on July 25, 2020. https://my-ibisworld-com.proxy.libraries.rutgers.edu/gl/en/industry/h4911-gl/major-companies

Table A.50 Overnight couriers

2000	2020	2030
Federal Express (U.S.)	United Parcel Service	FedEx
United Parcel Service (U.S.)	FedEx	United Parcel Service
Airborne (U.S.)	Deutsche Post DHL Group (Germany)	Deutsche Post DHL Group

Source: Gonzales, Eddie (2020), "Global Courier & Delivery Services," IBISWorld, July 2020, accessed on July 25, 2020. https://my-ibisworld-com.proxy.libraries.rutgers.edu/gl/en/industry/h4921-gl/major-companies

Table A.51 Paper and pulp companies

2000	2020	2030
International Paper (U.S.)	Oji Holdings Corporation	International Paper
Oji Holdings Corporation (Japan)	International Paper	Oji Holdings Corporation
Georgia-Pacific (U.S.)	Stora Enso AB (Finland)	Stora Enso AB

Source: Leach, Nathaniel (2019), "Global Paper & Pulp Mills," IBISWorld, August 2019, accessed on July 25, 2020. https://my-ibisworld-com.proxy.libraries.rutgers.edu/gl/en/industry/c1511-gl/major-companies

Table A.52 PBX equipment manufacturers

2000	2020	2030
Lucent (U.S.)	Cisco (U.S.)	Cisco
Northern Telecom (Canada)	Avaya (U.S.)	Avaya
Siemens/Rolm (Germany)	NEC (Japan)	Mitel (Canada)

Source: Buckley, Sean (2018), "Cisco, Avaya Retain Dominant PBX Market Share, but Segment Drops 8% on Delayed Spending, Cloud Migration, says Analyst," *Fierce Telecom*, March 16, accessed July 25, 2020, https://www.fiercetelecom.com/telecom/cisco-avaya-retain-dominant-pbx-market-share-but-segment-drops-8-delayed-spending-cloud

Statista (2020), "Ranking of Telecom Infrastructure Companies by Brand Value in 2020" accessed July 25, 2020. https://www.statista.com/statistics/500041/telecom-infrastructure-brand-value/

Note: Huawei may also be a major player, but little information is available about their production of PBX equipment

Table A.53 Personal computer companies

2000	2020	2030
Compaq (U.S.)	Lenovo (China)	Lenovo
Dell (U.S.)	Hewlett-Packard	Acer (Taiwan)
Hewlett-Packard (U.S.)	Dell	Hewlett-Packard

Source: Statista (2020), "Market share held by the leading personal computer vendors worldwide in 2019," accessed July 25, 2020. https://www.statista.com/statistics/267018/global-market-share-held-by-pc-vendors/

Table A.54 Pharmaceutical companies

2000	2020	2030
Johnson & Johnson (U.S.)	Johnson & Johnson	Johnson & Johnson
Pfizer (U.S.)	Novartis (Switzerland)	Roche
Roche (Switzerland)	Roche	Novartis

Source: Statista (2019), "Pharmaceutical Market Worldwide," accessed July 25, 2020. https://www-statista-com.proxy.libraries.rutgers.edu/study/10642/global-pharmaceutical-industry-statista-dossier/
Macrotrends (2020), "Merck Revenue 2006–2020," accessed July 25, 2020. https://www.macrotrends.net/stocks/charts/MRK/merck/revenue
Koronios, Eva (2020), "Global Pharmaceuticals & Medicine Manufacturing," IBISWorld, March 2020, accessed on July 25, 2020. https://my-ibisworld-com.proxy.libraries.rutgers.edu/gl/en/industry/c1933-gl/major-c

Table A.55 Power plant companies

2000	2020	2030
Alstom (France)	State Grid Corporation of China	State Grid Corporation of China
General Electric (U.S.)	Enel (Italy)	Enel (Italy)
Siemens (Germany)	EDF (France)	Kepco (South Korea)

Source: Verdict Media Limited (2019), "The Ten Biggest Power Companies in 2018," Power Technology, March 19, accessed July 25, 2020. https://www.power-technology.com/features/top-10-power-companies-in-the-world/

Table A.56 Quick service restaurants

2000	2020	2030
McDonald's (U.S.)	McDonald's	McDonald's
Burger King (U.S.)	Yum! Brands (U.S.)	Yum! Brands
Tricon Global (U.S.)	Burger King	Subway

Source: Statista (2020), "Brand Value of the 10 Most Valuable Quick Service Restaurant Brands Worldwide in 2020," accessed July 25, 2020. https://www-statista-com.proxy.libraries.rutgers.edu/statistics/273057/value-of-the-most-valuable-fast-food-brands-worldwide/
Couillard, Lucie (2020), "Global Fast Food Restaurants," IBISWorld, May 2020, accessed on July 25, 2020. https://my-ibisworld-com.proxy.libraries.rutgers.edu/gl/en/industry/g4621-gl/major-companies
Note: Tricon Global is now Yum! Brands. Subway is expected to take the third global spot because of a global shift toward healthier eating

Table A.57 Railroads

2000	2020	2030
Union Pacific Corp. (U.S.)	Union Pacific Corp. (U.S.)	Deutsche Bahn (Germany)
Canadian Pacific Ltd.	Canadian Pacific Ltd. (Canada)	SNCF (France)
Burlington & Santa Fe (U.S.)	CSX (U.S.)	Indian Railways

Source: Statista (2020), "World's largest railway companies as of May 2020, based on market value," accessed July 25, 2020. https://www-statista-com.proxy.libraries.rutgers.edu/statistics/260683/the-largest-energy-railway-companies-worldwide-based-on-market-value/

Table A.58   Security systems makers

2000	2020	2030
Sensormatic (U.S.)	Honeywell International (U.S.)	Honeywell International
Knowgo (U.S.)	Checkpoint Systems (U.S.)	Checkpoint Systems
Checkpoint (U.S.)	Johnson Controls International (Ireland)	Johnson Controls International

Source: Savaskan, Devin (2020), "Electronic Article Surveillance Product Manufacturing," IBISWorld, February 2020, accessed on July 25, 2020. https://my-ibisworld-com.proxy. libraries.rutgers.edu/us/en/industry-specialized/od5723/major-companies

Table A.59   Semiconductor chip manufacturers

2000	2020	2030
Intel (U.S.)	Intel	Intel
Texas Instruments (U.S.)	Taiwan Semiconductor (Taiwan)	Taiwan Semiconductor
Applied Materials (U.S.)	Qualcomm (U.S.)	Qualcomm

Source: Reiff, Nathan (2020), "The Top 10 Semiconductor Companies," Investopedia, June 24, accessed July 25, 2020, https://www.investopedia.com/articles/markets/012216/ worlds-top-10-semiconductor-companies-tsmintc.asp

Table A.60   Shipbuilders

2000	2020	2030
Todd Shipyards Corp. (U.S.)	China Shipbuilding Industry Corporation	China Shipbuilding Industry Corporation
Anangel-Amer Shipbuilding (Greece)	Mitsubishi Heavy Industries (Japan)	China State Shipbuilding Corporation
Conrad Industries Inc. (U.S.)	Hyundai Heavy Industries (South Korea)	Hyundai Heavy Industries (South Korea)

Source: Wikipedia (2020), "List of the Largest Shipbuilding Companies," accessed July 25, 2020. https://en.wikipedia.org/wiki/List_of_the_largest_shipbuilding_companies

Table A.61   Steel companies

2000	2020	2030
Corus Group PLC (U.K./Netherlands)	ArcelorMittal (Luxembourg)	China Baowu Group
Pohang Iron & Steel ADS (South Korea)	China Baowu Group	ArcelorMittal
USX-US Steel Group (U.S.)	HBIS (China)	HBIS

Source: World Steel Association (2017), "World Steel in Figures 2017," accessed July 25, 2020. https://www.worldsteel.org/en/dam/jcr:0474d208-9108-4927-ace8-4ac5445c5df8/ World+Steel+in+Figures+2017.pdf

Table A.62 Tire manufacturers

2000	2020	2030
Goodyear (U.S.)	Bridgestone	Michelin
Michelin (France)	Michelin	Bridgestone
Bridgestone (Japan)	Goodyear	Zhongce Rubber Group Co. (China)

Source: Chen, Sisi (2020), "Tire Manufacturing China," IBISWorld, March 2020, accessed on July 25, 2020. https://my-ibisworld-com.proxy.libraries.rutgers.edu/cn/en/industry/2911/major-companies

Statista (2020), "The world's largest tire producers in FY 2019, based on tire-related revenue," accessed July 25, 2020. https://www.statista.com/statistics/225677/revenue-of-the-leading-tire-producers-worldwide/

Table A.63 Tobacco companies

2000	2020	2030
Philip Morris (U.S.)	China National Tobacco Corporation	China National Tobacco Corporation
Japan Tobacco	British American Tobacco	British American Tobacco
British American Tobacco (U.K.)	Philip Morris (U.S.)	Phillip Morris International

Source: Irigoyen, Santiago (2019), "Global Cigarette & Tobacco Manufacturing," IBISWorld, November 2019, accessed July 12, 2020. https://my-ibisworld-com.proxy.libraries.rutgers.edu/gl/en/industry/c1131-gl/major-companies

Note: As noted earlier for cigarette vending, China National Tobacco Corporation has a commanding lead with over 40% of global market share, followed by distant competitors Philip Morris and British American Tobacco

Table A.64 Toy makers

2000	2020	2030
Mattel (U.S.)	Bandai Namco (Japan)	Sony (Japan)
Hasbro (U.S.)	Lego (Denmark)	Microsoft (U.S.)
Electronic Arts (U.S.)	Hasbro (U.S.)	Nintendo (Japan)

Source: Statista (2019), "Worldwide Revenue of Major Toy Companies in 2018," accessed July 25, 2020. https://www-statista-com.proxy.libraries.rutgers.edu/statistics/241241/revenue-of-major-toy-companies-worldwide/

Table A.65 Web portal companies

2000	2020	2030
Yahoo (U.S.)	Google (U.S.)	Google
AOL (U.S.)	Yahoo	Baidu
MSN (U.S.)	Baidu (China)	Qihoo 360 (China)

Source: Statista (2019), "Online Search Usage," accessed July 25, 2020. https://www-statista-com.proxy.libraries.rutgers.edu/study/15884/search-engine-usage-statista-dossier/

Newton, Erik (2017) "BrightEdge SEO Blog," BRIGHTEDGE, accessed July 25, 2020. https://www.brightedge.com/blog/international-search-engines

Table A.66 Wireless carriers

2000	2020	2030
Verizon Wireless (U.S.)	China Mobile	China Mobile
Cingular (U.S.)	Verizon	Vodafone (U.K.)
AT&T Wireless (U.S.)	Deutsche Telecom (Germany)	Singtel-Airtel (Singapore)

Source: Ross, Olivia (2019), "Global Wireless Telecommunications Carriers," IBISWorld, August 2019, accessed July 25, 2020. https://my-ibisworld-com.proxy.libraries.rutgers.edu/gl/en/industry/i5111-gl/major-companies

Cingular Wireless LLC (2005), "Consolidated Financial Statements," Securities and Exchange Commission Archive, accessed July 25, 2020. https://www.sec.gov/Archives/edgar/data/732717/000073271706000008/ex99.htm

Note: Vodafone may buy out its American partner Verizon to propel itself to the global three

Note

1. Simpson, Jeffrey, Marc Jaccard, and Nic Rivers (2007), *Hot Air: Meeting Canada's Climate Change Challenge*, McClelland & Stewart Toronto, p. 164.

Index[1]

A

Aadhaar biometric database, 85
A&P, 59, 147
Abbott, 262
Accenture, 148, 179, 181, 197
Accor, 259
Acer, 147, 183
Acquire, 48, 117, 151, 185, 233
Acquisition, 2, 3, 7, 10, 12, 19, 31n15,
    32n15, 41, 46, 48, 54, 58, 60,
    62, 77, 104, 117, 136, 139,
    145–148, 155, 162, 197, 198,
    210–217, 233, 235, 236, 241
ACS, 257
Adapt, 80, 105, 137
Adidas, 6, 90
Advertising agencies, vii, 148
Aegon, 259
Aerospace, 17, 54, 140, 155, 157, 158,
    161, 206, 208, 233, 235–240
Aetna, 259
Affordability, 111–112, 180, 187, 202,
    210, 211, 216, 233

Africa, 49, 115, 176, 181, 182, 185,
    203, 204, 212, 228, 231,
    243, 245
AGCO, 251
Aging, 49, 73, 76–82, 85, 92, 93, 175,
    176, 187, 233
Agrarian, 177
Agricultural Bank of China, 141
Agricultural equipment, 104
Agriculture, 107, 149, 181
Airbnb, 83, 103, 105, 110, 144, 146,
    197, 215
Airborne, 264
Airbus, 17, 40, 58, 140, 154, 157,
    206, 236
Aircraft manufacturing, 12,
    17, 154–158
Airline industry, 12, 144, 159–161
Airlines, vii, 3, 9, 12, 13, 20, 23, 79,
    84, 108, 110–112, 115, 139,
    140, 146, 157, 159–161,
    236, 240
Alaska Air, 3

---

[1] Note: Page numbers followed by 'n' refer to notes.

© The Author(s) 2020
J. Sheth et al., *The Global Rule of Three*, https://doi.org/10.1007/978-3-030-57473-4

Alaska Airlines, 111
Alcan, 181, 212
Alcoa, 212
Alexander the Great, 227
Alibaba, 7, 29, 117, 137, 180, 232
Allianz, 261
Allstate, 262
Alphabet, 105, 119
Alstom, 266
Aluminum, 3, 18, 22, 150, 178, 180,
     181, 212, 240
Aluminum industry, 3, 240
Amazon, 7, 8, 21, 29, 40, 43, 44, 48,
     53, 56, 60, 75, 76, 104, 110,
     118, 137, 162, 163, 180,
     221n42, 232, 237
Amazon Prime, 21
Amazon Web Services (AWS),
     2, 40, 235
AmBev, 197
AMC Entertainment, 263
AMC Theaters, 263
America, 3, 42, 44, 77, 89, 145, 152,
     175, 176, 178, 181, 182, 184,
     185, 187, 204, 205, 212
American, vii, 1, 12, 77, 84, 107, 112,
     139, 142, 157, 159, 184, 206,
     210, 211
American Express, 258
American International Group, 261
American Motors, 8, 46
America West Airlines, 159
Amgen, 255
AMPS, 78, 119
Amul, 88
Anangel-Amer Shipbuilding, 267
Anchor stores, vii, 5, 33n27, 91
Andersen, Arthur, 148, 250
Android, 79, 114, 119
Anheuser-Busch, 18, 40, 60, 197, 212
Anheuser-Busch InBev, 197
Anthem, 261
Antitrust, 34n37, 49, 159, 212
AOL, 114, 137

Apollo, 1, 151
Apple, 47, 60, 79, 83, 91, 106, 111,
     114, 118, 119, 135, 136, 141,
     146, 163, 202, 203, 206,
     215, 232
Appliances, vii, 27, 74, 75, 88, 104,
     136, 142, 163, 178, 180, 187,
     201, 235
Applied materials, 267
ArcelorMittal, 135, 198
Arch Coal, 257
Argentina, 49, 184
Artificial intelligence (AI), 85, 93, 109,
     181, 196, 215–217, 229
Artificial market structure, 138
Asahi, 254
Asia, 142, 144, 147, 156, 178, 180,
     181, 184, 185, 228
Asian sovereign funds, 184, 185
Asset Turnover, 19
Association of Southeast Asian Nations
     (ASEAN), 87, 142, 144,
     145, 175
AT&T, 1, 2, 40, 50, 149, 235, 241
AT&T Wireless, 269
Attila the Hun, 227
Australia, 49, 175, 176, 181, 184,
     213, 214
Auto industry, 8, 153
Automation, 73, 84, 92, 107–109,
     112, 123, 181, 197, 213
Automobile, 10, 12, 13, 16, 22, 27,
     40, 73, 77, 83, 104, 111,
     113, 121, 129n30, 142,
     151–157, 177, 196, 197,
     201, 206, 215, 217,
     232, 235
Autonomous Vehicles, 197
Avaya, 257, 263
Aviation, 14, 17–19, 156, 158,
     235, 236
Avis, 25, 50
AXA, 261
Azure (Microsoft), 2, 40, 235

B

Baby-Bells, 1
BAE Systems, 259
Baidu, 76, 163
Bandai Namco, 268
Banking, 3, 23, 57, 80, 139, 144, 161,
    179, 199, 221n42, 240, 243
Bank of America, 144
Bank of New York, 253
Bank of New York Mellon, 253
BASF, 180
Bausch & Lomb, 258
Bausch Health Companies, 258
Baxter, 262
Bechtel, 259
Bed Bath and Beyond, 53
Beer, 12, 18, 19, 40, 52, 76, 86, 102,
    197, 206, 209
Belgium, 254
Bell Labs, 48, 135
Bentley, 54
Berkshire Hathaway, 60, 116, 212
BestBuy, 21
BF Goodrich, 1, 59, 141, 150,
    155, 156
BHP, 263
BHP Billiton, 257
BIC, 15
Big four accounting, 148
Bing, 50
Bitmain, 253
Blackstone, 116, 180
Blockbuster, 21, 110
Blockchain, 114, 181, 229, 232
Blue Ocean Strategy, 48
BMG, 264
BMW, 54, 76, 153
Boeing, 17, 18, 40, 51, 58, 145, 154,
    157, 158, 206, 235, 236, 240
Booking Holdings, 264
Born-global, 146
Boston Consulting Group(BCG), 25,
    56, 91, 138

BP, 89
BPO, 196
Brand, 1, 2, 6, 7, 13, 14, 18, 20–22,
    34n36, 43–46, 52, 54, 55,
    59–61, 73, 77, 82, 90, 92, 103,
    108, 110, 113, 121, 122, 136,
    141, 148, 149, 151, 155, 157,
    168n34, 179, 183, 196, 198,
    200–202, 205–209, 213, 214,
    217, 232, 237, 238
Brand image, 45, 61, 92
Brand proliferation, 45
Branson, Richard, 229, 230, 244
Brazil, viii, 24, 26, 146, 149, 175, 184,
    195, 199, 202, 212, 214, 233
Brexit, 3, 137, 144, 195
Brick and mortar, 56, 77, 110, 162
Bridgestone, 1, 141, 151,
    155–157, 237
Brin, Sergey, 229
Bristol-Myers Squibb, 3
British-American Tobacco, 141
British Tobacco, 2
Broadband, 80, 113, 179
Brooks Brothers, 57, 59
Buffet, Warren, 60, 116, 212, 229
Bureaucracy, 20
Burger King, 266
Burlington & Santa Fe, 266
Business leaders, 26, 137, 228, 243
Business-to-business (B2B), 44, 59, 60,
    84, 85, 87, 203, 204, 237, 240
Business-to-consumer (B2C), 84, 112,
    203, 204, 237

C

Cable TV, 139, 241
Cadbury Schweppes, 255
Cameco Corp., 263
Canada, 44, 140, 177, 181, 184, 212
Canadian Pacific Ltd., 266
CAN Capital, 262

Canfor, 260
Canon, 162
Capitalism, 101, 105, 114, 183, 185,
    186, 229–231, 244
Cargill, 260, 262
Carnegie, Andrew, 116
Carnival, 49, 52, 54
Carrefour, 260
Cash inflow, 74
Cash outflow, 74
Casio, 77, 83
Category killers, 21
CDMA, 78, 79, 119
Celgene, 3, 146
Cell phone, 75, 88, 115, 203
Cemex, 60, 199
CFM International, 251
Chalco, 252
Channel conflict, 43, 61
Chappell, Warner, 264
Charter, 80
Chase Manhattan, 208
Checker, 8, 80
Checkpoint Systems, 267
Chesapeake, 3
China, viii, 17, 23, 24, 26, 44, 49, 50,
    60, 75, 76, 86, 89, 94, 113, 117,
    135–137, 141–149, 153, 157,
    158, 160, 161, 175–178,
    180–185, 187, 195, 199, 201,
    203, 204, 207, 208, 210,
    213–215, 217, 231–233, 236,
    238, 243, 245
China Baowu Group, 135
China Communications Construction
    Company, 259
China Construction Bank, 141
China Mobile, 50, 203, 210
China National Tobacco Corporation,
    141, 209
China Shenhua Energy Company
    Limited, 263
China Shipbuilding Industry
    Corporation, 267
China State Shipbuilding
    Corporation, 267
China Telecom, 50
China Unicom, 50
Chipotle, 53
Chrysler, 8, 12, 16, 18, 19, 22, 27, 40,
    46, 52, 76, 80, 151–153, 235,
    240, 242
Churchill, Winston, 228
Cigna, 261
Cigna Corp., 261
Cinemark, 263
Cinepolis, 263
Cineworld, 263
Cingular, 242
Cisco Systems, 256
Citigroup, 253, 262
Citizen, 54, 77, 83, 177, 184, 186
Climate change, 43, 183
Cloud, 2, 23, 40, 114, 162, 181
Cloud services, 2
CNH Global, 251
Coal, 178, 199
Coal India, 257
Coca-Cola, 12, 40, 48, 49, 51, 54, 76,
    119, 122, 145, 149, 180,
    206, 240
COFCO, 260
Coffee, 44, 45, 83, 149
Coinstar, 238, 239
Collaboration, 138, 234, 237–239,
    241, 245
Collusion, 14, 241
Colonies, 198
Columbus, Christopher, 117
Comcast, 1, 80
Commercial Aviation Corporation of
    China (COMAC), 158, 236
Communism, 142, 145, 146, 175, 198
Compaq, 120

Competition, vii, viii, 5, 13–15, 18, 21, 41, 45, 51, 55, 56, 59, 62, 82, 91, 102, 103, 111, 112, 115, 118–120, 123, 124n1, 132n67, 136, 140, 143, 149–153, 156–159, 176, 195, 199–201, 213, 215, 217, 232, 234, 239, 241, 243

Competitive advantage, 13, 19, 55, 109, 117–118, 123, 204, 207, 212–215, 231, 244

Competitive dynamics, 13, 125n5, 233

Competitive markets, 3, 4, 11, 23, 24, 27, 28, 138, 139, 151, 164, 176, 204, 229

Competitors, viii, 1, 4, 7, 8, 12–14, 16, 23, 42–44, 47–61, 81, 102, 104, 107, 116, 135, 136, 139, 146, 148, 151, 162, 164, 199, 201, 202, 232, 235, 237, 238, 241, 242, 245

Complementary diversification, 76, 92

ConAgra, 260

Conglomerates, 44, 53, 60, 74, 90, 119, 122, 146, 179, 196, 197, 210, 216

Conrad Industries Inc., 267

Conscious Capitalism, 105, 183

Conservation, 187

Consol Energy, 257

Consolidation, vii, 3, 8, 10, 11, 18, 23, 27, 29, 56, 80, 104, 139, 140, 144, 146–147, 149, 153, 159–161, 164, 197, 235, 236, 240, 248n22

Constellation Brands, 18, 53

Consumer electronics, vii, 21, 75, 140, 142, 147, 178, 183, 187, 201, 215, 217

Consumer packaged goods (CPG), 44, 45, 49

Consumer psychology, 13, 14

Consumption, 7, 14, 49, 76, 78, 79, 83, 85–87, 89, 108, 110, 123, 179, 207, 233

Convergence, 1, 85, 125n5, 143, 162, 240, 242, 248n22

The Cooper Companies, 258

Cooper Tire, 1, 151

Coors, 18, 51, 60

Core compentency, 46, 59, 109, 157, 204

Corona, 18

Corporate, 3, 19–21, 26, 28, 29, 41, 44, 45, 126n11, 152, 196, 234

Corus Group PLC, 267

Costco, 260

Cost leadership, 55, 68n61

Cost structure, 11, 21, 29, 240, 248n22

Covid-19, 3, 25, 57, 81, 160, 182, 247

Creation of Standards, 9, 29

Creative destruction, 101, 105, 229

Croc, Ray, 230

Cross, 15

Crossing the Chasm, 101, 103–104

Cruise lines, 13, 49, 52, 54, 243

C-Suite, 41

CSX, 266

Cultures, 41, 85, 88, 104, 106, 142, 152, 163, 180, 206, 214

Currency reserves, 185

Customer intimacy, 47

Customers, 1, 6–8, 14, 20–24, 26, 27, 29, 34n36, 42–44, 49, 55, 59, 74, 82, 90, 103, 104, 106, 113, 116, 117, 120, 155, 159, 179, 186, 202, 206, 210, 211, 213, 217, 238–241, 245

Customer support, 45, 61

D

Daewoo, 139, 162
de facto standard, 9, 10, 90, 119, 123
Defensive, 28, 47–60, 148, 179, 242
Dell, 3, 32n15, 84, 136, 147, 162,
    163, 183
Deloitte, 3, 24, 148
Delta, vii, 12, 139, 140, 159
Dematuring, 82–83
Democracy, 147, 184–186
Demographic, 7, 55, 85–86, 93, 243
Denbury, 3
Deregulation, vii, 23, 26, 79, 140, 143,
    144, 146, 159, 160, 240
Descaling processes, 10
Detergent, 44, 45
Deutsche Bahn, 266
Deutsche Post DHL Group, 264
Deutsche Telecom, 40, 147
DHL, 51
Diageo, 254
Diamond, 44, 90, 208, 231
Diaspora, 205–206, 211, 213, 217
Dickinson, Becton, 262
Differentiation, vii, 20, 45, 47, 52, 53,
    55, 56, 68n60, 68n61, 91,
    118–119, 123, 124n1, 125n5,
    215, 240
Diffusion of innovations, 101,
    103–104, 107
Digital advertising, 40
Digital Equipment Corporation, 120
Digital revolution, 227, 232, 243, 244
Diminishing returns, 12, 90, 228–229
DirecTV, 1, 79
Discounting, 7
Discretionary income, 89, 179
Dish Network, 1
Disney, 21, 53, 54, 241
Disruption, 137, 229
Disruptive, 84, 101, 123, 137, 201
Distribution channels, 22, 29

The ditch, viii, 4, 7, 12, 13, 15–19,
    25, 28, 29, 39, 40, 46, 53,
    55–59, 61, 62, 147, 152, 156,
    157, 159, 160, 235, 237,
    240, 242
Divestiture, 12, 60
Divestment, 122
Dollar Shave Club, 2, 54
Dollar Thrifty, 25
DoorDash, 2, 110
DOW, 256
Dow Chemical, 122
Drucker, Peter, 57, 58, 70n71,
    97n24, 106, 116, 137,
    216, 232
Dunkin Donuts, 53
Duopoly, 2
DuPont, 120

E

Eastern European bloc, 198
eBay, 110, 114
E-commerce, 211
Economic development, 87, 88, 216,
    227–239, 243
Economic growth, 3, 175–177, 187,
    195, 198, 216
Economics, vii, viii, 2–4, 14, 17, 24,
    28, 55, 81, 83, 87, 88, 94,
    97n24, 102, 107, 108, 137, 139,
    140, 142, 143, 145, 148, 161,
    164, 175–178, 184, 187, 195,
    196, 198, 211, 216,
    227–239, 241
Economies of scale, 8–10, 12, 19, 20,
    22, 24, 29, 42–45, 74, 78,
    81–82, 93, 207, 240, 241
EDF, 266
Education, 14, 88, 89, 114, 179,
    180, 186, 211, 216, 230,
    231, 244

Efficiencies in scale, 9, 77, 78, 82, 90, 93, 243
Efficiency, 8–10, 14, 18–20, 27, 29, 42, 58, 73, 74, 77, 78, 82, 90, 92, 93, 101, 105, 123, 146, 159, 241, 243
eHarmony, 50
Electrolux, 136, 201, 235
Electronic Arts, 268
Emerging-market multinational companies (EMNCs), 196, 197, 199–217
Emerging markets, viii, 28, 42, 49, 60, 75, 76, 86–94, 115, 132n67, 141, 145–149, 177, 179, 180, 185, 186, 195–217, 232, 233, 238, 243
Empirical, 14, 25–26, 29, 56, 62, 83, 125n5, 138
Employees, 6, 14, 26, 27, 29, 42, 55, 104, 120, 148, 181, 186, 230
Employment, 26, 29, 195, 216, 238
EnCana, 3
Enel, 266
Energy, vii, 18, 40, 43, 87–89, 109, 122, 127n11, 145, 181, 184, 209, 216
Engel, Joel, 135
Enterprise, 25, 44, 77, 79, 88, 111, 121, 162, 178, 179, 187, 196, 198, 202, 229
Entrepreneurial marketing, 58, 126n11, 127n11
Entrepreneurs, 54, 62, 81, 87, 88, 90, 117–118, 123, 126n11, 229–231, 244
Entrepreneurship, 90, 105–107, 116, 178, 187, 227, 229–232, 243, 244
Entry and exit barriers, 3, 8, 73, 80, 93
Epson, 163

Ericsson, 198
Ernst & Young, 24
ERP, 197, 202
Estée Lauder, 258
E-tailers, 7, 29, 56
Europe, 2, 13, 50, 57, 78, 79, 108, 136, 138, 140–142, 144, 145, 149, 153, 154, 156, 159, 181, 182, 184, 205, 228
European Union (EU), 40, 81, 87, 111, 119, 120, 141, 142, 144, 145, 195, 211, 236
Evoked sets, 13, 14, 29
Exclusive rights, 24, 29
Exclusivity, 39, 45, 46, 61, 82
Executive compensation, 39, 41
Expedia, 264
Experimental campaigns, 58
Exporters, 177, 187, 198, 199, 208
EY, 148

F

Facebook, 23, 40, 48, 50, 104, 114, 127n11, 146, 178, 180
Farming equipment, 177, 187
Fast follower strategy, 48
Fast-moving consumer goods (FMCG), 44, 88, 216
Federal Express, 264
Federal Reserve, 129n30, 239
FedEx, 51, 116
Ferrero SpA, 256
Finance, 118, 161, 163, 164, 228, 243
Financial services, 47, 75, 209, 221n42, 232, 244
Firestone, 1, 141, 151, 156, 237
Five forces, 55, 234, 237, 239, 245
Fixed costs, 11, 20, 21, 29, 36n46, 81, 240
Flipkart, 48

Focus, 8, 10, 17, 22, 23, 29, 45–49,
54, 55, 61, 68n60, 68n61, 74,
75, 82, 84, 85, 91, 92, 102, 109,
116, 123, 125n5, 154–157, 180,
185, 198, 204, 210–216, 228,
233, 235, 240
Folgers, 45
Foot Locker, 5, 6, 20
Ford, Henry, 12, 107, 111, 114
Ford, 8, 12, 18, 19, 40, 60, 74, 80,
107, 109, 111, 114, 151–153,
196, 235, 240
Foreign ownership of assets, 24, 29
Fortune 500, 137, 164, 230
Fox, 241
Foxconn, 106, 206
Fox Entertainment Group, 259
Fragmented market, 10
Franchising, 54
Free markets, 2, 27, 79, 138, 143, 145,
178, 185, 203
Fujitsu, 256
Full-line generalists, vii, 4, 5, 8, 10–13,
17–21, 25, 28, 29, 74, 90–92,
102, 140, 161, 164, 236, 239,
241, 245

G

GameStop, 5
Gandhi, Mahatma, 228
Garments, 199, 208, 212
Gates, Bill, 118, 229, 230
Gatorade, 13, 19, 53, 54
GDP, 109, 115, 118, 143, 175, 177,
181, 182, 187, 188n1, 195
General Electric (GE), 27, 47, 49, 50,
60, 88, 136, 146, 158, 180, 201,
210, 211, 235, 236
Generalists, vii, viii, 4–8, 10–14,
17–23, 25–29, 33n28, 39–62,
74, 81, 82, 90–92, 102, 125n5,
137, 140, 147, 158, 161, 162,

164, 215, 235, 236,
239–243, 245
General Motors (GM), 8, 10, 12, 13,
18, 19, 40, 45, 51, 60, 74, 76,
80, 119–121, 147, 151–153,
156, 180, 235, 240
Generic strategy, 41, 47, 55, 61,
68n60
Genghis Khan, 197, 227
Gentex, 53
Geopolitical alignment, 163, 195, 206,
227–239, 243
Geopolitics, 184–186
Georgia-Pacific CP, 260
Germany, 75, 89, 139, 142, 143, 153,
176, 177, 184, 199, 200, 213
Gibson, William, 232
Gilead Sciences, 255
Gillette, 2
Glass-Steagall Act of 1999, 75
Glencore, 260, 263
Global brands, 148, 198, 206, 207
Global competitors, 139, 164
Global full-line generalist, 140,
161, 164
Globalization, 120, 136, 138–146,
157, 169n36, 195, 197–199,
216, 228, 233, 235, 240,
248n22
Global leaders, 50, 51, 54, 104,
135–137, 141, 150, 151, 180,
187, 199, 212, 215–216, 235
Globally-conceived, 146
Globally-conceived tech firms, 146
Global Rule of Three, viii, 28, 101,
135–160, 227, 233, 235,
238–243, 245, 247
Goldman Sachs, 161
Goldman Sachs Group, 255
Goodrich, Benjamin Franklin, 1, 59,
151, 155–157, 235, 237
Goodyear, 1, 141, 150, 151,
155–157, 237

Google, 2, 9, 40, 48, 50, 60, 104, 105, 111, 146, 163, 180, 202
Google Cloud, 2, 40, 235
Governmental intervention, 10, 29
Government mandate, 78–80, 90, 93
Grab, 54, 197
Great Britain, 75, 198
The great recession, 3, 17, 122
Gree Electric appliances, 136, 201
Greenfield investments, 211
Growth, vii, viii, 3, 7, 8, 10, 12, 13, 16, 17, 24, 27–29, 39, 41, 43, 46, 49, 53, 54, 56–58, 60, 62, 73–76, 85–93, 101, 103–106, 109, 114, 117, 122, 123, 124n1, 136, 148, 175–177, 179–181, 183, 184, 187, 195–203, 213, 216, 233, 235, 243, 245
GrubHub, 1, 2, 110
GSM, 78, 79, 119
Gucci, 86
Guerilla/surprise marketing, 58

H

Haier Group, 252
Hair care, 204
Hanes, 110
Harry's Edgewell Personal Care, 2
Hasbro, 268
Haworth, 264
HBIS, 267
HBO, 53
Healthcare, 54, 80, 85, 87, 88, 91, 114, 179–181, 204, 216, 259
Health care industry, 80
Heineken, 206
Heinz-Kraft, 212
Henderson, Bruce, 25
Hershey, 256
Hertz, 20, 25, 51
Hewlett-Packard (HP), 204

Hilton, 20
Hindalco, 179, 199, 212
Hitachi, 74
HNI, 264
Home appliances, 136
Home Depot, 51
Home markets, 77, 136, 140, 146, 161, 164, 199, 203–205, 209, 210
Honda, 19, 47, 151, 153, 157, 185, 202
Honest Tea, 53, 54
Honeywell International, 267
Hongqiao Group, 252
Household support services, 179
Housing, 87, 88, 178, 216
HP, 51, 81, 84, 92, 118, 136, 141, 147, 162, 183, 202, 210
HSBC Holdings, 253
Huawei, 135, 141, 149, 163, 179, 198, 199, 203
Hughes Electronics, 79
Humana, 261
Hyundai, 139, 162, 202
Hyundai Heavy Industries, 267

I

IBM, 2, 12, 13, 48, 50, 51, 58, 85, 109, 119–121, 136, 137, 145, 147, 148, 163, 179–181, 197, 204, 232
ICBC, 141
IHH, 204
IKEA, 52, 106, 146
Ikon Office Solutions, 264
Immigrant, 177, 205, 231
InBev, 197, 212
Incumbents, 10, 13, 16, 48, 76, 77, 83, 110, 115, 118, 132n67, 136, 141, 142, 144, 148, 150, 151, 156, 176, 201, 203, 213, 221n42, 231, 232, 237

India, viii, 1, 24, 26, 49, 52, 77, 85, 89, 94, 109, 113, 135, 137, 139, 142–146, 149, 160, 161, 175–181, 183–185, 187, 195, 197–199, 204–208, 210–215, 231–233, 236, 243, 245
Indian Railways, 266
Indonesia, 175, 184, 202, 210, 233
Industrial economy, 177
Industrial organization, 101, 138, 241, 248n22
Industry, vii, 3, 39, 73–94, 101–123, 136, 150–157, 159–161, 180, 196, 229
Industry life cycle, 83, 243
Industry revolution, 10, 87, 107, 108, 175, 187, 198, 200, 227, 228
Industry structure, 25, 39, 102, 103, 123, 234, 239, 248n22
Inflation, 17
Information age, 108, 137
Information technology (IT), 109, 147, 148, 162, 177, 179, 181, 196, 202, 205, 208, 221n42, 227
Infrastructure, 9, 41, 78, 79, 108, 114, 115, 145, 147, 149, 162, 177, 179, 181, 182, 184, 185, 187, 195, 198, 199, 203, 210, 216, 238, 245
Inner circle competitors, 4, 14, 27
Innovation, 8, 12, 22, 29, 34n36, 40, 47, 48, 52, 61, 84, 88, 90, 93, 105–107, 109, 111, 112, 116, 137, 142, 155, 156, 178, 180, 181, 183, 187, 195, 206, 210–211, 216, 229, 233, 237, 238, 241, 245
Innovative pricing, 58
Integrated operations, 19, 29
Intel, 81, 120, 121, 162, 180, 183
Interbrand, 7, 54
Interfor, 260
Internal synergies, 19, 29

International Monetary Fund (IMF), 139, 143, 187
International Paper, 265
Internet, 80, 85, 93, 111, 113, 114, 142, 163, 179, 238, 245
Internet Service Providers (ISPs), 80
Interpublic, 148
Interpublic GR OF COS, 250
Inventory turns, 7
Investment, 22, 40, 47, 48, 52, 54, 75, 76, 79, 91, 107, 108, 118, 145, 147, 149, 156, 157, 160, 161, 177, 181, 182, 184, 185, 187, 197, 204, 211, 214, 232, 233, 237, 240, 243, 252, 260
Investors, 10, 14, 16, 27, 47, 53, 54, 87, 142, 181, 197, 232
Invisible hand, 229
Iridium, 59, 77
Iron ore, 199
iTunes, 108, 110

J

Jaguar, 196
Japan, 1, 23, 50, 81, 83, 93, 113, 117, 136, 138, 140–142, 144–146, 149–151, 153, 155, 156, 161, 175, 176, 184, 185, 187, 195, 197–199, 209, 213, 232, 233, 236
Japan Tobacco, 268
JBS, 262
JC Penney, 4, 5, 7, 46, 57, 137, 201
JD, 260
Jiangsu Hengrui, 255
Jiayuan, 50
Jobs, Steve, 229
John Deere, 202
Johnson & Johnson, 258, 262, 265
Johnson Controls Internationals, 145, 267
Jones Apparel Group Inc., 252

JP Morgan, 60, 90, 116, 161
JP Morgan Chase, 144
Jumei, 86

K

Kay Jewelers, 5
Keiretsu, 185
Kenya, 115, 181, 211
Kepco, 266
Keurig Dr Pepper, 12, 242
KFC, 53, 180
Kim, Chan, 48
Kiva.org, 87
KKR, 117, 180
Kmart, 6, 20, 42, 47, 204
Knowgo, 267
Kodak, 48, 60, 77, 118, 132n67
Korea, 83, 144, 149, 198, 232, 233
KPMG, 24, 148
Kraft, 212
Krispy Kreme, 53, 54
Kroger, 59, 206
Kubota, 251

L

Latin America, 145, 176, 181, 204,
    205, 212
Lean inventory, 7
Lean manufacturing, 9
Lego, 268
Lenovo, 51, 136, 141, 147, 199, 204
Leo Chen, 86
Leveraged buyout, 59
Levi's, 46, 201
Levi Strauss, 252
Lexus, 22, 45, 47, 112, 202
LG, 136, 139, 140, 162, 163
Licensed economy, 24, 29
Lifecycle, 28, 56, 60, 73, 101, 103,
    123, 124n1, 125n5, 138, 164
The Limited, 55, 57, 58

LinkedIn, 53, 197
Lockheed Martin, 158, 236
Loews Cineplex, 263
Loews Corp., 262
L'Oréal, 44, 54, 86, 147, 148
Lowe's, 121
Loyalty, 7, 68n61, 113
Lucent, 198
Lucent Technologies, 256, 257
Lululemon, 8
Lyft, 13, 49, 149
LyondellBasell, 256

M

Ma, Jack, 229, 230, 244
Macy's, 4, 5, 7, 21, 137
Mahindra & Mahindra, 199, 202, 204
Major barriers to trade, 24, 29
Malaysia, 175, 182, 185, 204, 233
Margin-driven players, 4, 15, 20
Margin vs. volume dichotomy, 6
Market capitalization, 51, 56, 105,
    121, 137, 157, 237
Market concentration, 26, 96n20, 241
Market-driven economy, 139, 164
Market expansion, 10, 11,
    74–76, 92, 243
Market penetration, 74, 92
Market share, 1, 2, 4, 11–19, 25–29,
    34n36, 34n37, 35n37, 39–41,
    44, 45, 48–51, 53, 55–58, 61,
    62, 68n60, 74, 82, 90, 103, 104,
    112, 118, 119, 125n5, 135, 136,
    140, 141, 149–151, 156, 157,
    160, 162, 163, 206, 211, 235,
    240, 242
Markets with a high degree of vertical
    integration, 24
Markets with combined ownership and
    management, 24, 29
Marriott, 261
Mars Inc., 256

Mars Wrigley, 256
Maserati, 86
Massey Energy, 257
Masstige, 86
Mastercard, 162
Match Group, 50
Matsushita, 136, 140
Mattel, 268
Maturity, mature markets, viii, 4, 28,
    73, 76–82, 84, 90, 92, 93, 101,
    104, 123, 212–217
Mauborgne, Renee, 48
Maxtor, 257
Maxwell House, 260
MBA, 14, 234
McDonald's, 42, 60, 180
MCI, 1, 22, 40, 50
Medtronic, 262, 263
Mega-brands, 43
Megadeals, 2
Meiji Holdings, 256
Mercedes-Benz, 106
Mergers, 1–3, 12, 13, 18, 24, 28,
    34n36, 34n37, 41, 58, 74, 76,
    77, 80, 90, 93, 104, 117–119,
    123, 139, 140, 144, 146–149,
    153, 157, 158, 181, 197, 212,
    235–239, 242
Mergers and acquisitions (M&A), 2, 3,
    12, 31n15, 32n15, 40, 41, 48,
    54, 61, 104, 120, 147, 149–151,
    153, 158, 187, 235–237, 242
Merrill Lynch, 254, 255, 262
Metals, 3, 204
Metro-Goldwyn-Mayer Inc., 259
Mexico, 44, 60, 146, 184, 199, 210,
    212, 214
Michelin, 1, 59, 141, 150, 151,
    155–157, 237, 240
Micro-finance, 88, 216
Microsoft, 2, 40, 48, 77, 81, 104, 108,
    118, 120, 121, 135, 146, 180,
    183, 235

Middle class, 86, 89, 90, 93–94,
    177, 187
Midea Group, 213
Military, 17, 87, 154, 155, 178, 182,
    227, 228, 236, 243
Miller, 18, 40
Miller, Herman, 18, 40, 197, 212
Mini Cooper, 240
Minimum efficient scale (MES),
    81–82, 96n20
Minivan, 19, 22, 40, 52
Mitel, 265
Mitsubishi, 21, 74, 138
Mitsubishi Chemical Holdings, 256
Mitsubishi Heavy Industries, 267
Mitsui, 113, 138
Mobile network, 49, 211
Modelo, 18
Model T, 8, 9, 60, 107
Molbak, Jen, 238, 239
Molson Coors, 18
Mondelez, 212
Mondelez International Inc., 122
Monopolistic competition, vii, 5, 102,
    103, 123, 124n1
Monopoly, vii, 10, 14, 23, 24, 79, 86,
    93, 103, 114, 144, 145, 154,
    157, 241–243
Monsanto, 255
Mont Blanc, 15
Morgan Stanley, 161
Morgan Stanley Dean Witter,
    255, 262
Motorola, 59, 79, 135, 136
Mozilla, 50
M-Pesa, 115, 211
MSN, 268
Multinationals, 28, 132n67, 137,
    143–145, 148, 183,
    186, 195–217
Munich Re, 262
Musk, Elon, 229, 230, 244
Mutual forbearance, 51

N

Nanotechnology, 187, 216
Nationalism, 142
"Natural" market structure, 138
NBCUniversal, 259
NEC, 265
Nestle, 44, 45, 88, 90, 206
Netflix, 21, 53, 110, 111, 213
The New Deal, 86, 233
Newell Rubbermaid, 15
Newfield, 3
Niche, vii, viii, 5, 8, 12, 13, 16, 19, 27,
    29, 39, 47, 51, 53–59, 62,
    68n61, 77, 83, 91, 104, 125n5,
    147, 149, 153, 162, 164, 201,
    202, 208, 240–243
Nike, 6
Nintendo, 268
Nokia, 77, 79, 135, 146, 147
Non-users, 49
Nordstrom, 5
Nortel Networks, 256
North America, 2, 76, 138, 140, 141,
    156, 161, 187, 195, 202, 212
North American Free Trade Agreement
    (NAFTA), 87, 142, 145
Northern Telecom, 265
Northwest Airlines, 159
Norwegian, 52, 54
Novartis, 122
Novelis, 212
Novo Nordisk, 255

O

Offensive, 28, 47–60, 148, 242
Oil industry, 3, 73
Oji Holdings Corporation, 265
Oligopolistic competition, 5
Oligopoly, vii, 102, 103, 123, 138
Olsen, Ken, 120
Omega, 112

Omnichannel, 8, 43
Omnicom, 148
Omnicom Group, 250
Omnipresence, 43, 44, 61
One World alliance, 159
Online Dating Market, 50
Operations, 8, 19, 20, 22, 23, 29, 44,
    46, 49, 61, 79, 81, 107, 110,
    116, 118, 144, 145, 160, 180,
    199, 207, 240
Oracle, 2, 162, 197
Organization, 6, 23, 47, 49, 56, 57, 73,
    82, 88–90, 101, 104, 106, 109,
    111, 116–117, 119, 122, 123,
    125n5, 138, 155, 186, 239,
    241, 248n22
Original equipment manufacturer
    (OEM), 51, 156, 207–208,
    211, 217
Ottoman Empire, 228
Outsourcing, 10, 79, 81, 92, 109–110,
    122, 123, 177, 198, 205,
    208, 216
Overhead, 20, 44, 108, 235

P

Pabst, 40
Panasonic, 21, 140
P&G, 2, 43–45, 90, 237
Paradigm, 4, 40, 77, 119, 124n1, 162,
    164, 180
Passenger car tires, 151
Patent rights, 3, 12
Pay TV, 1
Pay TV market, 1
PC manufacturer, 51, 58, 81, 104,
    137, 147
Pechiney, 252
Pelikan, 15
Pen manufacturing market, 15
Penn Virginia, 3

PeopleExpress, 13
People's Insurance Company of China, 261, 262
PepsiCo, 12
P/E ratio, 39, 51
Performance, 4, 10, 12, 13, 25, 26, 28, 29, 41, 49, 56, 58, 68n60, 68n61, 81, 82, 97n24, 104, 125n5, 202, 210, 240, 245
Personal computers, 118–120, 136
Petrochemical products, 199
Pfizer, 31n15, 163, 238
Phantom generalist, 7
Pharmaceutical industry, 24, 87, 102
Pharmaceuticals, 3, 24, 80, 88, 103, 122, 146, 180, 199, 201, 216, 240
Philip Morris, 141, 197
Philip Morris International, 268
Phillips, 47, 78, 92, 136, 210
Pillsbury, 59
Pilot, 15, 16
Ping An Insurance, 261
Pioneer, 48, 61, 77, 103, 105, 111, 118, 124n1, 205
Pirelli, 141, 151, 156
Pizza chains, 43, 59
Pohang Iron & Steel ADS, 267
Polman, Paul, 43
Population, 42, 49, 85, 89, 93, 113, 146, 175–177, 181, 184, 195, 204, 211, 216, 233
Porsche, 13, 53, 54, 86, 240
Porter, Michael, 55, 68n60, 68n61, 234
Positioning, 19, 21–22, 28, 29, 43, 45, 61, 180
Postmates, 2
PowerChina, 259
Prada, 86
Prahalad, C.K., 87
Pratt & Whitney, 235, 236

Premium, 5, 6, 22, 29, 33n28, 54, 82, 85, 162, 164, 200–202
Preview Travel, 264
Price concession/cuts, 46, 51, 66n38
Price elasticities, 51
Price premium, 6, 82
Price wars, 41, 49, 51, 56, 60, 61
PricewaterhouseCoopers, 24
Princess, 258
Private equity, 3, 53, 60, 90, 91, 116, 117, 121, 122, 158, 180, 185, 187, 232, 236
Private sector, 87, 145–146, 185
Procter & Gamble (P&G), 49
Procurement, 6, 41, 45, 74, 81, 93, 101, 161, 164, 183, 234–236, 240, 241
Procurement costs, 6
Product expansion, 74, 75, 92
Product line, 10, 19, 40, 44, 49, 74, 90, 110, 122, 125n5, 146, 236
Product/market specialists, 4, 5, 7, 8, 11, 13, 20–22, 28, 53, 62, 140, 161, 242
Professional services, 24, 208
Profitability, 20, 25, 26, 53, 59, 82, 97n24, 103, 104, 109, 138, 153, 164, 234, 241, 242
Profit Impact of Market Strategies (PIMS), 25
Proof-of-concept, 2, 103
Propel, 3, 238, 242
Proprietary, 12, 119, 200
Protectionism, 142, 209, 214
Publicis, 148
Publicis Groupe, 250
Publicis Omnicom, 148
Puma, 253
Purchasing Power Parity (PPP), 88, 90, 143, 177, 187
PVH, 252
PwC, 148

Q

Qihoo 360, 268
Qualcomm, 31n15, 79, 162
Quality, 16, 46, 82, 88, 112, 113, 156,
    180, 185, 201, 206, 207, 209,
    210, 216, 238, 241
Quest Diagnostics, 255

R

Railroads, 10, 78, 96n24, 97n24, 111,
    114, 116
Rapid prototyping, 58
Rationalization, 3, 27, 139, 144, 240
Raytheon, 83, 235
Raytheon Technologies, 235, 237
Razor market, 2
RC Cola, 12, 22, 242
Recycling, 43, 212
Red Bull, 39, 53, 60
Reebok, 253
Reform, 87, 177, 182, 187
Regulated monopoly, 79, 93, 114, 242
Regulation, 10, 23, 29, 56, 73, 74, 78,
    79, 86–87, 114, 115, 141, 159,
    183, 215, 235, 238, 239, 245
Reliance Jio, 52, 211
Renault, 8, 19, 46, 152, 153
Renewable energy, 43
Research and Development (R&D),
    12, 40, 48, 53, 81, 91, 146, 147,
    155, 157, 180, 201, 210, 233
ResearchGate, 53
Research in Motion, 118
Resource-based view, 124n1, 208
Resources, 10, 13, 16, 23, 27, 28,
    34n36, 57, 79, 80, 90, 109, 111,
    122, 125n5, 137, 142, 143, 163,
    175–187, 198, 199, 208, 209,
    211, 213–217, 228, 231, 233,
    241, 244
Restructuring, 27, 80, 91, 122, 139,
    147, 148

Retail, 7, 13, 19–21, 26, 44, 56, 59,
    75, 77, 113, 136, 137, 206, 216,
    232, 244
Return of equity, 39
Return on assets (ROA), 25, 26, 39,
    51, 56, 240
Reverse brand life cycle, 200–203,
    213, 217
Revitalization, 10, 28, 83, 93, 101
Reynolds American, 2
Ricardian economics, 83
Ricardian theory of comparative
    advantage, 197–198
Ride-sharing, 197
Rio Tinto, 181
Rivalry, 19, 51, 178, 234, 237
RJR Nabisco, 117
Roche, 265
Rockefeller, John D., 90, 116, 118
Rogers, Everett, 107
Rolex, 112
Rolls-Royce, 54, 154, 235
Royal Caribbean, 52, 54
Rule of Three, 1–29, 39, 41, 44, 46,
    53, 54, 56, 58, 61, 62, 74, 77,
    104, 110, 112, 122, 125n5,
    138–144, 148, 149, 151, 152,
    159, 161, 163, 164, 233, 235,
    239–242, 245
Rural, 42, 89, 94, 179, 204, 210
Rusai, 252
RyanAir, 108

S

SAB, 197, 212
SABMiller, 18, 60, 197
Safeway, 59, 206
Salesforce, 2, 44, 46, 232
Sales promotions, 41, 49, 51, 66n38
Samsonite, 44
Samsung, 60, 80, 83, 135, 136,
    139–141, 162, 163, 202

Sanders, Colonel, 230
S&P 500, 121, 137, 164
Sara Lee Brands, 260
Scarcity, 182, 187, 216, 233
Schick, 2
Schlitz beer, 242
Schumpeter, Joseph, 101, 105, 229
Schwab, Klaus, 227
Scope diversification, 58, 62
Scope economies, 10, 14
Scope of offerings, 21
Seagate, 257
Search firms, 137
Sears, 5–7, 20, 42, 46, 47, 59, 121,
     137, 157, 201, 204
Seiko, 54, 77, 83, 112
Sensormatic, 267
Service malls, 7
Seventh Generation, 54
Shakeouts and mergers, 74, 77,
     118–119, 123, 242
Shared infrastructure, 9, 29, 240
Shared standards and costs, 93
Shareholders, 16, 26, 29, 51, 120,
     186, 212
Shenhua Energy Company, 257, 263
Sheraton, 261
Shipbuilding, 140, 144, 243
Shopping mall, 4–7, 28, 58, 91
Short production runs, 7
Siemens, 47, 198, 203, 210
Siemens/Rolm, 265
Silicon Valley, 39, 117, 146, 197, 230
Singapore, 116, 175, 197, 209
Singtel-Airtel, 269
Size distribution, 56
Sky Team, 159
Smartphone, 60, 75, 76, 83, 85, 91,
     113, 115, 118, 119, 135, 137,
     141, 177–179, 201
Smartwatches, 83, 108
Smith, Adam, 124n1, 185, 229
Snapple, 12, 53, 54

SNCF, 266
Socialism, 145
Social media, 39, 48, 49, 127n11,
     179, 186
Softbank, 117
Software, 23, 60, 121, 177, 179, 183,
     187, 196, 208
Sony, 24, 79, 91, 92, 118, 136, 140,
     163, 183, 209
South Africa, 184, 195, 197, 199, 202,
     212, 233
South Korea, 135, 136, 139, 142, 144,
     177, 184, 199
Southwest Airlines, vii, 111, 159, 161
Specialists, vii, 1, 2, 4, 6–8, 12, 13, 15,
     17–22, 25–29, 33n28, 34n36,
     36n46, 39–62, 80–82, 102,
     125n5, 136, 139–141, 151–153,
     158, 161, 162, 164, 215, 237,
     240, 242, 245
Speed, 20, 29, 40, 42–44, 48, 61,
     112, 210
Spin-off, 2, 3, 91, 122, 157, 212
Sports Authority, 20, 47, 57
Sprint, 1, 22, 40, 52, 60, 235, 242
Stakeholder, 14, 26, 27, 29, 39, 41,
     105, 138, 164
Star Alliance, 140, 159
Starbucks, 58, 83, 86, 149, 162, 180
Start-up, 8, 10, 50, 73–74, 92, 104,
     109, 126n11, 146, 229, 230,
     232, 238, 241, 243
State Grid Corporation of China, 266
State Street, 253
State Street Bank and Trust, 253
Steel, 60, 83, 103, 116, 135, 140, 142,
     156, 178, 182, 197–199, 201
Steelcase, 264
Steel industry, 76, 150, 198
Steinway, 57, 202
Stock keeping unit (SKUs), 5, 109
Stock market returns, 25, 39, 240
Stone and Webster, 259

Stora Enso AB, 265
Strange bedfellows, 181, 187
Strategic options, 47, 54, 62
Strategic vendor, 14
Strategy, vii, viii, 4, 13, 15, 16, 19–21,
    26–28, 39–62, 74, 76, 89–91,
    116, 119–121, 123, 124n1, 138,
    155, 162, 164, 176, 186,
    195–217, 229, 233, 234, 238,
    242, 243
Stuck in the middle, 26, 55, 56, 58, 59,
    68n60, 68n61, 79–81, 236, 240
Studebaker, 8, 80, 151
Subway, 266
Suleiman the Magnificent, 228
Sumitomo, 138, 151
SunTrust, 3, 144
Supermarkets, 59, 89, 110, 121, 147,
    162, 205
Superniche, 13, 33n28, 53, 54
Supernicher, 13, 29, 53, 62
Supply chain, 7, 42, 78, 81, 108, 114,
    132n67, 161, 164, 203
Sustainability, 43, 88, 90, 94, 183, 208,
    215, 216, 233
Swatch, 112
Switzerland, 112, 139
Synergy, 19, 20, 23, 29, 44, 162, 164

T
Taiwan, 184, 198
Taiwan Aerospace, 17, 157
Taiwan Semiconductor, 267
Target, 4, 5, 7, 8, 17, 24, 46, 55, 61,
    62n1, 158, 211
Tariff, 76, 142, 178, 203, 232
Tata, 77, 179
Tata Consultancy Services (TCS),
    179, 196
TDMA, 78, 119
Technology, 8, 12, 14, 22, 28, 31n15,
    40, 76–80, 84–85, 88, 90, 92,
    93, 101, 104, 108, 112, 114,
    115, 117, 118, 120, 123,
    132n67, 146, 153, 156, 178,
    180, 183, 187, 198, 200, 203,
    207, 211–213, 216, 227, 229,
    232, 233, 237, 243, 248n22
Telecommunications, 19, 22–24, 27,
    56, 114, 138, 145, 178, 179, 209
Television (TV), vii, 1, 77, 78, 83–85,
    88, 91, 96n24, 104, 114, 136,
    139, 147, 161, 163, 178, 185,
    208, 211, 241
Temasek, 116, 185
Tencent, 117, 137, 178, 197
Tesla, 46, 47, 53, 83, 153, 202, 213
Texas Instruments, 79
Theory of mutual forbearance, 51
Theory of vacating markets,
    83–84, 93, 213
Thermo Fisher, 262
3M, 49, 76, 115
Tiffany, 8, 75
Time Warner, 2, 149, 241
Timex, 77, 112
Tire industry, 141, 150–151,
    156, 157
Tire market, 151, 156
Tires, 1, 27, 51, 59, 141, 150, 151,
    155–157, 237, 243
T-Mobile, 40, 58, 147
Tobacco industry, 141
Tobin's q, 39
Todd Shipyards Corp., 267
Toshiba, 136
Toyota, 19, 22, 45–47, 54, 151–153,
    185, 202, 206, 209, 235
Trade, viii, 24, 29, 87, 88, 109, 114,
    119, 142, 143, 145, 168n34,
    169n36, 175, 177, 178, 182,
    184, 187, 188n1, 195, 198, 203,
    214, 216, 228, 232, 242
Trade triad, 144
Trade wars, 3, 76, 148, 185, 195

Traditional, 4, 44, 47, 52, 58, 61, 82, 85, 86, 92, 101, 103, 105, 109, 111, 112, 121, 123, 132n67, 137, 143, 148, 153, 162, 164, 184, 196, 197, 202, 207, 210, 216, 234

TransformCo, 6

Transportation, 26, 49, 56, 83, 88, 89, 96n24, 97n24, 216

Travelocity, 264

Triad power, 28, 141, 143, 163, 175–187, 238

Tricon Global, 266

Trump, Donald, 3, 31n15

TUI Group, 264

Turkey, 146, 184, 199, 204, 208, 211, 233

Turkish airlines, 160

Tyson, 262

U

Uber, 2, 13, 49, 83, 103, 105, 110, 117, 144, 149, 197, 213, 215, 221n42

Uber Eats, 2, 110

Umbrella branding, 21, 44

Under Armour, 6

Unicorns, 195, 216, 229, 232

Unilever, 2, 43–45, 49, 54, 76, 90, 179

Union Pacific Corp., 266

UnionPay, 162

Uniroyal, 51, 59, 141, 157, 237

United Airlines, 20, 140

United Artists, 263

UnitedHealthCare, 261

United Health Group, 261

United Kingdom, 57, 176, 177, 181, 184, 185, 239

United Parcel Service, 264

United Technologies (UT), 157, 158, 235–237

Universal, 88, 163, 184, 230, 244

Universal Rule of Three, 161–163

Urban, 5, 75, 115, 179, 211

Urban Office, 264

USAA, 53

US Airways, 12, 159

U.S. hair care market, 44

USX-US Steel Group, 267

V

Value-add, 81, 183, 198, 208, 231

Value chain, 55, 110

Value creation, 27, 39, 105

Vanguard, 25

Variable costs, 20, 21, 81, 88, 108

Vatican, 228

Venture capital, 117

Vera Wang, 39

Verizon, 1, 235, 242

Verizon Wireless, 147

Vertical integration, 10, 24, 29, 79, 199

VF Corporation, 252

Viacom, 259

Victoria's Secret, 7, 55, 57

Viking Cruises, 54

Vinci, 259

Vinyl, 83

Virgin America, 3

Virgin Atlantic, 13

Visa, 162

VistaKon, 258

VMware, 3, 32n15

Vodafone, 52, 147, 210

Volatility, 90, 91, 187

Volkswagen, 47, 54, 147, 153

Volume players, 17–19, 23, 29

Volvo, 196, 240

W

Walden Books, 20, 47
Walmart, 42, 44, 48, 56, 58, 137, 204, 221n42, 237
Walton, Sam, 42, 204
War, 3, 19, 40, 41, 49, 51, 56, 60, 61, 76, 78, 109, 136, 148, 155, 156, 175, 176, 185, 187, 195, 203, 228, 232, 242
Warner EMI, 264
Warner Media, 259
Watch industry, 83
WD-40, 53
Wealth, 105, 118, 142, 144, 145, 177, 216, 228, 229, 231, 244
WeChat, 23
Weigao, 262, 263
Western Digital, 257
Westfield, 58
West Fraser Timber, 260
WeWork, 117
Weyerhaeuser Co., 260
Whirlpool, 136, 201, 235
White goods, 51
Whole Foods, 7, 137, 162, 206
WildHorse, 3
Wilkinson, 2
William-Sonoma, 60

Windows OS, 79
Wireless communications, 1, 3, 59, 78
World Trade Organization (WTO), viii, 24, 26, 87, 145, 187
WPP, 148
Wuling, 45

X

Xerox, 48, 145
Xiaomi, 203, 204
Xinfa, 252

Y

Yahoo, 117
Yamaha, 21, 202
Yanzhou Coal Mining, 263
Yum! Brands, 266

Z

Zaibatsu, 113
Zappos, 110
Zara, 4, 7, 8
Zhongce Rubber Group Co., 268
Zuckerberg, Mark, 229, 230

CPSIA information can be obtained
at www.ICGtesting.com
Printed in the USA
LVHW081946230821
695903LV00002B/23

9 783030 730833